Edward B. Segel

*The New Guide to the
Diplomatic Archives
of Western Europe*

Edgar Anderson
Marvin L. Brown
Lino G. Canedo
Manoel Cardozo
Lynn M. Case
Robert Claus
Vincent Confer
Raymond L. Cummings
Fritz T. Epstein
Keith Eubank
Luther H. Evans

Willard A. Fletcher
Kent Forster
D. P. M. Graswinckel
Vincent Ilardi
Raymond E. Lindgren
Arthur J. May
Mme. G. Pérotin
Yves Pérotin
Mary Lucille Shay
Florence Janson Sherriff
Daniel H. Thomas
Domna Visvizi-Dontas

The New Guide to the Diplomatic Archives of Western Europe

Edited by
Daniel H. Thomas
and
Lynn M. Case

University of Pennsylvaina Press

The numbers in the text and footnotes of each chapter (such as "No. 65") refer to the numbered bibliography at the end of that chapter. In the case of last-minute changes in the bibliographies, there was no overall renumbering because of cross-references already established in the text; hence the appearance in some instances of omitted entries.

Contents

Preface

THIS is a scholar's *Baedeker* or *vade mecum* for locating and using most efficiently the materials in the diplomatic archives of Western Europe. Our objectives are to offer information, advice, and, hopefully, answers to numerous questions which arise from the time research in documents is seriously considered until the investigation is far advanced, if not completed. We trust it will be welcomed by archivists as well as researchers.

The favorable response to the first guide (1959) encouraged us to expand and update it, and we have profited by the criticisms of its reviewers. Three new chapters deal with Finland, Greece, and Luxemburg, and two subsections with the International Labour Organisation and the International Telecommunication Union. We have eliminated the chapter on "Public Opinion and Foreign Affairs," but have given more attention to periodical collections in the various states. A major change occurs in the chapter on Germany. When the earlier guide appeared, the German materials were widely scattered in Allied countries. Now they are returned to West and East Germany, but are still dispersed in such cities as Bonn, Coblenz, Freiburg im Breisgau, Merseburg, and Potsdam, as well as in the capital cities of former German states, such as Munich, Stuttgart, and Hanover. Bavaria has been made a subsection of the German chapter. We deem ourselves especially fortunate to have the archivist-historian Fritz T. Epstein as the author of this chapter, because he knows intimately the states and relocation of these complicated and scattered archives. Other new authors are Edgar Anderson, Marvin L. Brown, Raymond L. Cummings, Luther Evans, Kent Forster, Vincent Ilardi, Raymond E. Lindgren, Madame G. Pérotin, Yves Pérotin, and Domna Visvizi-Dontas.

The chapters usually contain four categories of information. The first, a history of the principal depositories, is a background which should aid in comprehending the arrangement and most effective use of the materials. The next, and perhaps most helpful section is a description of the organization, arrangement, and classification of the records, which should enable the investigator to expedite research by avoiding faulty starts and diversions and going more directly and quickly to the pertinent materials. A third type of information includes such varied matters as the administration of the depositories, the present officials, regulations concerning admission and use of documents, the hours of the reading rooms, and the dates of closing because of extended holidays, vacations, or cleaning — how many researchers have travelled to distant depositories only to learn that they were closed for a fortnight or longer! Also, this section usually indicates the extent of reference works on the shelves of the reading rooms, whether microfilming and duplicating services are available, the most useful libraries in the area, their archival collections and facilities for research, and a convenient district for lodging in a particular city. Finally, most chapters contain a bibliography both of the principal collections of published documents and of the most useful printed guides and inventories. In this connection users are advised that, in order to save space and eliminate frequent repetition, *the editors have written "See No.   ", rather than "See No.   in the bibliography at the end of the chapter."*

We have felt justified in departing from the strict western European orientation of our work and have included chapters on "Greece" and "Finland," as well as "International Organizations," trusting that purists will show forbearance.

The specialists chosen to write the various chapters have our gratitude for immediately comprehending the objectives and nature of the cooperative work, perhaps because they had experienced the frustrations inherent in research in unfamiliar archives. We are grateful also to the late William E. Lingelbach for a bequest to subsidize a new guide, a gift which explains its modest price.

Contributors to this volume have received immeasurable aid and information from archivists and librarians in the many

depositories. We are all indebted to these patient and accommodating partners in research, whether or not they are identified in
the text. May this book be a boon to them by eliminating some of
the more common and recurring questions by researchers, but
may it also attract more scholars to their reading rooms. Readers
are reminded that, in recent years, obliging archivists have
multiplied their reciprocal agreements with foreign counterparts
to exchange microfilms of extensive collections. Consequently,
before going abroad for research, one should ascertain whether
his own nation's archives now possess copies of some of the
requisite documents.

March 1, 1975   Daniel H. Thomas
                                  University of Rhode Island

                                  Lynn M. Case
                                  University of Pennsylvania

*The New Guide to the
Diplomatic Archives
of Western Europe*

1   AUSTRIA

Arthur J. May

University of Rochester

and

Marvin L. Brown, Jr.*

North Carolina State University

HISTORY

In 1749 Maria Theresa ordered Theodor Anton Taulow von Rosenthal to assemble family and state papers of the Hapsburg domains in a single repository, thus laying the basis for the establishment of the world's greatest archives, the institution that came to be known in the Napoleonic era as the *Haus-, Hof-, und Staatsarchiv* (referred to hereafter as HHSA).[1] The *Kriegsarchiv* (War Archives) had already been founded in the period of Eugene of Savoy, and to this day it remains separate; but by the early nineteenth century the HHSA became the repository for family, court, and state parers, including diplomatic correspondence, which had only recently, in 1742, been shifted from court to state chancery archives. Extremely old material of different sorts is to be found in the HHSA, the oldest document of which is a letter of 816 from Emperor Louis the Pious to the Archbishop of Salzburg

---

*The fine first-edition chapter by the late Professor May has been to some extent rewritten and updated by Professor Brown for this revised second edition.

[1] The monumental work of Ludwig Bittner, the *Gesamtinventar des wiener Haus-, Hof-, und Staatsarchivs*, 5 vols. (Vienna, 1936–1940), especially I, 9-82, is the greatest source of information about the development of the *HHSA*. An excellent recent survey by Rudolf Neck, "The Haus-, Hof-, and Staatsarchiv: its history, holdings and use," *Austrian history yearbook*, VI-VII (1970–1971), 3-16, concisely covers the whole scope.

granting immunity from imperial taxation.[2] By 1807, after the dissolution of the Holy Roman Empire, all diplomatic material was placed in the HHSA under Kaunitz's Court and State Chancery, which conducted foreign affairs. Thus, from its early days the HHSA has been especially associated with diplomacy.

In the Napoleonic era the HHSA not only gained its name and quantities of documents from the Imperial Court Council and the Imperial Court Chancery of the defunct Holy Roman Empire, but it also was threatened by the victories of French armies and the schemes of Napoleon to establish in Paris an archives for all Europe. Many documents were removed from Vienna for safety and, after Napoleon's victory at Wagram in 1809, many cartloads of material were carried off to Paris. Later, in accordance with the settlements in the Congress of Vienna, this material was returned to Vienna. Austrian territorial acquisitions of this period, of course, enhanced the holdings of the HHSA with the addition of documents from such sources as the Republic of Venice and the Archbishopric of Trent.

By 1852 the HHSA gained the material that had been in the archives of the Archbishopric of Mainz. These were significant because the archbishop had been the Archchancellor of the Holy Roman Empire. Another gain was the addition from Belgium of the records of Hapsburg officials in the Austrian Netherlands, from the time of Charles V until the end of the eighteenth century.

However, besides additions, the middle part of the nineteenth century also brought losses and changes for the HHSA. When Lombardy was lost in 1859 and Venetia seven years later, the archival material belonging to these provinces was transferred to Italy, and certain documents of particular interest to Hungary were sent to Budapest as a result of the *Ausgleich* of 1867.[3] Under

[2] This document, together with ninety-nine other resplendent jewels of the *HHSA*, has been magnificently reproduced in facsimile in Leo Santifaller, ed., *1100 Jahre österreichische und europäische Geschichte in Urkunden und Dokumenten des Haus-, Hof-, und Staatsarchiv*, 2 vols. (Vienna, 1949).

[3] For a short account of the archives of Hungary, consult Dionys Janóssy, "Das Archivgesetz in Ungarn," *ibid.*, I, 13-20.

the Dual Monarchy, the HHSA became the common property of the two partners, although only one Magyar, Arpád von Károlyi, ever served as its director.

The desirability of a specially-designed building to store the Viennese archival treasures came under discussion as early as the 1850s, but only in 1902, under Gustav Winter, did the idea become a reality when an archives building was completed at the rear of the historic chancellery. The physical merging of the foreign ministry and of the HHSA indicated the closeness that already existed. The archives building on the Minoritenplatz was envied and imitated after its construction, and it remains an appropriate repository for all the material of the HHSA.

The HHSA suffered significant losses as a result of World War I, with successor states making claims on the holdings of the defunct Hapsburg Monarchy. The Treaty of Saint-Germain stipulated that the Republic of Austria should negotiate with the successors of the deceased empire for "an amicable arrangement on all objects which ought to form part of the intellectual patrimony of the ceded districts. . . ." At the time it was feared that much of the material would have to be surrendered, especially as Czechoslovakia and Italy pressed their cases. Although Czechoslovakia succeeded in gaining extensive holdings, the Austrian appeal to the principle of origin generally was applied. The archivists of the negotiating states greatly respected the acting director of the HHSA at that time, Professor Oswald Redlich, who had been the teacher of some of them. Thanks to him, Austria came out of the arrangements better than might have been the case. Although the losses to Italy were relatively light, the Czechs took considerable Bohemian, Moravian, and Silesian material. Hungary, on the other hand, dealt sparingly with HHSA documents. To this day the Hungarians have a permanent archivist at the HHSA, and relations appear to be very satisfactory.[4] Some compensation for archival losses of this era came as important families deposited their archives in the HHSA. As of 1939, the archives building held more than two hundred

4 Neck, *loc. cit.*, pp. 13–14.

collections of papers, about one-hundred fifty thousand bundles and cartons of documents, some sixty thousand parchment records, fifty thousand manuscripts, and a considerable body of newspaper materials.

In 1938 Austria was incorporated into the German Reich, and with the loss of sovereignty came the danger that the holdings of the HHSA would be transferred to other archives. Fortunately this fate was avoided, but the stamp of the swastika was literally placed on many of the diplomatic documents. Aerial attacks damaged the archives during World War II, and on orders from Berlin, the riches of the HHSA and other Viennese archives were carried into hiding in various places, ranging from cellars in the capital to salt mines in the country. Unfortunately some of the material was carried to a point in Lower Austria where there were sharp engagements with the advancing Russians, resulting in the destruction of the *Akten des älteren Staatsrates* (records of the old Council of State), the most serious of the losses. Fortunately, the diplomatic correspondence escaped.[5] Following the war an *Österreichisches Staatsarchiv* was organized on July 26, 1945, the first division of which was the HHSA, a step that was taken before the reassembling of the holdings.

Almost from the beginning, limited access to the materials of the HHSA was granted to historical investigators.[6] However, throughout the nineteenth century the cautious, vigilant paternalism that pervaded the whole Austrian administration ruled in the HHSA. It was feared that secret papers might be examined less to achieve impartial history than to distort or discredit the conduct of Hapsburg diplomacy. Permission to consult the diplomatic archives was granted only to scholars that the regime thought to be completely trustworthy. Even Leopold von Ranke, who in 1868 described the HHSA as "the most important archives for German history,"[7] had been denied in 1863 the privilege of

---

[5] R. John Rath, "The war and the Austrian archives," *Journal of central European affairs,* VI (1946–47), 392–396; Neck, *loc. cit.,* pp. 6–7.

[6] See Walter Pillich, "Staatskanzler Kaunitz und die Archivforschung, 1762–1792," in Santifaller, *1100 Jahre,* I, 95–118.

[7] Neck, *loc. cit.,* p. 3.

studying the correspondence of Prince Kaunitz with the Austrian ambassador in France of more than a century earlier. Likewise, Treitschke was denied the use of Austrian documents, while various investigators were allowed to see dispatches from foreign posts, but not instructions to them. In the late nineteenth and early twentieth centuries some liberalization of this policy set in, but selectivity in the material available was still the case when Eduard von Wertheimer wrote his monumental biography of Count Julius Andrássy, foreign minister during the 1870s.[8] The abolition of censorship for older material following World War I made possible a more authoritative treatment of the career of Andrássy, compelling revisions in Wertheimer's analyses and judgments.

Beginning with Rosenthal, a notable line of directors has administered the HHSA, displaying industry and sagacity in the discovery, classification, and description of documentary materials. The leaders have been flanked by competent and skillful archivists who have set standards for others. Directors and their colleagues have consistently engaged in scholarly pursuits, with the principle still pervailing that the archival staff resembles a learned academy, in the language of one director, not a set of bureaucratic state servants.

Apart from enlarging the archival collections substantially, Joseph von Hormayr, director from 1808 to 1813, produced historical studies on his native Tyrol that glowed with romantic color and provincial pride. A fiery patriot, Hormayr exploited his familiarity with the contents of the archives in the cause of his country; for his flair for effective pamphleteering he was likened to Thomas Paine. After helping organize the Tyrolian rebellion of 1809, Hormayr fell into disfavor at the Viennese court and eventually drifted into the service of Bavaria.

One of the most notable directors of the HHSA was Alfred von Arneth. No doubt his greatness as a historian brought glory to the HHSA. He wrote a wide variety of works, including important

---

[8] Eduard von Wertheimer, *Graf Julius Andrássy*, 3 vols. (Stuttgart, 1910–13).

biographical studies, notably of Maria Theresa and Eugene of Savoy. He was famous for developing the concept that historical documents were for the historian and not just the regime, whatever may have been the rules governing accessibility of documents during his term as director (1868–97). His successor, Gustav Winter, was also an outstanding historian, earning distinction as an authority on the economic and legal history of Austria.[9]

Possibly the most distinguished archivist of his generation, Ludwig Bittner presided over the HHSA from 1925 to 1940 and continued to have charge of the *Reichsarchiv Wien,* the designation given by Hitler to the HHSA. Respected throughout the world as an archival administrator and scholar of front rank, Bittner was chosen in 1933 as chairman of a commission on diplomatic history by the International Congress of Historians. Three major monuments honor his memory and bear witness to his indefatigable energy and unusual competence as an editor.

In collaboration with other well-known Austrian scholars, though the main burden fell on his own shoulders, Bittner prepared the *Österreich-Ungarns Aussenpolitik von der bosnischen Krise 1908 bis zum Kriegsausbruch 1914,* 9 vols. (Vienna, 1930). Part of his energies during World War II was devoted to arranging a supplement to this massive collection, necessitated by the discovery of additional documents. With the help of eleven other outstanding scholars, he issued the *Gesamtinventar des wiener Haus-, Hof- und Staatsarchivs,* 5 vols. (Vienna, 1936–1940), for which he wrote a lengthy and brilliant introduction on the history of the HHSA. Again in collaboration he commenced publication of *Repertorium der diplomatischen Vertreter aller Länder seit dem westfälischen Frieden bis 1930.* The first volume, covering from 1648 to 1715, appeared in 1936, and the second, from 1716 to 1763, finished in the midst of World War II, appeared in 1950, after Bittner's death.

[9] For biographies of the officials of the HHSA, see Bittner, *Gesamtinventar,* I, 3–166.

Bittner's life is symbolic of the importance of the German question for Austria. An ardent partison of the union of the Austrian Republic with Germany, Bittner applauded the *Anschluss* in 1938. But as World War II drew to an end, with Soviet armies taking their zone around Vienna, Bittner and his wife committed suicide in April of 1945.

Since World War II Professor Dr. Leo Santifaller, Dr. Gebhard Rath, and Dr. Richard Blaas have carried on the high traditions of their predecessors.

ORGANIZATION OF THE COLLECTIONS

Members of the courteous staff of the HHSA are the ultimate guides to the searcher in Vienna, but in a large measure Bittner's *Gesamtinventar* is the effective pathfinder which first should be studied. This indispensable work was hailed immediately on its appearance as an extraordinary model for other archives to imitate, and it is difficult to see how it could be improved upon, considering the extent and complexity of the material. Unfortunately it is not widely distributed, but some of the major research libraries in the United States possess it, where it can be studied before investigations in Vienna are undertaken.

The *Gesamtinventar* is in five volumes, published as part of the total *Inventare österreichischer staatlicher Archive,* the first volume of which is of the most interest to researchers in the field of diplomatic history. In addition to sections of general interest about the HHSA, it contains the section on *Österreichische geheime Staatsregistratur,* under which is the division of the *Staatskanzlei (Ministerium des Äussern).* Of particular interest to the student of the period 1848–1918 is the *Politisches Archiv* (*Gesamtinventar,* I, 442–451). Here are forty *Bestände,* generally dealing with different countries where Austria had diplomatic representation. This correspondence is largely arranged chronologically according to dispatches, instructions, and *varia.* Paralleling these ministerial *Bestände* are the archives of *Botschaften* (embassies), *Gesantschaften* (legations) and *Konsulate* (consulates), returned from posts abroad. Of particular interest among these *Gesantschaftarchive* are those returned from Constantinople.[10] However, some of the most interesting material, principally dealing with the great treaties, is separately classified in the *Geheimakten*. Likewise, within certain of the *Bestände* devoted to given countries, one finds cartons for given topics, such as the negotiations for a triple alliance between Austria, France, and Italy, 1868–1870 (Frankreich — IX, carton 182). These *Bestände* contain cartons specially devoted to internal developments within certain countries, such as the seven comprising the correspondence of the special agent, Georg Klindworth, who kept the Ballhausplatz informed about events in France from 1869 through 1875. In *Bestand* XXXX [*sic*], which bears the designation *Interna*, one finds, among other things, copies of the correspondence of Richard Metternich and Joseph Hübner.[11]

The *Administrative Registratur* (*Gesamtinventar*, I, 451–461) contains information of interest for the study of later diplomacy. For pre-1848 study, the section of *Deutsche Staaten* (I, 511–528) and *Äusserdeutsche Staaten* (I, 528–584) are to be noted. While the second and third volumes of the *Gesamtinventar* do not contain as much of interest for diplomatic history as the first, the fourth has some particularly useful information. Private archives, such as those of Count Stadion, are listed here (IV, 409–448). These important papers of statesmen are grouped among the *Nachlässe* (IV, 375–406), including the papers of men like Baernreither (IV, 409–411). The fifth volume is devoted to supplements and an index.[12]

[10] Neck, *loc. cit.*, pp. 11–12. The letter of Dr. Richard Blass of May 16, 1973 is gratefully acknowledged for information on the returned Constantinople archives.

[11] Marvin L. Brown, Jr., "France in the Haus-, Hof-, und Staatsarchiv," *French historical studies*, III (1963), 272–277.

[12] A colossal *Generalkatalog* (1908), comprising 100 handwritten volumes, lists the resources of the HHSA and their location in the archives building. In 1873 Constantin Böhm published in Vienna *Die Handschriften des Haus-, Hof-, und Staatsarchivs*, and a supplement appeared the following year. Unprinted supplements followed, but all are out-of-date, owing to transfers of documents to other countries and the ravages of war. New inventories are being developed.

In recent years significant new acquisitions have been made by the HHSA. Papers of Archduke Friedrich have been added to the *Hausarchiv*. *Nachlässe* of Richard Schmitz, Lexa von Aehrenthal, Friedrich Funder, and Ludwig Flotow have enriched the holdings of personal papers.

ADMINISTRATION, REGULATION, AND FACILITIES

The overall supervision of the Austrian State Archives is in the hands of the General Director, Dr. Walter Goldinger, with Dr. Richard Blaas directly in charge of the HHSA. While the great bulk of material of interest for diplomatic history is in the HHSA, in some instances the papers of Austrians who served in the diplomatic corps still remain in the possession of their families or have been deposited in *Landesarchive*. Current information on the location of specific collections not in the HHSA may be obtained by addressing: Österreichisches Staatsarchiv, General-Direktion, 1010 WIEN, Minoritenplatz 1, Austria.

As a standard rule, archival material after 1925 is closed. Some exceptions may be made for internationally-recognized scholars by special permission of the chancellery. Some of the private papers deposited in the HHSA may be seen only with the permission of the families, or after a stated period of time. The recently-acquired *Nachlässe* are in this category; as are the papers of Khevenhüller, Macchio, Lützow, Baernreither, and Stadion. A case in point is the rich and diversified *Nachlass* of Archduke Francis Ferdinand. Following World War I the heirs of the archduke granted access to this collection to a few scholars.[13]

Permission to conduct research in the HHSA is regulated by an ordinance, published in the *Gesantinventar* (I, 77–78), requiring the scholar to present a copy of any work he may publish that is based on his researches in the HHSA. This regulation does not include doctoral dissertations.

---

[13] Robert J. Kann, "Emperor William II and Archduke Francis Ferdinand in their correspondence," *American historical review*, LVII (1951–1952), 323–351. See p. 323, n. 1; p. 324, n. 2.

The staff of the HHSA not only is most helpful to the foreign investigator, but also it does not require any special kind of references. The staff encourages previous communication from the researcher as to the material he desires before his arrival, and it would particularly like to know the specific cartons he desires, so they can be ready on his arrival. The general rule is that five cartons a day may be ordered, and these should be ordered a day in advance: Material may be microfilmed at two schillings a copy, or xeroxed at three schillings a copy. Whole cartons may be microfilmed, but xeroxing is restricted to smaller amounts. The HHSA will accept requests for microfilming by persons unable to visit Vienna. Services for the transcription of some of the more difficult documents in German script may be arranged through the office of the director. Arrangements in special cases may also be made by mail to search for and transcribe certain documents.

The *Benützersalle* of the HHSA is open from 9:00 A.M. to 6:00 P.M. Monday through Friday. Varying in length from year to year is a vacation from mid-December until the start of the new year. Other official holidays include Epiphany, Eastertide, Ascension Day, Whitsuntide, Corpus Christi Day, Saint Mary's Ascension Day, All Saints' Day, and Saint Mary's Conception Day. The *Österreichische Nationalbibliothek*, the library of the University of Vienna, and the library of the history faculty at the university are available at similar times to the researcher, in addition to the library of the HHSA.[14]

It is advisable to live within easy walking or riding distance of the Inner City. Prices which seemed cheap to the American traveler in the days of the occupation and for sometime thereafter are no longer the case. Nevertheless, satisfactory arrangements in Austria can be made by the visiting scholar. Austrian Tourist

[14] Data on these libraries may be found in Ernst Trenkler, "The history of the Austrian National-Bibliothek," *Library quarterly*, XVII (1947), 224–231; Johann Gans, "Bibliotheca redivivia, the University Library of Vienna," *Library journal*, LXXIII (1948), 993–995; Hugo Alker, *Die Universitätsbibliothek Wien* (Vienna, 1953); see also Josef Stummvoll, "Austrian libraries, past and present," *Library quarterly*, XX (1950), 33–38, and Lawrence S. Thompson, "Research libraries in Vienna," *American-German review*, XIV (1947), 24.

Information, 545 5th Avenue, New York, N. Y., will furnish extensive information about accommodations and a variety of other matters.[15]

BIBLIOGRAPHY

Printed Collections of Documents
The principal printed collections of Austrian diplomatic papers are:
1. Arneth, Alfred. "Die Relationen der Botschafter Venedigs über Österreich im 18. Jahrhundert," *Fontes rerum Austriacarum,* II/22 (1863).
2. Bittner, Ludwig. *et al.,* eds. *Österreich-Ungarns Aussenpolitik von der bosnischen Krise bis zum Kriegsausbruch 1914.* 9 vols. Vienna, 1930. This monumental series, which runs into 8,144 pages, was prepared in three years and printed in eight months. For an analysis consult O. H. Wedel, "Austro-Hungarian diplomatic documents, 1908-1914," *Journal of modern history,* III (1931), 84-107.
3. Chroust, Anton. "Gesandtschaftsberichte aus München, 1814-1848," *Schriftenreihe zur bayrischen Landesgeschichte,* XXXIII (1939), XXXVI-XXXVIII (1941-43).
4. Demelitsch, F. "Aktenstücke zur Geschichte der Koalition vom Jahre 1814," *Fontes rerum Austriacarum,* II/49/2 (1899).
5. Fiedler, Josef. "Die Relationen der Botschafter Venedigs über Deutschland und Österreich im 17. Jahrhundert," *Fontes rerum Austriacarum,* II/22, 27 (1866-67).
6. "Die Relationen der venetianischen Botschafter über Österreich im 16. Jahrhundert," *Fontes rerum Austriacarum,* II/30 (1870).
7. "Josef II und Graf Ludwig Cobenzl Briefwechsel (1780-1790)," *Fontes rerum Austriacarum,* II/53, 54 (1901).
8. Gachard, M. *Documents inédits concernant les troubles de la Belgique.* 2 vols. Brussels, 1858.
9. Gooss, Roderich. *Das wiener Kabinett und die Entstehung des Weltkrieges.* Vienna, 1919.
10. *Diplomatische Atenstücke zur Vorgeschichte des Krieges 1914.* Ergänzungen und Nachträge zum Österreich-Ungarischen Rotbuch. Vienna, 1919.

---

[15] The staff of the Austrian archives, especially Dr. Anna Banna, are thanked for information in this section.

11. Mendelssohn-Bartholdy, R. *Brief von Friederick von Gentz an Pilat.* Leipzig, 1868.

12. Oechsi, W. *Die Anfänge des Sonderbundes nach österreichischen Gesandtschaftsberichten.* Zürich, 1914.

13. Pribram, Alfred F. "Privatbriefe Kaiser Leopolds an den Grafen F. E. Pötting," *Fontes rerum Austriacarum,* II/56, 57 (1903-4).

14. Prokesch-Osten, Anton von. *Dépêches inédits du Chevalier de Gentz au hospodar de la Valachie.* 3 vols., 1867.

15. Reinöhl, Fritz von. "Der Fall Jeftanović-Sola-Gavrila, Grossserbische Umtriebe vor und nach dem Ausbruch des I. Weltkrieges," *Veröffentlichungen des Reichsarchivs Wien,* I (1944).

16. Schlesier, M. *Mémoires et lettres inédits du Chevalier de Gentz.* 1841.

17. Schlitter, Hans. *Napoléon à St. Hélène. Rapports officiels du Baron Stürmer.* Paris, 1886.

18. "Die Berichte des I. Agenten Österreichs in den Vereinigten Staaten, Baron de Beelen Bertholff . . . 1784-1789," *Fontes rerum Austriacarum,* 45/2 (1891).

19. *Correspondence secrète entre le Comte A. W. Kaunitz, ambassadeur à Paris, et le Baron Ignaz de Koch, secrétaire de l'Impératrice Marie Thérèse, 1750-1752.* Paris, 1899.

20. *Fürst von Kaunitz, Philipp Cobenzl und Spielmann. Ihr Briefwechsel, 1779-1792.* Vienna, 1899.

21. *Brief und Denkschriften zur Vorgeschichte der belgischen Revolution.* Vienna, 1900.

22. *Geheimkorrespondenz Josefs II. mit seinem Minister in den österreichischen Niederlanden, Grafen Ferdinand Trauttmannsdorff (1787-1789).* Vienna, 1902.

23. *Les correspondances des agents diplomatiques étrangers en France avant la révolution.* 1896.

24. Srbik, Heinrich, and Oskar Schmid, "Quellen zur deutschen Politik Österreichs, 1859-1865," *Deutsche Geschichtsquellen des 19. Jahrhunderts,* XXIX-XXXIII (1934-38).

25. *Urkunden und Aktenstücke des Reichsarchivs Wien zur reichsrechtlichen Stellung des burgundischen Kreises.* 3 vols. Vienna, 1944-45.

Guides and Reference Works

The best general historical account of the resources in HHSA for the study of diplomacy is Bittner's description in Volume I of the *Gesamtinventar.* Other works with bearing upon the subject are:

26. Bittner, Ludwig. "Das wiener Haus-, Hof- und Staatsarchiv in der Nachkriegszeit," *Archivalische Zeitschrift*, XXXV (1925), 141-203.

27. "Die zwischenstaatlichen Verhandlungen über das Schicksal der österreichischen Archive nach dem Zusammenbruch Österreich-Ungarns," *Archiv für Politik und Geschichte*, III (1925), pp. 58-96.

28. "Zur Neuorganisation des österreichischen Archivwesens," *Festschrift für Waldemar Lippert* (1937), pp. 36-41.

28a. Bemis, Samuel F., and Grace G. Griffin, *Guide to the Diplomatic History of the United States, 1775-1921*. Washington, 1935. In Austria, pp. 928-931

29. Brown, Marvin L., Jr. "France in the Haus-, Hof-, und Staatsarchiv," *French historical studies*, III (1936), 272-277.

30. Coreth, Anna. "Das Schicksal des k.u.k. Kabinettsarchiv seit 1945," *Mitteilungen des österreichischen Staatsarchivs*, IX (1958), 514-525.

30a. Degras, Jane. *Calendar of Soviet Documents on Foreign Policy, 1917-1941*. London, 1948. On Austria, pp. 38, 77, 118, 149.

31. Gross, Lothar. "Das Haus-, Hof-, und Staatsarchiv in Wien," *Archivalische Zeitschrift*, XXXV (1925), 134-140.

32. *Jahrbuch der österreichischen Wissenschaft*, 2 (1950), 146-148.

33. Neck, Rudolf. "The Haus-, Hof-, und Staatsarchiv; its history holdings, and use," *Austrian history yearbook*, 6-7 (1970-1971), 3-16.

34. Rath, R. John. "The war and the Austrian archives," *Journal of Central European affairs*, 6 (1946), 392-396.

35. Redlich, Joseph. "Family, Court, and State Archives in Vienna," *Transactions of the Royal Historical Society*, 4th ser. 4 (1920), 49-61.

36. Reinöhl, Fritz von. "Zur Geschichte der wiener Zentralarchive," *Archivalische Zeitschrift*, 36 (1926), 220-226.

37. Santifaller, Leo. *Festschrift zur Feier des zweihundertjährigen Bestandes des Haus-, Hof,- und Staatsarchiv*. 2 vols. Vienna, 1949.

38. Schlitter, Hans. "Die Rückstellung der von den Franzosen 1809 aus Wien entführten Archive," *Mitteilungen des Instituts für österreichische Geschichtsforschung*, XXII (1091), 108-122.

39. Seidl, Jakob. "Österreichische Archive," *Archivi d'Italia*, II (1935) 234-244.

40. "Das österreichische Staatsarchiv," *Mitteilungen des österreichischen Staatsarchivs*, I (1948), 3-19.

41. "Das österreichische Staatsarchiv, dessen Abteilungen und führenden Beamten in den letzten fünfzig Jahren," *Festschrift*, I, 127-138.
42. Stropp, Robert. "Die Akten des k.u.k. Ministerium des Äussern, 1848-1918," *Mitteilungen des österreichischen Staatsarchivs*, 20 (1967), 389-506.
43. "Neuordnung und Neuaufstellung der Archivbehelfe des Haus-, Hof-, und Staatsarchivs," *Mitteilungen des össterreichischen Staatsarchivs*, 27-28 (1964-1965), 611-639.
44. Winter, Gustav. "Die Gründung des Haus-, Hof-, und Staatsarchivs," *Archiv für österrreichische Geschichte*, 92 (1903), 1-82.
45. *Das neue Gebäude des k.u.k. Haus-, Hof-, und Staatsarchivs in Wien*. Vienna, 1903.
46. Winter, Otto Friedrich. "Der Bestand 'Archivbehelfe' des wiener Haus-, Hof-, und Staatsarchivs," *Mitteilungen des österreichischen Staatsarchivs*, 5 (1953), 316-345.
47. Wolf, Gustav. *Geschichte der k.k. Archive in Wien*. Vienna, 1871.

At this point may be noted the principal documentary collections pertinent to diplomatic history, together with references to the *Gesamtinventar* and to scholarly articles in which the records in question are discussed.[15]

Imperial Court Chancery:
48. *Gesamtinventar*, I, 330-353.
49. Gross, Lothar. "Die Geschichte der deutschen Reichshofkanzlei von 1559 bis 1806," *Inventare österreichischer staatlicher Archive*, I. Vienna, 1933.
50. Kaiser, Hans. "Die Archive des alten Reiches bis 1806," *Archivalische Zeitschrift*, XXXV (1925), 204-220.

Archives of the Archchancellor of Mainz:
51. *Gesamtinventar*, I, 393.

Secret Austrian State Register:
52. *Gesamtinventar*, I, 397-398.
   Gross, Lothar. "Der Kampf zwischen der Reichskanzlei und österreichischer Hofkanzlei um die Führung der auswärtigen Geschäfte," *Historische Vierteljahrschrift*, XXII (1925), 279-312.

State Chancery:
53. *Gesamtinventar*, I, 401-421.
54. Mayr, Josef K. "Geschichte der Staatskanzlei im Zeitalter des Fürsten Metternich," *Inventare österreichischer staatlicher Archive*, II. Vienna, 1935.

55. Postkurse, *Inventare österreichischer staatlicher Archive*, III. Vienna, 1935.
56. Reinöhl, Fritz von. "Die österreichischen Informationsbüros im Vormärz," *Archivalische Zeitschrift*, XXXVI (1926), 261–288.
57. Stix, Franz. "Zur Geschichte und Organisation der Wiener Ziffern-kanzlei," *Mitteilungen des österreichischen Instituts für Geschichtsforschung*, LI (1937), 131–160.

Ministry of Foreign Affairs:
58. *Gesamtinventar*, I, 442–466.
59. Wiedermayer, Rudolf. "Geschäftsgang des k.u.k. Ministerium des Äusseren," *Archivalische Zeitschrift*, XL (1931), 131–152.

Diplomatic Papers by States:
    a. German States
60. *Gesamtinventar*, I, 511–528.
    b. Non-German States
61. *Gesamtinventar*, I, 529–584.

Correspondence of Statesmen:
62. *Gesamtinventar*, I, 587–594.
    This section contains selections of the papers of Count F. E. Pötting, Prince Eugene of Savoy, Count Karl Cobenzl, Prince Wenzel A. Kaunitz, Counts Rudolf and Francis Colloredo, and others.)

Diplomatic Collection:
63. *Gesamtinventar*, I, 594–596.
    This section is made up of copies of documents from European archives, for the period 1605–1726, assembled by Baron Johann F. Dumont von Karlscroon, publisher of the *Corps universel diplomatique*.)

State Charters (Staatsurkunden):
64. *Gesamtinventar*, III, 97.

State Treateis:
65. *Gesamtinventar*, III, 127–128.

Belgium:
66. *Gesamtinventar*, IV, 81–360.
67. Brandi, Karl. "Die politische Korrespondenz Karls V," *Nachrichten Göttingen*, I (1931), 251–258.
68. "Die Überlieferung der Akten Karls V im Haus-, Hof, und Staatsarchiv Wien," *Berichte und Studien*, V, VI, VII, XI, Vienna, 1931–33.

69. Laenen, I. *Les archives de l'état à Vienne au point de vue de l'histoire de Belgique* (Brussels, 1924).

Manuscript Collection:
70. *Gesamtinventar*, III, 137–291.
71. Böhm, Constantin. *Die Handschriften des Haus-, Hof- und Staats-archiv.* Vienna, 1873; Supplement, Vienna, 1874.
(This section contains correspondence of diplomatic officials, some originals, some copies.)

Private Papers (*Nachlässe*):
72. *Gesamtinventar*, IV, 375–406.
73. Reinöhl, Fritz von. "Politische Nachlässe des 19. Jahrhunderts in den staatlichen Archiven Österreichs," *Korrespondenzblatt des Gesamtvereins der deutschen Geschichts-und Altertumsvereine* (1925), 209–220.
(This section contains papers of both public personalities and private citizens.)

Works containing Austrian treaties and other diplomatic engagements, as well as data on Austrain diplomatic personalities and Red Books are:
74. Bittner, Ludwig. "Chronologische Verzeichnis der österreichischen Staatsverträge," 4 vols., *Veröffentlichungen der Kommission für neuere Geschichte Österreichs.* I (1902), VIII (1909), XIII (1914), XV (1917).
(The first volume in this series covers the period 1526–1763; the second, 1764–1847; the third 1848–1911; the final volume is an index and supplement.)
75. "Bericht über die Ausgabe einer internationalen Bibliographie der Farbbücher und anderen diplomatischen Aktenpublikationen," *Bulletin of the international committee of historical sciences*, XVI (1932), 411 ff.
76. *Repertorium der diplomatischen Vertreter . . .*, I (1936), xi.
77. *Corpus pacificationum. Systematische Zusammenstellung der Friedensverträge, 1792–1913.* Berlin, 1917.
78. *Repertorium der diplomatischen Vertreter aller Länder seit dem westfälischen Frieden.* 2 vols. Vienna, 1936, 1950. (The first volume covers the period 1648–1715; the second, 1716–63.)
79. Bruns, V. In *Fontes iuris gentium* (on Red Books), series B, section I, vol. I, 1932, p. 38 for the period 1856–71; vol. II, 1937, p. 16 for the period 1872–78.

80. Gooss, Roderich. "Österreichische Staatsverträge, Fürstentum Sie-
    benbürgen (1526-1690)," *Veröffentlichungen der Kommission für
    neuere Geschichte Österreichs,* IX (1911).
81. Kotasek, Edith. "Die Herausgabe der österreichischen Staatsver-
    träge durch die Kommission für neuere Geschichte Österreichs,"
    Mitteilungen des österreichischen Staatsarchiv, I (1948), 248-254.
82. Pribran, Alfred F. "Österreichische Staatsverträge, England," 2
    vols., *Veröffentlichungen der Kommission für neuere Geschichte
    Österreichs,* III (1907), XII (1913). (The first volume covers the
    period 1526-1748; the second, 1749-1813).
83. *Die politischen Geheimverträge Österreich-Ungarns, 1879-1914.*
    2 vols. Vienna, 1920.
84. *The secret treaties of Austria-Hungary, 1879-1914,* 2 vols. Cam-
    bridge, Mass., 1920-21. English edition of the preceding item.
85. Srbik, Heinrich. "Österreichische Staatsverträge, Niederlande,"
    *Veröffentlichungen der Kommission für neuere Geschichte Öster-
    reichs,* X (1912).
86. Übersberger, Hans. "Österreich und Russland seit dem 15. Jahr-
    hundert," *Veröffentlichungen der Kommission für neuere Ge-
    schichte Österreichs,* II (1906).

For guidance on the general content of collections outside the custody
of HHSA, the following descriptions will be found helpful:

87. *Jahrbuch der österreichischen Wissenschaft,* II (1950), 163, 174, 226,
    295.
88. Jaksch, August. "Katalog des Graf Gössischen Familienarchivs,"
    *Veröffentlichungen der Kommission für neuere Geschichte Öster-
    reichs,* XXVIII (1932), 3-54.
89. Küfstein, Karl. *Das Küfsteinische Familienarchiv* (1906).
90. Martin, Franz. "Das gräflich Kuenburgische Archiv im Langenhof
    zu Salzburg," *Mitteilungen des k.k. Archivrats,* II (1916), 99-149.
91. Nösslböck, Ignaz. "Das Archiv des Reichsgaues Steiermark," *Das
    Johanneum,* VII (1942).
92. Seidl, Jakob. "Privat- und Adelsarchive in Österreich," *Archivi
    d'Italia* (1934), 42-49.
93. "Archivalienschutz in Österreich," *Archivalische Zeitschrift,*
    XLIV (1936), 149-163.
94. Zibermayr, Ignaz. *Das oberösterreichische Landesarchiv in Linz
    im Bilde der Entwicklung des heimatlichen Schriftwesens und
    der Landesgeschichte.* 3d ed., Linz, 1950, pp. 196 ff., 206, 302 ff.,
    306 ff.

2   BELGIUM

Daniel H. Thomas
University of Rhode Island

LE SERVICE DES ARCHIVES DU MINISTÈRE DES AFFAIRES ÉTRANGÈRES

HISTORY

THE Belgian *Service des Archives,* one of the youngest depositories of western European diplomatic archives, has had an adventurous as well as a significant history. Although a secretary-archivist was one of the first positions created in the new ministry of foreign affairs in 1831, the authorities did not establish the *Service des Archives* until 1863 and did not make it adequate in concept and personnel until 1875. As if to compensate for the neglect, the government then made it a "division" and appointed, as chief and director, Emile Banning, a scholar with experience as a librarian. Except for a few short intervals, it has been housed with the ministry of foreigh affairs.

The examination of the holdings by the new archivists confirmed what they feared — the records were far from complete. They filled most of the gaps in the instructions to their diplomatic agents and in the agents' reports by having the consulates and legations forward their files to the ministry. Still other documents were retrieved from the residences of former foreign ministers.[1]

The method of classification chosen by the archivists was to place political documents on subjects of special interest in separate dossiers, but to arrange the bulk of the political records by countries and in chronological order. Then the staff went to

---

[1] Pp. 3-6 of reprint of No. 28; November 29, 1878, with addenda, January, 1880, of No. 18.

extraordinary lengths to prepare the contents of certain categories for rapid and efficient use. Able analysts summarized the contents of each document, and then they skillfully bound the summaries and the pertinent documents in black morocco leather with the title imprinted on the back. These nine hundred volumes form an invaluable collection for the busy researcher interested in the period to about 1890. The First World War interrupted the summarization, and thereafter the amount of material was too extensive for the staff to analyze. The authorities of the *Service des Archives,* hereafter referred to as the Service, did not abandon the practice until they became convinced that an experienced person could summarize an average of only twenty-four documents a day.[2] Thereafter the archivists have had to be content with listing only the subjects of a documents.

Charles Seeger succeeded Banning in 1898, and he constructed a pleasant and fireproof room, the *Salle de Fer,* in which the relatively small number of volumes were shelved and research tables provided. Once the Service outgrew these facilities, decades passed before the government provided the present quarters which were specifically constructed for the preservation and use of the documents and where the Service and the ministry's library were adjacent. Alfred De Ridder, who succeeded Seeger as chief of the Service, was the most prolific author-editor among the functionaries in the division. While second in command, he was chiefly responsible for having the Service made a depository for the *Correspondance politico-commerciale,*[3] an objective that the archivists had in mind from the beginning. The duties of the staff were increasing rapidly when disaster struck in 1914.

When the Germans overwhelmed the Belgian defenders in August of that year and the government fled Brussels, the officials had time to remove only ten cases of documents. Upon the fall of the capital, the Germans learned that numerous diplomatic and

---

[2] Based on information furnished in November 1948 and May 1949 in interviews with A. Henri Lambotte, then Chief of the Service and Director.
[3] P. 6 of reprint of No. 28.

other documents were still in Brussels. Pius Dirr, a Bavarian archivist, claimed to be the discoverer of the materials and of their potential value to the Central Powers. In a short time German propagandists began to make frequent use of them. Indeed, never before in wartime had such extensive use been made of diplomatic records. Starting with publications in the *Norddeutsche Allgemeine Zeitung* on October 13,1914, the Germans published a stream of Belgian documents that continued until 1919. The imperial propagandists sometimes made extravagant claims in their introductions and comments which the documents did not substantiate. To illustrate, Germany accused Belgium and Britain of plotting aggression against Germany. In the *Norddeutsche Allgemeine Zeitung* of November 25, 1914, Berlin charged Belgium with having "determined from the outset to join Germany's enemies and to make common cause with them."[4] "There are no palliations, no extenuations" for the Anglo-Belgian military conversations of 1906, the Germans announced in 1915 in an introduction to a volume of Belgian documents, characterizing them "a record of a monstrous crime."[5]

The Allied Powers countered by pointing out inconsistencies between the charges and the documents produced as supporting evidence, and by publishing some of their own records. Thus began a famous polemic that lasted a quarter of a century.[6] Throughout the war the Belgians were at a disadvantage, since the mass of their archives was in the hands of the invaders.

In 1916 the imperial authorities decided to go about the study of the Belgian material in a more thorough and systematic fashion. For this duty they chose Bernhard Schwertfeger, a military historian and officer. He notified Berlin that the documents did not justify the charge that there was a "Belgian departure from the precepts of neutrality" and proposed that Germany admit that the Belgian diplomats were capable and

---

[4] Pt. II, p. 847 of No. 14.

[5] P. xii of No. 8.

[6] The views of a number of the participants in this well-known and lengthy polemic are treated in No. 13.

neutral observers and publish a still larger selection of their reports, in which they described German policy in the most favorable light. Instead, Berlin dissolved the archival section and transferred Schwertfeger to Berlin in 1918,[7] but did permit him to proceed with the publication of numerous Belgian documents — five volumes appearing in 1919 under the title *Zur europäischen Politik: 1897-1914*. They were probably a factor in the postwar decision to publish extensive collections of German documents culminating in the renowned *Die grosse Politik*.[8]

A tremendously discouraging task awaited the personnel of the Service upon the liberation of Brussels in 1918. Returning to their quarters in the rue de Louvain, the archivists found the offices in great disorder and much of the unbound material scattered and some damaged beyond use. Immediate postwar problems included the backlog of unclassified material, numerous new documents related to the treaties, training new personnel, and acquiring adequate quarters.

When order replaced chaos and the Service began to function properly once again, it opened the archives to private scholars. A significant addition in this period was the acquisition of copies of numerous and valuable Austrian documents consisting of instructions to the Austrian envoys in Brussels and envoys' reports for the years 1833-1902, as well as a number of miscellaneous documents dealing with Belgian affairs. They are open to investigation on the same conditions as the documents of Belgian origin.

The most radical action of the period was the preparation of the records for rapid evacuation in case of another invasion by storing the volumes in wooden cases. They were about a yard in length, with hinged fronts and clasps and hand-holds cut in the ends to facilitate rapid evacuation. When puzzled visitors — including researchers from Germany—inquired about the unor-

---

[7] Schwertfeger to the author, November 20, 1950, and March 9, 1951, in which he quoted portions of an unpublished report to General Bissing dated May 26, 1916. See also pp. 169-170 of No. 17, and pp. 44, 94, and *passim* of No. 20.

[8] P. 295 of No. 21.

thodox and ungainly arrangement, the personnel freely acknowledged their suspicion that in another war the Germans would attempt a second seizure of the documents and that the materials were habitually boxed so they could be rushed to a sanctuary. Moreover, the staff drafted secret plans for evacuation.

When the Second World War began in 1939, Belgium was not at first invaded. Nevertheless, various ministries transferred a number of documents — *archives mortes* — to hiding places in Brussels and completed plans for the rapid evacuation of the others to the port of Ostend. A. Winandy, who had been in charge of the Service, had retired by the latter season; Charles Lecharlier was chief and A. Henri Lambotte was assistant director.

The Nazis invaded Belgium on May 10, 1940, and two days later the Belgians began the evacuation of the remaining ministry records to Ostend. When the Germans broke through the French forces near Sedan and dashed to the Channel coast, the Belgians decided on a final evacuation. While the cases were being loaded on two ships bound for England, German dive bombers approached and the ships quickly put to sea without some of the boxes. These, fifteen hundred in number, were moved overland to Poitiers. None of them contained diplomatic documents, however.

Lambotte followed the 125 tons, some two thousand cases (four fifths of which were Service records), to England. The British authorities soon offered a relatively safe depository for the duration — a portion of the Caernarvon Castle in Wales. When the curious Welsh neighbors asked about the contents of the boxes, they were satisfied with Lambotte's reply, "whiskey and cigarettes." Here, in the Queen's Tower of the famous medieval structure, Lambotte stored his cargo. Where archers once stood guard, he set up a small office and was soon able to serve the government in exile. Still concerned about the safety of the archives, officials added a concrete roof over the tower to protect them from incendiary bombs. When it appeared that the Nazis might invade Britain, the determined Belgians envisaged a third evacuation, this time to Canada.[9]

All this was as yet unknown to the German authorities, who had indeed decided to seize the documents, as in 1914. The Nazis trained one special detachment of *Sonderkommando* to seize the diplomatic and other archives of Belgium and another to obtain those of the Netherlands. The motorcycle detachment dashed into the heart of the city and placed certain offices and buildings under guard until a thorough search could be made. A full day passed before the other troops occupied the Belgian capital.[10] Thus the Belgian and Dutch archives became one of the first military objectives when the fighting spread to western Europe.

The Germans quickly realized that much of what they sought was missing. Nevertheless, they collected all papers thought to be of interest, called in their ambassador to verify this, and shipped the records to Berlin.[11] Actually, the archivists had left no material of value in the Service. The Nazi group, led by Baron von Künsberg, one-time Secretary of Legation, began a search for the missing cases of documents, traced them to Ghent, and then Ostend, only to discover that the cases had disappeared. Learning that some had been trucked into France, Künsberg continued the chase to that haven for Belgian émigrés,[12] located the fifteen hundred cases, and shipped these to Berlin. But the Nazis were in for still another frustration, for these documents likewise proved to be of little interest. Learning that the ones most sought had been shipped to England,[13] the tenacious Künsberg began to

[9] Pp. 3–5 of reprint of No. 16; information furnished by Lambotte.

[10] Memo., Berlin, May 11, 1940, Ad. Protocol A. 8191; tel., Kordt to the German foreign office, May 17, A09001; and Zeitsschel to the Service of Protocol, German Embassy, Brussels, May 23, No. 16, D, 511204-5-6, of No. 19.

[11] Künsberg to the German foreign office, Brussels, May 30, and note, Künsberg to Halem, Berlin, October 8, Rgen 1/4–179, of No. 19.

[12] Tel., Künsberg to German foreign office, May 29, apparently from Ostend, HNOX 906, of No. 19. On the last day of May, a United Press despatch contained a report that the Belgian diplomatic archives had been "almost entirely located and continue to arrive at Poitiers by truck." (*New York Times*, June 1, 1940, p. 2, c. 2.).

[13] Note, Künsberg to Halem, October 8, Rgen 1/4–179 and supplementary report by Berswordt, May 15–June 14, 18. XIII. 40, of No. 19.

compile a list of the personnel of the Service who had gone to England and tried to secure their addresses in exile, an investigation he pursued as late as January of 1941.[14] Only when the English Channel once again proved to be an adequate moat for Britain did he abandon the effort to search out and seize the Belgian documents. Lambotte, the ingenious archivist, and his colleagues took the deepest pride in the successful evacuation of the documents. "This was our first success against the Germans," he has declared. "The British have their Dunkirk and we have our Ostend!"

After four and a half years, that is, in November, 1944, the Service-in-exile could return home with its documents intact. This success of the Belgian government was in direct contrast to the experience of several states that had not taken similar precautions. Archivists of the Netherlands, for example, burned many of their prewar records in 1940 as the Nazi forces approached The Hague. Many Quai d'Orsay records fell into German hands and some were removed to the Reich, while others were lost in a fire during the hostilities in liberating Paris. The Nazis seized documents at Oslo and used some in the "White Book No. 4" in an effort to bolster the claim that Norway had forsaken neutrality before the invasion. They transported some Greek government materials to the Fatherland after the fall of Athens, delayed returning these for some years, and left the files in great disorder.[15]

With the return of peace, the Belgian archivists secured roomier quarters and soon opened the archives with Lambotte as chief. Nevertheless, the war experiences were still fresh in the minds of the postwar authorities. They had thwarted the invaders in 1940 but, deciding that the same method would not succeed in a later

[14] Note, Künsberg to Lutter, Berlin, September 4; Künsberg to Barben, Berlin, November 16, Rgen 1/4-248; Bargen to the German Foreign Office (intended for Künsberg), Brussels, January 13, 1941, Rgen 7/4-248 Ang. II (also marked D.511169); Künsberg to the Special Group in the German Foreign Office, Berlin, January 31, number D.11168 (also marked K/LG-153 42), all in No. 19.

[15] For an interesting review of the treatment and use of archives during wars in recent centuries, see Ernst Posner, "Public records under military occupation." *American historical review*, XLIX (January 1944), 213–227.

invasion, they drafted new plans for evacuation. The Service began to microfilm its materials, one purpose being that, if again threatened, perhaps the archivists could fly the less-bulky films to a friendly haven and destroy the significant originals. Many films are now stored in an atomic bombproof shelter, and the timetable for "securing" the documents is three days.[16]

P. Desneux has been the Chef du Service since 1952. He has maintained the traditions of careful protection of the documents, while extending the most cordial welcome to researchers. He is internationally known also for his innovative approach to the classification of documents.

ORGANIZATION AND CLASSIFICATION

The history of the *Service des Archives* helps clarify the arrangement of its materials. When the staff first gave serious attention to their documents — summarizing each and binding them — the archivists placed most of the materials in the general collections described below and arranged the others in special dossiers on topics of particular interest. As time passed, they put an increasing amount of materials in special dossiers and modified other early practices.

The general collections are:

1. *Arrêtés royaux et ministériels,* 1830–   Arranged chronologically in bound volumes.
2. *Correspondance politico-commerciale,* 1830–   Records of negotiations and information on commerce, finance, emigration, colonization, the Red Cross, health, social problems, arms, etc.
3. *Correspondance politique,* 1830–
   a. *Légations.* Correspondence with diplomats accredited to foreign states; most frequently arranged by the state to which the diplomat is accredited — Allemagne (after 1870), Grande Bretagne, etc.

[16] For a sparkling review of the Service and an introduction to the use of its documents, see No. 27.

    b. *Consulats.* Reports from and communications to the consulates on political matters; arranged by locality of consulates until 1903, but after that date placed with the *Légations* correspondence.

    c. *Départements ministériels et autorités belges,* 1830–
In the main, correspondence of ministers of foreign affairs and commerce with other ministers, the king's secretary, and local authorities. Volume 5, for example, contains correspondence on such matters as *Arbitrage du Roi entre les Etats-Unis et le Chili, Troubles dans le Hainaut, Mission de Général Chazal* (1866), and *Mission chinoise en Belgique.*

The unusual interest in the Belgian documents and the need to maintain greater security were major factors in a decision by the archivists to depart from their practice of imprinting titles on the bindings; consequently they now divide the dossiers into the *unnumbered,* which bear their titles, and those which are *numbered* with the titles listed only in catalogues. The need for greater security is also the reason some catalogues are not open to examination.

The unnumbered dossiers. Most of the earlier records — a good majority of those of the nineteenth century and some after that time — are in this group. They are the ones usually bound in black morocco leather and canvas; hence, they are familiarly known as *les volumes noires* and *les séries noirés reliées.* The first pages of the bound volumes contain useful *Tables chronologiques,* which indicate the number of the document, the date, the sender, the receiver (if the document is a piece of correspondence), and the summary.

Much of the material found in the unnumbered dossiers is the *Correspondance politique — Légations* and *Consulats.* After the documents in this category had been bound, a number of other pieces were forwarded to the Service, summarized, and bound; given the name *Compléments reliés,* they contain documents of the period 1830–70. Documents received still later were not analyzed, and these are known as *Suppléments non-reliés*. As mentioned earlier, the *Correspondance politique — Consulats* was not classified separately after 1903, but was placed with the legation's correspondence.

The unnumbered dossiers also include some of the special dossiers. These contain not only pieces of *Correspondance politique*, but also private papers, memoranda, and even newspaper clippings. Two sample titles are *Conférence de Londres, 1830-39,* 18 vols., and *Convention des forteresses, 1831-1873,* 2 vols. Attention is called to *Missions étrangères, 1830-70,* six volumes of correspondence with foreign diplomats accredited to Brussels until 1870, after which the correspondence is placed in the numbered dossiers. The *Papiers Lambermont,* 11 vols., constitute one special dossier; another is *Notes et mémoires,* 4 vols., containing significant comments and opinions of various officials of the ministry on a number of subjects.

As could be anticipated, materials relating to Africa constitute an important segment of the Belgian Service. One large special collection is *Afrique.* Although most of the dossiers in this collection are numbered, and hence will be described later, eight are unnumbered and are among *les volumes noires,* which have the summaries of each document included in the volume. Researchers are reminded that although documents were collected and placed in the special dossiers and in *Afrique,* there may be other significant materials in other unnumbered and numbered collections. As an illustration, political records related to the Congo may be found also in the *Correspondance politique,* both *Légations* and *Consulats.*

A subject guide for the earlier materials (to 1914), the *Tables de rubriques,* is a large card catalogue that is available to the investigator upon the consent of the chief of the Service. In addition, there are more recent, comprehensive, and extensive guides and *fichiers* which are most useful.

The numbered dossiers. In general, most of these materials bear a date after 1900, although some go back to 1830. The two principal series of numbered dossiers are the *Série politique* and the *Archives politico-commerciales*. The political dossiers bear numbers from 1 to 1,999 and above 10,000. The political-commercial are numbered 2,000 to 10,000. These numbered dossiers, too, contain instructions, reports, clippings, notes, and memoranda. The titles of these dossiers, with their divisions and subdivisions, have been typed and placed in binders which researchers may consult with the consent of the archivist. To cite examples, the first of the numbered political dossiers is a major collection on the *Grand Duché de Luxembourg,* and over six pages are needed to indicate its contents; in contrast, *Belgique-Panama: Divers, 1904 et 1924,* is a very small dossier. Examples of dossiers bearing numbers greater than 10,000 are the *Pacte de Locarno, Désarmement,* and the *Politique belge d'indépendance et la neutralité de 1936.*

The political dossiers include the *Archives des Affaires étrangères, Vienne, 1832–1901.* This multivolume collection of copies of Austrian correspondence contains instructions of Austrian envoys accredited to Brussels, their reports, some dispatches relating to Belgium and sent by other Austrian diplomats, and correspondence between Belgian kings and the emperors and chancellors of Austria. Most of the copies are typewritten. This valuable collection is no longer unique. The archivists are steadily adding microfilms of similar materials from depositories in France, Great Britain, Germany, Spain, Switzerland, and the United States. Reciprocity is so often the case that foreign scholars studying their own country's relations with Belgium are advised to check their home archives rather than assume that research in Brussels is essential.

The *Archives politico-commerciales* (numbered from 2,000 to 10,000) are arranged by subject and subtopics. *Négociations commerciales,* for example, has sections on *Belgique-France, Belgique-Pays-Bas,* etc. *Questions financières* is divided into states and then into aspects of the questions, such as *Emprunts, Budgets,* etc. Other dossiers are devoted to such subjects as *Les chemins de fer europeens, L'émigration,* and *Les tentatives de colonisation.*

The archivists maintain a *fichier* for the political and the politico-commercial dossiers.

The Service is a major depository for records relating to the Congo. As the area assumed significance, some materials were arranged in special dossiers and became a portion of the unnumbered *séries noires reliées.* As the area became still more significant, the archivists decided to make a *grande collection* of these Congo documents. Therefore the collection entitled *Afrique,* which was mentioned above, contains both unnumbered special documents and numbered dossiers. The numbers of the latter bear the prefix "Af." As illustrations, Af 1-1 contains the correspondence of the consulate at Trondheim on the colony of the Congo from 1908–1913, and Af 1-13 has *Papiers Strauch-Correspondance avec Léopold II au sujet du Congo.* This African collection has a special index. In 1962 the Belgian Ministère des Affaires étrangères received both the *Archives africaines métropolitaines* and the great majority of the archives from the Congo itself. The materials transferred amounted to seven hundred tons, and some have not been catalogued. Most of the records on the Congo and the continent of Africa are now in the numbered dossiers.

The dossiers in the *Collection presse,* also among the numbered, deserve special mention. There are well over sixteen hundred dossiers at the time of this revised edition. They contain clippings and copies of articles on a great variety of subjects from both Belgian and foreign newspapers and periodicals. The contents are primarily editorials or political news items, but some are from commercial and technical journals. The materials come from an office that systematically clips articles and from embassies and consulates. However, when reports from the latter deal specifically with the articles, the clippings are usually left with the reports. Practically all the items are in the period since the 1860s. Some titles have only a single folder (or *farde*) with a dozen articles, such as *Anarchisme (1893–1914),* which has twenty-six items. Other subjects have many volumes of articles, as for example, *Presse étrangère. Analyses. (1914–1922) Violation du droit des gens par les Allemands. (Déportations, etc.) Divers,* which consists of thirty-two volumes and has an estimated seven hundred items. Together with the thousands attached to the reports in the *Correspondance politique,* the articles make the Belgain Service a good starting point for research on many aspects of press opinion during the period since 1860. The fifty-year rule does not apply to this collection. A special card index lists the titles alphabetically.

Finally, there are numbered *Dossiers du personnel* which contain the records of individuals engaged in administering foreign affairs. These files have a separate index and are accessible only with the approval of the chief of the Service.

Although the correspondence concerning treaties is deposited in the *Service des Archives,* the treaties themselves are in the *Service des Traités* of the Ministry of Foreign Affairs. Special authorization must be secured before they are opened to investigators.

Two of the valuable collections of private papers in the Service are those of the Beyens family (most significant for relations with France) and the Anethan family (for relations with the Vatican); their use is restricted to established scholars who secure the authorization of the family.[17]

ADMINISTRATION, REGULATIONS, AND FACILITIES

Admission to the archives is by a written application to the Ministre des Affaires étrangères, 2 rue Quatre Bras, 1000 Bruxelles. The applicant should give the place and date of birth,

[17] Information on these archives was cordially given by Lambotte, P. Desneux, who succeeded Lambotte, their staff, and Professor J. Willequet, Chef du Service historique. Arnold J. Briddon also helped the author comprehend the arrangement of unfamiliar materials. The research was made possible by sabbatical leaves, a C.R.B. Fellowship by the Belgian American Educational Foundation, a Fulbright Scholarship, and other grants.

profession or position, the research topic, its dates, and the purpose of the study. Foreign nationals should inclose a letter of introduction form their embassies. Although the mailing address of the Service is 2 rue Quatre Bras, the usual entrances are 58 rue aux Laines and 1 rue du Cerf.

After receiving authorization to use the archives, the investigator should present himself to the Chief of the Service and explain in more detail the scope and objectives of the study. The chief and researcher will then draft a list of dossiers pertinent to the subject, a list that is retained in a large envelope. To obtain a volume, the reader should indicate the name or number on the envelope and sign upon receiving the volume; he should request a signature upon returning it. Further regulations governing the use of the reading room are mimeographed and are on the tables. With few exceptions, the materials open to investigation are those antedating fifty years; another year is automatically opened on January 1. Researchers may apply to a "Commission diplomatique" for authorization to examine more recent documents — to 1940 at this writing. Their use is subject to certain restrictions such as no microfilming. The members of the staff are extraordinarily cordial and know their materials well. The hours of the reading room are 9:00 A.M. to 12:00 A.M. and 2:00 P.M. to 5:00 P.M. Monday through Friday. Noon meals are available in the building and, if a member of the staff remains in the Service offices, readers may work there between 12:00 A.M. and 2:00 A.M.. There is no summer or annual closing, nor are there more than the usual number of national and religious holidays. The reading room has a coin machine for duplicating documents; microfilming is available also, and forms for requesting this service are on the research tables.

A limited number of scholars are permitted to use the library of the Ministry of Foreign Affairs. Application should be made to E. Duquenne, who has an accommodating staff. This library of some 300,000 titles adjoins the Service, and they have a common reading room.

ADDITIONAL ARCHIVES AND LIBRARIES

The extensive and rapidly expanding *Archives générales du Royaume* have much to offer diplomatic historians interested in both the period before and during Belgian national history. Very useful lists and *aperçus* of the collections in the *Archives générales* are available,[18] and the collections in the provincial archives — which are located in the principal cities of the provinces and which also contain documents of diplomatic interest — will soon have a volume which lists and describes their contents. These descriptions also contain the number of *articles* of each collection, that is, the number of categories or subjects into which the papers are classified. Although the *articles* vary in the amount of material they contain, they do convey some idea of quantity. Practically all of the collections have been inventoried, many in great detail; all the collections mentioned here have inventories, unless otherwise noted.

As might be expected, these *Archives générales* contain much material on Burgundy's relations with other states. Also, there are many pieces of correspondence of Charles V, Philip II, and Emperor Charles VI, including instructions and reports from envoys to various foreign states. There are collections on the relations of the Low Countries with the Empire from 1506-1711, and on the correspondence of the Spanish envoys at The Hague with the king of Spain and others, 1648-1702. Another collection is *Archives diplomatiques des Pays-Bas (1815-28)*, which consists of copies with some documents predating 1815. Still another is the more numerous *Gouvernement provisoire, Régence, et Congrès national* (1830-31).

The most significant collections of private papers, most of which are voluminous, include: *Papiers E. Banning,* 160 *articles*; *Papiers de Borchgrave,* primarily those of Baron Emile de Borchgrave, 285 *articles*; *Papiers Ch. de Broqueville,* very numerous but not inventoried or open to research as the present edition is

---

[18] No. 11.

published; *Papiers Forthomme, 145 articles; Papiers de H. J. W. Frère-Orban, 1,092 articles; Papiers H. Jaspar, 258 articles; Papiers J. Van Den Heuvel, 1854–1926, 54 articles; Papiers P. Hymans, 530 articles* which contain over four hundred brochures; *Papiers de Jena-Baptiste Nothomb, 1805–81, 223 articles; Papiers P. Poullet et archives de la famille Poullet, 295 articles; Papiers Ch. Rogier, 137 articles; Papiers Baron Rolin-Jaequemyns, Papiers E. Schollaert et J. Helleput,* 200 *articles* relating to foreign affairs; *Papiers Baron Stassart, 2,043 articles; Papiers de Theux de Meylandt, 205 articles;* and *Papiers S. Van de Weyer, 294 articles.* Some of these collections contain numerous press clippings. In addition to the fifty-year restriction of the *Archives Générales,* donors have placed restrictions on some of the private collections. To examine these, researchers should direct written requests to the Archiviste en Chef, C. Wyffels, rue de Ruysbroeck. Mlle. A. Scufflaire is Chef de Département.[19] Admission cards available at the entrance, and the hours are 9:00 A.M. to 6:00 P.M. including Saturdays. Pending additional storage space on the premises, users must request some collections in advance, and the waiting time varies. The inventories and some reference works are on open shelves of the reading room. Microfilm and photostat services are available. Two neighboring institutions are the *Bibliothèque royale* and the *Centre de Recherches et d'Etudes historiques de la Seconde Guerre Mondiale.*

King Baudouin announced in 1963 the decision to make the royal archives accessible to scholars. Appropriately, the choice for the location of these *Archives du Palais Royal* was a wing of the palace in Brussels. The documents presently open are primarily those of Kings Leopold I and II, although a few predate 1831 and some are from the reigns of the three succeeding monarchs. Most of the papers of Leopold I have been lost, and extensive research has not disclosed the exact fate of the missing documents. The papers of the later monarchs have had better fortune. Emile

[19] The author is indebted to them for much of the information on which this description is based.

Vandewoude has published the first of several projected inventories.[20]

Although the first two Leopolds were noted for both the number of their correspondents — foreign and domestic — and frequency of their correspondence — official and private — more of their letters are available elsewhere than in their own palace. Nevertheless, a number are in the *Fonds Léopold I* and *Cabinet du Roi Léopold II,* the latter containing some 1,440 letters exchanged between the monarch (or his principal secretary at his direction) and Belgian statesmen, particularly between 1880 and 1909. Major collections of other documents are the *Papiers Conway, Papiers Kinkin, Papiers van Loo, Papiers du Comte de Flandre, Fonds Congo,*[21] *Papiers M. L. Gérard, Fonds dit du Havre,* and *Cabinet du Roi Albert Ier.*

The fifty-year restriction and other conditions for use of the *Archives générales du Royaume* apply to the *Archives du Palais Royal,* the latter being under the administrative supervision of the former, but remaining the property of the crown. Applicants for research in the *Archives du Palais Royal* should send the usual information on qualifications for research and the topic to Le Chef du Cabinet du Roi, Palais Royale, 2 rue Ducale, 1000 Bruxelles, well in advance of their anticipated research. Emile Vandewoude is the Archivist.[22] The reading room at 2 rue Ducale is accessible by appointment; its telephone is 02-13.07.70. There is no set date for summer or vacation closing of the royal archives.

The numerous documents relating to the Congo are widely dispersed. As shown earlier, a number are in the *Service des Archives* of the foreign ministry, but some are in the *Archives générales du Royaume,* the *Archives du Palais Royal,* in the *Musée Royal du Congo belge,* and a great number of documents and microfilms are in the *Archives africaines* at Place Royale 7, which was once the *Service des Archives* of the *Ministère des Colonies* and later of the *Ministère des Affaires africaines.* E. Van

[20] No. 22.

[21] See the detailed inventory in No. 23.

[22] The author is grateful to him for his aid in describing these archives.

Grieken and Madeleine Van Grieken-Taverniers have histories of
the latter archives down to 1959[23]. Archivists have published
various inventories and descriptions of them[24], and unpublished
inventories are available under the same fifty-year rule as the
documents. A small proportion of the documents have been
carefully summarized.

To gain access to the *Archives africaines,* scholars should apply
to the Chef du Service, Mme. M. Van Grieken-Taverniers, 7 Place
Royale, 1000 Brussels, giving precise identification of themselves
and their research interests, with foreigners presenting letters of
introduction from their embassies. There is no set date for
summer closing, so the request should be made well in advance of
projected research. The reading room is open from 9–12:00 A.M.
and 2–5:00 P.M. Mondays through Fridays, and microfilming is
available.

The *Bibliothèque africaine* of the same address shelves some
three hundred thousand volumes. It subscribes to more than
fourteen hundred periodicals and maintains an index of their
articles. The library is strong in pertinent newspapers as well.
Since 1946 it has published 10 issues a year of *Bibliographie
africaine,* and it has an annual *Catalogue des acquisitions.* The
reading room contains many reference works on open shelves and
has adequate space for researchers. The hours are 9:00 A.M. to 1:00
P.M. and 2:00 P.M. to 5:00 P.M. Mondays through Fridays, and
microfilming is available.

The largest Belgian library is the *Bibliothèque royale Albert
I*[er], the history of which can be traced to the Dukes of Burgundy
in the fifteenth century. First opened to the public in 1772, it
became the *Bibliothèque royale de Belgique* in 1837, was made
the *Dépot légal* of all printed works of the country in 1966, and
became a memorial to King Albert upon the construction of the
present building. Efficiently housed on the Mont des Arts and

[23] See Nos. 24 and 25.
[24] See No. 24, which describes the private papers and some materials going back
to 1878; No. 25; and the inside cover of No. 15, which has some 26 titles of articles
describing selected materials.

staffed by well-trained librarians, its acquisitions now approach three million volumes. This library has 180 Belgian newspapers and subscribes to seventeen thousand periodicals. The subject and author catalogues do not include the publications of some international organizations such as the European Communities; these are in *inventaires-catalogues* and constitute a portion of the Section des Documents Officiels, with a separate reading room.

Most sections of the library are open until 9:00 P.M. except Saturdays and the eves of *jours fériés,* when they close at 7:00 P.M.; the special sections are usually open from 9–12:00 A.M. and 2–5:00 P.M. Interlibrary loans may be arranged. University professors may apply to le Conservateur en Chef for space in the *Salle de Travail,* where they may leave volumes for a reasonable period of time. A cafeteria, complete with a pleasant terrace, is on the fifth floor.

A researcher wishing to consult the rapidly expanding documents of the European Communities (Coal and Steel, Common Market, and Euratom) should explain his qualifications for and the purpose of his research and request their use from the Central Archives and Documentation Service (Division IX/D/1-SCAD) of the Commission of European Communities, 200 rue de la Loi, 1040 Brussels. This Service publishes a Bulletin on Documentation and, in time, will prepare further guides to the materials which will, of course, be of increasing interest. Research may be conducted during the usual office hours.[25]

All of the archives and libraries described here are within walking distance of each other, at least for the more vigorous. The large and small hotels and the declining number of pensions in the neighborhoods of Porte de Namur and Porte Louise are the most conveniently located.

Since Belgium is both a newcomer to the family of western European nations and a small state, students of diplomatic history tend to overlook or underestimate the value of materials

[25] Mr. C. J. Martens kindly supplied the information on the Communities' archives.

maintained there, unless the topic concerns the country directly. Actually, Brussels is a good location for research on innumerable topics. Some advantages have been explained: the sympathetic interest of the archivists, the organization and arrangement of documents, the typewritten copies of Austrian documents, films of other foreign documents, the numerous materials on Africa, the outstanding press collection, and the voluminous private papers. Another major reason is that Belgium's successive diplomats, headed by its first two monarchs, were vigilant observers, reporters, analysts, and students of the foreign scene. They appear to have been so by inclination; certainly their small state's precarious location, and for a time its neutralized status, would have forced them to be so. To a greater degree than other states, the very existence of the country could depend on the accurate interpretation of the policies of other states and on international amity; as a consequence, the Brussels officials were activists in their search for avenues to peace. Finally, Belgium's early industrial development caused a strong interest in custom's unions starting in the early decades of the Zollverein, well over a century before the Common Market.

BIBLIOGRAPHY

Printed Collections of Documents
1. Académie royale de Belgique. Commission royale d'Histoire. *Documents diplomatiques belges, 1920-1940.* Published by Ch. de Visscher and F. Vanlangenhove. 5 vols.; Brussels, 1964-66.
2. Notte, Charles. "Document Notte. Stanley au Congo, 1879-1884," *Bulletin des séances de l'A.R.S.C.*, published by the Académie royale des Sciences coloniales, XXV (1954), 1124-79, 1428-61.

Alfred de Ridder, one-time Director of the Service, frequently quoted entire documents in his numerous publications. The five following titles are among those in which he was more editor than historian.
3. *La Belgique et la Prusse en conflit, 1834-38.* Brussels and Paris, 1919.
4. *La crise de la neutralité belge de 1848, le dossier diplomatique.* 2 vols. Brussels, 1928. After forty pages of comment, each of 477 documents is summarized briefly and quoted almost *in toto*.

5. *Histoire diplomatique du traité de 1839 (19 avril, 1839)*. Brussels and Paris, 1920.
6. *Le mariage du Roi Leopold II*. Brussels, 1925. Consists primarily of Belgian documents dealing with Franco-Belgian relations, 1851–56.
7. *Les Projets d'union douanière franco-belge et les puissances européennes, (1836–1843)*. Brussels, 1933.

When the Germans occupied Brussels in the war of 1914–18, they selected and published a number of documents during and following hostilities, including the next two titles.

8. *European politics during the decade before the war as described by Belgian diplomatists*. Documents issued by the Imperial German Foreign Office, 1915.
9. *Zur europäischen Politik, 1897–1914: unveröffentliche Dokumente in amtlichem Auftrage*. Edited by Bernhard Schwertfeger. 5 vols. Berlin, 1919. A second edition under the title *Amtliche Aktenstücke zur Geschichte der europäischen Politik, 1885–1914* was published in Berlin in 1924. It had three supplementary volumes, which contained some additional Belgian materials published during the war.

Conventions and treaties that were negotiated, whether they were ratified or not, may be found in:

10. *Recueil des traités et conventions concernant le royaume de Belgique*. Edited by Baron de Garcia de la Vega and continued by Alphonse de Busschère. 21 vols. Brussels, 1850–1914.

Guides and Reference Works:
11. An earlier work, *Les Archives générales du Royaume à Bruxelles. Aperçu des fonds et des inventaires* (edited by H. van Haegendoren, Brussels, 1955) has been superseded by *Répertoire des inventaires des archives conservées en Belgique parus avant le 1er janvier, 1969* (edited by L. Nicodème, Brussels, 1970), and supplements appear regularly in the quarterly, *Archives et bibliothèques de Belgique*.
11a. Bemis and Griffin, *Guide*. On Belgian MSS, pp. 924–928.
12. A *Bibliographie de Belgique* has been published periodically since 1838 (except 1868–76), with some variation of source and of title and with supplements.
12a. Degras, *Soviet Documents*. On Belgium, pp. 14, 107, 171, 218.
13. De Ridder, Alfred. *La violation de la neutralité belge et ses avocats*. Brussels, 1926

14. *Diplomatic documents relating to the outbreak of the World War.* Edited by James B. Scott. London, 1916.

15. Duchesne, A. *Le Musée royal de l'Armée et d'histoire militaire au point de vue de la documentation historique coloniale.* Brussels, 1958.

16. Lambotte, A. H. "Les archives des affaires étrangères pendant la guerre," *La revue générale belge* (April 1947).

17. Lancken Wakenitz, Oscar Freiherr von der. *Meine dreissig Dienstjahre — 1888-1918. Potsdam — Paris — Brussels.* Berlin, 1931.

18. "Organisation de la direction des archives au Département des Affaires étrangères." A special dossier in the *Service des Archives, Ministère des Affaires étrangères,* Brussels.

19. Reports and memoranda by members of the German *Sonderkommando,* which was assigned the task of seizing the Belgian documents in 1940. Photostatic copies are on deposit in the Belgain *Service des Archives.* It is difficult to cite these German materials properly and consistently, for they have not been given uniform classification.

20. Schwertfeger, Bernhard. *Der geistige Kampf um die Verletzung der belgischen Neutralität.* Berlin, 1919.

21. Thomas, Daniel H. "History of the diplomatic archives of Belgium," *The American archivist,* XV (1952), 291-302. A more detailed account of the history of the Service written at the same time.

22. Vandewoude, Emile. "Les archives royales à Bruxelles," *Archives et bibliothèques de Belgique,* XXXVIII (1967), 176-192.

23. *Inventaire des archives relatives au développement extérieur de la Belgique sous le règne de Leopold II.* Brussels, 1965.

24. Van Grieken, E. and Madeleine Van Grieken-Taverniers. *Les archives inventoriées au Ministère des Colonies,* published by Académie royale des Sciences coloniale, classe des sciences morales et politique, new series, Vol. XII. Brussels, 1958.

25. Van Grieken-Taverniers, Madeleine. "L'histoire de l'Etat indépendant du Congo et les archives du Ministère du Conto belge et du Ruanda-Urundi," *Archives, bibliothèques, et musées de Belgique,* XXX (1959).

26. *Inventaire des archives des affaires étrangères de l'Etat indépendant du Congo et du Ministère des Colonies (1885-1914)* published by the Académie royale des Sciences coloniales, classe des sciences morales et politiques, new series, Vol. II. Brussels, 1955.

27. Willequet, Jacques. "Les archives du Ministère des Affaires étrangères," *Archives, bibliothèques et musées de Belgique,* XXII (Number 1, 1951).

28. Winandy, A. "Les archives du Département des Affaires étrangères," *Expansion belge, revue mensuelle illustrée* (October 1913). By a former director of the Service.

3 DENMARK

Edgar Anderson
California State University, San José

HISTORY

RIGHT in the center of Copenhagen rises the stately Christianborg Palace, formerly the residence of the Danish royal family and presently the seat of the Danish *Rigsdag* (Parliament), the Foreign Ministry, and the Supreme Court. A building to the east of the palace houses the Danish State Archives (*Rigsarkivet*).

The present small kingdom of Denmark occupies a strategically important position at the entrance to the Baltic Sea; as a consequence, the issue of the Danish Sound dues has been an international problem of great importance. Many wars have been fought to eliminate or lessen this control over the gateway to the Baltic, and in these and other wars Denmark lost most of its numerous and widespread provinces and colonies. Nevertheless, a number of Danish public servants, social reformers, scientists, and men of letters have left their influence on the development of civilization and social life in these areas.

As checkered as the history of the country is, so is also the history of the Danish archives. Copenhagen has not always been the capital of Denmark. During the Middle Ages the archives followed the kings from one residence to another. The Cathedral of Roskilde, commissioned by Bishop Absalom in 1170, was one of the first depositories; centrally located on the island of Zealand, it is to Danish history somewhat as Westminster Abbey is to English history. The Cathedral of Lund, now a part of Sweden, has served as the site for the Danish royal archives, as has Vordingsborg Castle in the southern part of Zealand. The founders of the Kalmar Union, Queen Margrete (1387–1412) and King

Erik (1412-39), housed their archives in Kalundborg, on the western side of Zealand.

King Frederik III (1648-70), who established absolute monarchy in Denmark, also laid the foundation for the *Geheimearkiv* (privy archives) when he appointed Peder Schumacher (later Count Griffenfeld) as the royal librarian and archivist in 1663. Finally the archives were moved to Copenhagen, first to Rosenborg Castle, one of the royal residences built by Christian IV, and in 1720 to the present location near the Christianborg Palace. Frederik I (1523-33) and Christian III (1534-58) had set up the so-called joint archives at Gottorp in Schleswig, and these were transferred to Copenhagen in 1734, as were the ducal archives of Gottorp not long thereafter.

Under a succession of able and intelligent privy archivists, such as Hans Gram, J. Langebek, and G. Schönning, from 1730 to 1780, the archives became an important center of research. The first well-edited collection of Danish documents pertaining to the Middle Ages, *Scriptores rerum Danicarum medii aevi*, was published from 1772 to 1834. Later, as the collections accumulated rapidly and caused concern among the archivists, their attempt at a solution was the unfortunate destruction of many documents of historical value.

In 1848 Caspar Frederik Wehner became the privy archivist and, thanks to his initiative, most of the ministerial archives up to 1750 were also deposited in the privy archives. After the war of 1864, Prussia forced Denmark to surrender a large portion of her Schleswig-Holstein archives.

In 1883 the privy and state documents were united under a single head, the *Geheimearkivar* (privy archivist). Adolf D. Jörgensen, a trained archivist, became the chief and soon made major changes in the organization and classification. He abandoned the impractical system of listing each separate document on a card and adopted the principle of provenance, the institutional source of the document. Also, in 1889 he divided the *Rigsarkiv* (main archives) into two sections: *Afdeling I*, corresponding to the old privy archives and providing a reading room for visitors, and *Afdeling II*, the current governmental archives with a loan office for the government ministries.

Provincial archives were set up in Copenhagen, Odensee, and Viborg between 1890–93, and in 1933 at Aabenraa, and were placed under the chief archivist's administration. A noted American expert on Scandinavian archives, Dr. Waldemar Westergaard, has pointed out that the Danish state archives system was more highly centralized than most European countries. This made it possible to integrate the functions of the provincial archives with those of the *Rigsarkiv* so as to avoid duplication and possible friction.

The *Rigsarkivar* (the Archivist of Denmark) is also a member of the *Erhvervsarkiv*, the Board of Business Archives, originally a private institution established in 1944 in order to collect the archival deposits from commercial firms, banks, factories, etc. These archives, now having an official function, are not, however, under the direct administration of the *Rigsarchivar*.

The structure of the two sections of the *Rigsarkiv* was altered in 1956 and 1958, respectively, by the establishment of a secretariat and a section for technical services (photographing and conservation). In 1971 the *Rigsarkivar* also took over the administration of the Archives of the Army.

ORGANIZATION AND CLASSIFICATION

The *Rigsarkiv* (State Archives, hereafter called the RA) is the depository for the central administration of the state, its ministries, and its bureaus, and for the private papers of its leading personages. The *Landsarkiver* (archives of the provinces) house materials pertaining to the activities of ecclesiastical as well as lay officials of various ranks. Of importance to genealogists and students of Danish emigration are the files of parish registers going back even to the seventeenth century and available to researchers when the last entries are at least thirty years old. Entries on burials are accessible after ten years. Probate records from the archives of private estates and judicial offices are deposited after thirty to fifty years.

The RA is divided into:

Section I — Government records prior to 1848; reading room; conservation and photographer's studio; Xeroxing.

Section II — Government records since 1848; accessions from and loans to government offices.

Section III — Former Archives of the Army, containing records of army units (records of the central administration of the army belong to Sections I and II).

Section IV — "Private" archives of nonofficial origin; Manuscript Collection; Library.

The Secretariat can be considered as a fifth section; it handles management, budget, programs for microfilming, and records management, in collaboration with the administration.

The oldest and most precious group of manuscripts (mostly parchments) in the RA is the "Oak Cabinet" collection, deposited in the "Oak Cabinet Vault." The main sections in this highly important collection, dealing with princely or foreign relations, are: (a) older archives of the Danish royal house from Waldemar II to Christian VII (1230–1766); newer archives since the year 1766 (from 1839 open only with royal assent); (b) materials concerning the Kalmar Union, the Council of State (1438–1660), and the estates; (c) papers on the relations with the church (1419–1536); (d) documents on relations with Schleswig, Holstein, Norway, Iceland, the Faroes, Greenland, and Sweden; (e) correspondence on foreign relations to about 1700, arranged under the separate states concerned and treaties (1700–80); (f) archives of princes in territories formerly Danish, such as the "joint archives" (mainly from the period 1460–1669); the Glücksborg archives (1564–1773), consisting of parchments only, the papers being located elsewhere; and (g) the oldest private archives. (Of the above (g) includes sources dealing with the events up to about 1600.) For the sections listed above, there are printed guides only for the collection of private archives and the archives belonging to King

Christian II during his exile from 1523 to 1531 (Emilie Andersen, *München Samlingen,* Copenhagen, 1969). The reading room has a detailed card index, folio registers, and a chronological list of all parchments and the oldest paper letters (especially before 1513) in the "Oak Cabinet" collection.

Of great international importance are the Öresund (Sound) customs archives (1624-1857) and the Sound Dues accounts (1497-1856), published in part by Nina E. Bang. The correspondence that accompained this published material is still unpublished, but it is indexed in folio catalogues kept in the reading room. Among commercial archives, those of the East Asiatic and West India and Guinea companies are particularly interesting (see Kristian Erslev, *Rigsarkivet og hjaelpemidlerne til dets benyttelse. Sn Oversigt* [Copenhagen, 1923], pp. 57-66; and the guide *Asiatiske, vestindiske og guineiske handelskompagnier* by J. O. Bro-Jørgensen and Aa. Rasch [Copenhagen, 1969]). For Norway, Iceland, and Schleswig-Hosltein, formerly under the Danish crown, the RA has retained the so-called *Forestilling-sprotokoller* containing collegial representations on matters requiring royal signature and the resulting royal resolutions, whereas most of the original accompanying documents have been turned over at different times to Norwegian, Icelandic, and Prussian archives.

Denmark's correspondence with foreign states was carried on by two departments or chanceries up to 1676. The Danish chancery handled the letters to Sweden and Russia written in Danish. Letters to other European countries, including Poland, composed in German or Latin, were ordinarily written in the German chancery. Copybooks of Latin letters are preserved from the 1560s, and drafts of such letters from about 1650. Copybooks of outgoing letters in German are preserved from the 1540s; drafts of such letters are preserved for later dates. Copybooks of instructions to envoys and of *pleinpouvoirs* exist from the 1530s. From 1676 to 1770 all foreign correspondence was carried on in the foreign department of the German chancery under two sections, a "general" and a "special." The former includes an *Ausländische*

Registrant (foreign register), 1677-1756; and a more important *Geheimeregistratur* (privy register), 1676-1770, with political communications to foreign princes and to Danish envoys abroad. For the period 1736-60 there is a "protocol of confidential foreign reports, the deliberations concerning them and ... the royal resolutions," with extracts from the letters of Danish envoys abroad, the council of state's discussions of them, and the resulting royal resolutions. The "special" section of the German chancery includes the correspodence with each country arranged chronologically from the beginning, to include (1) correspondence with the country's ruler and papers resulting from negotiations with his representative in Denmark; (2) dispatches from the Danish envoy in that state; and (3) the archives of the Danish mission in that country, including instructions and letters from Copenhagen, copybooks, incoming letters, drafts of dispatches, and related materials.

During the regime of Count Johann Friedrich Struensee, a radical change was made in the German chancery. In 1771 the foreign department of this chancery was elevated to a new position as a department for foreign affairs. In 1848 its name was changed to Foreign Ministry. Its "general" section for 1770-1847 contains protocols of representations made to the king and, for 1785-1847, journals of incoming letters and various miscellaneous topics (matters pertaining to navigation, customs, transit trade, etc.). Like the previous period, the "special" section covering the time span from 1771 to 1848 is arranged under various countries. The reading room has card indexes to the foreign administration archives to 1848 and also a guide to the foreign administration archives entitled *Tyske Kancelli II*, by Arthur G. Hassø, Erik Kroman, and Carl S. Christiansen (Copenhagen, 1962).

Information pertaining to military matters before 1660 must be sought in the Danish and German chanceries. The archives for the "colleges" — after 1848, the ministries — for land and sea forces established thereafter, important for foreign policy, are located in Sections I and II, and those of individual elements of the land (and air) forces in Section III. As mentioned before, there are no longer separate Army Archives.

When royal absolutism in Denmark came to an end in 1848 and ministries replaced the administrative colleges, an extensive reshuffling of their functions occurred. In addition to the ministries for foreign affairs and for land and sea forces, there was also a special ministry for Schleswig (1851–64), for Holstein and Lauenburg (1852–64), and for Iceland (1874–1904).

An alphabetic survey of private papers in the RA: *Private Personarkiver i Rigsarkivet,* published in 1972, states the family name of persons whose papers have been deposited in the RA, with a short notice about the dates and quantities of the papers. A survey of the records of private institutions now in the RA will follow. A useful, detailed guide to private papers for the period before 1660 is Erik Kroman's *Privatarkiver før 1660 i Rigsarkivet* (Copenhagen, 1948; 188 pp.), which lists the collections alphabetically from Aagaard to Örtzen, describes their contents, and identifies senders and recipients of the letters. A thorough index enhances its usefulness. Included among these papers are numerous letters on parchment, royal missives, and "open letters" from German, Swedish, and Danish rulers, letters to and from private persons at home and abroad, drafts and transcripts of correspondence, and a variety of miscellaneous documents. In 1952 Henny Glarbo published a continuation of Kroman's guide — *Privatarkiver 1660–1800.* For the nineteenth century the guide is Kr. Erslev's *Privatarkiver, fra det 19 Aarhundrede* (Copenhagen, 1923). For acquisitions of nineteenth century papers and others received since 1923, researchers must rely on a manuscript catalogue in the RA and the alphabetic survey mentioned above, but the RA plans to issue up-to-date surveys of the private papers.

Collections of private papers deposited at the RA are numerous. For the period prior to 1800 one can mention at random the papers of these families: Bernstorff, Bielke, Brahe, Gyldenstierne, Krag, Milan, Munk, Oxe, Rantzau, Reventlow, Rosenkrants,

Sehested, Trolle, Ulfeldt, etc. Among the most important private papers of the nineteenth century are those of J. G. Adler, C. A. Bluhme, C. C. Hall, A. F. Krieger, T. A. Regenburg, A. F. Tscherning, and P. Vedel.

The *Kongelige Bibliotek* (Royal Library) in Copenhagen, too, has a large manuscript division which contains many collections of personal papers of political and diplomatic figures. A student of Danish affairs will be well advised to consult two catalogues: E. Gigas, *Katalog over det kongelige Biblioteks Haandskrifter vedr. Norden, saerlig Danmark* (3 volumes; Copenhagen, 1903–1915), and C. Behrend, *Katalog over det kgl. Biblioteks Haandskrifter vedrörende Dansk Personalhistorie* (Copenhagen, 1925). Since the publication of these catalogues, numerous subsequent acquisitions have been made, however.

A short but useful guide to the RA materials other than private papers is Kr. Erslev's *Rigsarkivet og Hjaelpemidlerne til dets Benyttelse* (Copenhagen, 1923). Guides to the materials found in the RA have been regularly published since 1886. There are now two general series: The *Vejledende Arkivregistraturer* (I–XV) (Iventories) and the *Foreløbige Arkivregistraturer* (Preliminary Inventories). For diplomatic relations with Sweden and Russia, the student may consult the previously mentioned book by Hassø, Kroman, and Christiansen — *Tyske Kancelli II* (pp. 33–35). The internal department of the German Chancery has been well covered in Johanne Skovgaard's *Tyske Kancelli I og de dermed beslaegtede Institutioner* (Copenhagen, 1946), partly based on F. J. West's long preliminary labors. Skovgaard's guide is especially useful for the Schleswig area and also contains some documents on the treaties of Westphalia and Nimwegen, on imperial diets in Regensburt and Frankfurt, and on the *Niedersächsischer Kreis, Bremen und Verden, Oldenburg und Delmenhorst, Stift Lübeck, Stadt Hamburg,* and other areas.

The already menitoned series published by the RA under the title of *Vejledende Arkivregistraturer* also has sections, originally prepared by J. Bloch, which are devoted to various governmental bodies such as: *Rentekammeret* (1660–1848), the exchequer, now replaced by Jens Holmgaard's *Rentekemmeret 1660–1848* (Copenhagen, 1964); *Generaltoldkammeret* (1760–1848), the commerce commission or college, which will be replaced in the near future by a new guide prepared by J. O Brø-Jorgenson, and *Finanskollegiet*.

Of interest to students of international relations are records of the overseas trade of Danish companies in which the government was a shareholder, the companies having a semiofficial position. A good guide to the East Asiatic, West Indian, and Guinean merchant companies recently has been compiled by J. O. Bro-Jørgensen and Aa. Rasch: *Asiatiske, vestindiske og guineiske handelskompagnier* (Copenhagen, 1969). The Danish West India and Guinea affairs came under the Danish customs administration after 1760, but the colonies in the East Indies, taken over by the Danish crown in 1777, were placed under the college of commerce.

There is as yet no printed catalogue of diplomatic correspondence in the Department for Foreign Affairs, 1771–1848 (*Undenrigske Anliggender*). The researcher, however, may consult a detailed card index listing materials of later years.

ADMINISTRATION, REGULATIONS, AND FACILITIES

Ministerial records are generally accessible after fifty years. Special limitations (eighty or one hundred years) apply to cases involving persons, to private papers, to records of the royal house, and to problems of national security. Census materials are available up to 1895, but special permission for access to later censuses may be granted for securing statistical information. Access to the materials available in the provincial archives is governed by similar rules. The private archives in public depositories are normally available when the documents are at least eighty years old; access to more recent materials requires the permission of the *Rigsarkivar* or, in certain cases, the representatives of the donors.

The address of the *Rigsarkiv* is Rigsdagsgården 9, DK-1218 Copenhagen K. The *Rigsarkivar* (The Archivist of Denmark), Dr. Johan Hvidtfeldt, is in general charge of the RA staff. The *Overarkivar* (Chief Archivist), Dr. Sune Dalgård, is head of Section I; the *Overarkivar*, Niels Petersen, of Section II; Colonel (ret.) E. Weigaard Jørgensen of Section III (Army Archives); the *Overarkivar*, Dr. Vello Helk, of Section IV; and the *Overarkivar*, Sigurd Rambusch, of the Secretariat.

No introduction of any kind is needed at the RA. Readers may receive a leaflet with a few simple rules by applying to the officer in charge at the reading room desk. The reading room has a small but useful selection of recent works on Danish history. Adjoining it is a room with a large collection of seals and a room for microfilm readers.

No typewriters or microfilming equipment belonging to private persons may be used. The RA accepts orders for microfilms at a price, as of the present, of 50 øre per exposure. Enlargements can be provided at the following rates: 9 × 12 cm., 4.00 kroner; 13 × 18 cm., 5.00 kr.; 18 × 24 cm., 6.25 kr.; 24 × 30 cm., 7.50 kr.; 30 × 40 cm., 10.00 kr. Black and-white or color or color diapositives can be provided (sizes 5 × 5 cm. and 7 × 7 cm.) at rates between 8.00 and 12.00 kr. Xerox copies can be made at the price of 50 øre per copy. Minimum price of an order acceptable to the studio has been set at 10.00 kroner.

Hotel rates at present vary from 50 to 240 kr. per night for a single room and 106 to 330 kr. per night for a double room. It is advisable to reserve rooms in advance. Inquiries regarding hotel accommodations should be directed to Danmark's Turistraad, Banegaardspladsen 2, DK-1570 Copenhagen V, (Phone 13 70 07 and 11 14 15). Fortunately for researchers, the *Rigsarkiv* is centrally located with convenient traffic facilities.

BIBLIOGRAPHY

In addition to the guides mentioned below, see those discussed above in the sections on history and organization. Caspar Frederik Wegener's *Aarsberetninger fra det kongelige Geheimearkiv* (7 vols., Copenhagen,

1852-83) is an important source for the history of the RA during Wegener's tenure as its chief archivist (1848-82), including reports on acquisitions, problems of reorganization, and publication of selected groups of historical MSS. Further development of the RA is reflected in Adolf Doitlev Jörgensen's detailed and authoritative account, *Udsigt over de danske Rigsarkivers Historie* (Copenhagen, 1893, 329 pp.). Jörgensen replaced Wegener in the office of chief archivist and initiated the classification of the materials according to provenance. Most of the credit for this work is due to Vilhelm Adolf Secher, who first served as Jörgensen's assistant and later became state archivist. Jörgensen's book traces both principal acquisitions through the centuries and losses such as those to Norway (1820ff. and 1850ff.) and to Prussia (1873ff.). Of some interest is the list of archival officials from 1523 to 1882. At the end of the book, a selection of documents from the fifteenth century to 1882 illuminates the checkered history of the archives. Jörgensen also inaugurated a series of RA-sponsored publications — *Meddelelser fra det kongelige Geheimearkiv og . . . Kongerigets Arkiv* (the title was later changed to *Meddelelser om Rigsarkivet*), which was a revised and improved version of Wegener's *Aarsberetninger*. Of particular interest is the volume for 1883-85, which contains Secher's history of the Danish chancery and a classified *registratur* of its contents to 1848, the first printed guide of its kind, and reflects the author's application of the principle of provenance (*Hjemmehörs Principet*), explained in greater detail in the volume of 1906.

Three books describe periods of the "civil central administration" from 1848 to 1935: G. N. Kringelbach's *Den civile Centraladministration 1848-1893* (1894); L. Laursen's *Den civile Centraladministration, 1894-1913* (1921), and H. Jörgensen's *Den civile Centraladministration, 1914-1935* (1936). *Den danske civile Centraladministrations Embedsetat 1660-1848* (1889) provides a list of Denmark's civil officials, but G. N. Kringelbach's *Civile Direktioner og Kommissioner samt andre overordnede Myndigheder under Enevaelden* (1899) supplies information on directorates, commissions, and higher authorities under absolutist kings.

Emil Marquard's *Danske diplomater i Utlandet* (1952) presents information about the Danish diplomats abroad until the beginning of World War I.

Haandbog for lokalhistorikere (1952-56), edited by Johan Hvidtfeld, contains much information for users of Danish archives, especially in the field of local history.

Of great importance to the students of Danish history are several compilations, containing listings, calendaring, or reproductions of documents found in the RA, starting with *Repertorium diplomaticum regni Danici mediaevalis* by Kr. Erslev and W. Christiansen (13 volumes in two series, 1894-1939). *Diplomatarium Danicum* (1938 ff.), published by the Danish Society of Language and Literature, contains medieval documents from 1250 in facsimiles, printed text, and Danish translation. A very important collection of Danish-Norwegian treaties is *Danmarks-Norges Traktater 1523-1750* (1907ff.). So far eleven volumes have been published, including the documents from 1523 to 1700. The first nine volumes have been edited by L. Laursen. C. S. Christiansen has edited Vols. X and XI. *Kabinetsstyrelsen i Danmark 1768-1772* (3 vols., 1916-23), edited by H. Hansen, has reproduced the "cabinet orders" issued by Struensee and other statesmen.

Dansk Arkivvaesen: Historie, Orgnaization og Virksomhed (1935, originally published in German in the *Archivalische Zeitschrift*, Vol. 41) by the former *Rigsarkivar*, Axel Linvald, contains a brief account of the history, organization, and activities of the Danish archives. It also contains valuable notes to all the more important printed materials on the subject, and comparisons with the practices and problems of foreign archives. Harald Jørgensen's *Nordiske Arkiver* (1968) is of more general character, dealing with the history and organization of archives in all of the Scandinavian countries.

An article by F. J. West, "Arkivalier vedr., Hertugdömmet Sleswig eller Sönderjylland," in *Fortid og Nuted*, III (pp. 40-65), has served as a guide to RA's archival materials on Schleswig until the publication of H. Hjelholt's article, "Den dansk-tyske Arkivudveksling i April-May 1936: Hvad vi fik, og hvad vi afstod," in *Fortid og Nutid*, XII (1937-38), pp. 1-12, and A. Linvald's "Dansk-tyrsk Arkivudveksling," in *Historisk Tedskrift*, 10 R., Vol. IV, pp. 109-120. A very important guide to the historical literature and sources bearing on Schleswig's history is *Vejledning i Studiet af Sönderillyllands Historie* (1944), by Troels Fink and Johan Hvidtfeldt.

Of some use are two guides to the Archives of the Army prior to its incorporation in the RA: Knud C. Rockstroh's article, "Oversigt over de vigtigste Afdelinger af Krigsministeriets Arkiv og Vejledning med Hensyn til Benyttelsen," in *Fortid og Nutid*, II (1920), pp. 170-76; and Carl von Kohl's *Haerens Arkiv* (1946).

The archives of the City Hall of Copenhagen can also be of some use. Among other collections they contain the largest part of the archives of the earliest college of commerce, under designations such as *Politiog Kommercekollegiets Resolutionsprotokoller* in three volumes (1704-12 and 1722-30), *Missivprotokoller* in (5 Vols., 1704-30), and its *Memorialprotokoller* in 8 Vols.,1704-27). One can recommend Oluf Nielsen's

"Bidrag til Kobenhavns Raadstuearkivs Historie," in *Danske Samlinger,* IV, pp. 234–49; and Axel Linvald's "Meddelelser fra Raadstuearkivet 1923ff.," in *Historiske Meddelelser ... om Köbenhavn* (1924 ff.), as useful guides to these archives.

The University of Copenhagen also contains certain archives, although its collections for the period prior to 1900 have been taken over by the RA. A person interested in the collections of manuscripts found in the Library of the University should consult Victor Petersen's "Universitetets Arkiv gennem Tiderne," in *Ex Biblioteca universitatis Hafniensis* (1920) and Alfred Krarup's *Katalog over Universitetsbibliotekets Haandskrifter,* I–II (1929, 1935).

A special committee appointed by the Danish Royal Academy of Science and Letters (*Det Kongelige Danske Videnskabernes Selskab*) has listed and evaluated historical manuscripts in private possession. An account of its work for the period from 1923 to 1931, "Kommissionen til Undersögelse af de i dansk Privateje bevarede Kilder til dansk Historie 1923ff.," has been published by the former Archivist of Denmark, Axel Linvald, in *Oversigt over det danske Videnskaberned Selskabs Forhandlinger* (1923ff.).

Identification of the authors of unsigned manuscripts is always a serious problem. A collection of approximately fourteen hundred photostats of specimen hands brought together by W. Christensen offers certain assistance in this area. Two paleographic studies, *Middelalderlig Skrift: Skriftspröver og Transkriptioner* [1951] by Erik Kroman, and *Skriftspröver fra Tiden efter Reformationen til Midten af 19. Aaehundrede* [2nd ed., 1948], can be highly recommended.

All books and pamphlets published by the Danish State Archives, as well as provincial archives from 1852 to 1973, are listed in *Skrifter udgivet af Rigsarkivet og Landsarkiverne 1852–1973* by Michael Hertz and Karen Kraft (Copenhagen, 1973), and can be considered as the most valuable guide to the various collections found at the Danish archives.

In preparation for research in Denmark, historians might also find helpful Bemis and Griffin's *Guide* (on Danish MSS, pp. 932–933); and Degras' *Soviet Documents* (on Denmark, pp. 77, 117, 149, 185, 230).

Waldemar Westergaard produced the first study on the Danish archives in English, the valuable chapter on Denmark which appeared in the first edition of this *Guide*. This chapter of the *New Guide* is partly based on his initial study. The author is deeply indebted also to Michael Hertz, Assistant Keeper of the *Rigsarkiv*, for his kind collaboration and valuable assistance.

4 FINLAND*

Kent Forster
Pennsylvania State University

HISTORY

IF, as most scholars maintain, language and historical conscious-
ness are important ingredients of nationalism, then the location
of the Finnish National Archives across the street from the
brooding statue of J. V. Snellman is, however coincidental, most
appropriate. For while Snellman began his promotion of Finnish
as the national language in the 1860s, it was in this same decade
that the National Archives (originally the "State Archives") were
founded and, through the encouragement of the writing of Finnish history became another stimulant of Finnish nationalism.

Archival development in Finland, however, commenced long
before the establishment of the National Archives. Following the
unification with Sweden in the twelfth century, documentary
material about the Finns began to accumulate — much of it
inevitably in Stockholm. But when the Grand Duchy of Finland
was transferred to Czarist Russia, one of the stipulations of the
Treaty of Hamina (1809) was the delivery by Sweden to the Finns
of all archives pertaining to the latter. This led in 1817 to the
initial Finnish archival organization, known as the Archives of
the Senate. By the middle of the nineteenth century a trained
archivist was in charge of these archives' classification and
organization. The reign of Alexander II, well remembered as that
most sympathetic to all affairs Finnish, saw the opening of the

*Grateful acknowledgment is made to the American Philosophical Society,
whose grant from the Penrose Fund enabled the author to undertake this study.
He is also indebted for invaluable assistance rendered in Helsinki by Arkistonhoitaja Veikko Litzen and Arkistonhoitaja Markku Järvinen of the Valtionarkisto, by
Dr. Risto Ropponen, Director of the Sota-arkisto, and by Mr. Heikki Impola of
the Ulkoministeriön-arkisto.

Senate Archives to the public in 1859 and their reconstitution ten years later as Finland's State Archives. By 1890 the present classically colonnaded building in Rauhankatu had been constructed and in 1971 the new modern building behind the old one was opened.

National independence introduced, among many things, a new archival era. The documentary material became so voluminous that the State Archives, now referred to as the National Archives (though the Finnish title of *Valtionarkisto* remains) were designated as the repository for mainly national matters; materials of more local import were assigned to six subsidiary provincial archives. Such a division served to emphasize further the role of the National Archives as the foremost center for historical research in the country.

To so identify the National Archives, however, requires a caveat for students of Finnish foreign policy. The latter, as smiling archivists and librarians in Helsinki are likely to point out, is essentially a contemporary subject. To be sure, there are facets of Finland's earlier history which may fall within the range of diplomatic historians — such as relations between the pre-Reformation Papacy and its Finnish clergy, or between medieval Viborg and the Hansa. Moreover, there is the story to be told of Finnish opinions on international issues before the gaining of independence. But, since in the Russian period whatever autonomy St. Petersburg accorded its Grand Duchy was not in the realm of international politics, and a somewhat similar situation marked the centuries when Finland was united with Sweden, a clearly-identified Finnish foreign policy begins only in 1917. Consequently, the scholar confronts all of the advantages and disadvantages surrounding research in recent history.

On the one hand, there exist copious and relatively complete records. Frequent fires may have destroyed much of the grist for the medievalist's mill but aside from deliberate burnings such as that of the P. E. Svinhufuud papers, the contemporary record has few gaps. In addition, the whole of Finland's foreign policy has evolved in an age of assiduous recordkeeping, abetted by the typewriter, teletype, the carbon-copy habit, and filomania. But, if the data exist, access to them is also affected by their recency. Like all governments, Finland has restrictions, closing most of its diplomatic files covering the last 40 years, or more than half of the history of its external relations as a nation-state. Thus, the researcher meets obstacles which cannot be overcome either by his own persistence and diligence or by the good will of Finnish archivists, though the latter evince much of this, partly because Finns generally are gratified by foreigners' interest in their country and partly because the archivists are usually trained and practicing historians.

This restricted access applies not only to the National Archives, but also to the category of diplomatic archives next to be considered. Following the outbreak of the Russian Revolution and the Finnish gravitation toward independence, the former Imperial Senate and a newly-appointed regent acted as a provisional government in charge of, among many matters, foreign policy. After initial assignment of this responsibility to a Senatorial Committee on Constitutional Law, the Senate in October, 1918, created a Department for Foreign Affairs (*Ulkoasiaintoimitus-kunta*) under the leadership of Senator Otto Stenroth. The written records of these two bodies and of the Senate's plenary actions comprise the first official records of Finnish diplomacy, and are today part of the archives of the Ministry of Foreign Affairs (*Ulkoasiainministeriö*). This ministry replaced the Department of Foreign Affairs in November, 1918, when it assumed the vital tasks of securing foreign recognition and launching the republic as a sovereign member of the nation-state system. From this time until the present, it has accumulated the characteristic files of a foreign office. The repository of these files, as well as of the 1917–1918 records noted earlier, is the Foreign Ministry Archives (*Ulkoasiainministeriön arkisto*).

The Ministry of Foreign Affairs, including its archival division, may be reached in a two-minute walk from the National

Archives along Snellmankatu to Helsinki's historic Senaatintori. The former offices of the Grand Ducal Senate, in the Empire-style structure forming the east façade of the *Senaatintori*, have been the quarters of the ministry since 1918, and are entered from the Ritarikatu side.

Another major archives are those of the War Ministry (*Sotaministeriö*), located in the long, gray, fortress-like building in Siltavuorenranta. Their holdings cover the military history of the Finns as far back as 1812, and contain more than fifteen miles of shelved records. Especially voluminous is material on the two wars with Russia in 1939–1944; other items of interest to students of foreign policy are the reports and correspondence of Finland's military attachés abroad and of the Finnish Supreme Command (*Pääesikunta*).

The Ministry of Education (*Opetusministeriö*) preserves the documentation of Finland's international relations in the fields of educational, scientific, and cultural exchange. Outside the United Nations until 1956 and therefore unaffiliated with UNESCO, Finland's international activities of this nature before this date were confined largely to Scandinavia. Since then, however, such exchanges multiplied rapidly, and the government has undertaken to preserve their record in the ministry most concerned with them.

From the executive center of the government, the trail of research in foreign policy leads across the inner city of Helsinki to the parliament in Mannerheimintie. As with all parliamentary systems, the power exercised over foreign affairs by the Finnish legislature remains unclear. The Diet, which replaced the old Estates in the constitutional reform of 1906, was, at the time of independence, the scene of much debate on international affairs, but policy formulation was exercised first by the Senate and then by the president and foreign ministry. Should contemporary efforts by the Diet to assert itself more vigorously in foreign policy prove successful, its records will assume larger import for the student of diplomacy. But in any case he will be interested in the

Diet debates and the reports of its Foreign Affairs Committee. The former, since they are published, may be found in a number of libraries and the National Archives, but the latter reports are only in the Diet Library (*Eduskunnan kirjasto*). Organized in 1872 to serve — as it still does — the deputies of the Diet, this library has also evolved into an academic study center. Contributing to such a function is its collection of recently-published works in various languages on Finnish foreign policy, a periodical section of international dimensions, and the best appointed public reading rooms in Helsinki. The library is located in the north wing of the Diet building, but plans exist for its placement in a new annex to be situated directly in the rear of its present location.

Among university archives, the library of the University of Helsinki is the most important. A venerable institution chartered by Queen Christina at Turku (Åbo) in 1640, its library has acquired an extensive manuscript collection which includes the personal papers of some political personalities. It further contains an inventory of all major unpublished private papers now held by all libraries (but not "archives") in Finland. Since the early nineteenth century, the library has stood on the west side of the Senaatintori, and is another element in the great complex built early in the Russian period when the capital was moved to Helsinki. Its rotunda and galleries no doubt impress architectural historians more than diplomatic historians, since the latter find its facilities cramped.

Outside Helsinki there are two other university libraries of interest. Turku (Åbo) not only lost the political captaincy of Finland in the early nineteenth century, but also its university — the present University of Helsinki. To compensate for this amputation, a Swedish-speaking university, the Åbo Academy, and a Finnish-speaking university, Turku University, were founded shortly after the achievement of national independence. The two institutions adjoin, the Academy midst the park surrounding the Cathedral, Turku University in its new modern setting on the hill beyond. The libraries of both are recently constructed, and are so attractive that the student of international politics must regret that they do not contain more material of interest to him. Nonetheless, there are private papers of relevant figures in the Academy's holdings, while Turku University is curator for the private library (not the papers) of Juho K. Paasikivi.

A few remaining categories of source materials deserve mention here, though they will not be referred to again in the subsequent parts of this chapter. One comprises the private papers which have not been deposited in any of the archives just reviewed. Most notable of these are Carl Gustaf Mannerheim's papers which are held by the Mannerheim Foundation (*Mannerheim säätiö*). They are presently closed to all except the Swedish academician and family friend, Stig Jägerskiöld, already author of the first volumes of a Mannerheim biography. Papers of other important leaders also have remained in family custody, thus presenting the scholar with the formidable task of both discovering what collections of this kind exist and of gaining access to them.

The other category is the records of Finland's political parties. Both the directives and decisions of each party's leadership committee, as well as the documentation of its party congresses, contain material of interest to foreign policy researchers. Each party's headquarters in Helsinki holds this data.

Finally, attention is directed to the Finnish Institute of International Affairs (*Ulkopoliittinen instituutti*). Modest in its facilities at Museokatu 18A, it seeks to promote research and information in international politics and in pursuit of this objective has inaugurated press archives of prominent foreign newspapers. Articles in these journals which deal with Finnish foreign relations have been catalogued at the Institute.

ORGANIZATION AND CLASSIFICATION

The National Archives

As noted above, Finland's National Archives (*Valtionarkisto*) occupy a central place for historians in general and for diplomatic historians in particular. Its collection of the personal papers of the Republic's presidents, prime ministers, and foreign ministers is impressive. Included are those of the first president, K.J. Ståhlberg; of the six times foreign minister, Rudolf Holsti; and of Väinö Tanner, prime minister and foreign minister. And to these will be added, in 1984, the papers of Juho K. Paasikivi. These unpublished materials are listed alphabetically by author in the Archives Catalogue for Private Papers (*Yksityiskokoelmat*). The latter is a four-volume work kept in the main reading room. Each of its listings indicates the nature of the papers and the restrictions, if any, pertaining to their use.

Certain files of the Foreign Ministry are also in the National Archives. These may be categorized as "inactive," since they deal with aspects of foreign policy now concluded. A separate list of these documents indicated the following: documents concerning the Åland Islands, 1917–22; documents concerning conferences with Estonia, Latvia, and Lithuania, 1919–26; documents concerning the League of Nations; documents of the Tartu Peace Conference, 1920; press reports from Finnish legations abroad, 1918–52, and reports from Finnish legations abroad, 1918–30. Maps and treaties constitute two other noteworthy items. A collection of the former contains political frontier maps and a list thereof, the "Map Collection" (*Rajakarttoja*), and is in the main reading room. The treaties are printed public pacts to which Finland is a signatory, and are available in the same place.

Archives of the Ministries

The Ministry of Foreign Affairs Archives (*Ulkoasiainministeriön arkisto*). Here are found the usual documentary records of a foreign office, including: ministerial directives; protocols of the Foreign Affairs Committee of the Council of State, 1946–   ; reports from Finnish consulates abroad, and reports from Finnish legations and embassies abroad, 1930–   . The larger part of these documents are filed under topical headings and then under country name with various subheadings. The ministry has no plans for publication of a comprehensive foreign documents series, but from time to time publishes materials of selective interest such as: *The Finnish Blue Book* (1940); *Suomen asetuskokoelman sopimussarja* [*Finnish Statutes and Covenants Series*] (1933–   ); *Suomen itsenäisyyden tunnustaminen* [*The Recognition of Finnish Independence*] (1937); *Suomen ja Venäjän välsten Tartossa pidettyjen rauhanneuvottelujen pöytäkirjat* [*Minutes of the Finno-Russian Peace Negotiations at Dorpat*] (1923); and *Ulkopoliittisia lausuntoja ja asiakirjoja* [*Foreign Policy Statements and Documents*] (1959–   ).

War Archives (Sota-arkisto). As already noted, only a small part of the extensive holdings of these archives pertain directly to foreign policy, but they are conveniently filed under the following headings:

General Headquarters. Foreign Section. Reports, correspondence, miscellaneous papers, 1919–44.

Reports, correspondence, and miscellaneous papers of the military attachés of Finland assigned as indicated:

    Berlin, 1929, 1932–41.

    Bern, 1943–45.

    London, 1933–35.

    Moscow, 1926, 1929, 1931, 1933–34.

    Paris, 1919–26, 1929–42.

    Riga, 1921, 1924–26, 1934.

    Stockholm, 1923–29, 1934, 1939–40.

    Warsaw, 1920, 1924–25, 1929, 1933–34.

Ministry of Education (Opetusministeriö) Archives. The materials here are organized and filed for administrative purposes only. They include:

Minutes and reports of international educational, scientific, and cultural congresses in which Finland has participated.

Records of Finland's activities in UNESCO (some parts of these are in the National Archives).

Records of international exchange programs in which Finland has participated, including numbers, specialties, and nationalities of persons, exchanged.

Diet Library (Eduskunnan kirjasto). In addition to the complete proceedings of the Finnish Diet, which appear under the title *Valtiopäivät pöytäkirjat* and are available also in the National Archives and a number of other libraries, this repository contains the records of the parliament's Committee on Foreign Affairs (*Ulkoasiainvaltionkunta*) for January 10, 1918 through July 13,1918, and for the period since April 1, 1919. These are not voluminous, filling not more than a single filing box per year. A third holding consists of the personal unpublished papers of Askari Tokoi — a unique item, since no other personal papers collection is here.

University Libraries

University of Helsinki Library (Helsingin Yliopiston kirjasto). The private papers collection are in the library's manuscript division and are accompanied by a special card catalogue (*Käskirjoituskokoelma*). Among the more important are the papers of Gustaf J. Ramstedt and of Jarl W. Söderhjelm. An inventory list of all private papers collections in the libraries of Finland is, as of this writing, untitled and unpublished but available for individual use upon request in the manuscript division.

Library of the Åbo Academy. While the private papers in this library are primarily those of literary figures, some of politicians are to be found. All are in the manuscript division, where a catalogue is available. The papers of Edward Westermarck represent the most prominent holding of political interest.

Turku University Library (Turun Yliopiston kirjasto). The Paasikivi private library, consisting of six thousand volumes, is the single item here which may be of use to diplomatic historians. The volumes are in large part shelved in a room exclusively for them, arranged topically, and catalogued both topically and by author. The extensive marginal notations made by Paasikivi make these volumes of considerable significance for students of this man.

The Finnish Institute of International Affairs (Ulkopoliittinen instituutti). The institute's newspaper files date from 1965 and, except for most recent editions, are on microfilm.

ACCESS AND FACILITIES

Although not more restrictive than most governments and less so than some, Finland exercises very considerable control over access to source materials on foreign policy. The basic law applicable to all Finnish archival holdings bearing on foreign affairs, national defense, certain economic matters, and individual privacy rights is as follows:

1) Documents and papers for the last twenty-five years are classified as closed;
2) Documents and papers for the period between twenty-five and forty years ago may be made available with the explicit permission of the Council of State;
3) Documents and papers more than forty years old are open to Finnish citizens and may be made available to non-Finns with the permission of the ministry concerned.

This makes clear that a foreigner must secure permission for access to diplomatic source materials in the various ministries and in the National Archives, though not for access to university libraries.

In applying for permission for access, applicants should be as explicit as possible in describing their projects and the nature of the materials they wish to consult. Since permission sometimes may entail action by more than one archivist (for example, a request to the National Archives to see a certain document in its possession may have to be approved also by the Foreign Ministry or a family), it is advisable to submit applications in triplicate. The archives receiving the application will then act as a clearing house for the applicant. One may expect a response normally within a week from the National Archives, three weeks from the Ministry of Foreign Affairs.

All prospective researchers, whether concerned with classified or unclassified materials, are well advised to correspond in advance with the directors of archives and libraries in which they wish to work. Names and addresses of such officials, as well as the hours and facilities of the various archives and libraries are given below.

National Archives. Prof. Tuomo Polvinen, Director, Valtionarkisto, Rauhankatu 17, Helsinki 17. Hours: Monday through Friday, 8:00 A.M. to 5:00 P.M. Copy services and work space available.

Foreign Ministry Archives. Mr. Reino Kuusi, Chief of Archives, Ulkoasiainministeriön arkisto, Ritarikatu 2B, Helsinki 17. Hours: by appointment. No copy services; work space available.

War Archives. Dr. Risto Ropponen, Archivist, Sota-arkisto, Siltavuorenranta 16, Helsinki 17. Hours: Monday through Friday, 8:00 A.M. to 4:00 P.M. and by appointment. Copy services and work space available.

Ministry of Education Archives. Mr. Kalervo Siikala, Director of the Department of International Affairs, Opetusministeriö, Rauhankatu 4, Helsinki 17. Hours: by appointment. No copy services; very limited work space.

Library of the Finnish Diet. Mr. Henrik Schauman, Chief Librarian, Eduskunnan kirjasto, Eduskuntatalo, Helsinki 10. Hours: Monday through Friday, 9:00 A.M. to 4:00 P.M., Saturday, 9:00 A.M. to 2:00 P.M.. Copy services and work space available.

University of Helsinki Library. Mr. Henrik Grönroos, in Charge of Manuscript Division, Helsingin Yliopiston kirjasto, Unionkatu 36, Helsinki 17. Hours: Monday through Friday, 9:00 A.M. to 4:00 P.M. Copy services and work area available.

Åbo Academy Library. Mrs. Gôta Tegengren, Librarian, Handriftsavdelningen, Åbo Akademis bibliotek, Åbo 2. Hours: Monday through Friday, 9:00 A.M. to 3:00 P.M., and evenings by special appointment. Copy services and work space available.

Turku University Library. Mr. Heikki Eskelinen, Librarian, Turun Yliopiston kirjasto, Turku 2. Hours: Monday through Friday, 10:00 A.M. to 4:00 P.M. Copy services and work space available.

The Finnish Institute of International Affairs. Museokatu 18A, Helsinki 10. Hours: Monday through Friday, 9:00 A.M. to 6:00 P.M., Saturday, 9:00 A.M. to 1:00 P.M. No copy services; public reading room only.

BIBLIOGRAPHY

1. Järvinen, Markku, ed. *Valtionarkiston Opas.* Helsinki: Valtion painatuskeskus, 1970. The only extant guide to the National Archives and a very helpful one. An English edition is in preparation for publication.

2. Julkunen, Martti, and Lehikoinen, Anja, eds. *A select list of books and articles in English, French, and German on Finnish politics in the 19th and 20th centuries.* Turku: Auraprint, 1967. A number of bibliographies of the works cited herein are of considerable assistance in determining the existence of primary materials on diplomatic history.

3. Kluge, Reinhard, and Schetelich, Eberhard. *Das Archivwesen der Republik Finnland.* Berlin: Staatlichen Archivverwaltung der Deutschen Demokratischen Republik, 1966.

4. Nivanko, Eino, ed. *Suomen Tieteellisteen kirjastojen opas.* 3rd. ed. Helsinki: Valtioneuvoston kirjapaino, 1962.

5. Nurmio, Yrjö. "Suomen arkistolaitos ennen ja nyt," *Liiketeloudellinen Aikakauskirja,* IV (1962), 264–274. A short historical account of the National Archives by a former director.

6. Passivirta, Juhani, *L'administration des affaires étrangères et la politique extérieure de la Finlande.* Turku: Turun Yliopisto, 1966. The best short description of the administration of foreign policy, it covers the period 1917–40.

7. Passivirta, Juhani, and Mylly, Juhani, eds. *Suomalaiset ja Diplomaattiura 1918-1968.* Turku: Auraprint, 1969. A directory of Finnish foreign service personnel.

8. *Routsista hankitut mikrofilmit valtionarkistossa.* Helsinki: Valtionarkisto, 1968. A list of microfilmed Swedish records concerning Finland.

9. *Suomen historiallinen bibliografia, 1544-1960.* 6 vols. Helsinki: Käsikirjoja, 1940-68.
10. *Valtionarkiston yleisluttelo.* Helsinki: Valtioneuvosten kirjapaino, 1956-66. A guide to the National Archives' holdings. Part One deals with materials pertaining to the Swedish period; Part Two with the Russian period, 1808-1917. Students of the era of national independence must await the appearance of Part Three.
11. See also Degras' *Soviet documents.* On Finland, pp. 36, 72, 116, 147, 184, 226.

5 FRANCE

Vincent Confer

Maxwell School of Citizenship and Public Affairs,
Syracuse University

ARCHIVES DU MINISTÈRE DES AFFAIRES ÉTRANGÈRES (AMAE)

HISTORY

THE habit of identifying the major European foreign ministeries simply by their street addresses may be regarded as a recognition of the timeless and institutional quality of these great agencies of the state. In modern France the Quai d'Orsay stands as a symbol of the continuity of foreign policy through domestic political vicissitudes unmatched in the annals of any other power. Its archives are the material legacy of the centruies since Richelieu, when French statesmen were never absent from the council tables of Europe and of the world — when indeed they sometimes were predominant there.

Yet the building that the French foreign ministry now occupies at 37 Quai d'Orsay (75007-Paris) was not the scene of the diplomatic triumphs of either Louis XIV or Napoleon I. It was constructed in the reign of Louis-Philippe, but the ministry did not move to the site until 1853. The AMAE are installed in the rear at the southern end of the west wing, facing upon the rue de l'Université.

In 1671 Louis XIV ordered the retention henceforth of all state papers by the crown. This marked the beginning of regular and careful preservation of the holdings of the foreign ministry.[1]

---

[1] Accounts of the early history of the archives are to be found in Nos. 2 and 6. The most detailed study of development down to the Third Republic is No. 3.

Fortunately for the historian, nearly all the papers of Richelieu and Mazarin were subsequently recovered from private holders. The diplomatic correspondence was thus nearly complete for as far back as 1624, and a not inconsiderable number of items from the sixteenth century were also obtained. These later acquisitions constitute the heart of the important series, *Mémoires et Documents*. Before 1880 admission to the AMAE for research was sanctioned only after special personal consideration of each candidate by the minister of foreign affairs. It was an exceptional favor, granted more often to foreigners as a diplomatic gesture toward the governments or parties that supported the applications. During the Peace of Amiens, Napoleon and Talleyrand admitted Charles James Fox with every show of courtesy for his research on the last two Stuart kings. Perhaps the first American to win access to these archives was Jared Sparks in 1828–29. Somewhat later came George Bancroft, when he was minister to Great Britain. He made a trip to Paris in 1847, and was well received by two fellow historians: Guizot, the premier, and Mignet, the keeper of the foreign ministry archives. Germans such as Sybel and Theiner were more likely to succeed in their quest than were French historians, who might have political theses to cultivate.

All attempts to regularize admission policy failed until 1880.[2] The change in that year was due in part to a growing interest in modern history in France. Some of that attention can be attributed to the effect of the Franco-Prussian War. Wounded national pride sought, perhaps unconsciously, the solace to be found in contemplating the more victorious past. It is not surprising that among the first Frenchmen to take advantage of the new liberality were Albert Sorel, who ultimately published his *L'Europe et la Révolution française,* and Gabriel Hanotaux, later the author of the *Histoire du cardinal de Richelieu*. Each devoted his research to an age when French policy had been eminently successful. But

[2] For an urbane account of the campaign to open the archives in the 1870s and 1880s, see the memoirs of Gabriel Hanotaux (No. 14).

even without the impact of 1870, modern history was coming into its own through the German school of historical scholarship and through the activities of such French historians as Gabriel Monod, who founded the *Revue historique* in 1876 and complained that ancient and medieval French history crowded out the more recent period in the faculties and in the training of young research men.

Nonetheless, the Quai d'Orsay had remained aloof, and more direct stimuli were required to open the AMAE. One of these was the precedent set by Great Britain, Prussia, Austria, and Russia. By 1875 all of them had announced policies providing easier access to their foreign ministry archives. This argument was cleverly used by Armand Baschet whose history published in 1875 was intended as much as a lever to pry open the French archives as a serious account of their development. Even then the reform came only after the triumph of the republicans in 1877–80. Mounting pressure forced the adoption in 1880 of the modern practice of appointing an official archival commission, composed of experienced diplomats and prominent historians as well as the leading officials of the archives, to handle applications in accordance with a general policy fixed by law or decree. A new keeper of the archives was appointed, and Gabriel Hanotaux became the youthful secretary of the new Commission for the Diplomatic Archives. Under Charles de Freycinet in the same year, the open date for research was set at 1815. Some ten years later, an American influence made itself felt through Benjamin Franklin Stevens, who was the first research worker to persuade the Quai d'Orsay to recognize photography as a method of reproducing manuscripts. He was even granted permission to set up a photographic room in the grounds of the ministry, where he copied many items of his famous twenty-five volumes of facsimiles.[3]

The Second World War inflicted upon the AMAE the greatest damage since its formation.[4] As the Germans approached Paris in

---

[3] No. 22.
[4] The losses and the restoration process are described in Nos. 18 and 20.

May, 1940, much of the diplomatic correspondence for 1935-40, as well as a part of that covering 1930-35, was burned in the courtyard of the archives. Of course, certain series of documents had been evacuated earlier to Touraine, but they were not safe. Some of them were abandoned by the captain of the steamer upon which they were being taken from Bordeaux to America, when the vessel was turned back by German aircraft. The remainder in Touraine was seized and returned to Paris for preliminary examination. Later the Germans carried away between four and five thousand cartons of post-1914 documents bearing on their primary interest: French participation in international conferences, 1919-39. Then a disastrous fire broke out in the southwest wing of the AMAE during the fighting that accompanied the liberation of Paris in August, 1944. It consumed many additional items dating from the same period that were still under examination in the offices of the archives.

These stunning losses were, fortunately, not wholly irreplaceable. The French recovered about eighteen hundred volumes of their diplomatic records in Germany after the war. The staff of the archives saw that much of the remaining correspondence to and from foreign posts could be reconstituted by bringing back to Paris the originals or copies of all incoming and outgoing correspondence kept regularly in the files of the French posts abroad during the years that were missing at the Quai d'Orsay. The identification of what ought to be found at each foreign post was expedited by the fortunate survival of the Quai d'Orsay's official registers of all documents received or dispatched (with two exceptions: outgoing dispatches for the second half of 1935, and both outgoing and incoming dispatches for the second quarter of 1940). Microfilm copies were made for retention in the archives. Still, certain gaps will remain in the 1914-40 holdings (see Note A in the next section).

ORGANIZATION AND CLASSIFICATION

(For quick reference, a list of the kinds of documents presently [1973] open for research in the AMAE is provided first.)

Available for research:

1. Political and commercial documents pertaining to:
   a. the states of Europe, to December 31, 1929.
   b. the United States, to December 31, 1929.
   c. the states of the Americas (except the United States), Asia, the Near East, and Africa (except Morocco and Tunisia), to May 31, 1918.
   d. Morocco and Tunisia, to December 31, 1916.
   e. the series: *Guerre 1914-18.*
2. The series: *Mémoires et Documents.*
3. Documents concerning the administrative and budgetary affairs of the ministry, to May 31, 1918.
4. The career dossiers of the personnel of the ministry, to 1870.
5. The papers of a number of eminent ministers of foreign affairs and diplomatists (*Papiers d'Agents*), to about 1914.

Note A. Archival losses during the Second World War have created difficulties for researchers concerned with peace plans in 1914-19, or with French participation in international conferences and the League of Nations after 1919. As a result of the fire of 1940 and subsequent German inspection, two series: *Paix 1914-1920* and *Internationale 1918-1940* (also known as Série Y) suffered the disappearance of 70 to 80 percent of their contents. Additional havoc was caused by the fire of 1944. In fact, *Série Y* was practically destroyed. What remains of the two series is still unorganized and will be made available only after the documents for Asian and African states down to 1929 have been opened for research. The most detailed account of these losses and reconstitutions is to be found in the general introduction written by Maurice Baumont and Pierre Renouvin for France, Commission pour la publication des documents relatifs aux origines de la guerre de 1939-45, *Documents diplomatiques français, 1932-1939*, Tome I (ler janvier-31 mars 1936), Paris, 1963, pp. vii–xiv.

Note B. The reconstitution and organization of the records for 1929-45 is proceeding at a pace that may permit the application of the thirty-year rule by 1976.

In the eighteenth century the foreign ministry adopted a classification that remains in effect for all materials accumulated down to 1897. It comprises three basic series: *Correspondance politique, Mémoires et Documents,* and *Correspondance consulaire et commerciale.* Each of these is subdivided into *fonds* (record groups). The *fonds* of the *Correspondance politique* bear the names of states, those in *Mémoires et Documents* are called after states or continents, and in the *Correspondance consulaire et commerciale* (including *Correspondance politique des consuls*) they are named for diplomatic or consular posts. Then one comes upon the individual documents, most of which are bound into stout volumes numbered chronologically within the *fonds.*

Except for the unwieldy series *Mémoires et Documents,* which grew to more than twenty-five hundred volumes, this system served well enough until the present century brought a vast increase in daily international communication, nearly all of it requiring preservation and classification. The First World War provoked a change. Three new series were begun in that period: *Guerre 1914-1918, Paix 1914-1920,* and *Internationale 1918-1940.* At about the same time, the old separation of political from economic correspondence had come to seem unrealistic. So, too, appeared the purely chronological subdivision of the mass of documents pertaining to a given country.

These considerations, combined with the traumatic events of 1940-44, led the AMAE to institute after the Second World War a fundamental reform in its system of classification — at least for everything since 1897 (1901 for consular material). In the first place, that year became a terminal date for *Mémoires et Documents.* Then four new series were created, consisting principally of what would have been collected under the now-terminated *Correspondance politique* and *Correspondance consulaire et commerciale.* They are:

Nouvelle Série: Europe-Levant 1897–   .
Nouvelle Série: Afrique 1896–   .
Nouvelle Série: Asie-Océanie 1896–   .
Nouvelle Série: Amérique 1897–   .

In addition to combining political and economic documents, these current series are notable for another innovation: they are subdivided first by country and then by *subject*, with the old chronologocal treatment applied only as the subdivision under subject.

I. *Correspondance politique*:

This series consists, in major part, of drafts and copies of communications sent by the French foreign ministry to its agents abroad, and of the reports of those agents in return. It also includes the correspondence between foreign diplomatic representatives in France and the French foreign ministry. Moreover, the series contains valuable minutes, notes, memorials, and drafts originating in the ministry, as well as reports, clippings, and varied enclosures that once accompanied the letters from French diplomats abroad.

Only slightly less important are the supplements to the *Correspondance politique*. There are two: *intercalaire* and *général*. The *Supplément intercalaire* consists mostly of papers that were once attached to the original dispatches, or have been acquired by the ministry at a later date. They are bound into volumes, generally on an annual basis, and these volumes form a regular part of a particular *fonds*, coming in their natural chronological place immediately after the ordinary volume for the year in question. The *Supplément général* contains very much the same kind of material, but usually a longer period is covered by each volume. It is shelved at the end of a particular *fonds*, and its volumes are renumbered in chronological order. The official inventories of the *Correspondance politique* include the supplements as well as the main series.

While it has been noted that the files of the Quai d'Orsay date in general only from the time of Richelieu, scholars interested in sixteenth century can not afford to neglect them. Depending upon the country, a certain number of documents from that period, especially the latter half, can be found in the *Correspondance politique*. For example, the first thirteen volumes for Switzerland deal chiefly with the sixteenth century; and twenty-two volumes are assigned to Rome for the years 1537–1601.

II. *Mémoires et Documents*:

This is one of the greatest, and certainly the most complex of the series in the French foreign ministry. Some of the major acquisitions of previously dispersed documents — when they came in through royal order, by purchase, or by legacy — are still visible in its structure. For example, Volumes 21 to 46 of the *Fonds France* in this series still bear the subheading *Lettres de Mazarin* and cover the years after 1646. The task of the investigator is complicated, however, by the fact that numerous letters of the great minister can be found in other volumes of the *Fonds France,* in other *fonds* of this series, and in the series *Correspondance politique.* The letters of Mazarin for 1642–46 are held by the *Bibliothèque Mazarine* (Paris), and copies of some of his outgoing letters for 1647–51 are located in the Free Library of Philadelphia. This dispersion is characteristic of the records left by many other French diplomats, even into the nineteenth century.

Mémoires et Documents also contains reports and memorials drawn up by the staff of the foreign ministry, as well as documents sent to France by its diplomats abroad which did not constitue a part of their regular correspondence. It will be noticed that the distinction between this material and some of the contents of the supplements to the *Correspondance politique* is not very sharp. Finally, other volumes deal with what are really internal administrative problems of France. These are found chiefly in the *fonds: France. Affaires intérieures* and *France. Petits fonds de province.* Each *fonds* in this series is arranged chronologically, and the constituent volumes are numbered consecutively, but there is also an overall, continuous enumeration from *fonds* to *fonds* in the following order of mention.

Perhaps the most important subdivision in the *Mémoires et Documents* is the *Fonds France.* This group of about five hundred volumes of manuscripts includes the papers of Richelieu, some volumes from the original Saint-Simon collection, a part of the Noailles family correspondence in the eighteenth century, and a wealth of other material. Associated with the *Fonds France* are four *fonds* of considerable interest. One of these is the *Fonds Bourbon*, sometimes known as the *Fonds des émigrés*. It contains correspondence dealing with royalist intrigues and counterespionage during the French Revolution. The *Fonds Saint-Simon* consists of eighty-four carefully inventoried volumes of manuscripts from the collection of the famous duke. Much of the material in the *Papiers de Bonaparte*, comprising forty-seven volumes, is now available in printed form. The *Cérémonial* concerns itself with precedence and etiquette at the French and foreign courts.

More than a hundred volumes have been assigned the title *France. Affaires intérieures et extérieures.* Among them are additional manuscripts of Richelieu and some of the volumes of Mazarin's correspondence. Here, too, can be found many of the manuscripts originating with the *"jurisconsultes et publicistes spéciaux"* in the era between the reign of Louis XV and 1930, when the policy of paying certain publicists for services to the state had not yet been officially abandoned.

About four hundred volumes in the *Fonds France et divers états* constitute a source for drafts of treaties, as well as for reports drawn up by the ministry on various subjects, They are arranged geographically. The next two *fonds* reveal the impossibility of separating foreign affairs from domestic matters, particularly in the old regime. *France. Affaires intérieures* contains more than six hundred volumes. It includes that part of the Mazarin papers which concern internal problems — for example, the Fronde; the correspondence of Fleury; royal ordinances on army, navy, and financial matters; and letters and memorials addressed to the foreign ministry by private French citizens. Some three hundred volumes in *France. Petits fonds de province* are devoted to the prerevolutionary administration of such provinces as Dauphiné,

Franche-Comté, Brittany, and Provence, which retained a right to special treatment as a result of the vagaries of political history.

There are, in addition, a few comparatively new *fonds*, such as *France. Commerce* which covers the years 1700–1830 (with emphasis on the eighteenth century) in thirty-six volumes of reports, memorials, letters from chambers of commerce, etc., that are useful for economic history and the study of colonial policy. The series *Mémoires et Documents* is concluded with a small *Supplément* composed of manuscripts which, for some reason, were not bound into one of the regular *fonds*.

III. Correspondance consulaire et commerciale:

Although it is the least known and the least inventoried of the three original series, the *Correspondance consulaire et commerciale* possesses great historical value. It is also the only series not entirely housed at the Quai d'Orsay. For consular correspondence and papers earlier than 1793, one must go to the *Archives Nationales,* because French consulates were controlled by the ministry of the navy until that year (except briefly in 1761–66). When the consulates became part of the ministry of foreign affaires in 1793, the two ministries divided the consular records accumulated up to that time. Those retained by the ministry of the navy were turned over to the *Archives Nationales* in 1898 and classified as: *Série Ministère de la Marine. Sous-série B⁷*. In 1929 and 1933 the Quai d'Orsay relinquished to the *Archives Nationales* most, but not all, of its consular holdings earlier than 1793, and these materials are found in: *Série Ministère des Affaires étrangères.* Sous-séries B^I et B^{III}.

Since the division of the files in 1793 seems to have been carried out unsystematically, the research worker nearly always will have to examine at least two of the subseries for a particular period or consular post. It is possible, however, to distinguish three major kinds of material and, in a general way, their location. The instructions and reports drawn up in France prior to January 1, 1756 are to be found in the navy subseries B^7 (registers 48-202).

For 1756-93 they are in the foreign affaires subseries B^I (registers 1-74). The correspondence sent in by consuls abroad was not so neatly divided. It can be noted only that most of the early manuscripts dating from the seventeenth century (and even from the sixteenth in the case of Morocco) can be studied in B^I (registers 75-1188), while B^7 (registers 204-462) covers mostly the last years of Louis XVI. The former has the larger number of manuscripts. Its bound volumes bear an inclusive enumeration applied by the *Archives Nationales,* but their former designation by post, by old volume number, and by years has been preserved. For example: *Sous-série B¹, Registre 843, Maroc,* vol. 19 (1786-89) in which the French vice-consul on February 2, 1786, acknowledges his instructions to treat the expected American agent to the sultan with a *"conduite amicale et prudente."*

When certain registers taken over from the navy in 1793 were filled out with manuscripts of slightly later date, the ministry of foreign affairs chose to retain them under its own control. They form a part of the series B^{II}, which still remains at the AMAE. Foreign affairs subseries B^{III} at the *Archives Nationales* covers in general the period 1750-1850, with an important number of earlier items and a few of later date. Most of its volumes represent the Mediterranean area and include correspondence with municipal authorities and private commercial enterprises, as well as reports and statistical tables.

Most consular documents after 1793 remain at the AMAE. They have been neither so well inventoried nor so well arranged and filed as have the other great series. Consequently, the staff may withhold some of them from use for the period after 1870, even though the regular open date is much later. From 1793 down to 1826, all consular manuscripts are arranged chronologically under the post or other consular jurisdiction rather than by country, and are called the *Correspondance consulaire.* A major change occurred in 1826. Thereafter, the consular material was divided into two parts: the *Correspondance politique des consuls* (not to be confused with the great series, *Correspondance poli-*

tique, described above) and the *Correspondance commerciale,* both including much material in addition to correspondence in the strict sense and together known as the *Correspondance consulaire et commerciale.*

The *Correspondance politique des consuls* was intended to distinguish the more political from the more economic matter in a rapidly growing consular network. From 1826 to 1830 it was either incorporated in the volumes of the *Correspondance politique* or filed as *volumes intercalaires* in that major series, but after 1830 it was given the distinct identity contemplated in the reform of 1826. Thenceforth, while it continued to be arranged by states rather than by posts, it was shelved separately from and directly after the corresponding *fonds* in the *Correspondance politique.* There has been some variation in its internal organization after 1830. In the case of certain countries, such as the United States, the correspondence with all consular posts was thrown together chronologically. In other instances, as for Italy both before and after unification, the documents for each post were classified separately and then chronologically. It is interesting to remark, too, that political matters involving Morocco were treated entirely within the *Correspondance politique,* although much of the material concerning that state originated with French consuls located there.

The *Correspondance commerciale,* with its emphasis upon trade and industrial opportunities, perpetuated, after 1826, the old arrangement by posts inherited from the *Correspondance consulaire.* Like the *Correspondance politique,* the consular series comes to a close at the end of the nineteenth century. That kind of material after 1901 is incorporated with the following new geographical series.

IV. The four current geographical Nouvelles Séries:

Designated as *Europe-Levant, Afrique, Asie-Océanie,* and *Amérique,* these series are the product of the reorganization of the archives mentioned above. Each is subdivided first into countries.

Occasionally, an area that was not a state will be included. For example, *Europe-Levant*, 1918-29, has headings like *Rive Gauche du Rhin 1921-29*, and *Rhin, Elbe, Oder*. The most significant innovation is the subdivision of the documents belonging to a country into subject headings rather than years. This was inspired by the problem of the researcher who must trace a specific topic in a nation's affairs across a considerable period of time. In the older series, where all the correspondence of a year is grouped together, the irrelevant material which a researcher must at least glance at was frustrating, although not usually overwhelming. This has changed since 1914, when in the subsequent twenty-five years the accessions of the AMAE equalled the total number of documents accumulated during the first three centuries.[5]

The aim has been to make the topical subdivisions as much alike for all countries as possible. Of course many states will require a certain number of special headings. The new policy also entailed some subsidiary decisions. If a document has importance for two or more subjects, it is cross-referred. The designation *"dossier générale"* is resorted to frequently as a device to cover items that do not fall under the more specific rubrics. And the infrequent documents which cannot be categorized are placed at the end of the national grouping as *"documents divers."* As an illustration of the new system, the major subdivisions for Belgium, 1897-1914, are listed:

Politique intérieure.
   (a)   *Dossier général.*
   (b)   *Question flamande.*
Questions dynastiques et cour.
Défence nationale.
   (a)   *Dossier général.*
   (b)   *Forts d'Anvers.*

[5] No. 20.

Politique étrangère.
- (a) *Dossier général.*
- (b) *Relations avec la France.*
- (c) *Relations avec l'Allemagne.*
- (d) *Relations avec les Pays Bas, l'Angleterre, et le Luxembourg.*

Finances.
- (a) *Finances publiques.*
- (b) *Banques, bourse.*

Affaires commerciales.
- (a) *Dossier général.*
- (b) *Relations avec la France.*

V. Papiers d'Agents:

The AMAE hold some private papers, including correspondence, of former personnel of the foreign ministry or foreign service. Those which are open for research have been designated by ordinance, most recently that of August 5, 1965. Some were bound separately (*e. g., Papiers Thouvenel,* 20 vols.), but form part of *Mémoires et Documents, Fonds France.* Others were put directly into volumes of that series (*e. g., Papiers Barante,* 1 vol.). The terminal date in most of these collections falls before 1890, although, in a few of the more recently opened, it comes down to a later year (*e. g.,* those of Hanotaux, 31 vols., 1870–1924; and of Delcassé, 25 vols., 1898–1915).

While nearly all of the sets of papers presently available are found in *Mémoires et Documents,* each is inventoried under the designation *Papiers d'Agents,* a series that also includes currently closed papers of more recent personnel. Among the personalities represented are: Favre, Freycinet, Gambetta, Ollivier, Pavie, Ribot, Rouher, Thiers, Waddington, and Walewski. It should be remembered that the private papers of certain diplomats are to be found in the *Archives Nationales* (*e. g.,* those of Guizot, Gramont, Persigny, and some of Thouvenel).

VI. Availability of guides and inventories:

The historian who is planning to do research in the above series will find that certain official printed inventories of part of the holdings are obtainable at the Library of Congress and some other American libraries. About sixty inventories or calendars, printed or typewritten, are available in the reading room of the foreign ministry archives. For the *Correspondance politique* the AMAE began a calendar that could not be continued on the same scale after the First World War because of a reduced budget and staff. Only three volumes were published.[6] As the title implies, they do not pretend to give a listing of all the documents. Unpublished, but available in the archives, is the volume that covers the *Fonds Etats-Unis* in this series. To carry the work down to 1871 and to include states not yet in print, the staff published in 1936 an even more summarized but still useful volume.[7] This was followed in 1961 by a continuation for 1871–96, which also includes the *Correspondance politique des consuls*.[8] These can convey an impression of the extent of the material available on a particular diplomatic mission or personage. For the years after 1897, there are typewritten bound inventories for the four new geographical series. There is also an unpublished *Tables analytiques de la Correspondance politique de l'origine à 1830.*

To assist research in the *Mémoires et Documents,* four inventories covering the *Fonds France* and the *Fonds France et divers états* have been published.[9] The first two deal with holdings down to 1814; the third carries the inventory down to 1830. All are provided with a good subject index. For the period since 1830 there is a printed volume that treats only the *divers états* of Europe. Other countries in these *fonds* are dealt with in a typewritten inventory. The *Fonds Bourbon* has also been pro-

[6] No. 10.
[7] No. 8.
[8] No. 9.
[9] Nos. 11 and 12.

vided with a published inventory.[10] A typewritten one is available for *France. Affaires intérieures et extérieures.* The *Fonds Saint-Simon* has been calendared in greater detail than most of the others.[11]

For the consular documents acquired by the *Archives Nationales* from the ministry of the navy (subseries B[7]), there is a published survey.[12] While the calendaring is brief, valuable footnotes are provided for certain volumes. The inventories for the two groups of consular records from the Quai d'Orsay have not been published, but microfilm copies are available in the Library of Congress, which will supply additional prints to other libraries or research centers.[13] For the consular papers since 1793, still in the possession of the foreign ministry, published inventories are generally lacking. The exception is the *Correspondance politique des consuls* for 1826-70.[14] Typewritten inventories are to be had for the personal papers in the series *Papiers d'Agents.* Another agency has made a survey of similar papers held elsewhere: Direction des Archives de France. Service Technique. *Enquête sur les papiers d'agents diplomatiques conservés dans les départements,* 1966. It should be added that most of the above inventories can be consulted in the *Bibliothèque Nationale (Salle des Manuscrits* or *Salle de Bibliographie)* at hours when the foreign archives are closed.

ADMINISTRATION, REGULATIONS, AND FACILITIES

The minister of foreign affairs is authorized by the French council of ministers to determine by ordinance, with the advice of the Commission for the Diplomatic Archives, the open date and the regulations governing the use of the documents. The commis-

[10] No. 13.
[11] A careful analysis of the Saint-Simon papers in this and other *fonds* can be found in No. 5.
[12] No. 17.
[13] Nos. 4 and 19. See also some suggestions made by Howard C. Rice, Jr., in Appendix A, 41-47, of No. 1.
[14] Included in No. 8 and continued in No. 9.

sion upon whose recommendation he makes his decision is a distinguished group of about forty statesmen, diplomats, archivists, and historians. The last category composes nearly one-third of the total. All members are appointed by the premier after nomination by the minister of foreign affairs.

The scholar seeking admission to the AMAE must remember that, even if his field of interest lies in the years before the official open date for the materials in which he is interested, this does not guarantee automatic admission. Not only will each project be considered in itself, but a proper protocol must be followed. Occasional disappointments can usually be traced to ignorance of procedure or to impatience with requirements and delays which, upon reflection, would be recognized as unavoidable in all countries, considering that the *bona fides* of a foreign applicant is naturally not so quickly perceived as it might be at home.

The first obligation of the researcher is a careful formulation of the subject to be investigated, the purpose for which this work is intended, and the expected duration of the visit to Paris. Above all, the applicant must avoid phrasing his topic in terms that are too general and elusive. The more precise and limited they are, the more likely they are to be accepted. Even if it seems possible that the research worker will find one line of investigation leading to another so that he will ultimately want to examine more materials than he requested at first, he should remember that there is no rule against asking for new, related material after one has been admitted to the AMAE and has exhausted the first supply of documents. Nor need any time be lost, for the chief of the archives can approve the new petition, unless it raises issues that only the commission can determine.

Upon arrival in Paris, a United States citizen should go in person to the office of the United States cultural attaché (2 rue Saint-Florentin, 75001-Paris), where he will show his passport, present a simplified version of his project as mentioned above, and indicate his institutional connection or other evidence of seriousness of purpose. He must ask for a supporting letter from the United States embassy. This official letter, which is required by the French government as an introduction to the foreign ministry, usually can be obtained within a few days. It refers, in a general way, to the objective the research worker has in mind.

The applicant is now ready to go to the *Service des Archives* of the AMAE. Entry is through the side gate on the rue de Constatine. Int the lobby,' he will be asked to present his letter from the cultural attaché and to fill out a form addressed to the archives. Then he will be directed to the third floor (in American terms), either to the secretariat of the archives in Room 264, or to the reading room, No. 266. He will have preliminary conversation with a staff member, who often will make valuable suggestions for effective approaches to the problem at hand. Should there be a question of borderline or unusual requests, the higher authorities of the archives might be consulted. At this time they are: Jean de Laloy, *Ministre plénipotentiaire, Chef du Service des Archives*; Maurice Degros, *Conservateur-en-Chef des Archives*; René Massigli, *Président de la Commission des Archives*; René de Vienne, *Secrétaire de la Commission des Archives*; and for the *Archives Nationales*, Jean Favier, *Directeur*. Once admitted, the researcher will be given a card that must be presented on his later visits to the archives, which will be made through a special entrance at 130 rue de l'Université.

An investigator interested in the consular records of France prior to 1793 will need to use the *Archives Nationales* (60 rue des Francs-Bourgeois, 75003-Paris). Again, he must go first to the office of the American cultural attaché, where he will ask for an official letter mentioning briefly his purpose and qualifications. When the letter is presented by the applicant at the office of the director, an admission card valid for the *Archives Nationales* and its brances usually can be obtained without much delay.

Plans for research in Paris must be determined in part by the dates of the annual holdiays. The AMAE are closed from March 1 to 15. For the *Archives Nationales*, the date is July 1 to 15. Neither institution will be open on the usual religious holidays, or on

July 14 and November 11. The daily hours are 2–7:00 P.M., except on Saturdays, when the times are 9:00 A.M. to 1:00 P.M. The *Archives Nationales* are open from 9:30 A.M. to 6:00 P.M., Monday through Saturday.

The regulations of the reading room in the AMAE require that volumes wanted for a certain day be requested the preceding afternoon. Normally, no more than three volumes can be delivered each day. They can be retained for a week at the reader's place. Ink may be employed for notetaking, but the use of typewriters is not permitted.

The AMAE will allow a person whose application has been approved to designate a second person to do the actual research in his name, but the second individual must also have the approval of the foreign ministry. While microfilming requires special authorization, this is ordinarily obtainable when scattered documents or limited series of documents are involved. No one will be allowed to microfilm a long, continous series of items without the consent of the Commission for the Diplomatic Archives, or of a subcommission designated by it. Such requests will normally be granted only to societies or institutions that can provide evidence of intent to publish. All microfilming must be done by the agency officially approved for this work by the archives. The cost for each negative frame (1973) is 0.68 francs, plus 2.70 francs for each volume.

If he expects to use materials at both the AMAE and the *Archives Nationales,* the investigator who is a stranger to Paris will find it most convenient to live in the Louvre section in the first *arrondissement.* But if the Quai d'Orsay is his daily objective, there are less commerical and perhaps quieter areas which he might choose. The AMAE lie on the Left Bank in the agreeable seventh *arrondissement.* The sixth and eighth also merit consideration, for they afford direct bus connections to within a block or two of the archives if one lives near such well-known streets as the boulevard Saint-Germain, the avenue Marceau, the boulevard Malesherbes, or the boulevard Raspail.

BIBLIOGRAPHY

Students of North American history are singularly fortunate in having access on their side of the Atlantic to copies of a large part of the manuscripts of the seventeenth and eighteenth centuries that bear upon the history of the United States and Canada, as well as a considerable number concerning Mexico and the Caribbean. The Archives of Canada in Ottawa hold a large collection of extracts of material relating to that country.[15] Since 1913 the Library of Congress has carried on, with the support of the Carnegie Institution of Washington, a monumental task of copying and photographing that has produced by far the most extensive collection in this country.[16] More recently, the joint program of the American Historical Association and the Library of Congress for microfilming selected historical documents has added to the holdings of the latter. Howard C. Rice, Jr., made available the unpublished inventories of the foreign ministry documents in the *Archives Nationales*. A. P. Nasatir prepared copies of the complete French consular correspondence relating to the United States before 1792.[17] For the latest accessions, the Division of Manuscripts should be consulted. The collection in the Library of Congress also contains the Benjamin Franklin Stevens facsimiles, transcripts, and catalogue index of manuscripts relating to American history from 1763 to 1784.[18]

The Bancroft Library of the University of California has microfilm copies of all the California material in the *Correspondance politique des consuls* (vols. 1–38), as well as some limited series of microfilms based upon other series in the foreign archives and related to such subjects as Mexico, New Grenada, Honolulu, and the Sandwich Islands.[19] The *Guide to the diplomatic history of the United States, 1775–1921* by Samuel F. Bemis and Grace Gardner Griffin gives references to other collections in the United States, as well as to numerous published works based in whole or in part upon the French foreign ministry materials. Important notes on collections of copies or transcripts in this country can be found also in the general preface of the Leland guide to the libraries and archives of Paris; the second volume in that work is the Leland, Meng, and Doysié guide to the American materials in the

[15] Some of it is listed in No. 21; all of it is available as photostats in the Library of Congress.

[16] A list of the series and volumes acquired down to 1942 can be found in Appendix A, 1065–70, of No. 15.

[17] A summary of this work appears in No. 1. See also No. 16.

[18] No. 22.

[19] No. 1, p. 48.

archives of the Quai d'Orsay.[20] In 1971-72 Nancy N. Barker translated and published the French correspondence with the Republic of Texas in a two-volume collection entitled *The French legation in Texas.* On areas other than North America comparatively little in the way of reproduction of the French records is available in the United States. The research worker should, however, consult the list of acquisitions by the Library of Congress printed in Appendix A of the Leland, Meng, and Doysié guide. For many fields of interest, extensive material may be found in the great published collections of documents in the foreign ministry archives. The more important of these are listed below.

Printed Collections of Documents

Avenel, Denis, ed. *Lettres, instructions diplomatiques et papiers d'état du cardinal Richelieu.* 8 vols. Paris, 1853-77.

Basdevant, Jules, ed. *Recueil dis traités et conventions en vigueur entre la France et les puissances étrangères.* 3 vols. Paris, 1918-20.

Chéruel, P. A., and Georges d'Avenel, eds. *Lettres du Cardinal Mazarin pendant son ministère.* 9 vols. Paris, 1872-1906.

Clercq, Alexandre et Jules de, eds. *Recueil des traités de la France depuis 1713 jusqu'à nos jours.* 23 vols. Paris, 1864-1917.

Doniol, Henri. *L'histoire de la participation de la France à l'éstablissement des Etats-Unis d'Amérique.* 5 vols. Paris, 1886-92.

France. Commission pour la publication des documents relatifs aux origines de la guerre de 1914-1918. *Documents diplomatiques français, 1871-1914.* 40 vols. Paris, 1929-55.

————. Commission pour la publication des documents relatifs aux origines de la guerre de 1939-1945. *Documents diplomatiques français, 1932-1939.* 2 series. Paris, 1963-

————. Ministère des Affaires étrangères. *Documents diplomatiques (Livres jaunes).* 229 vols. Paris, 1856-

————. Ministère des Affaires étrangères. *Les origines diplomatiques de la guerre de 1870-71.* 29 vols. Paris, 1910-32.

Sorel, Albert, Gabriel Hanotaux, and others, eds. *Recueil des instructions données aux ambassadeurs et ministres de France depuis les traités de Westphalie jusqu'a la Révolution francaise.* 25 vols. Paris, 1884-1929.

Guide and Reference Works

1. American Historical Association. Committee on Documentary Reproduction (Edgar L. Erickson, chairman). "Report and ap-

---

[20] No. 15.

pendices A and B," *Annual report of the American Historical Association, 1951.* Washington, 1952, I, 39–49.

2. Baillou, Jean, and Pierre Pelletier. *Les affaires étrangères* (Collection: "L'administration française," I). Paris, 1962, 131–133.

3. Baschet, Armand. *Histoire du dépôt des archives des affaires étrangères.* Paris, 1875.

3a. Bemis and Griffin, *Guide.* On French MSS, pp. 915–920.

4. Celier, Léonce. *Archives Nationales. Affaires étrangères. Répertoire numérique de la correspondance consulaire: sous-serie B¹* (typescript dated 1935).

5. Coirault, Yves. *Les manuscrits du Duc de Saint-Simon; bilan d'une enquête sur les archives diplomatiques.* Paris, 1970.

6. Delisle, Léopold. "L'origine des archives du Ministère des Affaires étrangères," *Bibliothèque de l'Ecole des Chartes,* XXXV (1874), 356–372.

6a. Degras, *Soviet documents.* On France, pp. 13, 60, 105, 141, 169, 218.

7. Dethan, Georges. "Les archives des affaires étrangères," *French historical studies,* IV, 2(Fall 1965), 214–18.

8. France. Ministère des Affaires étrangères. *Etat numérique des fonds de la Correspondance politique de l'origine à 1871.* Paris, 1936.

9. ———. *Etat numérique des fonds de la Correspondance politique et commerciale de 1871 à 1896.* Paris, 1961.

10. ———. *Inventaire sommaire des archives du Département des Affaires étrangères. Correspondance politique*:
Tome I. "Allemagne, Angleterre, Argentine, Autriche." Paris, 1903.
Tome II, partie I. "Bade, Bâle, Bavière, Brésil, Brunswick-Hanovre, Chili, Cologne, Colombie, Corse, Danemark, Dantzig." Paris, 1908.
Tome II, partie II. "Espagne." Paris, 1919.

11. ———. *Inventaire sommaire des archives du Département des Affaires étrangères. Mémoires et Documents*:
Tome I. "France," Paris, 1883.
Tome II. "Fonds divers," Paris, 1892.
Tome III. "Fonds France et Fonds divers. Supplément," Paris, 1896.

12. ———. *Inventaire des Mémoires et Documents. Fonds France et Fonds divers de Pays d'Europe jusqu'en 1896.* Paris, 1964.

13. ———. *Inventaire des Mémoires et Documents, France (Fonds Bourbon).* Paris, 1960.

14. Hanotaux, Gabriel. *Mon temps.* 4 vols. Paris, 1933. Especially vol. I, 321-331; vol. II, 17-19, 23-25, 38-48, 52-58.

15. Leland, Waldo G., ed. *Guide to materials for American history in the libraries and archives of Paris.* 2 vols. Washington, 1932-43. Vol. 2: Leland, Waldo G., John J. Meng, and Abel Doysié, eds. *Archives of the Ministry of Foreign Affairs.* Washington, 1943.

16. Nasatir, Abraham P., and Gary Elwyn Monell, eds. *French consuls in the United States. A calendar of their correspondence in the Archives Nationales.* Washington, 1967.

17. Neuville, D. *État sommaire des Archives de la Marine antérieures à la Révolution.* Paris, 1898.

17a. O'Neill, James E. "Copies of French manuscripts for American history in the Library of Congress," *Journal of American history,* 51 (1965), 674-691. For diplomatic records, see especially pp. 676-677, 678, 681.

18. Outrey, Amédée. "Note sur les pertes subies du fait de la guerre par les archives du Ministère des Affaires étrangères et sur les mesures qui ont été prises en vue de la reconstitution des documents détruits," *Cahiers d'histoire de la guerre,* 2 (October 1949), 31-33.

19. *Répertoire de l'ancien bureau des consulats* (manuscript dated 1935).

20. Ribier, Jean de. "Le dépôt des affaires étrangeres: nouvelles installations techniques," *La gazette des archives,* n.s., 19 (January 1956), 5-9.

21. Roy, Edmond. *Rapport sur les archives de France relatives à l'histoire du Canada.* Ottawa, 1911.

22. Stevens, Benjamin Franklin. *Facsimiles of manuscripts in European archives relating to America, 1773-1783.* London, 1889-98.

23. UNESCO. Conseil international des Archives. *Guide des sources de l'histoire de lAfrique,* Série 3: *Sources de l'histoire de l'Afrique, du Sud du Sahara dans les archives et bibliothèques françaises,* Tome I: *Archives.* Zug, Switzerland, 1971, pp. 651-691 (Ministère des Affaires étrangères).

24. Welsch, Erwin K., ed. *Libraries and archives of France: A handbook.* Pittsburgh, 1973, pp. 49, 73-75 (Ministère des Affaires étrangères).

6 GERMANY

Fritz T. Epstein
Indiana, Bonn, and Freiburg Universities

ARCHIVAL DISPERSIONS

THE history of Germany has dictated a rather unusual dispersion of diplomatic documents and a multiplicity of archival institutions. Until 1871 each German state was sovereign in foreign relations and therefore kept its own state and royal diplomatic records. These are still retained in separate state archives (*Staatsarchive* and *Landesarchive*) or in royal collections. However, after the establishment of the German Empire in 1871, foreign relations were conducted by the Empire with its Foreign Office (*Auswärtiges Amt*) in Berlin, and this federal ministry, with its separate archives, continued under the Weimar Republic, the Nazi Third Reich, and the present German Federal Republic (*Bundesrepublik Deutschland* — BRD). The present archives of the BRD, holding most of the Prussian and German diplomatic records since 1867, is called the *Politisches Archiv des Auswärtigen Amtes* (Political Archives of the Foreign Office), located in Bonn. Since the end of World War II and the division into the BRD (West Germany) and the *Deutsche Demokratische Republik* (DDR), East Germany, the DDR has had its separate *Zentrales Staatsarchiv* in Potsdam and Merseburg.

However confusing this evolution of sovereign states and archives may be, the situation is further complicated by the existence of still other related archives:

1. For the German Confederation (1815–66), there are unpublished records, as well as the printed proceedings of the so-called Frankfort Diet (No. 9).

2. For the provisional federal government at Frankfort, 1848–49, there are registers and records (No. 7).

3. Since Prussia had been a great power among the German states before the federal union in 1867, her archives are particularly important. A large part of them are found in the *Preussische Geheime Staatsarchiv* in Berlin-Dahlem. (See Nos. 42 and 48.)

4. Since military records are often closely related to diplomacy, one has to include the *Militärarchiv* and *Marinearchiv*, branches of the *Bundesarchiv* located in Freiburg-im-Breisgau holding also former state military records. (See No. 16.)

5. The royal and princely family archives (*Hausarchive*) often parallel the state archives on international relations. The *Brandenburg-Preussische Hausarchiv* is in the *Zentrales Staatsarchiv*(see No. 51.) Others are located in state archives in Wiesbaden, Marburg, Hanover, and Stuttgart. For discussions of those of the ruling houses of Bavaria, Wüttemberg, Baden, Hesse, Oldenburg, Brunswick, and Schaum-Lippe, see Skidmore in No. 15 and Ingeborg Koch in *Die Bundesfürsten und die Reichpolitik in der Zeit Wilhelms II: Die dynastischen Auslandbeziehungen* (Diss. Munich, 1961).

6. For diplomatic archives of German states now transferred to neighboring successor states, one has to search in these foreign countries and consult Nos. 110–112. For the special problems dealing with East Prussia, West Prussia, and Danzig, there are several helpful articles (Nos. 81–83).

7. Also in the Manuscript Division of the Library of Congress (Washington) are microfilm copies of the *Berichte des Ministers Residents Schleidens* to the Bremen Senate (1861-65). Russian archives contain material on Holstein; British archives contain material on Hanover; Dutch archives, on Geldern; and Danish archives, on Schleswig. (see Nos. 21–40.)

Some guides have been published on the German diplomatic archives dealing with certain world areas. Among these areas are: the United States, Latin America, and central Africa (see Nos. 8, 70, and 20).

All of this proliferation of states and archives requires that this chapter, like that on Italy, follow an organization different from the usual chapters in this book. The discussion of the central archives will be followed by those on state, local, and special repositories.

FEDERAL REPUBLIC OF GERMANY
(Bundesrepublik Deutschland — BRD)

POLITISCHES ARCHIV DES AUSWÄRTIGEN AMTES

The diplomatic archives (1867 to the present) of the North German Confederation, the German Empire, the Weimar Republic, the Nazi Third Reich, and the Federal Republic of Germany are all housed in the Federal German Foreigh Office under the new organizational title of *Politisches Archiv des Auswärtiges Amtes* (Political Archives of the Foreign Office — 5300 Bonn 1, Adenauer-Alle 99-103). The word "political" reminds us that these are working archives (*Arbeitsarchiv*), as well as an historical repository. The present Foreign Office needs constant access to its more recent holdings, but historians have access to the materials before 1945.

At the close of World War II, the Allies took possession of most of the German official records, including the Foreign Office files, which were transferred to Whaddon Hall in Great Britain. (See No. 32.) Here a Tripartite Project of American, British and French scholars arranged, microfilmed, and published parts of the surviving German diplomatic correspondence from 1918 to 1945. The microfilms are available in the National Archives (Washington), the Public Record Office (London), and the *Archives du Ministère des Affaires étrangères* (Paris). The Paris collection is limited to Franco-German relations, 1918-45. Microfilms of large segments of the German diplomatic documents of the earlier period of 1867-1918 have been made by the universities of California (Berkeley), Washington State, Florida, and Michigan and by St. Antony's College (Oxford). These also have been deposited in the National Archives (Washington), making its total German documentary collection about 37,200 rolls. On the Anglo-American custody, use, and return of the captured German archives, see Nos. 24, 25, 28, 30, 32, 36, 39, and 40.

At the same time as the transfer of the captured German diplomatic documents to Whaddon Hall, all the captured German military (army) files, the Nazi Party files, and private papers of German officials were sent to Alexandria, Virginia, under the custody of the U.S. Army's Adjutant General's Office. In this temporary repository a Committee for the Study of War Documents, under the auspices of the American Historical Association, proceeded to microfilm nearly thirty thousand rolls of these documents and later deposited them in the World War II Records Division of the National Archives (Washington). These military and party records have some materials related to diplomacy, and some of the Alexandria miscellaneous files are directly relevant, such as seventy-seven rolls of the Records of German and Japanese Embassies and Consulates, 1890–1945. For discussions of these microfilmed captured documents, see Nos. 16 and 37.

To aid the research historian in the use of these voluminous collections, several guides have been prepared. In the first place, at the beginning of each diplomatic microfilm group a data sheet has been included, furnishing a summary and indications of important material. For the period of 1867–1920, see No. 22. For the microfilmed Alexandria materials, see Nos. 34 and 37.

In addition to these catalogues and guides, two collections of a wide selection of these important German diplomatic documents (1918–45) have been and are being edited and published by the Tripartite Commission (joined by West Germany in 1960) under two titles: *Documents on German foreign policy* and *Akten zur deutschen auswartigen Politik* (Nos. 124 and 125). This large dual enterprise consists of five series: A (1918–25); B (1925–33); C (1933–37); D (1937–41); and E (1941–45). Series D has been completed in thirteen volumes in English translation (1950–70); series C has four volumes to 1936 and will be complete with Volume V. The German section of the Commission will prepare series A, B, and E in the original German text under the German title. Already six volumes of series B and three volumes of series E have been published, and the German group has brought out three volumes (to 1935) of the German original version of series C. They plan eventually to have German versions of all of both series C and D. Thus researchers should consult these printed series first, before undertaking work with the microfilms or with the originals in Bonn. For the printed diplomatic documents of Prussia and Germany before 1914, one should consult especially *Die auswärtige Politik Preussens* and *Die grosse Politik der europäischen Kabinette* (Nos. 138 and 128), as well as collections of Bismarck's correspondence (Nos. 132,135, and 140).

All the captured German documents in Great Britain and the United States were returned to the Federal Republic of Germany in progressive installments, beginning in 1958, and were deposited in appropriate German repositories (see No. 40). This meant that the *Politisches Archiv des Auswärtigen Amtes* at Bonn became the repository for the original copies of the official German diplomatic documents. For a discussion of the availability of these returned diplomatic documents, see No. 5.

This *Politisches Archiv* also makes a special effort to collect the private papers (*Nachlässe*) of former members of the Foreign Office and the diplomatic service. For a listing of some of these diplomatic *Nachlässe,* especially those of Brockdorff-Ranzau and of Stresemann, see the publications by Mommsen and Gatzke (Nos. 12 and 27).

BUNDESARCHIV

The *Bundesarchiv* (Archives of the Federal Republic of Germany) is the modern successor of the *Reichsarchiv,* which had been established in 1920 to house the noncurrent records of the Prussian and German ministries and governmental agencies — except, of course, the records of the Foreign Office, which had its own Political Archives. Among the earlier *Reichsarchiv* holdings, however, were military and economic records, closely related to international relations. The *Reichsarchiv* was also to conduct research on the history of the prewar Reich and on the military history of World War I, and to organize a reference service for its holdings. After the disruption of World War II and the capture of the German and Prussian state archives by the Allied Powers, these records became scattered in the Soviet Union, Great Britain, and the United States. Thus it was not until after the establishment of a German Federal Republic that, in 1950, the new *Bundesarchiv* was authorized as the successor to the *Reichsarchiv* and was organized and established in 1952 in Coblenz (54 Koblenz 1, am Wöllershof 12).

In addition to the previous functions of the *Reichsarchiv*, the *Bundesarchiv* was to collect the zonal and bizonal records of 1945 to 1949 and was to receive and administer all records returned by the Allied Powers, except those of the Foreign Office. Great Britain, the United States, and France began returning the captured Prussian and German records in 1958, while the Soviet Union returned the German-Russian correspondence and the major part of the Prussian and German ministerial archives to the German Democratic Republic (DDR). Thus the bulk of the materials which originated in the Reich ministries and agencies between 1871 and 1945 is to be found in the *Deutsche Zentralarchiv* of the DDR, including the *Reichskanzlei* (Chancellery) records from 1871-1919. The *Bundesarchiv* holdings are made up largely of the army and Nazi Party records returned from Alexandria, Virginia; the naval records returned from Great Britain; the three western zonal records, and the current Federal files since 1948.

Although the major diplomatic files are in the Political Archives of the Foreign Office (see above), there are many record groups deposited in the *Bundesarchiv* which are relevant to diplomacy:

1. Records of the *Reichskanzlei* (Imperial Chancellery) for 1919-45 (R 43 I & II). See No. 34.

2. Records of the ministries of Justice, Finance, Reparations

(*Wiederaufbau*), and Eastern Occupied Territories, 1941–45 (R 6). See No. 1a.

3. Records of the German Bureau for Peace Problems (*Deutsches Büro für Friedensfragen*, 1946) (Z 35).

4. Records of institutions and associations of Germans living abroad:

    a. *Reichskommissar für die Festigung deutschen Volkstums*, 1939–45 (R 49).

    b. *Deutsche Akademie*, 1925–45 (R 51).

    c. *Institut für deutsche Ostarbeit*, 1940–45 (R 52 IV).

    d. *Deutsches Auslandsinstitut*, 1917–45 (R 57).

    e. *Volksdeutsche Mittelstelle*, 1939–45 (R 59).

5. Records of institutions for cultural relations in southeast Europe (R 63), Latin America (R 40 & 63), and Spain (R 64 I & IV).

6. Records of Nazi Party organizations and activities concerning foreign countries:

    a. *Kanzlei Rosenberg, 1934–1945. Aussenpolitisches Amt der NSDAP* (Rosenberg Chancellorship, 1934–45. Foreign Policy Office of the Nazi Party) (NA 8).

    b. *Das Ahnenerbe*; Sven Hedin-Institut (NS 21).

    c. *Hauptarchiv der NSDAP*, 1935–45 (Main Archives of the Nazi Party), Section XXVIII (USSR) (NS 26). See No. 29.

    d. Reports of Captain Wiedemann and von Papen from Vienna, personal representatives of Hitler (NS 10).

    e. Personal papers of statesmen, diplomats, and military and naval attachés.

For other descriptions of the *Bundesarchiv* holdings, see Nos. 1a, 11, and 12.

MILITÄRARCHIV

As a branch of the *Bundesarchiv*, the *Militärarchiv* is located in Freiburg (78 Freiburg im Breisgau [Postfach] Wiesentalstrasse 1).

Here are all the files and record groups of the Prussian and German army, navy and air force, as well as those of the *Reichwehr* and *Bundeswehr* (imperial and federal defence forces) and the holdings of the former *Dokumentenzentrale* of the *Militärgeschictliches Forschungsamt* (78 Freiburg, Kaiser Joseph-Strasse 262). Among these records are correspondence and reports of German military attachés stationed around the world (1934-45). The naval attachés' reports are still held by the British Admiralty. Likewise, in this repository are the reports of the German military and economic advisers to Chiang Kai-Shek, reports of the German Armistice Commission of 1940 and the papers of General Wilhelm Groener's negotiations in 1919 with Colonel Conger (U.S. Army). On the German military archives and their holdings, see Nos. 6, 16, 25, 28 and 39.

AUSSENSTELLE FRANKFURT AM MEIN
(The Frankfort Branch)

Before World War II, these Frankfort archives had been a branch of the *Reichsarchiv*, and they continued to be a branch of the *Bundesarchiv*. Its holdings of particular diplomatic interest are the files of the German Confederation (1816-66) and of the Provisional Central Government (1848-51).

Among the record groups of the German Confederation are:

1. Files of the *Bundeskanzleidirektion*.
2. The protocols of the *Bundesversammlung*.
3. Files on the international conferences of Aix-la-Chapelle (1818) and of Verona (1822).
4. Records regarding German emigration to North America.

Among the record groups of the Provisional Central Government are:

1. Files of the National Assembly (1848–49).
2. Files of the Reich ministries (*Provisorische Zentralgewalt*), 1848–1849.

3. Agréments of foreign representatives (BTI/4–6).
4. The Schleswig-Holstein question (BTI/405–432).
5. Files of the *Reichsministerium für Auswärtige Angelegenheiten*, 1848–49.
6. Files of the diplomatic correspondence of the German envoys to Bern, Brussels, Copenhagen, London, Washington, Paris, and Stockholm.
7. Files of the correspondence of the *Abteilung für die Verhältnisse zum Ausland* (Department for Foreign Relations), 1849–51.
8. Military records, 1825–67, of the Confederation fortresses at Mainz and in Luxemburg, 1825–67.

For a discussion of the holdings of the Frankfort Branch, see No. 3.

PRUSSIA

GEHEIMES STAATSARCHIV PREUSSISCHER KULTURBESITZ

Originally the *Geheime Staatsarchiv* was the repository for the records of the Prussian Privy Council, the administrative authority of the Prussian state in the seventeenth and eighteenth centuries. It therefore contained the diplomatic correspondence of Prussia up to 1867. After that year, the Prussian correspondence housed here was limited to correspondence with other German states and with the Vatican. Until 1945 it was also the repository for the records of Brandenburg Province, the city of Berlin, and the royal archives of Brandenburg-Prussia (*Hausarchiv*).

After 1945 the *Geheimes Staatsarchiv* came under the jurisdiction successively of Greater Berlin, of Berlin Territory (*Land Berlin*), and finally, in 1954, of the German Federal Republic. In 1963 it was incorporated into the *Stiftung Preussischer Kulturbesitz* (Foundation for Prussian Cultural Holdings). During this period it became the collecting point for scattered records of the

Reich ministries and agencies. Unfortunately, from the point of view of centralized consolidation, the bulk of the former Prussian holdings (*Vor-Kriegsbestände*) are now held by the Merseburg Branch (*Abteilung*) of the *Zentrales Staatsarchiv* of the DDR [see end of chapter]. For some notable exceptions, see also immediately below.

Since some of the postwar holdings of the *Geheimes Staatsarchiv* were *Reich* records and not specifically those of Prussia or Berlin, an exchange of materials between it and the *Bundesarchiv* took place in 1969 (see No. 41). The *Reich* governmental and military records were transferred to the *Bundesarchiv* and to its military branch in Freiburg, and the Prussian record groups in the *Bundesarchiv* were transferred to the *Geheimes Staatsarchiv*. Included in the transfer to the *Bundesarchiv* branch in Freiburg were the private papers (*Nachlässe*) of military personalities after 1867. This means that the Gneisenau *Nachlass*, with materials on Prussia's relations with Great Britain and Russia prior to 1867, has been retained by the *Geheimes Staatsarchiv*. For the paucity of its remaining holdings, see No. 42.

Yet there are important record groups on Prussian diplomacy still held by the *Geheimes Staatsarchiv,* such as: 251 volumes of diplomatic correspondence with Austria, Belgium, Denmark, England, France, Greece, and the Netherlands, all between 1837 and 1867; copies of reports of German ministers in various countries, alphabetically arranged according to countries (Ägypten to Venezuela), and the Gneisenau *Nachlass* (mentioned above). Among other important collections are:

1. The Constitution and Administration of Alsace-Lorraine (by the Prussian State Ministry), 1871–1929, 24 vols.
2. World War I records concerning Poland and Lithuania and the armistice and peace with Russia, 1914–18, 45 vols.
3. *Seehandlung* (maritime trade — Prussian State Bank), financial relations with foreign countries, 1777–1942, 139 vols.
4. *Nachlässe* of Friederich Schmidt-Ott, especially papers relating to German-Russian cultural relations, 1925–34.

5. East Prussian representative at Berlin: *Vertretung beim Reichs- und Staatsministerium.*

6. Hohenzollern family correspondence with relatives abroad, in the *Brandenburg-Preussische Hausarchiv* (see no. 42 [Pt. II, pp. 265-278]).

For research regulations and facilities, write the *Geheimes Staatsarchiv Preussischer Kulturbesitz* (1 Berlin-Dahlem 33, Archivstrasse 12-14). For guides and descriptions of Prussian documentary material in both the BRD (West Germany) and the DDR (East Germany), see nos. 42-44 and 48-53.

STAATLICHES ARCHIVLAGER UND ARCHIVBESTÄNDE
DER STIFTUNG PREUSSISCHER KULTURBESITZ
(3400 Göttingen, Merkelstrasse 3)

This Göttingen branch of the *Stiftung Preussischer Kulturbesitz* is useful for diplomatic history, mostly for its important and valuable *Archiv des Deutschen Ordens* (Archives of the Teutonic Order). As a part of the former *Staatsarchiv Königsberg*, these Teutonic records were evacuated to West Germany, delegated to the *Niedersächsische Archivverwaltung*, and deposited in this Göttingen center. The collection contains correspondence (1198-1595) of the Order with European courts and cities, especially with Eastern Europe and the Vatican. For discussions of these archives, see Nos. 44, 45, and 46; and in *Archivum*, 15 (1969), 65-67. For derived printed sources, see No. 139.

BADEN-WÜRTTEMBERG

BADISCHES GENERALLANDESARCHIV
(75 Karlsruhe, Nördliche Hildapromenade 2)

This is the present successor to the original archives of the Duchy of Baden, established in 1803. It has a branch in Freiburg (*Badisches Landesarchivamt*) containing state and local materials for both North and South Baden. Its collections relative to diplomacy include correspondence of its envoys and consuls in most European and German states, in the United States and Brazil, and even as far away as in Hawaii and Persia. Among the private papers, those of Freiherr von Blittersdorf's reports from Russia from 1816 to 1819 are of special interest. Lists of the Baden diplomatic representatives and consuls will be found in the series of the *Hof- und Staats-Handbuch des Grossherzogtums Baden,* and the history and holdings of the *Badisches Generallandes-archiv* are treated in Nos. 55, 56, 57, and 59, as well as in the *Minerva-Handbuch: Archive* (1974).

HAUPTSTAATSARCHIV STUTTGART
(7000 Stuttgart 1, Konrad Adenauer-Strasse 4)

These archives were first established in 1489 by Duke Ulrich and contained state and ducal documents from as early as 1316. They continued to be the repository for the kingdom after 1806, and are now the central archives for the present territory of Baden-Wurttemberg. Among the record groups of the ducal period relating to foreign affairs are: *Kabinettsakten* (1550-1674); diplomatic reports of agents (1652-1805); treaties (1316-1729); customs (1347-1579); relations with foreign princes after 1354, and documents of annexed secular and ecclesisatical states.

For the period of the kingdom (1806-1919), the principal diplomatic collections are: files of the ministry of foreign affairs; files of the ministry of the royal house; legation files returned to Stuttgart; files of the German Confederation (1815-66); the house archives of the former ruling family; the military archives (1871-1918); *Flugschriften* (pamphlets) contained in many groups of legation reports, and emigration reports since 1750.

For guides and histories of the *Hauptstaatsarchiv Stuttgart,* see Nos. 54 and 58. Speical unpublished guides also exist in these archives for Wurttemberg's nineteenth century diplomatic correspondence with its legations in Paris, Vienna, and St. Petersburg.

STAATSARCHIV LUDWIGSBURG
(714 Ludwigsburg, Schloss)

These archives contain little of diplomatic nature. There are, however, legation reports before 1806 of minor German states with each other and with the Holy Roman Emperor. One special collection is the Geizkofler family papers, containing the *Nachlass* of the Reichspfennigsmeister Zacharias Geizkofler (1560–1617) about relations with Poland and the Italian states, especially concerning the Venetian mercenaries.

FÜRSTLICH HOHENZOLLERNSCHES HAUS- UND DOMÄNENARCHIV
(7480 Sigmaringen, Karlstrasse 32)

These princely archives are of particular value for the family correspondence on the Spanish throne candidacy of 1870, on Rumanian affairs from 1866 to 1939, and on the European Danube Commission. Use of the files of these archives since 1850 requires the permission of the legal owner, the Prince of Hohenzollern, who since World War II has authorized accessibility to scholars. The principal record group of these archives is Rubrik 53. No. 73. Sigmaringen 1870–1895. Personal *Akten Familien Archiv 1870* — three bundles dealing with the Spanish throne candidacy. For discussions and reproductions of these Hohenzollern-Sigmaringen archives, see Nos. 143a, 144, 145, 146, 147, and 152.

BAVARIA[1]

HISTORY

Bavaria (*Bayern*), second to Prussia in importance as a German state, became, under the Wittelsbach family, successively a duchy (1080), an imperial electorate (1648), a kingdom (1806), a member

---

[1]The help given in the preparation of this section on Bavaria by Dr. Bernard Zittel, *Generaldirektor der Staatlichen Archiveh Bayerns*, is gratefully acknowledged.

state of the Reich (1871), and a republican territory (*Land*) in the Weimar Republic and in the BRD. In addition to these historical transformations, Bavaria also acquired the Rhenish Palatinate (1214), the Upper Palatinate (1648), and some Swabian cities and principalities (1803). Hence her archives contain state and dynastic papers of all these periods and of all the acquired territories.

The organization of Bavaria's archives has likewise gone through several stages. In 1778 the earlier Munich documents archives were indicated as the main archives of all Wittelsbach territories, and in 1799 three independent archives were established in Munich: the *Geheime Landesarchiv* (of constituent territories), the *Geheimes Staatsarchiv* (Privy State Archives), and the *Geheimes Hausarchiv* (Privy House Archives). In 1929 all of these official record depositories were brought together to form the *Hauptstaatsarchiv* (Main State Archives) in Munich. In 1946 the *Kriegsarchiv* (Military Archives) were incorporated into the *Hauptstaatsarchiv*, and in 1970 all the Bavarian state archives were put under the direction of the *Generaldirektion der Staatlichen Archive Bayerns* (8 Munich 2, Arcisstrasse 12). For the history of the Bavarian archives, see Nos. 67, 68, and 69.

BAYERISCHES HAUPTSTAATSARCHIV
(8 Munich 2, Arcisstrasse 12)

These archives consist of four principal subdivisions, as described below.

I. The *Allgemeines Staatsarchiv* (General State Archives). While these archives do not contain the official diplomatic correspondence of Bavaria, they do contain:

1. Many early reports and memoranda on the history of Austria, Belgium, Bohemia, Denmark, Greece, Hungary, Italy, Serbia, Luxemburg, the Netherlands, Sweden, Switzerland, and the Vatican.
2. Records of the Thirty Years War (804 vols. and 541 fascicles) with sources for the history of Austria, Bohemia, Denmark, and Sweden.

3. Records of the 17th century wars against France and Turkey.
4. Records of the wars of the Spainsh and Austrian successions (1701–48).
5. The Jesuitica Section, containing Jesuit mission reports from North and South America, the Philippines, India, China, and Japan.

For descriptions of the holdings of these archives, see Nos. 60 and 158.

II. The *Geheimes Staatsarchiv* (Privy State Archives: Munich, Ludwigstrasse 14). This is the main repository for Bavarian diplomatic papers (correspondence, reports, and treaties) for all centuries up to 1919, established in 1769. These archives also contain the official diplomatic papers of all states, cities, and principalities annexed by Bavaria. Their holdings are divided into three time periods: 1208–1450, 1450–1795, and 1794–1969. Within these time periods the correspondence in each is subdivided into correspondence with Bavarian consulates, with the emperors and Reich officials, and with the foreign governments of France, the Vatican, England, Russia, Switzerland, the Netherlands, Savoy, Italy, Naples, and other German states. There are also here special diplomatic record groups, such as:

1. The Upper Palatinate and Zweibrücken preannexation correspondence, alliances, and peace negotiations.
2. The captured "Protestant Correspondence (1546–1624)" of the Protestant Union.
3. Bavarian correspondence with the German Confederation, 1816–1866.
4. Bavarian correspondence with the *Zollverein* (German Tariff Union).
5. Bavarian files on the International Commission for the Rhine.
6. Bavarian correspondence (1832–62) with King Otto of Greece, who was a Bavarian prince.

7. Bavarian correspondence with its own chairman of the Bundesrat Committee of Foreign Affairs (1871–1918).

8. Correspondence of Bavarian legations abroad after 1871, containing reports on the internal affairs of foreign countries, even though Bavaria no longer conducted direct negotiations.

III. The *Geheimes Hausarchiv* (Privy Family Archives: Munich, Ludwigstrasse 14). These archives contain large collections of the correspondence of the various branches of the House of Wittelsbach, whose ducal and royal lines had wide connections with European ruling families (see Nos. 67 and 157). The archives of some of the earlier dukes of Bavaria, a side line of the House of Wittelsbach, are deposited at Tegernsee. Special permission for use of materials is needed by the present heads of the ducal and royal houses, respectively. The older archives of the dukes of Leuchtenberg are of interest for relations with Russia, Sweden, Portugal, and Brazil from 1796 to 1840. For an ambitious program of publication of Bavarian diplomatic materials (1814–48), see No. 153.

IV. The *Kriegsarchiv* (Military Archives: Munich, Leonrodstrasse 37). These army archives were founded in 1887 and were renamed *"Heeresarchiv München"* during the Nazi regime. They contain records of military relations with other states from 1841 to 1921.

STAATLICHE ARCHIVE BAYERNS

This institution is a central administration for scattered regional and local archives, most of which have no collections on diplomatic relations. The few which do have diplomatic materials are:

Those of Bamberg for Oberfranken (Upper Franconia).
Those of Würzburg for Unterfranken (Lower Franconia).

Those of Amberg for Oberpfalz (Upper Palatinate) for the secularized ecclesiastical states and the mediatized principalities of the area.

The *Coburg Staatsarchiv* with its *Herzogliches Hausarchiv* (Ducal House Archives) for the dukes of Saxe-Coburg-Gotha, especially for the 19th century (see no. 62).

The state archives on foreign relations up to 1800 (see no. 61).

The *Landesregierung* (state government) archives, 1531–1858.

The *Ministerium* archives, 1801–1920.

INSTITUT FÜR ZEITGESCHICHT

This Institute for Contemporary History (8 Munich 19, Leonrodstrasse 46b) has much to contribute to diplomatic history since 1918 in both its Library and its Archives. Its Library contains sixty thousand volumes on German and diplomatic history since 1918, extensive files of more than eleven hundred newspapers of the period, and a massive collection of newspaper clippings from 1934 to 1945.

The rich holdings of the Institute's Archives include:

Records of the Nürnberg trials.

Records of German and foreign trials of Nazi criminals.

Microfilms of Nazi documentation from foreign depositories.

Tapes (*Zeugen-Schrifttum*) of interviews of important persons of contemporary history.

Many private papers (*Nachlässe*) of diplomats and military leaders, such as Dr. Hans Schäffer, Dr. Krekeler, Dr. Dietrich Sattler, and General Geyer von Schweppenburg.

The Institute's Archives also maintain information and locator files for papers and documents on the Nazi period held by private persons. For information on the Institute's Archives, see Nos. 64 and 65.

FREIE HANSESTADT BREMEN

STAATSARCHIV BREMEN
(28 Bremen, Präsident Kennedy-Platz 2)

A large part of the pre-World War II holdings of the Bremen archives, which had been evacuated to Bernburg-Saale and captured by the Russians, has been restituted to the DDR *Zentrales Staatsarchiv Potsdam*. Yet large record groups on Bremen foreign relations still remain in her *Staatsarchiv*, from which several studies have been written on the city's diplomatic and commercial relations. (See nos. 166–171). For a guide to the present holdings of these archives, see No. 70.

Researchers should also be reminded that the Manuscript Division of the Library of Congress (Washington) has microfilms of the *Berichte des Minister-Residents Schleiden* to the Bremen Senate, 1861–1865.

FREIE UND HANSESTADT HAMBURG

STAATSARCHIV

The diplomatic archives of Hamburg's *Senatsakten* suffered heavy damage by the great fire of 1842, but there is still a great deal of material on foreign affairs and foreign commerce (see listings in *Archivum*, 15 [1969], 59–60). Among modern record groups relative to foreign affairs are:

Files concerning the Czech leased Hamburg harbor (1929–38): *Deputation für Handel, Schiffahrt, und Gewerbe.*

Files on *Aussenhandel, Konsulatswesen, 1889–1938* under *Senatskommission für die Reichs- und auswärtigen Angelegenheiten.*

Files of the *Hanseatische Gesandtschaft Berlin, 1859–1914.*

Files of the reports of the Hamburg diplomatic and consular representatives in the eighteenth and nineteenth centuries.

Handakten of the German commissioner of the German-American Reparations Commission, 1922–34.

HESSEN

The territory of Hesse (*Hessen*) today comprises the old states of grand-ducal Hessen-Darmstadt, electoral Hessen-Kassel, ducal Nassau, and the city of Frankfort. Its diplomatic archives are therefore found in threee principal repositories.

HESSISCHES STAATSARCHIV DARMSTADT

For Hessen-Darmstadt the repository is the *Hessische Staatsarchiv* (6100 Darmstadt, Schloss), whose diplomatic holdings went back to the fourteenth century and extended into the twentieth. However, about two-thirds of its records were destroyed in World War II. (For descriptions, see Nos. 74 and 75.

For diplomatic history this archival repository possesses the following:

Staatsverträge (treaties with foreign states), fourteenth to twentieth centuries (Sec. 20, Group VIII).

Legation files and reports, sixteenth to nineteenth centuries (Sec. B 5).

Ministry correspondence with states, fifteenth to nineteenth centuries.

Reports from consulates.

Correspondence with the Rhine Confederation, 1804–14.

Correspondence of the Hessian representative to the Frankfort Diet, 1817–66.

Correspondence of the Hessian military commissioners of the Confederation, 1817–66.

The grand-ducal *Hausarchiv*, sixteenth to nineteenth centuries

— including letters of Nesselrode, Grimm, Catherine II, and Czar Paul.

Grand-ducal family archives, nineteenth to twentieth centuries.

Fischbacher Archiv: papers of Prince Alexander of Hesse (see No. 172).

The Dalwigk von Lichtenfels diaries (see No. 173).

HESSISCHES STAATSARCHIV MARBURG

For electoral Hessen-Kassel, the archives are located at 355 Marburg, Friedrichsplatz 15. Associated with these archives is the *Archivschule Marburg,* founded in 1949, which aids in the cataloguing and indexing of Hessian archival materials. The diplomatic and dynastic correspondence of the Landgravate of Hessen-Kassel begins to be important during and after the Reformation. In this period and during the Counter Reformation and the Thirty Years War there is a great deal of correspondence with Denmark, Sweden, England, France, and the Netherlands. In the eighteenth century there are interesting record groups concerning the Seven Years War, the Hessian troops in the American Revolution, and relations with the Holy Roman Emperor. Between 1815 and 1866 there exists the usual diplomatic and consular files of correspondence concerning German and foreign states. (For a listing of these holdings, see Nos. 72 and 73.)

There are also military files related to diplomacy: Group 4h — "Military Affairs"; Group 11 — "Military Cabinet"; and Group 12 — "War Ministry."

HESSISCHES HAUPTSTAATSARCHIV WIESBADEN

These contain the archives of the old Duchy of Nassau and its predecessors, and are located at 6200 Wiesbaden, Mainzerstrasse 80. Important for international relations are the following record groups:

171 *Altes Dillenburger Archiv,* fourteenth century until 1743, partly concerning the Dutch struggle for freedom.

131 Nassau-Usingen relations, especially with France.
150 Nassau-Weilburg, to the early nineteenth century, expecially with France and England.
151 *Weilburger Kabinett,* 1742–1816.
152 Weilburg Government, 1742–1806.
170 Nassau-Oranien, to 1814.
172 *Landesregierung zu Dillenburg,* sixteenth century to 1816.
205 *Regierung Wiesbaden,* 1803–16.
209 Legations of ducal Nassau, 1844–66.
210 *Staatsministerium* of ducal Nassau, 1806–66.
371 Grand-Ducal Frankfort, 1810–13.

For a description of all these holdings, see No. 78.

FRANKFURT-AM-MAIN: STADTARCHIV
(6 Frankfurt-am-Main 1, Karmelitergasse 5)

The diplomatic archives of the Free City of Frankfort (1816–66) were completely destroyed by an air raid during World War II (see no. 77).

For earlier periods, however, there are some important collections, such as:

Räte und Residenten, dealing with reception of foreign representatives, 1652–1806.
Reichssachen-Nachträge (Imperial affairs — supplement).
Reichssachen-Urkunden (Imperial affairs — records).
Kaiserschreiben (letters of emperors).

For discussions of the Frankfort City Archives, see Nos. 76 and 77.

NIEDERSACHSEN

NIEDERSÄCHSISCHES HAUPTSTAATSARCHIV IN HANNOVER

The Hanover State Archives of Lower Saxony (3 Hannover, Am Archive 1) contain the diplomatic collections of the Electorate of

Hanover (1705-1815) and of the Kingdom of Hanover (1815-66), and is now the central archives of the territory of Lower Saxony. During World War II these archives suffered heavy losses in all periods.

Record groups still surviving of special value for diplomatic history are:

Hann. 9a-h *Geheime Registratur, betreffend auswärtige Angelegenheiten des Kurfürstentums Hannover,* 1679-1825.

Hann. 39 *Verhandlungen des Bundestags in Militärangelegenheiten,* 1815-55.

Hann. 40 *Deutsche Kriegsflotte,* 1848-60.

Hann. 47-48a II *Welfenlegion und der Hann. Legion in Frankreich,* 1867-70.

Hann. 92 *Akten der Deutschen Kanzlei in London,* 1728-1837. Papers of the Royal House of Hanover.

For lists and descriptions of the diplomatic material in these Hanover archives, see *Archivum,* 15 (1969): 63-64 and No. 88.

NIEDERSÄCHSISCHES STAATSARCHIV OLDENBURG

The Oldenburg State Archives of Lower Saxony (29 Oldenburg, Damm 43) contain the following record groups (*Bestände*) relevant to diplomatic history:

2 Acta Holstein-Gottorp, seventeenth and eighteenth centuries.

6 Papers of the dukes of Oldenburg, eighteenth to twentieth centuries.

20 Oldenburg County, thirteenth century to 1773.

37-55 legation correspondence.

31 Oldenburg Cabinet Registry, 1774-1868.

35 treaties, 1778-1925.

38 Court and Privy Chancellery, 1848-84.

40 Diplomatic correspondence, 1774-1811.

41 Reichstag at Regensburg, 1778-1806.

42 Congress of Vienna, 1814–15.
43 Oldenburg Legation (Frankfort) to German Confederation, 1816–1866.
44 Oldenburg Legation in Vienna, 1838–66.
45 Oldenburg Legation in Berlin, 1858–85.
48 Oldenburg consulates, 1798–1866.
132 Ministry of the Grand-Ducal House and of Foreign Affairs, 1868–1913.
46 Oldenburg representation in the *Bundesrat,* 1888–1918.
47 Oldenburg representation in the *Reichsrat,* 1922–34.

For a description of these Oldenburg archives, see No. 86.

NIEDERSÄCHSISCHES STAATSARCHIV OSNABRÜCK

These archives (45 Osnabrück, Schlossstrasse 29) contain diplomatic papers of the *Fürstbistum* (ecclesiastical principality) of Osnabrück. They are particularly valuable for the period of the Thirty Years War and the Peace of Westphalia, when Cardinal Franz Wilhelm von Wartenberg (1625–61) was prince bishop, and for correspondence with European capitals between 1715 and 1728.

NIEDERSÄCHSISCHES STAATSARCHIV STADE

These archives at Stade (216 Stade, am Sande) are those of the Archbishopric of Bremen and, also of diplomatic interest, possess the famous Erskein Collection (so-called *Stader Reichsarchiv*). Alexander von Erskein, as War Commissioner of King Gustav Adolf during the Thirty Years War, had seized from conquered areas large collections of state documents and later, as Swedish administrator of Stade, he deposited them there. For descriptions of these collections, see Nos. 79 and 89.

NIEDERSÄCHSISCHES STAATSARCHIV WOLFENBÜTTEL

These archives in Wolfenbüttel (334 Wolfenbüttel, Forstweg 2) contain important diplomatic collections of both princely lines of

Lüneburg and Oldenburg, and its collection is one of the best in northwestern Germany. Among its most important record groups from 1154 to 1945 are: the complete archives of the ducal house of Brunswick-Lüneburg, alliances, treaties, correspondence with the Empire, German states, chancellery and foreign ministry files, correspondence of legations and consulates, correspondence with the German Confederation (1816–66), and with the *Bundesrat* and *Reichsrat* (1867–1929). Of interest to American history are the consular reports from St. Louis and the papers (*Nachlass*) of General F. A. Riedesel on the American Revolution. Likewise the papers of Karl G. Schroder are of importance on the Berlin-Bagdad Railroad and on the German-Portuguese Commercial Treaty, 1909–10. For a fuller description of these archives, see Nos. 84 and 85.

NIEDERSÄCHSISCHES STAATSARCHIV AURICH

These archives in Aurich (296 Aurich, Georgstrasse 50) contain primarily the state papers of the principality of Eastern Frisia (*Ostfriesland*) and of its successor reorganized governments from 1464 to 1945. Among its record groups are diplomatic correspondence with Denmark, England, France, the Dutch General States, Poland, Spain, and Sweden, and the personal papers (*Nachlässe*) of officials engaged in this diplomacy. For a fuller description of these archives, see No. 87.

NIEDERSÄCHSISCHES STAATSARCHIV BÜCKEBURG

These archives (4967 Bückeburg, Schloss) contain the records of the principality of Schaumburg-Lippe from the fifteenth century to 1933, including diplomatic correspondence, treaties, cabinet deliberations, and ruling family (*Haus*) archives. Also in this *Hausarchiv* are the protocols of the peace negotiations of Münster and Osnabrück (1644–48). Up to 1955 the British had refused to return fifty political and military files of the Nazi period. For a fuller description, see No. 80.

NORDRHEIN-WESTFALEN

HAUPTSTAATSARCHIV DÜSSELDORF

The Main Archives of North Rhine-Westphalia (4 Düsseldorf, Prinz Georg-Strasse 78) were established first in 1852 as Prussian provincial archives and were made the central archives of this territory (*Land*) in 1952. While these archives contain mostly local archives of Düsseldorf, Aix-la-Chapelle (Aachen), Cologne (Köln), Jülich-Berg-Clèves, and Mark, they do contain some diplomatic materials as well:

Materials on Belgium and the Netherlands (see No. 91).
Jülich correspondence with Denmark and Norway (1429–92), England (1458–1501), France (1423–1512), Spain (1492), Hungary (1425–80), and Venice (1580–97).

For general descriptions of the diplomatic holdings of these archives, see Nos. 92 and 98.

STAATSARCHIV MÜNSTER

The principal diplomatic holdings of these Münster State Archives (44 Münster [Westfalen], Bohlweg 2) are the papers of Prince Bishop Christoph Bernhard von Galen (1650–78). For a description see No. 94.

STAATSARCHIV DETMOLD

For diplomatic purposes these archives (493 Detmold, Willi-Hofmann-Strasse 2) are of limited value in having some holdings of the former state of Lippe (treaties and correspondence). See No. 93.

ARCHIV DER SOZIALEN DEMOKRATIE
FORSCHUNGSINSTITUT DER FRIEDRICH EBERT-STIFTUNG

Party archives will always contain correspondence and declarations on foreign policy, as well as some private papers (*Nach-*

lässe) of their leaders. In addition, these archives (53 Bonn-Bad Godesberg 1, Kölnerstrasse 149) contain exile files of party and leaders in Prague (1933-38) and in Paris and London (1938-45). For a description of these holdings, see No. 90.

RHEINLAND-PFALZ

STAATSARCHIV KOBLENZ

These are the central archives of the territory (*Land*) of Rhineland-Palatinate (54 Koblenz, Karmeliterstrasse 1-3) and contain diplomatic materials only in its older holdings, such as:

1 C relations of Kurtrier with France, Lorraine, and Luxemburg.

22 relations of Nassau-Saarbrücken with France and Lorraine.

These materials concern mostly boundary problems. For descriptions of holdings and reproduction of some documents, see Nos. 97 and 174.

SAARLAND

LANDESARCHIV

The archives of Saarland (6600 Saarbrücken, Am Ludwigsplatz 14) contain some diplomatic papers of the Saar territory for the period 1945 to 1957: the files of the Saar Ministry of Foreign Affairs and those of the Saar's Paris legation. For the period of 1920 to 1936 the archives are in the League of Nations Archives in Geneva, containing the records of:

The Governing Commission of the Saar Territory, 1920-35.

The Plebiscite Commission, 1934-35.

The Supreme Plebiscite Tribunal for the Saar Territory, 1935-36.

SCHLESWIG-HOLSTEIN

LANDESARCHIV SCHLESWIG-HOLSTEIN

Since Denmark conducted the diplomacy for Schleswig-Holstein from 1460 to 1864, these territorial archives (238 Schleswig, Schloss Gottorf) contain very little diplomatic material. Three exceptions to this situation are:

7 Anti-Danish correspondence of the Duke of Schleswig-Holstein-Gottorf with the Holy Roman Emperor, with German states (1544–1713) and with England, France, the Netherlands, Russia, Persia, Sweden, Spain, the Spanish Netherlands, and Denmark (1515–1713).

22 Correspondence of the Dukes of Augustenburg.

51 Records of the Provisional Government and *Statthalterschaft*, 1848–50.

For discussions of holdings and records exchanges with Denmark, see Nos. 100 and 101.

GERMAN DEMOCRATIC REPUBLIC

(DEUTSCHE DEMOKRATISCHE REPUBLIK — DDR)

Although this *Guide* had had to limit its scope generally to the diplomatic archives of Western Europe, where there is comparatively more accessibility to materials for Western scholars, some description and mention should be made of the archives of the German Democratic Republic, whose holdings on European diplomacy dovetail with those of the Federal Republic.

ZENTRALES STAATSARCHIV POTSDAM

This Central State Archives in Potsdam, better known to scholars by its former name of *Deutsches Zentralarchiv*, is the successor institution to the *Reichsarchiv* of the Weimar and Nazi periods. It is the principal collecting center for the files of the

German central administration between 1871 and 1945, and of the DDR's political, economic, and administrative files since 1945. This institution also is the administrative center with authority over the various local *Historische Staatsarchive* throughout the DDR, which house the records of the earlier independent German states, such as Saxony, Mecklenburg-Schwerin, etc., and which remain generally in their previous locations. The *Zentrales Staatsarchiv* also has a branch in Merseburg (see below) for Prussian materials.

Of special foreign policy interest, the ZSA at Potsdam possesses the following record groups:

Reichskanzlei, 1918–45.

Büro des Reichspräsidenten, 1919–34.

Büro des Präsidialkanzlei, 1934–39.

Grosses Hauptquartier, 1914–18.

Formation Reichskanzler und Auswärtiges Amt, 1917–19.

Vertreter des Reichskanzlers bei der Obersten Heeresleitung.

Kriegsstelle zur Vorbereitung der Wirtschaftsfragen fur die Friedensverhandlungen (*Spezialbüro* Dr. Helfferich), 1917–18.

Nachlässe of Fürst Chlodwig zu Hohenlohe-Schillingfürst (1819–1901), Baron Holstein (1837–1909), and Count Wolff-Metternich (1853–1934).

For descriptions of the holdings of the *Zentrales Staatsarchiv Potsdam,* see Nos. 102–109. A description of the holdings of the *Historische Archive* of the old former states in the DDR may be found in No. 109 (pp. 158–165). For documentary collections published from these archives, see Nos. 175–177.

ZENTRALES STAATSARCHIV MERSEBURG

Those Prussian state and royal archives not destroyed in World War II and not held in respositories in the Federal Republic (see above) are assembled in the ZSA branch at Merseburg. In addition to remnants of Prussian state and royal official files, there are private papers (*Nachlässe*) of many Prussian officials involved in diplomacy, such as those of Gerlach, Manteuffel, Hardenberg, Stein, Bunsen, Radowitz, Keudell, Usedom and others. Some Stein papers are in Schloss Coppenberg (BRD). They also contain the papers of such political writers as Moritz Busch and Georg Cleinow. For descriptions of the holdings of the ZSA branch in Merseburg, see Nos. 47, 50, and 51.

BIBLIOGRAPHY

Guides, References, and Descriptions of Archives
     German Federal Republic (Bundesrepublik Deutschland — BRD)

1. Bemis and Griffin, *Guide*. For German archives, pp. 924–928.
1a. Booms, H., and Boberach, H. *Das Bundesarchiv und seine Bestände*. Schriften des Bundesarchivs, vol. 10. 2nd rev. ed. Boppard-am-Rhein, 1970.
2. Born, Lester K. "The libraries and archives of postwar Germany," *American historical review*, 56(1950), 34–57.
2a. Degras, *Soviet Documents*. On Germnay, see pp. 19, 62, 107, 142, 171, 218.
3. Demeter, Karl. "Das Bundesarchiv, Abteilung Frankfurt-am-Main. Entstehung, Aufgabe, Tätigkeit," *Archivalische Zeitschrift*, 49 (1954) 11–125.
5. Epstein, Fritz. "Die Erschliessung von Quellen sur Geschichte der deutschen Aussenpolitik. Die Publikationen der Akten des Auswärtigen Amts nach dem beiden Weltkriegen. Ein Vergleich der Methoden," *Die Welt als Geschichte*, 22 (1962), 204–219.
6. Herwig, Holger. "Military Archives in Western Germany," *Military affairs*, 36 (1972), 121ff.
7. Latzke, Walther. "Die Registraturen der Reichsministerien der Provisorischen Zentralgewalt, 1848–1849," *Der Archivar*, 8 (1955), 187–198.
8. Learned, Marion Dexter, ed. *Guide to manuscript materials relating to American history in the German state archives*. Washington, 1912.
9. Meisner, H. O. "Die Protokolle des Deutsches Bundestages von 1816–1866," *Archivalische Zeitschrift*, 47 (1951), 1–22.
10. Mommsen, Wolfgang. "Die Akten der Nürnburger Kriegsbrecherprozesse und die Möglichkeit ihrer historischen Auswertung," *Der Archivar*, 3 (1950), 14–25.

11. ———. "Das Bundesarchiv im Strom unserer Zeit," *Der Archivar*, 26 (1973), 498-506.

12. Mommsen, Wolfgang A., and Denecke, Ludwig. *Verzeichnis der schriftlichen Nachlässe in deutschen Archiven und Bibliotheken*. Vol. I (Mommsen). *Die Nachlässe in den deutschen Archiven mit Ergänzungen aus anderen Beständen*. Vol. II (Denecke). *Die Nachlässe in den Bibliotheken der Bundesrepublik Deutschland*. 2 vols. Boppard-Rhein: Harald Boldt Verlag, 1969-71.

13. Nissen, Walter. "Zur Geschichte der Reichsarchividee im 19. Jahrhundert," *Archivar und Historiker*, (1956), 162-176.

14. Philippi, Hans. "Das Politische Archiv des Auswärtigen Amts. Rückführung und Übersicht über die Bestände," *Der Archivar*, 13 (1960), 199-218.

15. Skidmore, Thomas E. "A survey of unpublished sources on the central government and politics of the German Empire, 1871-1918," *American historical review*, 65 (1960), 848-859.

16. Stahl, Friedrich Christian. "Die Bestände des Bundesarchiv-Militärarchivs," *Militärgeschichtliche Mitteilungen*, 8 (1969): 599-608. Also in *Revue internationale d'histoire militaire*, no. 27 (1968), 307-313.

17. Stehlin, Stewart A. "Documents on German Foreign Policy," *AHA Newsletter*, 6 (1967), 12-14.

18. Ullrich, Johannes. "Das Politische Archiv des Auswärtigen Amts," *Archivum*, 11 (1963), 26-28.

19. Wagner, Alfred. "The administration of archives in Germany," *Archives*, 6 (1963), 67-77.

20. UNESCO. International Council on Archives and Interdocumentary Collections. *Quellen zur Geschichte Afrikas südlich der Sahara in den Archiven der Bundesrepublik Deutschland*. Vol. I (1970). English translation (1974).

Allied Captured German Archives

21. American Historical Association Committee for the Study of War Documents. *A catalogue of files and microfilms of the German Foreign Ministry Archives, 1867-1920*. Oxford, 1959.

22. American Historical Association Committee for the Study of War Documents. *List of archival references to material in the German Foreiv Ministry Archives filmed under grant from the Old Dominion Foundation*. ashington, 1958.

23. Birnbaum, John A. "The captured German records," *The historian*, 32 (1970), 564-575.

24. *Documents on German foreign policy* (see no. 125 below in Bibliography). For a discussion of this collection see its Genjal Introduction in Volume I of Series D.

25. Enders, Gerhart. "Die ehemaligen deutschen Militärakten nach 1945." *Zeitschrift für Militärgeschichte* (DDR), 8 (1969) 599-608.

26. Epstein, Fritz T. "Zur Quellenkunde der neuesten Geschichte; ausländische Materialien in der Archiven und Bibliotheken der Hauptstadt der Vereinigten Staaten," *Vierteljahrhefte für Zeitgeschichte*, (July 1954), 313-325.

27. Gatzke, Hans W. "The Stresemann papers," *Journal of modern history*, 26 (1954), 49-59.

20. Heinsius, P. "Aktenmaterial der deutschen Kriegsmarine. Seine bisherige Auswertung und sun Verbleib," *Die Welt als Geschichte*, 13 (1953), 198-202.

29. Heinz, Grete, and Peterson, Agnes F., compilers. *NSDAP Hauptarchiv. Guide to the Hoover Institution microfilm collection.* Stanfgd; 1964.

30. Humphrey, Richard A. "War-born microfilm holdings of the Department of State," *Journal of modern history*, 20 (1948) 133-136.

31. Kent, George O. *A catalogue of files and microfilms of the German Foreign Ministry Archives, 1920-1945.* Published under the auspices of the U. S. Department of State and the Hoover Institution on War, Revolution, and Peace. Stanford, 1972-

32. Kent, George O. "The German Foreign Ministry's archives at Whaddon Hall, 1948-58," *American archivist*, 24 (1961), 43-54.

33. Kent, George O., et al. *A list of archival references and data of documents fs from the archives of the German Foreign Ministry, 1867-1920, microfilmed at Whaddon Hall.* Whaddon Hall, 1957.

34. Loewenheim, Francis L. "Guides to microfilmed German archives: a review," *The American archivist*, 22 (1959), 445-449.

35. Lötze, Helmut. "Archivmaterialien aus der UdSSR," *Zeitschrift für Geschichtswissenschaft*, 8 (1960), 1177-1182. Now in the DDR.

36. Mommsen, Wolfgang. "Deutsche Archivalien im Ausland," *Der Archivar* (Dusseldorf), 4 (1951), 1-14.

37. National Archives of the United States. *Guides to the German records micro5rlmed at Alexandria, Va. Records of the German High Command and 54eld commanders.* 64 vols. Washington, 1958-

38. *Index of microfilmed records of the German Foreign Ministry and the Reich's Chancellery covering the Weimar period.* Ernst Schwandt, ed. Washington, 1958.

39. Poll, Bernhard. "Vom Schicksal der deutschen Heeresakten und der amtlichen Kriegsgeschichtsschreibung," *Die Welt als Geschichte,* 12 (1952), 61–68.

40. Wagner, Alfred. "Rückgabe von Quellen zur jüngsten deutschen. Geschichte aus Grossbritannien und den Vereinigten Staaten," *Der Archivar,* 15 (1962), 343–346.

Prussia (Preussen)

41. Booms, Hans. "Archivalienaustausch zwischen Bundesarchiv und Geheimem Staatsarchiv," *Der Archivar,* 23 (1970), 100–101.

42. Branig, Hans, et al. *Übersicht über die Bestände des Geheimen Staatsarchivs in Berlin-Dahlem.* Mitteilungen der Preussischen Archivverwaltung. Berlin, 1966–67. A description of the Prussian State Archives still held in West Germany (BRD) after the war.

43. Endler, Ranate. "Nachlässe in der Historischen Abteilung II des Deutschen Zentralarchivs," *Zeitschrift für Geschichtswissenschaft,* 19 (1972), 1160–1165. Papers of Prussian diplomats held in the DDR.

44. Forstreuter, Kurt. "Das preussische Staatsarchiv in Königsberg," *Veröffentlichen der niedersächisischen Archivverwaltung,* 3 (1955).

45. ——— . "Das Staatsarchiv Königsberg als Quelle für die allgemeine Geschichte," *Hamburger mittel- und ostdeutsche Forschungen,* 6 (1967), 9–35.

46. ——— . "Das staatliche Archivlager in Göttingen," *Zeitschrift für Ostforschung,* 3 (1954), 92–94.

48. Müller, Ernst, et al. *Übersicht über die Bestände des Geheimen Staatsarchivs zu Berlin-Dahlem.* Mitteilungen der Preussischen Archivverwaltung. Vols. 24–26. Leipzig, 1934–1936. A description of the Prussian State Archives before the losses in World War II.

49. Preuss, Sabine. "Veränderungen im Bereich der Nachlässe des Geheimen Staatsarchivs," *Der Archivar,* 25 (1972), 298–301.

50. Thieme, Horst. "Preussisches Geheimen Zivilkabinett—kapitalistische Epoche. Übersicht über einen Bestand im Deutschen Zentralarchiv [Gruppe Militär], Abteilung II, Merseburg," *Zeitschrift für Geschichtswissenschaft,* 17 (1970), 90–93.

51. *Übersicht über die Bestände des Brandenburg-Preussischen Haus-archivs zu Berlin-Charlottenburg.* Mitteilungen de preussi-schen Archivverwaltung, no. 27. Leipzig, 1936.

52. Zimmermann, Gerhard. "Das Geheime Staatsarchiv," *Jahrbuch der Stiftung Preussischer Kulturbesitz,* (1962), 303-323.

53. ———. "Neuerwerbungen des Geheimen Staatsarchivs," *Jahrbuch der Stiftung Preussischer Kulturbesitz,* (1964-65), 230-245.

Baden-Württemberg: with Hohenzollern-Sigmaringen

54. Gönner, Eberhard. *Das Haupt-Staatsarchiv Stuttgart.* Stuttgart, 1969.

55. *Inventare des grossherzoglich badischen General-Landesarchivs.* Veröffentlichungen der Staatlichen Archivverwaltung Baden-Württemberg. 4 vols. Carlsruhe, 1901-11.

56. Kaulfuss, G. *Das badsche Quellenmaterial für die Geschichte der Reichsgründung bei Ottokar Lorenz.* Ph. D. Dissertation. Halle-Wittenberg, 1912.

57. Krebs, Manfred, *Gesamtübersicht der Bestände des Generallandes-archivs Karlsruhe.* Veröffentlichungen der Staatlichen Archiv-verwaltung Baden-Württemberg, Vols. 1 and 2. Carlsruhe, 1954-1957.

58. Muller, Karl-Otto. *Gesatübersicht über die Bestände der staat-lichen Archive Württembergs in planmässiger Einteilung.* Veröffentlichungen der württembergischen Archivverwaltung, Vol. 2. Stuttgart, 1937.

59. Schafter, A. *Inventar der handgezeichneten Karten und Pläne fur europäische Kriegsgeschichte des 16.-19. Jahrhunderts.* Veröf-fentlichungen der württembergischen Staatlichen Archivverwal-tung, Vol. 25. Carlsruhe, 1971.

Bavaria (Bayern): with Coburg

60. Allgemeines Staatsarchiv. (Regulations and principal holdings), in *Minerva-Handbücher. Archive Abteilung,* 2nd Series. 1 (1932), 237-244.

61. Andrian-Werburg, Klaus Freiherr von. "Archive in Coburg," *Jahrbuch der Coburger Landesstiftung,* (1968), 79-126.

62. ———. "Das herzogliche Hausarchiv Coburg," *Mitteilungen für die Archivpflege in Bayern,* 17 (1971), 23-31. Correspondence of the Coburg house with European royalty.

63. "Bayerische Hauptstaatsarchiv," *Archivum,* 15 (1965), 40-54.

64. Hoch, Anton. "Das Archiv des Instituts für Zeitgeschichte," *Der Archivar,* 26 (1973), 295-308.

65. Institut für Zeitgeschichtem *Selbstverständnis, Aufgaben, und Methoden der Zeitgeschichte. Chronik, Bibliothek, Archiv, Publikationen, Personalia.* Munich, 1972.

66. Männer, Ludwig. "Die Neuordnung des Geheimen Staatsarchivs in München," *Archivalische Zeitschrift,* 46 (1950), 104-124.

67. Neudegger, M. J. *Geschichte der bayerischen und pfälzischen Archive der Wittelsbacher vom 13.-19. Jahrhundert.* 3 parts. Munich, 1881-96.

68. Ritter von Böhm, G. "Vorstand des Geheimen Haus- und Staatsarchivs [Bayerns]," *Archivalische Zeitschrift,* new series, 12 (1905), 79 ff.

69. United States Office of Military Government for Bavaria. *Postwar status of chief archival institutions in Bavaria.* Munich, 1948.

Bremen, Freie Hansestadt

70. Hauschild-Thiessen, Renate, and Bachmann, Elfriede. *Führer durch die Quellen zur Geschichte Latein-Amerikas in der Bundesrepublik Deutschland.* Veröffentlichungen aus dem Staatsarchiv der Freien Hansestadt Bremen, Vols. 37-38. Bremen, 1972.

71. Schwebel, K. H., et al. *Das Staatsarchiv Bremen.* Veröffentlichungen aus dem Staatsarchiv der Freien Hansestadt Bremen, no. 36. Bremen, 1968.

Hessen: with Darmstadt, Kassel, Nassau, and Frankfort.

72. Franz, Eckhart Gotz, ed. *Kurhessisches Ministerium der auswärtigen Angelegenheiten und des Hauses (1813) 1821-1867.* 2 vols. Marburg, 1972.

73. Dulfer, Kurt, ed. *Politische Akten nach Philipp dem Grosmütigen 1567-1821. Staatenabteilung.* 24 vols. Marburg, 1959-1973.

74. Eckhardt, Albrecht, and Hoferichter, C. H. *Das Hessische Staatsarchiv und das Stadtarchiv in Darmstadt. Übersicht über ihre Bestände.* Darmstadt, 1969. Discusses war losses, pp. 49-56.

75. Fink, G. *Geschichte des Hessischen Staatsarchivs zu Darmstadt.* Darmstadt, 1925.

76. Jung, Rudolf. *Das Frankfurter Stadtarchiv. Seine Bestände und seine Geschichte.* Frankfurt-am-Main, 1909.

77. Meinert, H. "Das Frankfurter Stadtarchiv im Zweiten Weltkriege," Archiv für Frankfurts Geschichte und Kunst, 5 (1948).

78. *Übersicht über die Bestände des Hessischen Hauptstaatsarchivs Wiesbaden.* Wiesbaden, 1971.

Lower Saxony (Niedersachsen: with Göttingen, Hannover, Königsbert, Oldenburg, Schaumburg-Lippe, Stade, and Wolfenbüttel)

79. Boulin, Herman. "Erskeinska samlinger i Staatsarchiv i Hannover," *Meddelanden från svenska riksarkiver*, (1936), 86–109. A discussion of seventeenth century German documents captured by the Swedes and deposited in Hanoverian archives.

80. Engel, Franz. *Die Schaumburg-Lippischen Archive und zentralen Reigstraturen*. Veröffentlichungen der Niedersächisischen Archivverwaltung, No. 4. Göttingen, 1955.

81. Forstreuter, Kurt. *Das preussische Staatsarchiv in Königsberg*. Veröffentlichung der Niedersächsischen Archivverwaltung, No. 3. Göttingen, 1955.

82. ———. "Das staatliche Archivlager in Göttingen," *Zeitschrift für Ostforschung*, 3 (1954), 92–94.

83. Joachim, Erich, and Hubatsch, Walther. *Regesta historico-diplomatica, Ordinis S. Mariae Theutonicorum, 1198–1595*. Göttingen, 1948.

84. Kleinau, Hermann. *Geschichte des Niedersächsischen Staatsarchivs in Wolfenbüttel*. Veröffentlichungen des Niedersächsischen Staatsarchivs in Wolfenbüttel, No. 1. Göttingen, 1953.

85. ———. *Übersicht über die Bestände des Niedersächsischen Staatsarchivs in Wolfenbüttel*. Veröffentlichungen der Niedersächsischen Archivverwaltung, No. 17. Göttingen, 1963.

86. Lübbing, Hermann. *Die Bestände des Staatsarchivs Oldenburg. Gesamtübersicht und Archivplan*. Oldenburgische Geschichtsquellen, Vol. 2. Oldenburg, 1943.

87. Möhlmann, Günther, and König, Joseph. *Geschichte und Bestände des Niedersächsischen Staatsarchivs in Aurich*. Veröffentlichungen der Niedersächsischen Archivverwaltung, No. 5. Göttingen, 1955.

88. Pitz, Ernst. *Übersicht über die Bestände des Niedersächsischen Staatsarchiv in Hannover*. Veröffentlichungen der Niedersächsischen Archivverwaltung, No. 25. Hanover, 1968.

89. Weise, Erich. *Geschichte des Niedersächsischen Staatsarchivs in Stade nebst Übersicht seiner Bestände*. Veröffentlichungen der Niedersächsischen Archivverwaltung, No. 18. Göttingen, 1964.

North Rhine-Westphalia (Nordrhein-Westfalen): with Düsseldorf, Köln, and Detmold

90. Jensen, Jürgen, and Krause, Werner. *Übersicht über die Archivbestände* [of the Social Democratic Party], pp. 8–10.

91. Oediger, Friedrich Wilhelm. "Die Bedeutung des Hauptstaats-archivs Düsseldorf für die niederländische Geschichtsfor-schung," *Nederlands Archievenblaad*, 70 (1966), 52 ffm

92. ———. *Das Staatsarchiv Düsseldorf und seine Bestände*. Vol. I. *Landes- und Gerichtsarchiv von Jülich-Berg, Kleve-Mark, Moers, und Geldern*. Siegburg, 1957. See especially p. 85.

93. Richtering, Helmut. *Die Bestände des Staatsarchivs und Personen-standsarchivs Detmold*. Veröffentlichungen der staatlichen Archive des Landes Nordrhein-Westfalen. Series: Archivführer und Kurzübersichten, No. 3. Detmold, 1970.

94. ———. *Die Bestände des Staatsarchivs Münster*. 2nd ed. Münster, 1971.

95. Stehkämper, Hugo. 'Der Nachlass des Reichskanzlers Wilhelm Marx," *Mitteilungen aus dem Stadtarchiv von Köln*, nos. 52–55 (1968).

Rhineland-Palatinate (Rheinland-Pfalz)

96. Ausfeld, E. *Übersicht über die Bestände des könglichen Staatsar-chivs zu Koblenz*. Mitteilungen der Preussischen Archivverwal-tung, Vol. 6. Coblenz, 1903.

97. Looz-Corswarem, Otto Graf von, and Scheidt, Hellmuth. *Repor-torium der Akten des ehemaligen Reichskammergerichts im Staatsarchiv Koblenz*. Veröffentlichungen der Landesarchivver-waltung Rheinland-Pfalz. Coblenz, 1957.

98. Schmidt, Charles. *Les sources de l'histoire des territoires rhénans de 1792 à 1814 dans les archives rhénanes et à Paris*. Paris, 1921.

Schleswig-Holstein (with Lübeck)

99. Brandt, A. von. "Das Lübecker Archiv in den letzten hundert Jahren. Wandlungen, Bestände, Aufgaben," *Zeitschrift des Ve-reins für lübeckische Geschichte und Altertumskunde*, 33 (1952), 33–80.

100. Hoffman, G. E.; Suhr, Wilhelm; and Hector, Kurt. *Übersicht über die Bestände des Schleswig-Holstein'schen Landesarchivs in Schleswig*. 1953.

101. Stephan, Walther. "Das deutsch-dänische Abkommen über den Austausch historischer Archivalien," *Archivalische Zeitschrift*, 42–43 (1934), 338–343.

German Democratic Republic (Deutsche Demokratische Re-publik DDR)

102. Harnisch, Hartmut. "Nachlässe im Staatsarchiv Potsdam," *Zeitschrift fur Geschichswissenschaft*, 21 (1971), 1088–1092.

Mentions papers of several German diplomats and the official German correspondence on China and Japan, 1859-1862.

103. Knabe, Lotte. "Die Neuordnung der Bestände des ehemaligen Reichsarchivs im Deutschen Zentralarchiv in Potsdam," *Archivmitteilungen*, 1 (1952), 43-44.

104. Lötzke, Helmut. "Archivalische Quellen zur deutschen Aussenpolitik bis zum Ende des Zweiten Weltkrieges," *Deutsche Aussenpolitik*, 2 (1957), 873-879.

105. ———. "Archivwissenschaft, Quellenkunde, und historische Hilfswissenschaften [in DDR]," *Zeitschrift für Geschichtswissenschaft*, 18 (1970), 815-828.

106. Lötzke, Helmut, and Brather, Hans-Stephen. *Übersicht über die Bestände des Deutschen Zentralarchivs Potsdam*. Schriftenreihe des Deutschen Zentralarchivs, Vol. I. East Berlin, 1957.

107. Mork, Gordon R. "The archives of the German Democratic Republic," *Central European history*, 2 (1969), 273-284.

108. Schmid, Irmtraut. "Der Bestand des Auswärtigen Amtes im Deutschen Zentralarchiv Potsdam," *Archivmitteilungen*, 12 (1962); 71-79, 123-132.

109. Staatliche Archivverwaltung (DDR). *Taschenbuch Archivwesen der DDR*. Berlin, 1971.

Successor States

110. Eder, Paul. "Archivfragen in den Friedensverträgen des 19. und 20. Jahrhunderts," *Korrespondenzblatt des Vereins für siebenbürgische Landeskunde*, 47 (1924), 9-17.

111. Paczkowski, Joseph. "La remise des actes en connexion avec les changements de frontières entre états," *La Pologne au Vᵉ Congrès international des sciences historiques*. Brussels, 1923. Warsaw, 1924.

112. Warschauer, Adolf. "Inventar des Breslauer Archivs," *Mitteilungen der preussischen Archivverwaltung*, 21 (1909).

Printed Collections and Special Items

German Federal Republic (Bundesrepublik Deutschland — BRD)

113. Berber, R., ed. *Europäische Politik im Spiegel der Prager Akten, 1933-1938*. Essen, 1941.

114. Bonnin, Georges, ed. *Bismarck and the Hohenzollern candidature for the Spainsh throne. The documents in the German diplomatic archives*. London, 1957.

115. Bulow, Bernhard W. von. *Kommentar: Die Krisis. Die Grundlinien der diplomatischen Verhandlungen bei Kriegsausbruch*. 3rd ed. Berlin, 1922.

116. Erdmann, Karl D.; Mommsen, Wolfgang; and Vogel, Walter; eds. *Akten der Reichskanzlei Weimarer Republik.* Boppard am Rhein, 1968–

117. Fester, Richard, ed. *Briefe, Aktenstücke, und Regesten zur Geschichte der Hohenzollern 'schen Thronkandidatur in Spanien.* Leipzig and Berlin, 1913.

118. (White Book Group) Germany. Foreign Office. *Aktenstücke zum Kriegsausbruch. Dem deutschen Reichstag vorgelegt am 4. 8. '14. Mit nachträglichen Ergänzungen.* Berlin, 1914.

119. ———. *Vorläufige Denkschrift und Aktenstück zum Kriegsausbruch.* Berlin, 1914.

120. ———. *Das deutsche Weissbuch über die Schuld am Kriege (mit der Denkschrift der deutschen Viererkommission zum Schuldbericht der Alliierten und Assoziierten Mächte).* Berlin, 1919.

121. ———. *Deutschland schuldig? Deutsches Weissbuch über die Verantwortlichkeit der Urheber des Krieges.* Berlin, 1919. An English translation by J. B. Scott, ed., *The German White Book concerning the responsibility of the authors of the war* [World War I]. New York, 1924.

122. ———. *Urkunden des deutschen Generalstabes über die miltärpolitische Lage in den letzten Jahren vor dem Kriege. Hat der deutschen Generalstab zum Kriege getrieben?* Berlin, 1918.

123. Sass, Johann. *Die deutschen Weissbücher zur auswärtigen Politik, 1870-1914. Geschichte und Bibliographie.* Berlin and Leipzig, 1928.

124. Germany. Foreign Office. *Akten zur deutschen auswärtigen Politik.* Series B. (1925-33), Vols. I–VI; Series C. (1933-1937), Vols. I (1 & 2), II (1 & 2); Series E. (1941-1945), Vols. I–III. Baden-Baden, 1969-73- .

125. United States. State Department. *Documents on German foreign policy.* Five Series. Series C. (1933-37), vols. I–IV. Series D. (1937-41), Vols. I–XIII. Washington, 1950-71- .

126. Kautsky, Karl; Montgelas, Graf Max; and Schücking, Walter; eds. *Die deutschen Documente zum Kriegsausbruch* [World War I]. 2nd ed. 4 vols. Berlin, 1927.

127. Kroll, Vincent. "Die Publikation der Akten zur deutschen Aussenpolitik zwischen den Weltkriegen," *Der Archivar*, 16 (Feb. 1963), 89–92.

128. Lepsius, Johannes; Mendelsohn-Bartholdy, Albrecht; and Thimme, Friedrich, eds. *Die grosse Politik der europäischen Kabinette, 1871-1914.* 40 vols. in 54. Berlin, 1922-1927. A collection of documents from the German Foreign Office.

129. Mendelsohn-Bartholdy, Albrecht, and Thimme, Friedrich, eds. *Die auswärtige Politik des deutschen Reiches, 1871-1914.* 4 vols. Berlin, 1928. An abbreviated edition of *Die grosse Politik.*

130. Scherer, André, and Grunewald, Jacques, eds. *L'Allemagne et les problèmes de la paix pendant la première guerre mondiale.* 2 vols. Paris, 1962, 1966. German documents on peace efforts, 1914-1917.

131. Schwertfeger, Bernhard. *Die diplomatischen Akten des Auswärtiges Amtes, 1871-1914. Ein Wegweiser durch das grosse Aktenwerk des deutschen Regierung.* 8 vols. Berlin, 1925-27.

132. Thimme, Friedrich, ed. *Die gesammelten Werke, Otto von Bismarcks.* 15 vols. Berlin, 1924-35.

133. United States. Department of State. *Nazi-Soviet relations, 1939-1941.* Washington, 1948. The German edition of the original texts is: *Das nationalsozialistische Deutschland und die Sowjetunion, 1939-1941. Akten aus dem Archiv des Deutschen Auswärtigen Amts.* Berlin, 1948.

Prussia (Preussen)

134. Barton, Irmgard von. *Die preussische Gesandtschaft in München als Instrument der Reichpolitik in Bayern von den Anfängen der Reichsgründung bis zu Bismarcks Entlassung.* Diss. zur Bayerischen Landes- und Münchener Stadtgeschichte, No. 2. Munich, 1967.

135. Bismarck, Otto von. *Bismarcks Briefwechsel mit dem Minister Freiherrn von Schleinitz, 1858-1861.* Stuttgart, 1905.

136. Branig, Hans, ed. *Briefwechsel des Fürsten Karl August von Hardenberg mit dem Fürsten Wilhelm Ludwig zu Sayn-Wittgenstein, 1806-1822.* Veröffentlichungen aus den Archiven Preussischer Kulturbesitz, Vol. 9. Berlin, 1972.

137. Dolezel, Stefan and Heidrum, eds. *Staatsverträge des Herzogtums Preussen.* Veröffentlichungen aus den Archiven Preussischer Kulturbesitz, Vol. 4. Berlin, 1971.

138. Historische Reichskommission Erich Brandenburg, Otto Hoetzsch, and Hermann Oncken, eds. *Die auswärtige Politik Preussens, 1858-1871* (1869). 12 vols. Oldenburg, 1933-1939. Part of 1866 and all of 1870 and 1871 were not completed.

139. Joachim, Erich, and Hubatsch, Walther, eds. *Regesta historico-diplomatica Ordinis S. Mariae Theutonicorum, 1198-1595.* 3 vols. Göttingen, 1960-1971.

140. Raschdau, T., ed. *Politische Berichte* [Bismarcks] *aus Petersburg und Paris, 1859-1862.* 2 vols. Berlin, 1920.

141. Schoeps, Hans-Julius. *Von Olmütz nach Dresden 1850-1851.*

Veröffentlichungen aus den Archiven Preussischer Kulturbesitz, Vol. 7. Berlin, 1972.

142. Sybel, Heinrich von. *Die Begründung des deutschen Reiches durch Wilhelm I.* 6th rev. ed. 7 vols. Munich, 1904. An English translation by M. L. Perrin, G. Bradford, and H. S. White, *Founding of the German Empire by William I.* 7 vols. New York, 1890-98. Based on the Prussian and German Foreign Office documents.

Baden-Württemberg: with Hohenzollern-Sigmaringen

143. Bach, August, ed. *Deutsche Gesandschaftsberichte zum Kriegsausbruch 1914. Berichte und Telegramme der badischen, sächsischen, und württembergischen Gesandschaften in Berlin aus dem Juli und August 1914m* Berlin, 1937.

143a. Becker, Josef. "Zum Problem der Bismarckschen Politik in der spanischen Thronfrage 1870," *Historische Zeitschrift,* 212 (June 1971), 529-607.

144. Bonnin, Georges. "The Sigmaringen Archives," in his *Bismarck and the Hohenzollern Candidature* (London, 1957), pp. 283-297. Contains documents reproduced from these archives.

145. Dittrich, Jochen. "Bismarck, Frankreich, und die Hohenzollernkandidatur," *Die Welt als Geschichte,* 13 (1953), 42-57.

146. ———. *Bismarck, Frankreich und die Hohenzollernkandidatur. Eine Untersuchung zur Frage von Schuld und Schicksal beim Kriegsausbruch von 1870 (mit einem Anhang von bisher unbekannten Briefen und Aktenstücken aus dem Fürstlich Hohenzollern 'schen Familienarchiv.* Diss. Freiburg University, 1948. Microfilm copies in the libraries of the University of Chicago and the University of Minnesota.

147. ———. *Bismarck, Frankreich und die spanischen Thronkandidatur der Hohenzollern. Die "Kriegschuldfrage" von 1870. Im Anhang* (pp. 351-412) *Briefe und Aktenstücke aus dem Fürstlich Hohenzollern 'schen Hausarchiv.* Munich, 1962.

148. Hoffmann, Paul. *Die diplomatischen Beziehungen zwischen Württemberg und Bayern im Krimkrieg und bis zum Beginn der italienischen Krise (1853-1858).* Veröffentlichungen der Kommission für geschichtliche Landeskunde in Baden-Württemberg, ser. A 23. Stuttgart, 1963. Utilizes Württemberg and Bavarian diplomatic correspondence.

149. Martenson, Sten. *Württemberg und Russland im Zeitalter der deutschen Einigung, 1856-1870.* Göppinger Akademische Beiträge, No. 4. Stuttgart, 1970.

150. Benz, Wolfgang, ed. *Politik in Bayern, 1919-1933. Berichte des württembergische Gesandten, Carl Moser von Filseck.* Schriftenreihe der Vierteljahrshefte für Zeitgeschichte, Vols. 22-23. Stuttgart, 1971.

151. Poschinger, Heinrich von, ed. "Eigenhändigen Auszeichnungen des Präsidenten des badischen Ministeriums des Auswärtigen, Rudolf von Freydorf, über die militärischen Einigungsversuche der süddeutschen Staaten," *Annalen des deutschen Rechts für Gesetzgebung, Verwaltung, und Volkswirtschaft,* 38 (1905): 1-30.

152. Zingeler, Karl Theodor, ed. "Briefe des Fürsten Karl Anton von Hohenzollern an seine Gemahlen Josephine, geborene Prinzessin von Baden," *Deutsche Revue,* 39 (1914), No. 2, 338-346; No. 4, 112-120.

Bavaria (Bayern): with Coburg

153. Andrian-Werburg, Klaus Freiherr von, ed. *Gesandtschaftsberichte aus München, 1814-1848.* 15 vols. Munich, 1935-51.

154. Bastgen, Boda, ed. *Bayern und der Heilige Stuhl in der ersten Hälfte des 19. Jahrhunderts. Nach den Akten des wiener Nuntius Severoli und der münchener Nuntien Serra-Cassano, Mercy d'Argenteau, und Viale Prelà, sowie den Weisungen des römischen Staatssekretariates aus dem vatikanischen Geheimarchiv.* Beiträge zur altbayerischen Kirchengeschichte, vols. 17 and 18. Munich, 1940.

155. Deuerlein, Ernst. *Der Bundesratsausschluss für auswärtige Angelegenheiten.* Regensburg, 1955.

156. Dirr, P., ed. *Bayerische Dokumente zum Kriegsausbruch und zum Versailler Schuldspruch.* Munich, 1925.

157. Druffel, A. von, et al., eds. *Briefe und Akten zur Geschichte des sechszehnten Jahrhunderts mit besonderen Rücksicht auf Bayerns Furstenhaus.* 6 vols. Munich, 1873-1913.

158. Duhr, Bernhard, ed. "Zur Geschichte des Jesuitenordens. Aus münchner Archiven und Bibliotheken," *Historisches Jahrbuch,* 25 (1905); 28 (1907). Reproduces reports on Jesuit missions to North and South America, the Philippines, India, China, and Japan.

159. Franz-Willing, Georg. *Die bayerische Vatikangesandtschaft, 1881-1934.* Munich, 1965.

160. Furnrohr, Walter. *Kurbaierns Gesandte auf dem Immerwährende Reichstag. Zur bayerischen Aussenpolitik 1663 bis 1806.* Göttingen, 1971.

161. Jelavich, Barbara, ed. *Russland 1852-1871. Aus den Berichten der bayerischen Gesandtschaft in St. Petersburg.* Veröffentlichungen des Osteuropa-Instituts, München, Vol. 19. Wiesbaden, 1963.

162. Reiser, Konrad. *Bayerische Gesandte bei deutschen und ausländischen Regierungen, 1871-1918.* Neue Schriften des Stadtarchivs München, No. 26. Munich, 1968. Discusses several episodes of Bavaria's relations with France, Austria-Hungary, and the Vatican.

163. Ritter, Monika. *Frankreichs Griechenlandpolitik während des Krimkriegs (im Spiegel der Französischen und bayerischen Gesandtschaftsberichte), 1853-1857.* Diss. Munich, 1967.

164. Ritter, M., et al., eds. *Briefe und Akten zur Geschichte des dreissigjährigen Krieges in den Zeiten des vorwaltenden Einflusses der Wittelsbacker.* 15 vols. Munich, 1870-1948.

165. Zittel, Bernhard. "Die Vertretung des Heiliges Stuhles in München, 1785-1934," *Der Mönch im Wappen. Aus Geschichte und Gegenwart des katholischen München,* (Munich, 1960): 419-494.

Bremen, Freie Hansestadt

166. Engelsing, Rolf. *Bremen als Auswandererhafen, 1683-1880.* Veröffentlichungen aus dem Staatsarchiv der Freien Hansestadt Bremen, no. 29. Bremen, 1961.

167. Glade, Dieter. *Bremen und der Ferne Osten.* Veröffentlichungen aus dem Staatsarchiv der Freien Hansestadt Bremen, No. 34. Bremen, 1966.

168. Kossok, Manfred. "Preussen, Bremen, und die Texasfrage, 1835-1845," *Bremisches Jahrbuch,* 49 (1964), 73-104.

169. Lührs, Wilhelm. *Die Freie Hansestadt Bremen und England in der Zeit des Deutschen Bundes, 1815-1867.* Veröffentlichungen aus dem Staatsarchiv der Freien Hansestadt Bremen, No. 26. Bremen, 1968.

170. Prüser, Jürgen. *Die Handelsverträge der Hansestädte Lübeck, Bremen, und Hamburg, mit überseeischen Staaten im 19. Jahrhundert.* Veröffentlichungen aus dem Staatsarchiv der Freien Hansestadt Bremen, No. 30. Bremen, 1962.

171. Wiedemann, Hans. *Die Aussenpolitik Bremens im Zeitalter der französischen Revolution, 1794-1803.* Veröffentlichungen aus dem Staatsarchiv der Freien Hansestadt Bremen, No. 28. Bremen, 1963.

Hessen: with Darmstadt
172.   Corti, Count Egon Caesar, ed. *Unter Zaren und gekrönten Frauen. Schichtsal und Tragik europäischer Kaiserreiche an Hand von Briefen, Tagebüchern, und Geheimdokumenten der Zarin Marie von Russland und des Prinzen Alexander von Hessen.* Leipzig, 1936.
173.   Schüssler, Wilhelm, ed. *Die Tagebücher des Freiherrn Reinhard von Dalwigk zu Lichtenfels aus den Jahren 1860–1871.* Deutsche Geschichtsquellen des 19. Jahrhunderts, Vol. 2. Darmstadt, 1920.

Rhineland-Palatinate (Rheinland-Pfalz): with Koblenz
174.   Looz-Corswarem, Otto Graf von, ed. *Kaiser und Reich unter Karl V. Urkunden und Akten im Staatsarchiv Koblenz.* Veroffentlichungen der Landesarchivverwaltung. Coblenz, 1964.

German Democratic Republic (Deutsche Demokratische Republik—DDR)
175.   DDR Ministerium für Auswärtige Angelegenheiten, ed. *Locarno-Konferenz, 1925. Eine Dokumentensammlung.* East Berlin, 1962.
176.   DDR and Soviet Union Foreign Ministries. *Deutsch-sowjetische Beziehungen von den Verhandlungen in Brest-Litowsk bis zum Abschluss des Rapallovertrages, 1919–1922.* 2 vols. East Berlin, 1968-71.
177.   Metschies, Karl. "Presseaussehnittsammlungen im Zentralen Staatsarchiv," *Zeitschrift für Geschichtswissenschaft,* 23 (1975), 88-91.

7 GREAT BRITAIN

Keith Eubank
Queens College

THE chief repository of the diplomatic archives of Great Britain is the Public Record Office, Chancery Lane, London. The history of the modern diplomatic archives of Great Britain began with the development of the State Paper Office as an adjunct of the office of the secretary of state. After the creation of the office of the secretary of state in the reign of Henry VIII came the need to find a site for storing records. In 1578 the State Paper Office was created to serve as a repository for the papers from the archives of the secretaries of state. The first official State Paper Office was located in rooms near the banqueting hall in Whitehall palace, and Dr. Thomas Wilson was appointed "clerk of the papers." He was succeeded by his nephew, Sir Thomas Wilson, who took over the duty of guarding the papers with the title of "keeper of the paper." Sir Thomas began the first attempt at a systematic arrangement of the papers, dividing them into domestic and foreign classes.

In spite of the labors of the early keepers, secretaries of state carried documents away with them when they left office. Gradually many of these documents found their way into the great manuscript collections in the British Museum, the university libraries, and many important private libraries.

During the reign of James I the papers of the State Paper Office were moved to the king's apartments in the tower, over the gateway which stood across what is now Whitehall. In 1705 some of the papers were moved to the lord chamberlain's lodgings at Cockpit, known as the Middle Treasury Gallery. The papers remaining in the tower over Whitehall were gradually forgotten as the tower fell into disuse; in time it became a pigeon house.

About 1763 they were discovered and moved to a house in Scotland Yard, where they lay until the constant overflow of the Thames, flooding the lower floors of the house, endangered them. In 1819 they were moved to an old house in Great George Street, where they remained until 1833 when, together with the papers in the Middle Treasury Gallery, they were moved to the new State Paper Office in St. Jame's Park.

Numerous parliamentary reports attested to the deplorable condition of the papers, but nothing definite was done until after a select committee of the House of Commons recommended that a central record office should be erected on the site known as the Rolls Estate in Chancery Lane. These recommendations, embodied in a bill passed in 1838, pertained only to the records of royal justice and revenue. Through an order in council of March 5, 1852, all departmental records were placed under the charge and superintendence of the master of the rolls. By 1861 the foreign office gave permission for the removal of all records through the reign of George III to the new office for the public records. Thus began the periodic transfers of the foreign office records to the Public Record Office, commonly known as the PRO.

The master of the rolls was responsible for the care and preservation of the documents of the foreign office entrusted to his custody. The foreign office, like every department, could retain any papers or documents that were needed for the work of the government. Under the provisions of the *Public Records Act 1967*, the period in which records remained closed was set at 30 years. On January 1 of each year the open date would be advanced one year. An exception was made to the "thirty-year rule" in regard to documents relating to the second World War; these papers were released by 1972.

When the crisis over Poland developed in August 1939, the planned evacuation of about three hundred tons of documents from the PRO began and continued after the declaration of war until more than eighty seven thousand bundles and cartons had been evacuated by 1942. Throughout the war the PRO was open for business, although a bomb destroyed one of the turrets. The evacuated documents were kept in seven repositories outside London for the duration of the war. In September, 1945, the reassembling of the documents, which numbered over half of a million, was begun, It was completed by June, 1946, without a single document being mislaid or lost.

The steady accumulation of records has made space a prime problem for the officials of the PRO. After storing a portion of the overflow in an abandoned air raid shelter, better housing was secured in 1952 at Ashridge Park, Hertfordshire. Most of the twentieth century materials are now housed in a building in Portugal Street, which is near Chancery Lane.

ORGANIZATION AND CLASSIFICATION OF THE PRO

The organization and classification of the materials in the PRO relating to foreign relations have evolved through the years, progressing from simplicity to complexity. The first classification began with the division into foreign and domestic state papers. The State Papers Foreign began in 1547 and continued until 1780. During this period the papers are classified as: general correspondence, foreign entry books, foreign ministers in London, news letters, treaty papers, treaties, archives of legations, ciphers, confidential, and various.

The most important of these, general correspondence, contains the correspondence with British ambassadors. The correspondence for the years 1547–77 is arranged chronologically with no pretense at arrangement by country, but in 1577 the arrangement was changed to chronological within each country. By 1700 the drafts of the letters to the ambassadors were filed separately from the ambassadors' dispatches. The confidential class contains intercepted correspondence from foreign ambassadors in London; some of this material is still in cipher, but most has been deciphered.

For the years 1781–1878 the classification varies: general correspondence, supplement to general correspondence, Great Britain and general, slave trade, king's letter books, letters to public offices, treaties, miscellaneous, seals, chief's clerk's department, embassy and consular archives, archives of commissions, and private collections.

The general correspondence class by this time was arranged by country and chronologically within this category. Under each year the drafts of letters to the embassy came first, then dispatches from the embassy followed by correspondence with British consuls, foreign consuls, foreign ambassadors, and correspondence with other government departments and with private individuals in Britain.

Further changes in classification and arrangement came with the materials for the years 1879–85. There were now three main classes: general correspondence, treaties, and embassy and consular archives. Much of the arrangement for the period 1885–1906 is similar to this period.

The general correspondence for the years 1879–85 is arranged by country chronologically beginning with the drafts of dispatches to ambassadors, followed by dispatches from embassies, recorders of telegrams (the full message before it was shortened for telegraphing), correspondence with embassies about consular matters, correspondence with embassies over commercial matters, correspondence with consuls, departments of the British government, commercial negotiations, and dossier type files.

The treaties class contains the protocols of the treaties, ratifications of the treaties, miscellaneous matters, and the chief clerk's department papers. The embassy and consular archives class comprises the correspondence in the files of these offices, letter books, registers, and miscellaneous documents.

There is a slight variation in the arrangement and classification for the years 1885–1906. The separate class for treaties disappears and treaties are placed after telegrams in the general correspondence class.

After 1906, general correspondence was classified by department classes: Africa, new series (ending 1913), commercial (ending

1920), communications (1936–   ), consular, contraband (ending 1920), dominions information (1929-33), library, news
(1916–   ), political, prisoners of war and aliens (1915-19), and
treaty. The political class (F.O. 371) contains the records for all
political departments arranged alphabetically by country and
subject for the years 1906-20. Since 1920 the records have been
arranged separately for each year.

Beginning in 1906 the papers dealing with a subject are filed
together; the registry number of the first paper becomes the file
number for that subject. Indexes to the general correspondence
after 1906 are available in the search rooms in the PRO. These
volumes contain the lists of the papers by year, country, or subject
and with the appropriate file number. It is necessary to know the
file number in order to call for the particular volume.

In addition to the regular diplomatic archives of the British
foreign service, the PRO has transcripts from foreign archives
including Milan, 1428-1786; Rome, fifteenth to eighteenth centuries; Swedish archives, sixteenth to eighteenth centuries; Spanish
archives, fifteenth to seventeenth centuries; the Venetian manuscripts, 1485-1787; and Baschet's transcripts of the dispatches of
the French ambassadors to England, 1509-1714.

In addition to the official dispatches, a large amount of the
business of the Foreign Office through the years has been conducted by the foreign secretaries, diplomats, and Foreign Office
officials through private correspondence. Often these letters am-
plify negotiations reported in the official dispatches, and they
might contain gossip as well as strong personal opinions which
the diplomat or the Foreign Office official might not wish to insert
in an official dispatch. This private correspondence was advanta-
geous because it went directly to the person to whom it was
addressed without the time-consuming route official dispatches
had to take through the Foreign Office bureaucracy. In the
nineteenth century, diplomats, Foreign Office officials, and foreign secretaries often took this correspondence with them when
they resigned or retired and, as a result, some of these collections

remained in private hands. More recently, however, foreign secretaries, diplomats and Foreign Office officials have been required to leave behind their private papers relating to official affairs which have been unregistered. As a result of this practice, there are a number of private collections in the PRO which include material on foreign affairs.

Among these collections are the following private papers: Arthur Aston, Rio de Janeiro, Paris, and Madrid, 1827-43; Sir Benjamin Bloomfield, St. Petersburg and Berlin, 1823-71; Lord Clarendon, 1867-70; James Henderson, Colombia, 1818-31; Francis James Jackson and Sir George Jackson, Prussia and the United States 1763-1856; Lieutenant General Sir J. L. A. Simmons, the Russo-Turkish War; Stratford Canning, Lord Stratford de Redcliffe, 1808-63; Sir William White, Turkey and the Near East 1857-90; Lord Tenterden, 1873-82; Woodbine, Paris, Buenos Aires, 1813-55; Lord Cowley, Paris, 1852-67; Lord Hammond, Turkey and the Foreign Office, 1831-34, 1854-73; Howard de Walden, 1817-34, Sweden and Portugal; Sir Edward Malet, Berlin, 1884-95; Baron Stuart de Rothesay, 1801-14, Madrid and Lisbon; Andrew Snape Douglas, Palermo and Naples, 1811-14, 1816-18, 1822; Lord Cornwallis, Flanders, 1794, Congress of Amiens, 1801-02, and the American Revolution; Sir John Nicholl, 1798-1808; Sir William Stuart, Turkey, Russia, Argentina, Uruguay, Greece, the Netherlands, 1864-88; Lord John Russell; the First and Second Earls of Granville; the Earl of Carnavon; Lord Satow, 1865-1902, Japan, Siam, Uruguay, Morocco, China, and the second Hague Peace Conference; Sir John Ardagh, 1867-1900; the First Earl of Chatham; and William Pitt the Younger.

More recent additions of private collections include the papers of the following: A. J. Balfour; Sir Francis Bertie, 1896-1918, Italy and France; James Bryce; Henry Bulwer; Alexander Cadogan; George Canning; Lord Robert Cecil; Austen Chamberlain; Viscount Cranborne, fifth Marquess of Salisbury; First Marquess of Crewe; Lord Cromer; Eyre Crowe; Philip Currie; Lord Curzon; Ronald McNeill, later First Baron Cushendun; Eric Drummond;

Sir Charles Eliot; Sir Edward Grey; Lord Halifax; Charles Hardinge; Cecil Harmsworth; Arthur Henderson; Neville Henderson; Sir Samuel Hoare; Lord Inverchapel; Lord Kitchener; Lord Lansdowne; Frank Lascelles; J. Ramsay MacDonald; Lord Milner; Arthur Nicolson; Marquess of Reading; Walter Runciman; Thomas Henry Sanderson; Orme Sargent; Viscount Simon; Cecil Arthur Spring-Rice; Sir William Tyrrell; Sir Francis Hyde Villiers; and Ralph Follett Wigram.

ADMINISTRATION, REGULATIONS, AND FACILITIES OF THE PRO

The Keeper of Public Records is Mr. J. R. Ede, Public Records Office, Chancery Lane, London, W. C. 2. In order to use the PRO the researcher must use the appropriate form to apply for a "student's ticket" to the Search Department, where he will do his work. Foreign scholars should present a letter of introduction from their university or institution. The ticket is valid for five years. In addition, the researcher will sign the register of the PRO every day upon arrival.

After the researcher has obtained his ticket, registered, and found a seat in the Search Department rooms (seats are often at a premium in the summer), he will find the lists of documents in the bound volumes, both printed and typescript, around the walls of the rooms. A ticket must be filled out for each volume that the researcher wishes to consult. Whenever possible, the documents should be requested a day in advance. Some documents are kept in a repository in Ashridge and should be ordered two days in advance. Twentieth-century materials are located in the Land Registry building on Portugal Street, which is near Chancery Lane.

All records are produced for the researcher subject to the "thirty year rule." Anyone desiring to see documents after that date will first have to obtain the permission of the department concerned; such permission is granted only in very exceptional circumstances.

At present, the PRO is open every day except Sunday and such legal holidays as Good Friday, Saturday before Easter, Easter Monday, Saturday before Whitsunday, Whitmonday, August Bank Holiday, Christmas and December 26 (Boxing Day). In October the Search Department is closed for a short time for cleaning. Anyone planning to use the records during October should write ahead to ascertain the exact dates the PRO will be closed. Researchers may work in the Search Department daily from 9:30 A.M. to 5:00 P.M., except Saturdays when the hours are 9:30 A.M. to 1:00 P.M. Documents to be used on Saturdays must be ordered during the regular weekday hours.

Through its own facilities and personnel, the PRO offers microfilming and photocopying services for the researcher. Owing to the lack of space, private microfilming is not permitted. Applications for microfilming must specify the context in which the reproduction will be used or will appear. The authorities also must approve any caption or description that will be used. The PRO will, however, microfilm only complete volumes of documents.

The PRO is not immediately adjacent to a residential area or to hotels. The nearest area of London where the scholar can find accommodations is Bloomsbury, which includes the University of London and the British Museum. It is best to make reservations well in advance of the trip.

Information regarding accommodations for visitors in London can be obtained by contacting the British Tourist Authority, which has offices in Chicago, Dallas, Los Angeles, New York, Toronto, and Vancouver.

ADDITIONAL ARCHIVES AND LIBRARIES

There are a number of other archives, libraries, and organizations in Great Britain that can be of value to the scholar studying British foreign relations. Prominent among these is the famous British Museum Library (recently renamed the British Library), a complex of libraries and service departments, of which the most useful division for research in diplomacy is the Reference Division. The Library's Reading Room and Department of Manuscripts will remain housed with the British Museum on Great Russell Street until new quarters are constructed in the 1980s; its extensive Newspaper Library of British and foreign journals is on Colindale Avenue near the Colindale Underground Station. The British Library has a Lending Division which loans to libraries. It is strong in more recent monographs, serials, and British and American doctoral theses. Now it has a reading room open to the public at Boston Spa, Weatherby, West Yorks. Many state papers of the fifteenth through the eighteenth centuries that were retained by their owners when they retired are now in this repository. They are found in such famous collections as the Harley MSS., Cotton MSS., Stowe MSS., and Lansdowne MSS.

For the convenience of the student there is a manuscript class catalogue in the manuscript room of the British Library. Two groups of materials are of special interest. The first of these is state letters, foreign, consisting of single copies of letters relating to British foreign relations. The items are catalogued chronologically beginning with 1588 and continuing up into the late nineteenth century.

A second collection contains state papers, mainly of the sixteenth, seventeenth, and eighteenth centuries, although some material from the nineteenth century is also included. This is miscellaneous foreign correspondence for the most part, and it is composed of official correspondence of Denmark, France, Germany, Greece, Italy, the Low Countries, Portugal, Poland, Russia, Scotland, Spain and its colonies, Sweden, Switzerland, the Turkish Empire, Africa, and the United States. There is much material here relating to French foreign relations in the sixteenth through the eighteenth centuries.

The British Library possesses collections of private papers of officials of the British government that did not reach the PRO. Among the better known are the papers of Canning, Newcastle, Hastings, Auckland, Wellesley, Peel, Russell, Napier, Wellington, Campbell-Bannerman, the Grenvilles, Cobden, Dilke, Aberdeen, Clive, Townshend, Balfour, Robert Cecil, Paget, Ponsonby, and Charles James Fox. In addition there are the papers of Baron Lexington, Vienna, 1694–97, Spain, 1712–13; Francis Drake, 1790–1813, Genoa, Germany, Sardinia, and Corsica; Prince Christopher Lieven and Princess Dorothea Lieven; some papers of Frederick II of Prussia; Sir Thomas Chamberlayne, Spain, 1559–69; William Blathwayt, 1695–1701; James Vernon, 1697–1702; Sir Charles Hamilton, Naples, 1761–1803; Charles John Bentinck, 1730–65; Baron Heytesbury, 1801–32, Naples, Vienna, Malta, Barbary States, Spain, Portugal, and Russia; Cardinal Pole; Sir Benjamin Keene, 1727–39, 1749–57, Madrid, 1745–49, Lisbon; Sir Arthur Layard, 1861–66, Foreign Office, 1869, Madrid, and 1877–80, Constantinople; and the Palmerston Letter Books.

The Beaverbrook Library, now located in the House of Lords Library, is a private collection of books and papers, relating to twentieth-century politics, and it contains the private papers of Beaverbrook, Lloyd George, and Bonar Law.

One of the most important institutions for historical research in London is the Institute of Historical Research, part of the University of London. The library of this institution is particularly useful in the study of international affairs, and it contains much of the library of G. P. Gooch. Those who have research degrees or who have published their work may use the facilities of the institute upon application and payment of a fee.

The facilities of the Royal Institute of International Affairs in Chatham House also are available. The library of this institute contains a complete set of League of Nations publications, a press clipping service for articles on international affairs, and a collection of books and unpublished documents belonging to John Wheeler Wheeler-Bennett.

The library of the Royal Empire Society, London, will be useful for those studying the diplomacy of the empire and the commonwealth. The National Maritime Museum and the National Army Museum both have manuscript collections dealing with naval and military affairs.

Each of the departments of the British government that deals with foreign relations matters has a departmental library that may be of use. These libraries are not open to the general public, however, and the request to use their collections must be made in writing. The Foreign Office Library possesses a limited amount of recent manuscript materials. Special permission to use this material may be granted to a qualified scholar who has exhausted other sources and who makes a specific request in writing. The War Office Library does not contain any manuscripts, because they have been sent to the PRO. It is an excellent reference library and the scholar may use it after obtaining permission by writing to the director of the Library. The Admiralty Library is one of the finest naval reference libraries in the world and may be used by the researcher who applies for permission in writing to the director of the library. A similar procedure should be followed in seeking permission to use the collections in the library of the India Office and the Commonwealth Office.

Researchers who are in or near London for extended periods may wish to apply for membership in the London Library, 14 James Square, S. W. 1. The subscription fee is nominal, and volumes may be taken from the library.

The General Register House, Edinburgh, Scotland, is the Scottish equivalent of the PRO and possesses many items that relate to the history of diplomacy of the sixteenth, seventeenth, and eighteenth centuries. Because the accumulation of materials is not as extensive as in the PRO, the procedure for calling for the documents is simplified. Lists are available for the collections.

One of the largest collections comprises the official papers of the Scottish sovereigns. Among the collections in the General Register are the Elphinstone MSS., containing letters of James V, James VI, and Mary Stuart; the Tyninghame letter book, correspondence of James V; papers of the Regent Mar, 1571-72; Reay papers containing correspondence of Gustavus Adolphus; the

Society of Antiquaries collection, which includes correspondence of Mary Stuart; second Earl of Stair, 1715–19, Paris; Hopestoun MSS., 1536–95; Alex Gibson, 1807–13, Danzig; and the Newbattle Collection, containing letters to Charles II while in exile.

A list is available in the General Register House of the Buccleuch muniments which are in the Dalkeith House. These contain Townshend correspondence for the years when he was chancellor of the exchequer; correspondence with Pitt, Newcastle, Burke, and others is also included. Access to these documents requires the permission of the Duke of Buccleuch.

The National Library of Scotland contains papers of Rosebery, Haldane, and Lothian.

There are some papers of interest in the Public Record Office of Northern Ireland in Belfast. These include the Abercorn papers relating to the Duke of Manchester, 1699–1701, France, and Anglo-French relations in the early eighteenth century; Earl Macartney, 1795–96; and correspondence of the Count of Provence. This repository also possesses a quantity of important materials relating to Anglo-Irish history.

The John Rylands Library of Manchester, England, possesses a catalogue of the younger Pitt's papers, mostly of the 1780s and 1790s. There are six volumes with a lengthy description of each letter and occasional extracts; also included are transcripts of correspondence between Pitt and George III relating to foreign affairs. The catalogue was compiled by Edward Tomlinson, Bishop of Winchester, Pitt's tutor, before Pitt's papers were scattered and many were lost. This library possesses consular correspondence and the papers of the first Marquis of Bute, 1776–83. The Stapleton MSS. deal with British affairs in the West Indies for the late seventeenth and eighteenth centuries. There is also the correspondence of Charles T. Beke while in Abyssinia. The Rylands Library contains a great deal of material dealing with the East India Company's activities, and for this subject the Bagshame muniments, the Melville papers, and the Pitt papers are useful. This library has copies of letters from the correspondence of the ambassadors of Henry VIII.

The Bodleian Library of Oxford University contains materials of value in the study of seventeenth-century foreign affairs. The Rawlinson MSS. have diplomatic documents pertaining to the reigns of Charles II and James II. The Clarendon MSS. and Carte MSS. would be of use in studying the activities of the royalists during their exile at the time of the Civil War. For the eighteenth century, the Bodleian Library has the correspondence and diplomatic papers of Thomas Villiers, first Earl of Clarendon of the second creation, 1738-46; the correspondence of the Fourth Earl of Clarendon, 1853-58, 1861-66. Asquith's papers are also in this library.

There are papers in the college libraries at Oxford. The papers of Lord Salisbury are at Christ Church; New College has those of Milner, University College has Atlee's, and Churchill College will have Bevin's.

The University Library at Cambridge contains items of value. These include a number of state papers of the reign of Henry VIII relating to foreign affairs. There is also material relating to the diplomatic correspondence of Cardinal Wolsey, Reginald Pole, Elizabeth I, James I, James II, Cardinal Mazarin, the younger Pitt, Lord Carteret, 1742-45, the Duke of Newcastle, 1740-64, and certain popes. There are some items of diplomatic correspondence of the eighteenth century. The library also contains the papers of Charles Hardinge, Hoare, and Baldwin.

The papers of Joseph and Austen Chamberlain, as well as Neville Chamberlain, are in the library of the University of Birmingham. The Runciman papers are at the University of Newcastle. The University of Wales has the complete diaries of Thomas Jones.

PAPERS IN PRIVATE HANDS

Two other organizations in Great Britain can be of value to the scholar studying British foreign relations.

The oldest is the Historical Manuscripts Commission, appointed in 1869 to collect information on manuscript materials which were in private hands and to publish such as seemed worthy of publication. In addition, the commission was to make abstracts and catalogues of documents and to issue reports periodically. Since 1869 the commission has reported on manuscripts of over four hundred private owners and two hundred corporate bodies. Many of these volumes are still in print and can be obtained through H. M. Stationery Office.

The Historical Manuscripts Commission can be of value for the independent scholar in arranging introductions if he wishes to use private archives. Under no circumstances should one write directly to the family since, in all probability, he will be denied use of the papers.

In 1945 the Commission was enabled to make a more comprehensive survey of manuscripts in private hands in the form of the National Register of Archives, also in Quality Court. Such a step became imperative as the breakup of the estates continued, with the resulting loss of private archives. From modest beginnings the register's work has expanded to cover reporting on collections of manuscripts, obtaining access to manuscripts for students and arranging for tranfer of the archives to more suitable repositories. The work of the register has proceeded with creation of voluntary county committees which, with the owner's consent, furnished reports to the register on the location and extent of individual archival accumulations. There reports formed the basis of an index to papers still in private hands. A bulletin of the Register's work has been published periodically with selected summaries of the reports, and current numbers can be obtained from the National Register of Archives. At present the Register contains the most complete set of indexes and list of manuscripts collections in the United Kingdom. This is the place for the researcher to begin any search for manuscripts remaining in private hands.

Among the many collections examined through the work of the National Register of Archives are the papers of the First Earl of Kimberley; the First to the Fourth Dukes of Portland; the correspondence of the Earl of Portland, now on deposit in the

Nottingham University Library, and the Wentworth Woodhouse papers deposited in the Sheffield City Library, which contain correspondence of Burke and the Marquis of Rockingham. Other private collections include the papers of the Duke of Wellington; the First and Fourth Earls of Sandwich; Lord Galway's papers, including reports of Sir John Goodrich and correspondence of General Monckton; diplomatic correspondence of the Younger Pitt, Peel, Russell, and Gladstone in the possession of the Earl of Harrowby; correspondence of Spencer Perceval, 1800-18; the First Duke of Manchester, 1697-1707, Venice and Paris; additional Peel, Wellington, and Canning papers in the possession of Major General E. H. Goulburn; Canning correspondence in Leeds Library; and the papers of William Dacres Adams, private secretary of the Younger Pitt. Other papers still in private hands are those of Lord Grantham, First Lord Granville, Earl of Harrowby, Earl Bathhurst, Castlereagh, Palmerston, Earl of Malmesbury, Earl of Derby, Earl of Kimberley, Lord Lansdowne, Marquess of Reading, Viscount Simon, and Lord Halifax.

BIBLIOGRAPHY

Printed Collections of Documents
1. *British diplomatic instructions, 1689-1789,* James F. Chance, *Sweden 1689-1727* (London, 1922), *Denmark* (London, 1926), *Sweden 1727-1789* (London, 1928), and L. G. Wickham Legg, *France 1689-1721* (London, 1925), *France, 1721-1727* (London, 1927), *France 1727-1744* (London, 1930), *France, 1745-1789* (London, 1934). These are arranged chronologically according to ambassador; the main sources are the PRO, the British Museum, and a few private papers.
2. *British and foreign state papers* (London, 1841-   ). Begun in the nineteenth century by Sir Lewis Hertslet, librarian of the foreign office; it is a collection of the principal documents relating to international affairs that have been made public since 1814.
3. *British documents on the origins of the war.* Ed. by G. P. Gooch and Harold Temperley. 11 vols. London, 1926-38.
4. *Calendar of state papers, Edward VI and Mary.* Ed. by W. B. Turnbull. 2 vols. London, 1861.

5. *Calendar of state papers foreign, Elizabeth, 1558-1589.* Ed. by Joseph Stevenson, A. J. Crosby, A. J. Butter, S. C. Lomas, and A. B. Hinds. 21 vols. London, 1863-1931.

6. *Calendar of state papers and manuscripts relating to English affairs existing in the archives and collections of Venice and in other libraries of northern Italy, 1603-1643.* Ed. by Rawdon Brown, Cavendish Bentick, Horatio Brown, and A. B. Hinds. 26 vols. London, 1864-1947.

7. *Calendar of state papers, Milan, 1385-1618.* Ed. by A. H. Hinds. London, 1912.

8. *Calendar of state papers, Rome, 1558-1578.* Ed. by J. M. Rigg. 2 vols. London, 1916-26.

9. *Calendar of state papers, Spanish, 1485-1558.* Ed. by G. A. Gergenroth. Pesrual de Gayogas, M. A. S. Hume, and Royall Tyler. 13 vols. London, 1862-1954.

10. *Documents on British foreign policy, 1919-1939.* Ed. by E. L. Woodward and Rohan Butler. London, 1947-

11. *Letters and papers, foreign and domestic of the reign of Henry VIII, 1509-1547.* Ed. by J. S. Brewer, James Gairdner, and R. H. Brodie. London, 1862-1932.

12. *Manual of collections of treaties and collections relating to treaties.* Ed. by D. P. Myers. Cambridge, 1922.

13. *Notes on the diplomatic relations of England.* Editor in chief, C. H. Firth. *Lists of ambassadors from England to France and from France to England.* Ed. by S. C. Lomas. Oxford, 1906. *List of diplomatic representatives and agents, England and north Germany, 1698-1727.* Ed. by J. F. Chance. Oxford, 1907. *List of diplomatic representatives and agents, England and France, 1698-1763.* Ed. by W. G. Wickham Legg. Oxford, 1909. *List of English diplomatic representatives and agents in Denmark, Sweden, and Russia, and of those countries in England, 1689-1762.* Ed. by J. F. Chance. Oxford, 1913.

14. *Recueil des instructions données aux ambassadeurs et ministres de France, 1648-1789; Angleterre, 1648-1690.* Ed. by J. J. Jusserand. 4 vols. Paris, 1929.

15. *Reports of the Royal Commission on Historical Manuscripts.* London, 1870-   . Invaluable for calendars and extracts of documents from private archives examined by the commission. The eighteenth report (1917) contains a useful guide to the materials for diplomatic history for the years 1509-1783 that have been calendared in these reports. See also Nos. 43 and 75.

16. *Sessional papers.* Parliament. London, 1803- . Included in these are accounts of diplomatic correspondence laid before parliament. A list of available microprints can be obtained from the Readex Microprint Co., Chester, Vermont.

Guides and Reference Works

17. Andrews, Charles M. *Guide to the materials for American history, to 1783, in the Public Record Office of Great Britain.* 2 vols. Washington, 1912-14. Correspondence with Europe and the United States: I, 26-41.

18. *Manuscript materials in the British Museum for the history for the United States to 1783.* Washington, 1908.

19. *Archives.* The journal of the British Records Association, published twice yearly.

20. Barwick, G. F. *The ASLIB directory, a guide to sources of specialized information in Great Britain and Ireland.* London, 1928.

21. Bemis, Samuel F., and Grace G. Griffin, *Guide to the diplomatic history of the United States, 1775-1921.* Washington, 1935. On British archives, pp. 890-96; on British published diplomatic documents, pp. 838-41.

22. *Bodleian Library record.* Published three times a year; useful for information of the latest acquisitions.

23. *British Museum quarterly.* Contains articles relating to newly acquired manuscripts.

24. *Bulletin of the Institute of Historical Research.* Semiannual journal.

25. *Bulletin of the John Rylands Library.*

26. *Bulletin of the National Register of Archives.* The latest information on new reports of private papers which have been examined; annual report on new acquisitions in repositories.

27. *Catalogue of the manuscripts preserved in the library of the University of Cambridge.* 5 vols. Cambridge, 1856.

28. Craster, H. H. E. *The Western manuscripts in the Bodleian Library.* (Number 43 in *Helps for students of history.*) London, 1921.

29. Davies, Godfrey. *A student's guide to the manuscripts relating to English history in the seventeenth century in the Bodleian Library.* (Number 47 in *Helps for students of history.*) London, 1922.

30. Degras, *Soviet documents.* On Britain, pp. 10, 56, 101, 139, 167, 217.

31. Dennis, Faustine. "British manuscripts project," *American documentation.* I (1950), 130-132.

32. Deputy Keeper of the Public Records. *The hundred and first report.*

London, 1939. Current reports are valuable for recent information of developments at the PRO, and past reports are useful in the study of the history of the Public Record Office.

33. *The hundred and second report.* London, 1940.
34. *The hundred and fourth report.* London, 1942.
35. *The hundred and eighth report.* London, 1946.
36. *The hundred and twelfth report.* London, 1950.
37. Edwards, Edward. *Libraries and founders of libraries.* London, 1864.
38. *First report of the royal commission on public records appointed to inquire into and report on the state of the public records and local records of a public nature of England and Wales.* Cd. 6361. London, 1912.
39. Galbraith, H. V. *An introduction to the use of the public records.* Oxford, 1934. Useful to the scholar beginning his first research in the PRO.
40. Gilson, Julius P., *A student's guide to the manuscripts of the British Museum.* (Number 31 in *Helps for students of history*). London, 1930. Valuable lists of the ambassadors and envoys whose papers are found in the manuscript collections of the British Museum.
41. Griffin, Grace G. *A guide to manuscripts relating to American history in British depositories, reproduced for the Division of Manuscripts in the Library of Congress.* Washington, 1946.
42. *Guide to the Contents of the Public Record Office.* 3 vols. London, 1963,1968. A revision of Giuseppi's *Guide.*
43. *Guide to the public records. Part I. Introductory.* London, 1949. There is no completely up-to-date guide to the PRO, although one is in preparation. This is the introduction to the new guide and it explains much of the work of the PRO. Copies can be purchased from H. M. Stationery Office and the British Information Center, 30 Rockefeller Plaza, New York, N.Y. 10020.
44. Giuseppi, M. S. *A guide to the manuscripts preserved in the Public Record Office.* 2 vols. London, 1924. Useful but outdated.
45. Hall, Hubert. *Studies in English official historical documents.* Cambridge, 1908.
46. Harrod, L. M. *The libraries of greater London, a guide.* London, 1951. Includes the procedure for obtaining admission with a brief note on the contents of each library.
47. H. M. Stationery Office. *Sectional list number 17. Reports of the Royal Commission on Historical Manuscripts.* London, 1951.

List of reports which have been published through January 31, 1951; those still in print have been noted.

48. Historical Manuscripts Commission. *Guide to the Reports of the Royal Commission on Historical Manuscripts, 1911-1957.* London, 1966.

49. ——. *List of Accessions to Repositories in 1964.* London, 1965.

50. ——. *Record Repositories in Great Britain.* London, 1971.

51. Johnson, Charles. *The Public Record Office.* (Number 4 in *Helps for students of history*). London, 1916.

52. *Lists and indexes number XIV, list of volumes of state papers foreign preserved in the Public Record Office.* London, 1904.

53. *Lists and indexes number XVIII, list of admiralty records preserved in the Public Record office,* London, 1904.

54. *Lists and indexes number XXXVI, list of colonial office records preserved in the Public Record Office.* London, 1911.

55. *Lists and indexes number XLIX, list of diplomatic documents, Scottish documents, and papal bulls preserved in the Public Record Office.* London, 1923.

56. *Lists and indexes number LII, list of foreign office records to 1878 preserved in the Public Record Office.* London, 1929.

57. *Lists and indexes number LIII, an alphabetical guide to certain war office and other military records preserved in the Public Record Office.* London, 1931.

58. "Lists of foreign office records from 1878 to 1902 preserved in the Public Record Office." In typescript in the PRO.

59. *List and index of the publications of the Royal Historical Society, 1871-1924 and of the Camden Society, 1840-1897.* Ed. by Hubert Hall. London, 1925.

60. Martin, Charles T. *The record interpreter: a collection of abbreviations, Latin words and names used in English historical manuscripts and records.* 2d ed. London, 1910.

61. Matheson, Cyril. *A catalogue of the publications of Scottish historical and kindred clubs and societies, 1908-1927.* Aberdeen, 1928.

62. National Register of Archives (Scotland). *Reports of the National Register of Archives (Scotland).*

63. *Public Records of Great Britain. Microfilm.* Liechtenstein, 1972,1973. Selected PRO titles on microfilm available from Kraus-Thomson.

64. Public Record Office. *Index to Foreign Correspondence, 1920-1945* 107 vols. Liechtenstein, 1969-72.

65. *The Records of the Cabinet Office* to 1922. London, 1966.

66. *The Records of the Foreign Office, 1782-1939.* London, 1969. The best guide to the PRO for anyone working with Foreign Office documents.

67. Roberts, R. A. *The reports of the Historical Manuscripts Commission.* (Number 4 in *Helps for students of history.*) London, 1920.

68. Rye, Reginald A. *The student's guide to the libraries of London with an account of the most important archives and other aids to study.* London, 1927.

69. Scargill-Bird, S. R. *A guide to the various classes of documents preserved in the Public Record Office.* London, 1908. Superseded by Giuseppi (Number 39.)

70. Schmitt, Bernadotte E. "British foreign policy, 1919-1939," *Journal of modern history,* XXI (1949), 320-326.

71. "British foreign policy, 1931-1932," *Journal of modern history,* XXIII (1951), 153-157.

72. "Munich," *Journal of modern history,* XXV (1953), pp. 166-180.

73. *Scottish historical review.* Semiannual journal; October issue contains list of accessions to the Scottish Record Office.

74. *The Second World War. A guide to documents in the Public Record Office.* London, 1972.

75. Temperley, Harold, and Penson, Lillian. *A century of diplomatic blue books, 1814-1914.* Cambridge, 1938. The best guide to the Sessional papers.

76. Terry, G. Sanford. *An index to the papers relating to Scotland described or calendared in the Historical MSS Commission's reports.* London, 1908.

77. Thomas, F. S. *A history of the State Paper Office with a view of the documents therein deposited.* London, 1849.

78. *Notes of materials for the history of the public departments.* London, 1846.

79. Upton, Eleanor S., and Winship, George P. *Guide to sources of English history from 1603-1660 in reports of the Royal Commission on Historical Manuscripts.* Washington, 1952.

80. *Union list of microfilms.* Ann Arbor, 1951, revised. Lists of documents that have been microfilmed for the British Manuscripts Project; they include documents in the British Museum, Public Record Office, Cambridge University Library, Bodleian Library, Library of Congress, and certain private archives.

8   GREECE

Domna Visvizi-Dontas
Ministry of Foreign Affairs of Greece

HISTORY OF THE FOREIGN MINISTRY ARCHIVES

THE records of the Greek Foreign Ministry, dating from 1821, are the main source for the diplomatic history of modern Greece. The Foreign Ministry itself has had several stages of development over the last century and a half:

1821–28, the chancellor of state also acted as minister of foreign affairs under the provisional administration of the First National Assembly.

1828–32, a provisional secretary of state conducted foreign relations and was also secretary of the Merchant Marine under the presidency of Count John Capo d'Istria.

1833–46, the Secretariat of the Royal House and External Affairs was established by the government of King Otho.

1846–62, the name was changed by King Otho to that of Ministry of the Royal House and Foreign Affairs.

1863 to the present, the department has been called the Ministry of Foreign Affairs by the Second National Assembly and by the successive monarchies and republics, and has included a Records Office.

In 1919, under the general director of political affairs of the Ministry of Foreign Affairs, a separate Department of Historical Archives was established under the charge of a keeper of the records. The keeper received all files of closed questions (general, diplomatic, and consular correspondence, and miscellaneous papers), with the exception of those of the last two years. In pursuance of a royal decree of 1918, the staff of the Historical Archives began to calendar, classify, and systematically arrange all the papers of the ministry.

Before 1923 only the officials of the ministry had access to the records in the archives. After that date a few well-known scholars and well-connected amateurs were permitted to do historical research there.

During World War' II the Nazis, who occupied Greece, tampered with some of the documents and shipped others to Germany. Found there by American forces, they were eventually returned to Athens with no important loss or damage. Since 1945 the steady accumulation of documents has made space a prime problem for the ministry, and until a wing now under construction is completed, the organization, classification and research facilities will remain limited. The growing interest in modern history within Greece and elsewhere, and the mounting pressure for the use of the Greek diplomatic archives, brought about a decree in 1959 which fixed the present policy for access to and use of the Foreign Ministry Archives by private scholars.

There are many gaps in the instructions to the foreign service officers, and even more in the reports from these representatives. Until the embassies forward the remainder of their files to the home office, and until much more urgently required work is done, the archives of the ministry will disappoint some researchers. The very limited staff has at least prepared the bulk of records for use by giving a title to almost all volumes of the central administration records (covering some hundred years) and by drafting a catalogue.

ORGANIZATION AND CLASSIFICATION

The organization and classification of the Historical Archives of the Greek Ministry of Foreign Affairs developed from simplicity to complexity. The first classification began with the establishment of the Secretariat for Foreign Relations (consisting of a general secretary and a secretary) in 1822, and its was a very simple system, which remained in use until the creation of the modern state in 1833. For the years 1821 to 1825 the collection is scanty. From 1826 to 1833, however, there are letters from such personalities as Canning (Stratford), Capo d'Istria, Eyanrd, Blanquière; Admirals Cochrane, Codrington, de Rigny, Fabvier, Ricord, Heyden, and General Roche. Moreover, there is the correspondence of the ministers resident of the three Protecting Powers of Greece (England, France, and Russia), Dawkins, Rouen, and Panine, and the records of the Philhellenic committees. There is no diplomatic correspondence with the other states, since Greece had not yet established further diplomatic representation.

The years 1833–35, noted for the foundation of Greece as a modern European state, mark the beginning of more significant Greek diplomatic archives. By a Royal Act of 1833 they were classified as: general correspondence, archives of legations and consulates, official royal correspondence, treaty papers, treaties, and various — a classification which remains the basis of the more elaborate arrangement of today.

The most important records covering the years 1833–1913 are the general correspondence, which contain reports of envoys to the great European countries and of special missions, and drafts of dispatches of foreign ministers to envoys. The documents are arranged by country and in chronological order, with the drafts of dispatches of foreign ministers to the envoys usually found under separate cover and by years. In addition to external relations *per se*, the reports include files on such domestic affairs of foreign countries as national institutions and military, ecclesiastical, and educational matters.

Those legation archives which have been transferred to Athens contain invaluable information since they include not only the dispatches of the foreign ministers addressed to the Greek legations (especially to those in London, Paris, St. Petersburg, and Constantinople), and replies therefrom, but also communications of the other governments and their agents at Athens, and numerous official reports on internal events to justify Greek policy. In addition, there are sometimes copies of reports drawn up by

Greek provincial officials (usually on revolts) and sometimes letters of a more intimate nature, written by the foreign minister to the representatives in foreign capitals, by these representatives to each other, and, less frequently, by the representatives to the home government. These are arranged by country and within each country by year. A number of dispatches from and to legations in the nineteenth century are in French; after 1880 the dispatches are in Greek, while telegrams remain in French even after World War I.

The consular reports, starting in 1835, are arranged by city and chronologically. These important reports are much fuller than one might expect, especially those of the consuls in Turkey. The latter have good descriptions of the people and events — even in villages — which eventually brought about the successive revolts and dismemberment of the Ottoman Empire. Most of the consular reports contain enclosures — letters written by local worthies — on such matters as expenditure, military affairs, and political intelligence.

Although the basic arrangement of the records is by country and chronological, the archivists, in the face of the increased complexity of Greece's foreign relations, made more and more use of dossiers on particular topics; i.e., "The Cretan Revolt" (1866–1869), "The Congress of Berlin" (1878), and "The Annexation of Thessaly" (1881). Special subjects include treaties, with drafts of protocols, reports on negotiations, and related matters, and Greece's commercial conventions with European countries, the United States, and India. The originals of treaties, conventions, and agreements, and their ratifications, are kept separately in the Department for Legal Affairs.

The files described as "various" contain, under separate classification for each title, such important matters as landed property, piracy, brigandage, commerce and navigation, customs, etc. Those records are also arranged chronologically within each category.

ADMINISTRATION, REGULATIONS, AND FACILITIES

The Foreign Ministry records which are open for research are those antedating fifty years, although there are some restrictions as to subjects. At the time of this edition, some documents after 1919 have not yet been reorganized and catalogued, the date of their availability depending on the speed with which the staff can prepare them. In view of limited budgets and the enormous increase after 1919 in the number of items to be preserved, researchers should expect delays.

The scholar seeking admission to the archives should remember that even if the field of interest lies in the years before the official open date at the time of application, this does not guarantee automatic admission. Not only will each research request be considered in itself, but proper protocol must be followed, and occasional disappointments may occur. Application for admission should be a formal request to the Ministry of Foreign Affairs (2 Zalocosta St., Athens), with careful attention to the content. It should include a clear and specific statement of the subject to be investigated and the purpose of the study. Above all, the applicant must avoid phrasing the request in terms that are too general or elusive; the more precise and limited, the more likely they are to be acceptable. Finally, the applicant must include some indication that he has the training or experience to profit from access to the archives. Academic or other institutional connections, publications, or letters of recommendation will ordinarily serve the purpose.

The undersecretary of state for foreign affairs has final authority over all applications, but he will normally consult the appropriate director of political affairs upon whose recommendation he makes his decision. If favorable, the applicant will be informed withing days, the notification serving as entry card for a year. The entrance to the archives is the same as to the ministry (2 Zalocosta Street). The superintendent may confiscate notes of those whose aims are polemical rather than scholarly, or of those who seek to injure public or private interests, and the undersecretary may withdraw authorization to use the archives.

The annual closing is the whole month of August and, in addition, the legal national and religious holidays are observed. The hours are 9:30 A.M. to 1:30 P.M. except Sundays.

Researchers must request volumes a day in advance. Normally, no more than three will be delivered each day, but they may be retained for a week in the reading room. One may use ink for taking notes, but not a typewriter. The auxiliary facilities of the reading room are limited. While authorization is necessary for microfilming and photostating, this is ordinarily obtainable for scattered documents or limited series, but not for long, continuous files. Microfilming is difficult, however, since it cannot be done on the premises. A final reminder: the archives of the ministry are still in the process of being prepared for more efficient use, and researchers should expect lacunae among the documents and difficulties in consulting still-uncatalogued files, especially of the later periods, open to research.

A limited number of scholars are permitted to use the library of the Ministry of Foreign Affairs (same address), which, as a rule, is for the use of the staff.

The Greek Foreign Ministry lies in the center of Athens (near Constitution Square); thus it is well connected by public transportation to all areas of the city.

ADDITIONAL ARCHIVES

A number of documents which foreign ministers carried away when leaving office, together with their own private papers, are in manuscript collections of museums, other state archives, and libraries.

The General State Archives (Venizelos Street, Athens) contain some important collections. One is the voluminous papers of Ioannis Metaxas, the dictator who was foreign minister of Greece from 1936 to 1941. Not having been classified, they are arranged chronologically. The Metaxas papers contain memoranda, reports, and telegrams (notably from London and Berlin) to Metaxas; the correspondence Metaxas and Charilaos Simopoulos (ambassador in London)[1]; memoranda from the foreign ministry staff; memoranda and reports of Greek diplomatic missions to London and Berlin concerning commercial negotiations, etc.; memoranda and reports from the Supreme Staff of the Greek Army as to Greece's relations with her Balkan allies, France, and Great Britain, and miscellaneous papers of the conferences of the member states of the Balkan Pact. Access to these and other papers is by permission of the General State Archives.

A less significant set of papers is the Historical Archives of Alexander Mavrokordatos (1805-60), which consists of a mass of communications to him during his long public career; however, only a small percentage of which refers to foreign affairs. These are letters from foreign ministers and others during his ambassadorship in London (1835-41), in Constantinople (1841-44), and in Paris (1850-54).

Another collection in the General State Archives is that of Emmanuel Tsouderos, prime minister of the Greek government during its exile in the Middle East in World War II. These pertain to the foreign relations of the Greek government in exile from 1941-1944, the exiled government's relations with the resistance movements of Greece under German occupation, and letters on the political, diplomatic, and military situation of Greece during the years, 1947-1949. The Tsouderos papers are open to research by special permission, which is granted only in exceptional circumstances.[2]

The General State Archives are open daily from 9:00 A.M. to 1:00 P.M. and on Tuesdays and Thursdays from 5-10:00 P.M. as well. They are closed in August and on all public and religious holidays.

The Gennadeion Library (at Odios Soudias, Athens) has other

---

[1] Part of this correspondence is published in the four-volume work: *Metaxas, Memoirs* (in Greek) (Athens, 1951-1964).

[2] Tsouderos has used most of this material in his book *Diplomacy behind the scenes* (in Greek) (Athens, 1950).

Tsouderos papers, but these are miscellaneous materials from 1941 to 1944 and are of limited value to students of diplomatic history. They are open to research. Also, the Gennadeion Library manuscript collection has the newly-acquired papers of Konstantinos Musurus, minister of Turkey at Athens (1840-48), Vienna (1849-50), and ambassador at London (1851-85) — a diplomatic source of great interest. Section A consists of personal letters with few references to the affairs of Greece. Section B contains (a) autographed letters, in French, of the years 1840-70 from statesmen and prime ministers of the Ottoman Empire, and many autograph drafts of letters by Musurus to the above; (b) autograph drafts of reports of great significance, in French, to the Sublime Porte, 1841-51; (c) autographed letters from various patriarchs, British statesmen, and high officials in the Ottoman Empire; (d) a great number of documents relating to the 35-year service of Musurus as ambassador in London; and (e) a large collection of documents of Stephanos Musurus (1842-1907), son of Konstantinos Musurus, dealing with embassy affairs in London. But the Musurus collection of papers is still in the process of classification and organization, which, it is hoped, will be completed at an early date. This library is open daily from 8:30 A.M. to 1:00 P.M. and from 5-10:00 P.M., except on Saturday afternoons, public and religious holdiays, and in August.

The Benaki Museum (1 Odos Koumbari, Athens) acquired in 1962 the papers of the Greek statesman Eleutherios Venizelos. Their classification is: (1) state papers; Greek government, 1891-1935 (memoranda from officials and others to Venizelos); (2) state papers of the autonomous government of Crete, 1898-1911 (memoranda from officials to the provisional government, 1898-1906, and memoranda and letters from individuals to the High Commissioner of Crete, 1900-11); (3) private correspondence, 1896-1935 (political, diplomatic, administrative; and family matters). The Venizelos papers referring to political and diplomatic matters are subject to the fifty year rule, and access is through the Board of Trustees of the Museum.

The archives of Levidis, preserved by the Parnassos Philological Society in Athens, are a much less significant source. The society has published the diplomtaic documents of the years 1862 to 1863,[3] although there are some others scattered among these archives.

Outside Athens, the Historical Archives of Crete, in Canea, contain diplomatic documents which are important to the history of Crete. They consist of: (1) a small collection of the Greek consular archives of Crete for 1834–88; (2) the invaluable archives of the Russian consulate there 1839–1917; (3) the records of the international occupation by Italy, France, and England, 1898–99; (4) the records of the Cretan State, 1898–1913; and (5) the records of the Battle of Crete, of the German occupation, and of the resistance during World War II.

The oldest of all archives in Greece, and in some respects the richest, include no diplomatic materials. The Record Office of the Ionian Islands, in Corfu, contains the archives of the Ionian Senate and, thus, important materials on the Venetian (1386–1797), Russian, Turkish, French (1797–1815), and British (1815–64) periods of the history of the Ionian Islands.

BIBLIOGRAPHY

Printed Collections of Documents
1. Official Greek Document Publications (Athens, 1833–1971).
    By the Ministry of Foreign Affairs, concerning:
        the Musurus affair, the Pacifico affair
        the political situation in 1856, the Soulié affair
        the change in dynasty in 1862, the Greco-Turkish dispute (1868)
        the Ionian Islands, the Marathon brigandage
        the Russo-Turkish War of 1878, the northern frontier in 1882
        the blockade in 1886, the commercial treaty in 1855
        the Greco-Turkish War in 1896, the Crete affair
        the Greco-Turkish consular convention of 1900

[3] *The political events in Greece of 1862 and the Voulgaris papers in the Parnassos* (in Greek), ed., Maria Mantouvalou ("The Philological Society 'Parnassos', No. 1") (Athens, 1971).

> the Greco-Rumanian dispute, World War I (six books)
> Turkish treaty violations at Smyrna in 1911
> the commercial treaty with Austria in 1914
> peace negotiations with Bulgaria and Hungary in 1919
> Peace negotiations with Turkey in 1920
> observance of peace treaties, Greco-Bulgarian arbitration (1922)
> the Lausanne Conference of 1923, Italy's aggression in 1940
> the Cyprus question in 1954 and 1958
> the collection of Greek treaties.
>
>   By other Greek government authorities, concerning:
> the Bavarian alliance, Greek loans, Greek regeneration
> the International Financial Commission
> the ratification of World War I peace treaties in 1919
> the treaties on limited monarchy in Greece.

2. Soutzo, A. *Recueil des documents authentiques relatifs au droit public extérieur de la Grèce.* Publié par ordre et approbation du département de la maison royale et des relations extérieures. Athens, 1858.

3. Venizelos, Eleutherios. *La Grèce devant le Congrès de la Paix, 30 décembre 1918* (mémoire sur le traité de Sèvres). Athens, 1919.

Guides and Reference Works

4. Bemis and Griffin, *Guide.* On Greek archives, pp. 926–937.

5. Degras, *Soviet documents.* On Greece, pp. 42, 80, 119, 150, 188, 232.

6. Papadakis, N. J. *The activities of the Historical Archives of Crete, 1920–1933* (in Greek). Canea (Cret), 1933.

7. Tomadakis, N. B. "About archives and archival services in Greece," *Bulletin of the Historical and Ethnological Society of Greece* (in Greek), XI (Athens, 1956), 1–42.

8. Topping, Peter. "The public archives of Greece," *The American archivist*, XV (1952), 249–257.

9. Zakythinos, D. A. "The historical and monastic archives of Crete," *Yearbook of the Society for Cretan Studies* (in Greek), II (Herakleion, Crete, 1939), 505–526.

9   ITALY

Vincent Ilardi

University of Massachusetts, Amherst

and

Mary Lucille Shay

University of Illinois

INTRODUCTION[1]

THE *Ministero dell'Interno* has jurisdiction over the *Archivio Centrale dello Stato* in Rome and the ninety-two *Archivi di Stato* located in the provincial capitals, including the latter's thirty-one dependent *sezioni* or sub-archives created in selected communes. Whereas the *Archivio Centrale* holds the records of the central organs of the state after the unification of Italy, the *Archivi di Stato* are the repositories of government papers of the various former sovereign states before unification and of the provincial administrations. Within the Ministry, the *Direzione Generale degli Archivi di Stato* is charged with the supervision and administration of the various units, functioning through the *Consiglio Superiore degli Archivi* composed of archivists and university professors. Through a system of *Sovrintendenze*, one for each of Italy's eighteen regions, the Ministry also supervises and controls public records not deposited in the *Archivi di Stato* and private archives deemed of substantial historical interest.[2]

[1] In the preparation of this chapter, Vincent Ilardi is responsible for the Introduction and for the sections on Mantua, Milan, Modena, and Siena, and for their respective bibliographies. The authors wish to express their gratitude to the numerous archivists and librarians who have generously responded to their inquiries and aided their research over the years.

[2] Each year the first issue of the ministerial *Rassegna degli Archivi di Stato* contains the current list of the personnel comprising the commissions and of the directors and *sovrintendenti*.

The following necessarily brief descriptions of leading diplomatic repositories are designed to serve as a general orientation, particularly for young researchers. Printed guides and inventories will supply fuller descriptions and will provide additional information especially in reference to important documents of a diplomatic nature filed in smaller series not cited. Indeed, researchers should constantly bear in mind that the frequent intermingling of internal and external records, particularly in the earlier periods, the confused state of some of the repositories, the arbitrary classifications assigned to many of the series, the dispersal of archival records, as well as the more comprehensive nature characterizing diplomatic research in recent times, all point to the wisdom of proceeding carefully and systematically in the exploration of archives. In a few instances it is possible to begin research in the United States by consulting archival manuscript inventories and diplomatic series already microfilmed by American libraries and individuals.[3]

A summary description of the entire Italian archival patrimony is available in two publications of the Ministry — *L'ordinamento delle carte degli Archivi di Stato. Manuale storicl archivistico* (Rome, 1910), and *Gli Archivi di Stato italiani* (Bologna, 1944). They are now out of date but still useful. Since 1966 the Ministry has been preparing a two-volume *Guida Generale* of all state archives, the publication of which is still far in the future. As a result of this work, an ever-growing and perpetually revised central card catalogue of all the *fondi* comprising each archive will be assembled in Rome, facilitating periodic revisions of the guide. In addition, an effort is being made to provide a more uniform terminology for principal sections of archival records

[3] An extensive list of these holdings was published by Richard W. Hale, Jr., *Guide to photocopied historical materials in the United States and Canada* (Ithaca, 1961). More recent microfilm accessions in the Library of Congress are reported in its *Quarterly journal.* New holdings of other libraries and individuals have been reported periodically in the *News from the Center for the Coordination of Foreign Manuscript Copying,* published from 1967 to 1970 by the Library of Congress. Complete series of Italian diplomatic documents for the period 1450–94 have been microfilmed by the writer.

and for the files comprising them, which, at present, are known under a bewildering variety of names.

ARCHIVIO STORICO DEL MINISTERO DEGLI AFFARI ESTERI IN ROME[4]

HISTORY

The Kingdom of Sardinia had served as the nucleus for the unification of Italy and thus bequeathed some of its archival practices. According to the regulation of 1856, diplomatic papers were retained for ten years in the office of the secretary for foreign affairs. It was natural and even necessary that this practice be continued in the new kingdom. With the transferring of the capital to Florence in 1865 and to Rome in 1871, papers that belonged to the ten years preceding 1861 were moved. Some of these were returned to Turin, but not all. Other goups of documents pertaining to the Kingdom of Sardinia and the Archduchy of Tuscany are the legation archives that were sent to Rome after 1871.

The plans for the centralization of state papers in a national archives in Rome were not followed by the ministry of foreign affairs; the diplomatic papers have remained as a part of the foreign ministry's separate archives as in France and Belgium.

CLASSIFICATION AND ARRANGEMENT

From the preceding paragraphs, it is evident that the papers belong to two different periods: those before 1861, which supplement the archives in Turin and Florence, and those after 1861, which are the diplomatic papers of united Italy.

The legation archives of the Kingdom of Sardinia are an important part of the records before 1861. Even during the eighteenth century there developed the practice of keeping some

---

[4] Hereafter referred to simply as *Archivio storico.*

papers in the legations, and, after 1815, the practice became common. For the years 1815 to 1861, there are not the same kinds of documents in Turin as for the period preceding 1797. Prior to 1797 the originals of both the ambassadors' letters and the court's replies are in Turin. After 1815 only the orignials of the ambassadors' letters are in Turin; the court's replies are the copies that were preserved by the minister of foreign affairs and later turned over to the archives. Conversely, the papers that were sent from the legation archives which are in the *Archivio storico* are the copies of the ambassadors' letters and the originals of the court's replies.

The papers that pertain to the Kingdom of Sardinia (legations in eight countries), the legation of the Archduchy of Tuscany in Rome, and other papers have been classified, and since 1947 inventories have been published by the Ministry of Foreign Affairs in the series *Indici dell'Archivio storico*. (See Nos. 1-8 and 88-89.)

There are other inventories in typewritten copies, which may be consulted.

By far the most important documents in the *Archivio storico* are the diplomatic papers of united Italy, which are being published for 1861-1943 (see No. 9). A ministerial decree of September 20, 1946, established the "Commission for the Publication of Diplomatic Documents." Six years later two volumes were published; others have followed and will follow. There will be about one hundred volumes, which will contain papers from private and the royal archives, as well as from the *Archivio storico*.

ARCHIVIO DI STATO IN FLORENCE

HISTORY

In 1852 Archduke Leopold II appointed a commission to plan the union or centralization of the separate archives. The report of the commission was accepted, and a portion of the Palazzo Uffizi was selected as the depository. Three years later, the archives were opened. After 1859 the papers of the House of Lorraine were added.

CLASSIFICATION AND ARRANGEMENT

The usual basic groups of diplomatic papers are found in the fifteenth century records: instructions for envoys, letters to them and heads of states, and replies. Instructions and letters to envoys are filed in the series: *Signori — Carteggi — Missive — Legazioni e Commissarie — Elezioni e Istruzioni a Oratori*. Letters to rulers are in the series *Signori — Missive — Prima Cancelleria*. Letters from the *Signoria, Dieci di Balia*, and *Otto di Practica* to envoys are in the series *Missive Originali*. (See No. 7.)

The government developed some special practices: the *Signoria* frequently sought advice from groups of able citizens. The oldest group, the *Dieci di Balia* (1384–1531) at first advised about war, but in the fifteenth century it assisted in policy making, always under the *Signoria*. It sent envoys, corresponded with them and with rulers: *Dieci di Balia — Missive — Legazioni e Commissarie*, and received replies: the *Responsive*. Another group of records, the registers of *Consulte e Pratiche*, 1446–80, were kept of interviews with citizens whose advice was sought by the *Signoria*. These records ceased to contain anything about foreign policy when the Medici exercised influence.

The *Dieci di Balia* continued to exist when the second group, *Otto di Pratica*, was appointed. The latter (1480–1560) also corresponded with envoys (and rulers): *Lettere e Istruzione a Oratori* and the replies are in the *Responsive*.

The *Signoria, Dieci di Balia*, and *Otto di Pratica* appear also in the series of first drafts of instructions and letters to envoys and rulers: *Signori — Minutari*. These first drafts help to show the development of policy-making and sometimes this group of papers contains information that has been lost from other groups. Another source for filling gaps are two registers of the *Dieci di Balia, Sommari di Missive e Responsive e Ricordi*.

There are examples of misfiling. Some incoming letters belonging in the *Responsive Originali* may be found in the group of outgoing letters, the *Missive Originali*. Another example, some letters to envoys may be found in *Signori — Missive — Prima Cancelleria*.

Two series of miscellaneous papers are first, *Signoria, Dieci di Balia, Otto di Pratica — Legazioni e Commissarie — Missive e Responsive*; secondly, *Carte di Corredo — Legazioni e Commissarie*.

Treaties and agreements with other states are found in two groups: the *Archivio Diplomatico — Riformagioni — Atti Pubblici* and the *Capitoli*.

All the foregoing records do not complete the account of diplomacy. They give no evidence of the power of the Medici family, which was not a direct part of the government. The family papers, now in the archives of Florence, show the power of Cosimo de' Medici in policy-making, even policy reversing, and the power of this grandson, Lorenzo. Papers of other families, especially the Strozzi family, also in the archives, add to the knowledge of diplomacy. Two other parts of the archives are the Torrigiani papers and the *Archivio di Urbino,* which pertain to sixteenth century diplomacy.

In addition to the state archives, the archives of the Guicciardini family should be consulted. They are private, but permission to cousult them may be obtained.

When the last Medici ruler died in 1737, Francis of Lorraine became the archduke of Tuscany. He made only one visit to his new possession in the twenty-eight years of his reign. In great contrast, his son and successor, Peter Leopold, came to Florence in 1765 and for twenty-five years devoted a great deal of energy to the archduchy. He established a secretary of foreign affairs and left reports, which have recently been published. The first volume includes *"Relazioni politiche della Toscana con le corti estere"* and *"Ministri alle corti estere."* In the latter, he gave frank characterizations, favorable and unfavorable, of the envoys from Florence. (See Nos. 5 and 19-21.) These are, however, brief accounts. He was interested in good relations with other Italian states in order to improve the economic welfare of his subjects.

ARCHIVIO DI STATO IN GENOA

HISTORY

In 1817, the archives of Genoa were moved to the former criminal palace and, in 1881, the archives of the *Banco di San Giorgio* were transferred to the state archives.

By the close of the fifteenth century, Genoa had declined from her first great period: the loss of most of her possessions and the loss of trade in the eastern Mediterranean. At home, factions led her to accept French rule, 1458-61, then that of Milan, 1464-78, 1487-99, a total of twenty-nine years out of forty-one. Very few documents of this early period exist.

The second great period began about 1500, with trade and continuing diplomatic relations with European states.

CLASSIFICATION AND ARRANGEMENT

The documents of the government consisted of *Instructiones et Relationes, Istruzioni a Ministri,* and *Lettere a Minstri.* Envoys and consuls wrote *Relazioni di Ministri, Lettere Ministri,* and *Lettere Consoli.* The *Registri Litterarum* also contain some correspondence of the envoys. The archives of the *Banco di San Giorgio* and the collection made by Agostino Franzone in the seventeenth century should also be consulted.

Before Ciasca began to publish all the *relazioni* about Spain, Morandi and Vitale had published a few, but not such complete texts as Ciasca. (See Nos. 23, 26, and 115.) They also included *relazioni* about other states besides Spain. Morandi contrasted the report of San Martino di Baldissero, envoy of Turin in Vienna, with the report of Benedetto Viale, envoy of Genoa in London. Morandi warned readers not to judge these two reports by their length. Baldissero gave detail after detail; Viale's report ranked among the best of reports written by envoys from Genoa.

ARCHIVIO DI STATO IN LUCCA

HISTORY

In 1859 the archives were moved to Palazzo Guidiccioni.

From 1369 to 1400, and from 1430 to 1499, Lucca sent envoys occasionally. During the years 1400-30, Paolo Guinigi was in control. When Bongi prepared his inventory of the archives, he stated that some diplomatic correspondence might be found in the Guinigi family archives. These family papers are now in the state archives. In the sixteenth century, envoys were sent regularly and continued to be appointed as long as the republic lasted, until 1799.

CLASSIFICATION AND ARRANGEMENT

Diplomatic papers that have survived are in three divisions: 1. original instructions, reports, and letters, 1369-1799; 2. copies of the foregoing; 3. copies of letters from special ambassadors after 1480. Also preserved are many confidential letters from other persons and from spies. During the last years of the seventeenth century, Lucca began sending secondary representatives, called agents, whose duties were similar to those of consuls of a later period.

The Sardini family papers have been given to the state archives; members of the family served as ambassadors in a number of courts. Giulio Prunai, in a review, called Giovan Battista Domenico Sardini a most expert diplomat. He served in several Italian states for brief periods, and in Spain, 1733-38.

For negotiations after 1815, see No. 21.

ARCHIVIO DI STATO IN MANTUA

HISTORY

Although the origin of the *Archivio di Stato* in Mantua can be traced to the formation of the archives of the Commune (1199), the present *Archivio* began to develop as a central repository only after Mantua's annexation to the Kingdom of Italy in 1866 and, particularly, after the Commune deposited the state papers of the *Archivio Gonzaga* (1889). No general guide of the Archives has been published, and some of the *fondi* lack accurate inventories. The holdings of the *Archivio Gonzaga,* however, have been admirably described by Torelli (No. 36) and Luzio (No. 34). The latter is particularly useful for foreign affairs and is considered to be a model of its kind. The *Archivio* also possesses a multi-volume analytical but incomplete inventory of the Gonzaga diplomatic papers compiled by S. Davari which is still useful.

CLASSIFICATION AND ARRANGEMENT

The records of the *Archivio de Stato* form three principal *fondi* associated with various governments of the city: (1) the *Canossa,* Commune, and Signoria of the Bonacolsi up to their expulsion (1328), the Gonzaga (1328-1707), and the transitional period (1708-97) under Austria; (2) the Austrian domination, except for the French and provisional governments (1797-1866); (3) annexation to the Kingdom of Italy (1866-present).

The first *fondo,* up to the loss of Mantuan independence, is of particular interest for our purposes. With only fragments remaining of the communal archives, destroyed by fire in 1413, the Gonzaga papers, accumulated during four centuries of their rule, form the most extensive part. The *Archivio Gonzaga* has been rightly called the jewel of Italian archives, with particular reference to the massive size and, at times, crucial importance of its diplomatic holdings, despite the secondary rank of the Gonzaga, who were elevated to marquises in 1433 and dukes in 1530.

Although Mantuan diplomacy was already very active in the fifteenth century, it reached its apogee in activity, resourcefulness, and brilliance in the following century. At a time when one Italian state after the other was being annexed or reduced to vassalage by the national monarchies, this minuscule state was able to use its strategic position, its far-flung marriage alliances, and the skills of its diplomats to preserve its independence for another century and even to augment its territory by snatching Monferrato from Savoy. A number of Mantuan ambassadors compared with the best of the age, and some of them hold residence records probably unsurpassed in any age — Benedetto Agnello at Venice (1530–56) and Giustiniano Prandi in France (1610–73)! Under Duke Guglielmo (1550–87), the diplomatic service was reorganized as part of a general administrative reorganization, but after the death of this able ruler, the Duchy began a period of gradual decline during which Mantuan diplomacy lost much of this vitality and ability to prop up inept rulers and defend the anachronistic existence of their state.

The organization of the *Archivio Gonzaga* divides the records according to subjects designated by letters of the alphabet from A to Z. Apart from the fact that this arbitrary organization, which destroyed the historical origin of the *fondi*, has never been completed, researchers must deal with the reality that their own classification of their subjects of study may differ from the archivists' and they will thus be forced to search several series for the missing documents. The bulk of the diplomatic documents are found in Series E, which alone constitutes 1,600 *buste* (large envelopes) of the 3,719 that comprise the *Archivio Gonzaga* proper. This huge series is divided into sixty subdivisions corresponding to the various embassies, and one subdivision containing (1) correspondence with a few prominent individuals including the Marchesa Isabella d'Este (13 *buste*, 1504–22), Cardinal Ercole Gonzaga (43 *buste*, 1523–63, particularly important for research on the Council of Trent), etc., and (2) a miscellaneous collection of letters and reports coming from abroad (21 *buste*,

1552-1666). In each subdivision the documents are filed according to their nature; namely, (1) instructions to Mantuan envoys; (2) original letters received from heads of state; (3) incoming dispatches from Mantuan ambassadors, agents, and others residing abroad; (4, 5, 6) related documents and miscellaneous papers, including relations completed by ambassadors at the end of their mission, an imitation of the Venetian practice that Mantua initiated in the second half of the sixteenth century.

Among the most extensive subdivisions are those of Rome (233 *buste*, 1198-1241, 1303-1829), Milan (187 *buste*, 1344-1792), Venice (172 *buste*, 1331-1790), Ferrara (100 *buste*, 1164-1217, 1310-1781), France (86 *buste*, 1237, 1364-1708), Imperial Court (83 *buste*, 1311-1756), Florence (53 *buste*, 1345-1708), and Spain (44 *buste*, 1349-1734). It should be noted that the extensive files comprising the Imperial Court (*Corte Cesarea*) subdivision, combined with such subdivisions as *Diete Imperiali, Corti Elettorali, Fiandre, Innsbruck* and *Graz, Trento*, and *Danimarca*, reflect mostly the marriage ties of the Gonzaga with German princes and make the *Archivio Gonzaga* a prime source for Italo-German relations at this time. In all subdivisions, ciphered communications are generally accompanied by deciphered copies made by the chancery. In any case, cipher keys are available in the *Cifrari* (*buste* 423-425, 1395-1702), also part of Series E, which include some of the earliest ciphers used by an Italian state.

A great number of diplomatic documents can also be found in the files of internal correspondence that form Series F. This series is divided into four subdivisions. The first — F.II.6, *Lettere Originali dei Gonzaga* (92 *buste*, 1331-1708) — is composed of letters sent by the Gonzaga to members of their family, other princes, and individuals within and outside the Duchy which, for various reasons, remained or were returned to the chancery. Many were returned by Mantuan envoys at the end of their missions. Copies of most of the *Originali* can be found in the second and fourth subdivisions listed below. The second — F.II.7, *Minute della Cancelleria* (183 *buste*, 1344-1789) — preserves the first drafts of internal and external correspondence emanating from the chancery, along with some originals and copies of incoming correspondence, including a great number of copies of dispatches and other papers of foreign ambassadors. The third — F.II.8, *Lettere ai Gonzaga da Mantova e Paesi dello Stato* (514 *buste*, 1366-1783) — is composed of incoming correspondence from internal officials and castellans who report political news as well. In addition, this subdivision contains even some correspondence returned by Mantuan envoys and many undated or unclassified diplomatic dispatches received from other states. The fourth — F.II.9, *Copialettere dei Gonzaga* (614 registers, 1340-1706) — is a massive subdivision that recorded the final drafts of outgoing internal and external correspondence. In 1492 appropriate registers, called *Riservati*, were begun for letters dealing with foreign affairs, but this distinction was not respected consistently. These registers also contain a great number of dispatches from Mantuan ambassadors as well as some incoming correspondence from other states.

In view of the fact that the organization of the *Archivio Gonzaga* is arbitrary and remains, in any case, incomplete and not always consistent, one can find important diplomatic documents scattered literally in all its series. The most promising series, without excluding the others, are: *Autografi, Affari de' Confini, Affari di Famiglie Dominanti di Mantova*, and *Materie Ecclesiastiche*. Although several scholars, particularly Pastor, Luzio, and Quazza, have made frequent use of the Gonzaga diplomatic records, Luzio's complaint, voiced a half century ago, that these papers have never received the attention they deserve, remains true today. (See Nos. 34 and 37.)

ARCHIVIO DE STATO IN MILAN

HISTORY

The *Archivio di Stato* is the repository of the state records of Milan, under its various governments, prior to its annexation by the Kingdom of Sardinia in 1859: Duchy (1395-1796), Republic (1797-1805), Kingdom of Italy (1805-14), and Kingdom of Lombardy-Venetia (1815-59). The archives of the duchy were orignially housed in the *Castello Sforzesco,* from which they were subsequently (1781) transferred to the former Jesuit College of San Fedele. Beginning in 1872, they were combined with other government papers dispersed in several repositories and were centralized in their present location, the *Palazzo del Senato.* The *Archivio di Stato* has never published a general guide to its holdings. Summary descriptions of its *fondi* have been published by Vittani (No. 50) for the period up to 1943, and by Natale (No. 44) since then.

CLASSIFICATION AND ARRANGEMENT

After a major reorganization dating from the beginning of this century and still in progress, the holdings, at present, are arranged into twelve general divisions, as follows:

(1) Archivio Ducale (1395-1796)
(2) Archivio del Governo Republicano (1796-1805)
(3) Archivio del Regno d'Italia (1805-14)
(4) Archivio del Regno Lombardo-Veneto (1815-59)
(5) Atti di Governo (sec. XV-XIX)
(6) Archivio del Fondo di Religione (sec. XII-XVIII)
(7) Sezione Storica (sec. XV-XIX)
(8) Archivio Catastale (sec. XVIII-XIX)
(9) Archivio Notarile (sec. XIII-1863)
(10) Archivio del Regio Governo di Lombardia (1859-60)
(11) Archivio della Circoscrizione provinciale di Milano (post 1860)
(12) Acquisti-Depositi-Doni

(See No. 44.)

The first division, the *Archivio Ducale* (1395-1796), particularly its earlier section, the *Archivio Visconteo-Sforzesco* (1395-1535), is of prime importance for our purposes. After the

Sforza period, foreign policy decisions were made in the councils of foreign rulers, whose records, however, can be illuminated by reference to the papers of their governors and officials residing in Milan and deposited in the *Archivio di Stato*. The archives of the Commune of Milan, and of the early Visconti, were destroyed in past centuries. Only fragments of the papers of the last Visconti duke, Filippo Maria (1412–47), survived the turbulent period of the Ambrosian Republic (1447–50). On the other hand, except for relatively small losses, the Sforza archives have managed to resist the ravages of time to form, along with the *Museo Diplomatico* (a superb parchment collection dating from the eighth to the twelfth century, now being published), the most famous *fondo* of the *Archivio di Stato*. This is indeed fortunate, for the Sforza diplomatic documents are by far the most extensive in Europe in the second half of the fifteenth century; and they are so comprehensive that, if similar collections in other Italian archives had been destroyed, we would still be well informed about the diplomatic moves of all Italian states. This is the result of Milan's diplomatic leadership at this time, especially in the period of Francesco Sforza, 1450–66. The duchy pioneered the consistent use of resident embassies in all major Italian capitals, and it established the first, and most important, resident embassy of the age outside Italy — France and Burgundy. The enormous flow of correspondence was handled by the personal chancery of the Dukes, the *Cancelleria Segreta*, headed for thirty years by Cicco Simonetta, under whose leadership the chancery became a model of organization and efficiency. Regrettably, no inventory of this collection has been published, and the handwritten indexes (not really inventories, as they are called) are neither complete nor entirely accurate. This may partly explain the fact that these papers are imperfectly known to scholars, their significance being obscured by the well-known and publicized Venetian diplomatic records of the following centuries. A century ago, Osio conceived the overly ambitious plan to publish the whole corpus of the Visconti-Sforza diplomatic records, but at his death (1873), the publication ceased, having reached the last years of Filippo Maria (No. 59). Only fragments of the Sforza papers have been published, chiefly by Gingins-la-Sarra (No. 52) and Mandrot (No. 55). In recent tyears there has been a reactivation of these efforts (No. 54).

The present organization of the *Archivio Visconteo-Sforzesco* was created by Luigi Fumi, former director of the *Archivio di Stato* from 1907 to 1920, who changed the previous topical organization of the material to one conforming more closely to the historical origin of the various *fondi*. Under this reorganization, the remaining fragments of the *Visconteo* (19 *cartelle* or cartons and 17 registers) were separated from the *Sforzesco* proper. Inventories of the former were published by Manaresi (No. 42) and Vittani (No. 50). The *Archivio Sforzesco* was subdivided into the *Sforzesco avanti il Principato* (1411–51), also known as *Archivio del conte Sforza,* and the *Sforzesco Ducale* (1450-1535). The former consists of only twenty *cartelle* containing the personal papers and correspondence of Francesco Sforza, before he became Duke (see Natale, No. 57, p. CLXXIII). The latter holds the massive records of the Sforza dynasty, including the few remaining papers relative to the French domination of Milan (1499-1512; 1515-21; 1524-25). It is composed of (1) acts filed loosely and chronologically in *cartelle,* according to the following principal series: *Carteggio Estero* or *Potenze Estere, Carteggio Interno, Sommari, Cifrari, Trattati,* and *Potenze Sovrane;* and (2) acts inscribed in registers, divided into the series *Registri Ducali* and *Registri delle Missive.*

The *Carteggio Estero* or *Potenze Estere* (Inventory No. 1) is the principal repository of Milanese foreign policy records. This is a huge series containing the correspondence of the dukes with other rulers and with their ambassadors, informers, and persons residing in other states, together with relative miscellaneous papers. These papers are filed in subdivisions corresponding to the various embassies located in practically all Italian states, and in many outside Italy. The most extensive subdivisions are those of Genoa, Rome, Naples, Florence, Venice, and, outside Italy,

France-Burgundy. Researchers should bear in mind, however, that dispatches originating outside of the ambassadors' places of accreditation are filed in their respective subdivisions and occasionally in the *Carteggio Interno*, if written within the duchy. The *Carteggio Interno* contains papers and ducal correspondence with officials relative to the administration of the duchy, and it is subdivided according to its various districts (Inventory No. 1).

Intimately connected with the *Carteggio Estero* are the *Sommari* and the *Cifrari*. The former (cart. 1560–65, Inventory No. 2) contain summaries of diplomatic dispatches and of various secret reports from abroad, also filed according to their place of origin. They are important, particularly when the originals have not survived. In the *Cifrari* (cart. 1591, 1597) many of the cipher keys used in diplomatic correspondence are preserved. A more comprehensive collection of some two hundred Milanese cipher keys is deposited in the *Nationalbibliothek* of Vienna (Cod. 2398). This unique codex probably constitutes the earliest extensive collection of its kind, at least in Europe. It was recently published in facsimile, togehter with the extant keys at the *Archivio di Stato*, and a list and biographical sketches of the Milanese ambassadors by Cerione (No. 51). It should be noted that most of the dispatches in the *Carteggio Estero* are accompanied by deciphered copies made by the chancery, but they are not always complete or entirely accurate.

The series *Trattati* (cart. 1521–59, Inventory No. 2) includes originals and copies of treaties, ratifications, powers, credentials, contracts with *condottieri*, acts of investitures, and even some instructions and dispatches relative to these acts. The *Potenze Sovrane* (cart. 1455–85, Inventory No. 2), on the other hand, contains predominantly personal records of the dukes and members of their family, such as letters, marriage contracts, records of travel and expenditures, etc., which at times can be crucial for the elucidation of foreign policy.

In the *Registri Ducali* (214 registers, Inventory No. 4) are inscribed acts and records of negotiations dealing with internal as well as external affairs, such as treaties, ratifications, marriage contracts, investitures, contracts with *condottieri*, as well as some relative correspondence with rulers and ambassadors, the originals of which can generally be found in the *Carteggio Estero* and in the *Trattati*. In the *Registri delle Missive* (225 registers, Inventory No. 5) were copied the letters sent out by the ducal chancery to local officials and to ambassadors and foreign rulers, the latter usually dealing with matters peripheral to foreign policy. Few registers, however, are composed entirely of letters and instructions dealing with foreign affairs and occasionally one finds even copies of incoming dispatches. Each register normally contains letters addressed to various destinations in a way apparently reflecting the routes taken by the couriers.

Within the division, *Sezione Storica,* there are two series that contain some diplomatic documents — the *Autografi* and the collection *Famiglie*. The former is composed of autograph and allegedly autographed letters of rulers and prominent individuals, including ambassadors. This series is easily consulted through a five-volume handwritten inventory (Nos. 84bis, 85–87). The latter consists of a collection of papers about a great number of prominent Lombard families, some of whom were active in diplomacy (Inventory No. 90). Finally, the ever growing division, *Acquisti-Depositi-Doni,* should be checked by the careful researcher for additional diplomatic documents that are periodically deposited or acquired.

Outside of the *Archivio di Stato*, the *Biblioteca Ambrosiana* in Milan and the *Bibliothèque Nationale* in Paris have the most important collections of Milanese diplomatic documents. In the former, they can be found mostly in the Z-Sup. class, particlarly codices 88, 146, 219, 226–239, 247. In the latter, they form part of the large *Fonds Italien,* Codices 1583–96, fully described by Mazzatinti (No. 43) and partly published by Mandrot (No. 55). The Trivulziana Library, now combined with the *Archivio Civico* in the *Castello Sforzesco,* and the Brera Library, in Milan, also have additional codices useful for diplomatic research. (See Nos. 40, 41, 45, 48, 49.)

ARCHIVIO DI STATO IN MODENA

HISTORY

More than any other major Italian archival repository, the *Archivio di Stato* in Modena grew out of the papers of a ruling family — the Este — who ruled Modena and Reggio for five centureis and Ferrara for four. With the return of Ferrara to the Holy See in 1598, the Este transferred their capital and archives to Modena. These papers constitute the *Archivio Segreto Estense*, long held as private archives of the family, as is implicit in their title. The archives include the family papers dating from 781 combined with state records after the Este's rise to power in the thirteenth century, up to their expulsion by the French in 1796. The records of the Napoleonic period (1796–1814), those of the Hapsburg-Este dukes (1814–59), and those of the provincial organs of administration, after Modena's annexation to the Kingdom of Sardinia (1860), form three other principal *fondi* comprising the present *Archivio di Stato*. No general guide to the entire collection has been published, and most of the series of documents lack accurate manuscript inventories. The best recent summary description has been published by Filippo Valenti (No. 65).

CLASSIFICATION AND ARRANGEMENT

The *Archivio Segreto Estense* constitutes the most celebrated *fondo* of the *Archivio di Stato*. For centuries, these papers have lain in great confusion, partly through neglect by some of the rulers, and partly because of the meager efforts of past archivists. The great historian, Lodovico Antonio Muratori, who for fifty years (1700–50) was in charge of the *Archivio*, made little progress owing to the preoccupations of other duties and his natural inclination to concentrate his attention to his historical studies, rather than to the reordering of archival records. In recent years these collections have been undergoing an extensive reordering prior to the publication of a four-volume inventory, the first volume of which has been published (No. 62). This inventory deals with the subdivision *Casa e Stato*, summarily described earlier by Dallari (No. 63), who, however, included series from other subdivisions.

The *Casa e Stato* subdivision consists of a heterogeneous collection of family and state records arbitrarily formed by past archivists, mostly in response to specific needs of the court. The family records, more strictly defined, form the following series: (1) *Geneologie, storie e notizie di Casa d'Este*; (2) *Carteggi tra principi Estensi* (which include some correspondence with foreign princes); (3) *Documenti spettanti a principi Estensi* (wills, marriage and *condotta* contracts, records of disputes, voyages etc.); (4) *Corte* (court ceremonies, entertainment of foreign princes and dignitaries, order of precedence for ambassadors, etc.); and (5) *Dedizioni ed acquisti di città e terre*.

More pertinent to foreign affairs are the semi-private and state documents filed in two series. (1) The *Serie generale* is divided into parchment and paper documents, both of which register the dynastic rights of the Este and their conventions and treaties with other states. The former is composed of 1412 parchments dating from 781 to 1708 (*Cassette* 1-28). Summaries of these acts are available in a card catalogue at the Archives. The latter consists of paper documents of similar nature including acts of investiture, treaties from 1521 to 1767 (*Cassette* 50-54), charters, and one file (No. 58) containing *Patti e convenzioni commerciali tra Ferrara e Venezia* from 1191 to 1494. (2) The *Controversie de Stato* contains documents involving the restitution of Modena and Reggio to the Este by the Holy See following the arbitral sentence pronounced by Charles V (*buste* 494-499, 1530-37)), the dispute over precedence with the grand dukes of Tuscany (*buste* 500-508, 1570-93), and the devolution of Ferrara to the Holy See (*buste* 509-519, 1332-1814).

The bulk of the diplomatic documents, however, is located in the subdivision, *Cancelleria-estero*. This is one of the leading collections of the age, rivaling in size and importance the Gonzaga collection of Mantua. Like the Gonzaga, the Este were soldier-rulers of a relatively poor but strategically important state, who sought to preserve their possessions through their military skills, resourceful diplomacy, and an extensive network of marriage ties, including the royal houses of France, Austria, and England. As in the case of the Mantuan rulers, the Este attained their pinnacle of political power and fame as patrons of arts and letters from about the middle of the fifteenth century to the end of the sixteenth and declined thereafter for essentially the same reasons. It was at this time that Este diplomacy was able to play its most vigorous and crucial role. Unfortunately, very little is known about its organization, institutions, and overall significance. Its records have been utilized piecemeal for the study of particular diplomatic crises, partly because scholars have preferred to concentrate their attention on the men of letters and artists that made Ferrara one of the leading centers of Renaissance culture. The current reordering of the diplomatic files, and especially the publication of the planned inventory, hopefully will serve to arouse interest in this rich source, which has only been summarily described by Ognibene (No. 64). At present, this collection is difficult to use and defies accurate description, owing to the disorganized state of some of the series.

In the *Cancelleria-estero* subdivision, the correspondence of the Este with other princes and states forms the series *Carteggi con principi esteri in Italia e fuori d'Italia*, which includes, as sort of an appendix, their correspondence with foreign governing bodies, ambassadors, and bishops (*Carteggi con rettori di Stati e Città estere*). It comprises 650 *buste* of originals and copies beginning with the fourteenth century, filed according to the state or ruling house reflected in the correspondence. (Inventory No. 18).

The heart of the diplomatic collection is the celebrated series, *Carteggi di oratori e agenti presso le corti*, also known as

Carteggio ambasciatori. In addition to dispatches, these files contain ducal instructions and correspondence with agents, relatives, and friends residing abroad, much of which treat political matters. The series is composed of 1699 *buste,* 937 for Italian states and 762 for other states, subdivided according to the location of the various embassies. Virtually all Italian powers are represented as are many outside Italy, such as France (1470-1796), Germany (including Flanders and Austria, 1482-1793), England (1470-1779), Levant (Candia, China, Corfù, Dalmatia, Egypt, Greece, Turkey, 1505-1732), Malta (1583-1658), Poland (1520-1712), Spain (1468-1771), Switzerland (1531-1714), Tunis (1464-1573), and Hungary (1479-1739). Before the middle of the fifteenth century the documents are not plentiful, partly because some of the early records were destroyed by several fires in the sixteenth century, but mostly because the resident embassy had not been established. Duke Borso (1450-71) is credited with having established the first resident embassies at Venice, Florence, Rome, and Milan. A six-volume manuscript inventory (Nos. 12-17) lists chronologically the ambassadors and correspondents in the various files and gives valuable information about each diplomatic mission. There are, however, many omissions and errors.

The *Cancelleria-estro* also contains the following series, some of which are of great importance for the study of Estè diplomacy: (1)*Avvisi e notizie dall'estero* (130 *buste* and 14 volumes dated from 1393 to late eighteenth century) which consist of confidential reports by spies and news sheets, similar to newsletters, that formerly were often attached to ambassadorial dispatches; (2) *Sommari e copie di lettere* (two *buste,* 1468-1500) — summaries and copies of dispatches by foreign ambassadors, many of which were intercepted; (3) *Confini dello Stato* (192 *buste,* from the thirteenth to the eighteenth century) — records dealing with the inevitable border questions and controversies; (4) *Convenzioni e trattamenti con Stati esteri* (56 *buste,* 1393-1795) — documents regarding negotiations with other states in reference to the extradition of criminals and political refugees, extension of commercial privileges, etc.; (5) *Cifrario* (eight *buste* from the fifteenth to the eighteenth century) — cipher keys used in correspondence with ambassadors, foreign rulers, and with other members of the Este family; (6) *Documenti di Stati esteri* (196 *buste* from the eleventh to the eighteenth century). This is an extensive, miscellaneous collection of documents of all types, including dispatches, reports, instructions, treaties, memoranda, etc., often copies, emanating from other chanceries. Four subseries with self-explanatory titles, are of particular interest for diplomatic history purposes: (a) *Istruzioni ad oratori esteri in Ferrara e Modena e lettere dei medesimi in Italia;* (b) *Minute di lettere ducali ad oratori esteri in Italia;* (c) *Istruzioni ad oratori esteri e lettere dei medesimi fuori d'Italia;* and (d) *Minute di lettere ducali ad oratori esteri fuori d'Italia*. Maximum confusion reigns in these files, which are not even dated. Diligent research in the above-named series, particularly Nos. 1–2 and 6, is likely to result in the discovery of many important documents for Italian, as well as European, diplomacy.

As in the case of other archives of the age, diplomatic documents can be found scattered in other subdivisions that pertain mostly to internal affairs, such as the *Cancelleria — sezione generale*. Here the most promising series are the *Registri di lettere ducali* (47 registers, 1363–1592), and the *Minute di lettere ducali* (28 *buste,* 1403–1795). A summary inventory of this subdivision was published by Dallari (No. 63). Finally, in the subdivision, *Camera marchionale poi ducale*, there is the series, *Registri dell'ufficio del mese,* in which records for expenditures relating to ambassadorial travels, couriers, etc., can be found.

ARCHIVIO DI STATO IN NAPLES

HISTORY

Several decrees of Murat provided for a union of all records in Castel Capuano, but it was not large enough to house them all. In

1835 the former abbey of Saints Severino and Sossia was selected as the depository.

CLASSIFICATION AND ARRANGEMENT

Before the Second World War there were four major groups of papers: the Angevin, Aragonese, Farnese, and a portion of the Bourbon. Originally the Farnese papers belonged to Parma. When Don Charles became the first Bourbon king of Naples, he ordered that these papers be moved to Naples. After he succeeded to the Spanish throne, some of the papers were returned to Parma, but the greater part remained in Naples. When Louis Prosper Gachard, the Belgian archivist, went to Naples in 1868, he had some difficulty in finding this collection. It had lain almost forgotten in the Royal Palace. It was moved to the archives, arranged, and inventoried. When Francis II left Naples in 1860, the beginning of his exile, he sent away the papers of the last four Bourbon kings.

During the war these four groups of papers were moved for safekeeping to the Villa Montesano, near Nola. On September 30, 1943, the Germans set fire to the villa, and the losses were great. Practically all the Angevin papers, most of the Aragonese (see No. 7), and parts of the Farnese were lost (see No. 73). In addition, documents that had been lent by other archives for an exhibition and, upon the outbreak of war, had been transferred to the archives in Naples, were lost. This destruction explains the note in Inventory No. 322 in Venice.

A postwar addition consists of the return of most of the papers that Francis II sent away in 1860. Eventually they were housed in the Bourbon villa in Munich. During the Second World War all but one van load had been transferred for safe-keeping from the Bourbon villa to the Hohenschwangau castle. A German order forbade the van's departure. Later the Bourbon villa was destroyed in an air raid. During the postwar conversations about the transfer of the papers to Naples, it was said that the van, not allowed to proceed, contained most of the correspondence between the kings and their ambassadors. Italy obtained the return of the remaining papers to Naples, where they arrived in 1953. They have been arranged in the archives and an inventory printed. One part consists of thirty-one registers of Bernard Tanucci's correspondence from 1759 to 1774. Another part, the archives of various legations, contains correspondence from Berlin, Brussels, London, Madrid, and other capitals, of varying dates from 1778 to 1860.

For negotiations after 1815, see Nos. 75-78.

ARCHIVIO DI STATO IN PARMA

HISTORY

In 1592 Ranuccio I established the archives. Between 1621 and 1725, papers were brought to Parma from the Farnese palace in Rome and other family residences. After the death of the last Farnese ruler in 1731, Don Charles of Spain ruled Parma for three years. When he became king of Naples in 1734, he ordered that the Farnese papers be sent to Naples where they have remained.

From 1749 until the French revolution, Don Philip of Spain and his descendants ruled Parma.

CLASSIFICATION AND ARRANGEMENT

In spite of the loss of the Farnese papers, the present archives in Parma have a number of diplomatic papers. Inventories under the heading *Carteggio estero* list, for example, *Buste* numbered 6-85, France, 1359-1802; 86-101, Germany, 1472-1802; other countries and city-states are also listed. Under the heading *Corti e stati esteri*, 1741-1802, one part is the *Archivio du Tillot*, 1749-71; another, *Stato e affari esteri*, 1786-1802. Other diplomatic papers may be found for the period of Marie Louise's government, 1814-47, and, again, under the Bourbons, 1847-59.

ARCHIVIO DI STATO IN SIENA

HISTORY

The first enactments of the Sienese commune for the systematic preservation of its records go back to the beginning of the thirteenth century. These and other enactments adopted in subsequent centuries, were not fully respected. Official papers were allowed to lie in a disorganized state in several repositories, ranging from the Palazzo del Comune to selected monasteries. Lack of sound archival practices, unwise discarding policies of incompetent archivists, destructive raids by mobs, depredations by thieves, the usual dislocation of archival records during the Napoleonic period, and the transferral of a body of state papers to Florence after Siena's annexation to the grand duchy of Tuscany, all have contributed to a considerable diminution of the republic's archival patrimony, particularly in its earlier sections, up to the fourteenth century. It was only in 1858 that Grand Duke Leopold II of Tuscany provided for the centralization of the various repositories in the Palazzo Piccolomini, which remains the seat of the present *Archivio di Stato*. After the unification of Italy, the work of classification and reorganization began in a systematic way. In the last seventy years, and especially in the last twenty, several excellent inventories have been published, including a two-volume guide inventory of the entire collection (No. 80). In this respect, the *Archivio di Stato di Siena* has been one of the most active among Italian state archives.

This work of reorganization, and the publication of relative inventories, have served to highlight the historical significance of Siena's diplomatic files from the second half of the fifteenth century onwards, sources that hitherto had been most difficult to use and almost totally neglected. For, despite the republic's secondary importance in the diplomatic chessboard, its diplomacy assumed great significance at certain times in the last century of its independence, such as during the pontificate of the

Sienese pope, Pius II (1458-64) and in periods when Siena was trying desperately to fend off annexation attempts by Naples, Spain, the Empire, France, and Florence. At these times especially, the reports of Sienese diplomats provide another dimension in the analysis of Italian and European diplomacy, and they often fill the gaps in the collections of other states. On the other hand, Sienese dispatches on the whole do not have the crucial importance of those arriving at principal centers of power, nor do Sienese ambassadors have the same access to influential court circles often enjoyed by their colleagues of other second rank states like Mantua and Ferrara. For these reasons, and because of the availability of excellent printed inventories, we can be relatively brief in describing Sienese diplomatic holdings.

CLASSIFICATION AND ARRANGEMENT

Sienese diplomatic records form principally two general *fondi* — *Concistoro* and *Balia* — an arbitrary division made by earlier archivists. The *Concistoro,* a body of officials varying in size from nine to thirty-six, constituted the supreme magistracy, or *Signoria,* until the fall of the republic in 1555, when it was transformed into a judicial court of appeal. The *Balia,* on the other hand, was in origin a temporary commission of varying size, appointed generally by the General Council and/or the *Concistoro* from the thirteenth century onwards to carry out specific tasks normally requiring speed and secrecy in deliberation. One of these special commissions, or *balie,* created in 1455 gradually began to assume permanence and acquire an executive role independent of the *Concistoro* until it too was transformed into a purely administrative commission after 1555. For the series of documents comprising both *fondi,* we have two recently published inventories which also include brief sketches of the history and development of both magistracies (Nos. 81 and 82).

Within the *Concistoro fondo,* the series labeled *Carteggio* contains incoming internal and external correspondence addressed to the *Concistoro* by officials, as well as by ambassadors and foreign rulers. The letters are filed loosely in folders, which are bound in volumes or registers (Regs. 1773-2110, 1235-1572). Outgoing, internal, and external correspondence was similarly filed and bound in the series *Copialettere* (Regs. 1595-1769, 1363-1555). Important letters from heads of state and key treaties and conventions were copied in special registers, the *Copiari,* of which only three have survived (Regs. 1770-1772, 1400-1483). However, other copies, as well as originals, of these treaties can be found in two series within the *Diplomatico fondo* — the *Riformagioni* (around six thousand parchments, 814-1790), and the *Capitoli,* consisting of 274 fascicles and registers. A miscellaneous collection, known as *Legazioni e Commissarie,* contains credentials, instructions, envoys' copybooks, records of appointments of Sienese ambassadors, as well as originals and copies of diplomatic documents emanating from foreign chanceries. This is a rather disorganized series in which the twenty-odd registers contain documents spanning long periods of time, not necessarily in consecutive order. Cipher keys are collected in the *Cifrari e lettere cifrate* (Filza 2308, XIV-XVI centuries). Finally, the summary records, *Deliberazioni,* of the meetings of the *Concistoro* (Regs. 1-1399, 1338-1808) may be consulted during periods of diplomatic crisis, although they do not record the various opinions expressed. These can be integrated with the notes taken by notaries at these meetings, known as *Memoriali,* (Regs. 1400-1564, 1386-1580), which often contain additional details.

The diplomatic series of the *fondo Balia* parallel those of the *Concistoro,* since the two *fondi* were originally combined into one. We need only list them up to 1555: *Carteggio* (Regs. 488-780, 1455-1556); *Copialettere* (Regs. 396-474, 1455-1560); *Deliberazioni* (Regs. 1-163, 1455-1556); and the *Lupinari* (Regs. 257-323, 1480-1556), which contain the notarial notes of the meetings of the *Balia.*

ARCHIVIO DI STATO IN TURIN

HISTORY

In contrast to other Italian states, the House of Savoy did not begin to send resident ambassadors until after 1553, during the reign of Emmanuel Philibert. As early as 1351 Amadeus VI forbade entrance to the archives without his permission. In 1549 Charles III provided for the inspection of an official's residence, after his death, in order to prevent state papers from remaining in private collections. Both of these regulations were repeated by Victor Amadeus II in 1717 and 1720. His son and successor continued this interest in a striking way. Within six months after his accession, Charles Emmanuel III asked Philip Iuvara to submit plans for an archives building. Three years later, in 1734, it was completed and the documents were moved. With the exception of the years 1804-14, and during a portion of the 1940s, the papers that were transferred in 1734 have remained there until today, as have most of the subsequent papers to 1861.

In 1742 Charles Emmanuel III issued regulations regarding diplomatic papers. Ambassadors had to take an oath to give all their papers to the secretary for foreign affairs within a month after their return: that is, all copies of their letters written to the court and the original letters received from the court. Also, within the month, returning ambassadors were to submit reports of their missions. This was not an entirely new idea. A number of diplomats from the time of Charles Emmanuel I had prepared reports, but this part of the 1742 regulation was not always followed. After three years all such papers were transferred from the ministry to the archives, unless the papers pertained to unfinished business.

To such supervision can be attributed the rarity of gaps in these records. According to Nicomede Bianchi, director of the archives, 1870-86, the regulations were closely followed until 1797, but were not as carefully adhered to after 1815. Both the practice after the latter date and the unification of Italy affected the archives. In

1856 the rule was made that papers pertaining to ordinary matters must be transferred to the archives after five years, and papers pertaining to diplomatic questions transferred after ten years. This regulation meant that, with the changing of the seat of government to Florence in 1865 and to Rome in 1871, some of the papers were also moved. Some were returned to Turin after 1871, but not all. There is, therefore, a close relation between the archives in Turin and the archives of the ministry of foreign affairs in Rome for the years 1815–61.

CLASSIFICATION AND ARRANGEMENT

The diplomatic papers have been classified as *Materie politiche relative all'Estero,* with four subdivisions. The two most important subdivisions are *Lettere dei Ministri* and *Negoziazioni.* The *Lettere dei Ministri* are the ambassadors' orignial letters and the originals or copies of the court's replies, which are filed chronologically for each country in packetrs numbered consecutively. This subdivision contains very few enclosures sent by the envoys. If there are any missing letters, the copies in letter books, called *registri,* may be consulted. While these copies indicate what was put in cipher in the original, they do not indicate which letters were written by the ambassador and which by his secretary, as the originals do.

A newly-appointed ambassador received official instructions, letters to the sovereign and other members of the court to which he was accredited, and other papers. Upon the return of an ambassador, he usually submitted a report or *relazione.* All these instructions, copies of letters, lists, and reports are filed together, according to countries, in the subdivision *Negoziazioni.* If the instructions for only one ambassador are read, too narrow a view may be the result. What was old in the instructions may be found by comparing them with those to his predecessor. New instructions may be identified by the report of a predecessor.

Some of the enclosures sent by ambassadors were kept with their letters. Those that concerned the internal affairs of the foreign court were filed in a third subdivision, *Corti straniere*. For example, ambassadors in London sent pamphlets, parliamentary journals, reports of the national debt, copies of treaties, or correspondence with a third state. Such enclosures are by no means uniform or complete, and they are not always endorsed but they should not be neglected. Another subdivision is that of *Trattati nazionali ed esteri*, which is less important because of the printed edition of treaties.

The majority of the papers are logically filed. There are, however, a few special warnings. Some papers in *Negoziazioni* may be in a packet of miscellaneous items, generally the last one in a series. There may be supplementary papers in *Negoziazioni* and *Corti straniere*, which are called simply addition or first addition, second addition, final addition. Also, some packets may have two series of numbers.

There are many handwritten inventories. Those most important for diplomatic affairs are as follows: For the first subdivision, one should consult No. 151, *Indice del Carteggio diplomatico, Lettere dei Ministri*. This inventory consists of five parts, of which only the first two are valuable. The first lists for each foreign state, the ambassadors' dispatches from the early sixteenth century to 1814, the court's replies, and packet numbers. The second part contains similar information for 1814 to 1861. There are several inventories for the subdivision *Negoziazioni*; for example, No. 94, *Inventario delle Negoziazioni con Inghilterra e Olanda — Materie politiche*. For England, this inventory lists the items for 1281, 1554, 1603, etc., to 1794, with a brief summary that indicates the contents of each. Another inventory that supplements the preceding group is No. 165, *Carte politiche diverse, 1713–1860*. For the third subdivision, there are two parts in No. 100, *Inventario delle Scritture relative alle Corti straniere* and *Inventario d'Addizione delle Scritture relative alle Corti straniere*. (See Library of Congress films.)

Family papers given to the archives should be examined; some of these may be still in the hands of families in Turin or in

Piedmont. For post-1815 studies, the archives of the *Museo del Risorgimento* may have papers that supplement the archives. For negotiations after 1815, see Nos. 91–100.

ARCHIVIO DI STATO IN VENICE

HISTORY

In 1815 a decree from Vienna provided for a union of all the documents that were in three depositories. After 1822 they have been housed in the secularized monastery that adjoins the church of *Santa Maria Gloriosa dei Frati*. In 1866 many papers were taken by governmental order to Vienna, but all these, as well as others that had been taken after 1797 (and also those taken to Paris), were returned.

Of all the documents regarding Italian diplomacy, those in Venice have been the most famous, owing in part to the long period that the Republic maintained diplomatic relations, from before 1268 to 1797. As early as 1268, the Republic issued a law that required each ambassador, upon returning from a mission, to make a report (No. 127). In 1425 a law required that the report be written, and a law in 1533 repeated this stipulation. From these laws the renowned reports, or *relazioni*, have resulted. Despite an effort to maintain secrecy, copies of a number of the reports were made and may be found in various cities of Europe. There are many variations in some copies. Second- and third-hand copies may account for the variations.

While Austria still ruled Venice, the fame of the reports burst forth again as in the days of independent Venice. Ranke is justly accredited with this rebirth. In the 1830s, five volumes of reports were published by Luigi Cibrario, in Turin, Niccolò Tommaseo, in Paris, and Eugene Albèri, in Florence. Not one of these reports was from the Venetian archives. Albèri published nothing from the archives until 1855, using them in his last seven volumes (No. 101).

CLASSIFICATION AND ARRANGEMENT

The diplomatic papers are found in the archives of the College, the Senate, the Council of Ten, and the Inquisitors of State. The College prepared thé basic or formal instructions (*Commissioni*) for ambassadors, received letters from sovereigns (Lettere Principi), and admitted foreign ambassadors to audiences. After 1541 the records of these audiences were called *Esposizioni Principi* for all states except the papacy, which had its own subdivision, *Esposizioni Roma.* Prior to 1541 such records were filed under different headings, such as ambassadors, orators, France.

The archives of the Senate contain its deliberations, the dispatches from ambassadors, and their reports (No. 7). The deliberations were divided as *Misti,* 1293-1440; *Secreti,* 1401 (*sic*)-1630; and *Corti,* 1630-1797. A student's research is simplified if he is studying the last period, when foreign affairs were separated from domestic under the terms *Corti* and *Rettori,* respectively. In the earlier periods, a student must examine all papers to find those that are diplomatic. In the period of the *Misti,* the deliberations have been lost for 1293-1331, but an index of them remains. In the deliberations of the Senate are found the replies to ambassadors abroad or instructions supplementing the formal instructions.

After the invasion of Charles VIII, the Council of Ten became important in foreign affairs, and its papers may also help to fill the gaps between 1494 and 1554 in the dispatches to the Senate. Another source for the years 1496-1533 is the Sanuto diary. After 1579 the Inquisitors of state took an active part in foreign affairs. Letters to and from ambassadors abroad are in the separate archives of the Council of Ten and the Inquisitors.

The handwritten inventory of *Dispacci* has been published (No. 123). The inventory of *Relazioni* has received a new number, 322. The comments indicate whether the reports are still unedited or have been published. So recent a note as "destroyed at Naples, 30 September, 1943" reflects an unexpected effect of war (see the history of the archives in Naples, No. 73).

Some gaps may be filled by letterbooks of ambassadors and

copies of reports in the *Biblioteca Nazionale Marciana* and the *Museo Correr*. The latter has most of the Venetian family archives. The Querini-Stampalia library has the papers of some eighteenth century families, as well as other papers.

The *Fondazione Cini*, on the island of St. George, is gathering films of all papers dealing with Venetian history; for example, all the French and English dispatches sent from Venice. They may prove helpful to scholars who are reading dispatches from Paris and London.

ADMINISTRATION, REGULATIONS, AND SUGGESTIONS

THE ARCHIVI DI STATO AND LIBRARIES

Generally a passport is sufficient for permission to consult the inventories and documents, but sometimes a letter of introduction is requested; therefore, it is advisable to have one from the president of one's university that will be useful in archives and libraries.

Each archive has a reading room (*sala di studio*). Generally, requests for packets of papers (*mazzi, buste,* or *filze*) must be made the day before they are available. Generally, readers are limited to a number of packets per day, four in some archives. There are a few regulations which will be called to a reader's attention, such as the leaving of briefcases (also, purses sometimes) on a central table or in a checking room, the signing of a register each day or the signing of a register at departure each day in Venice, and the signing of a form in each packet consulted in Turin.

Each director decides the hours and annual closing; therefore, they are subject to change. Archives are generally open five hours from Monday through Friday, and fewer hours on Saturday. Generally, the annual closing is in August. Scholars should correspond with the director (or directors) about exact hours and annual closing, or unpleasant surprises may prevent a period of research.

Names of directors and addresses:

Florence	Prof. Guido Pampaloni	Uffizi Lunghi
Genoa	Prof. Domenico Gioffré	Via Tommaso Reggio 14
Lucca	Prof. Vito Domenico Tirelli	Palazzo Guidiccioni
Mantua	Dr. Giovanni B. Pascucci	Via Roberto Ardigò 11
Milan	Prof. Alfio Rosario Natale	Via Senato 10
Modena	Prof. Filippo Valenti	Corso Cavour 21
Naples	Prof. Jole Mazzoleni	Via del Grande Archivio 5
Parma	Dr. Maria Parente	Via Massimo D'Azeglio 45
Siena	Dr. Ubaldo Morandi	Via Banchi di Sotto 52
Turin	Count Gaetano Garretti	Via Alessandro Luzio 4
	di Ferrere	(Giardini reale)
Venice	Dr. Luigi Lanfranchi	Campo dei Frari 3002

Microfilming is done by a member of each archival staff, but a reader may experience some delay if there are many requests. There are some restrictions about filming, which will be explained by each archive.

Authors are expected to send a copy of a book or a reprint of an article to all archives whose materials have been used.

There is a library connected with each archives, but the shortness of the hours generally makes it more practical to use books in the *Biblioteca Nazionale* or other libraries in the late afternoon. The *Biblioteca Nazionale* of Florence and Rome have the word *Centrale* added. According to law, these two libraries receive copies of all books published in Italy, and a third copy is given to the main library of the region to which its subject matter applies. The main library in Milan, Naples, Turin, and Venice is also called *Biblioteca Nazionale*. There are other libraries in the cities, such as the *Biblioteca Reale* in Turin; the *Biblioteca di Storia Moderna e Contemporanea* in Rome. The latter has all the books published by the *Instituto Storico Italiano* of the University of Rome. The library and the institute are in the same building. Libraries also have annual closings, and sometimes shorter hours in the late summer or early fall.

In addition to the annual closings, all archives and libraries observe the following national and religious holidays. The national holidays: April 25, May 1, June 2, and November 4. The religious holidays: January 1, 6; March 19, Easter Saturday and Monday, Ascension Day (sixth Thursday after Easter), Corpus Christi (ninth Thursday after Easter), June 29, August 15-16, November 1-2, December 25-26 and, generally, 23, 24, 31. Each city has a patron saint, whose feast day is a holiday. Examples: June 24 in Florence, Genoa, Turin; September 19 in Naples, etc.

ARCHIVIO STORICO DEL MINISTERO DEGLI AFFARI ESTERI IN ROME

There are special statements to be made about receiving permission to consult papers in the *Archivio storico*. It is necessary to write a letter to the director stating the subject of research. This letter should be written well in advance of arrival in Rome. The reader should bring with him a letter of introduction from the president of his university, or in the case of a student, from his advisor. After arriving in Rome, a reader should telephone the archives office to make an appointment with the director. Upon arrival at the Ministry of Foreign Affairs, a reader must go to the Information Bureau to have a record made of the appointment, then he may proceed to the archive.

Papers of the last fifty years are not available for research. This restriction is offset, however, by the publication of documents for the years 1922-43 in *I documenti diplomatici italiani*, series 7, 8 and 9 (No. 9).

The address for the *Archivio storico* is *Ministero degli Affari Esteri*, Piazzale Farnesina. It is closed the entire month of August.

SUGGESTIONS ABOUT LIVING QUARTERS

The Touring Club Italiano and the Automobile Club d'Italia have a recommended list of hotels and pensions. The Touring Club publishes also comprehensive guides for all Italian cities ans special guides for Florence, Venice, Milan, Rome, and Naples. Michelin publishes a red guide for hotels and restaurants, and a green one for the monuments.

It is most advisable to make reservations in advance for a summer sojourn, especially in the large cities, by using air mail and sending international reply coupons for an air mail reply.

BIBLIOGRAPHY

Of capital importance for research in Italian archives are the following serial publications issued by the Ministero dell'Interno, Direzione Generale degli Archivi di Stato, Ufficio Studi e Pubblicazioni: *Pubblicazioni degli Archivi di Stato* (archival guides and inventories), 78 vols. published since 1951; *Pubblicazioni degli Archivi di Stato, Fonti e Sussidi*, 2 vols. since 1970; *Quaderni della Rassegna degli Archivi di Stato* (briefer guides, inventories, and miscellaneous archival aids), 41 vols. since 1960; *Rassegna degli Archivi di Stato*, 1954 — (successor to *Notizie degli Archivi di Stato* (1941-54). The Associazione Nazionale Archivistica Italiana, since 1968, has published the periodical, *Archivi e Cultura*, and a series of volumes, *Fonti e Studi*, all of which contain important archival studies. The following periodicals, all extinct, are also useful: *Revista delle Biblioteche e degli Archivi* (1895-1926); *Gli Archivi Italiani* (1914-21), succeeded by *Archivi. Archivi d'Italia e Rassegna Internazionale degli Archivi* (1933-61). An extensive bibliography of Italian publications on all phases of Italian archival organization and administration was published by Renato Perrella, *Bibliografia delle pubblicazioni italiane relative all'archivistica. Rassegna descrittiva e guida* (Quaderni della Rassegna degli Archivi di Stato, No. 24). Rome, 1963.

General Guides
1. *Gli Archivi di Stato italiani* ("Ministero dell'Interno, Ufficio centrale degli Archivi di Stato"). Bologna, 1944. A new edition is now being prepared, 1972-
2. *Archivum. Revue internationale des Archives*, XV (1965), published in 1969: "Italie," pp. 215-265 [includes descriptions of the *Archivio Centrale dello Stato* in Rome and of the *Archivi di Stato* in Florence, Genoa, Mantua, Milan, Naples, Palermo, Rome, Turin, and Venice].
2a. Bemis and Griffin, *Guide*. On Italian archives, pp. 937-939.
3. Camerani, Sergio. "Gli archivi italiani e la guerra in recenti pubblicazioni," *Archivio storico italiano* (1945-46), 196-200.
3a. Degras, *Soviet documents*. On Italy, pp. 27, 64, 109, 144, 175, 222.
4. Fish, Carl Russell. *Guide to the materials for American history in Roman and other Italian archives*. Washington, 1911.

5. Flammermont, Jules. "Rapport à M. le Ministre de l'Instruction publique sur les correspondances des agents diplomatiques étrangers en France avant la Révolution conservées dans les archives de Berlin, Dresde, Genève, Turin, Gênes, Florence, Naples . . . ," *Nouvelles archives des missions scientifiques et littéraires,* VIII (1896), 307-451.

6. Gómez Pérez, José. *Guía de los archivos de Estado italianos.* Madrid, 1961.

7. Ilardi, Vincent. "Fifteenth-century diplomatic documents in Western European archives and libraries (1450-94)," *Studies in the Renaissance,* IX (1962), 64-112.

8. Mazzoleni, Jole. *Manuale di archivistica, con appendice di note e fonti legislative.* Ed. by Catello Salvati. Naples, 1972.

Rome

Documents

9. *I documenti diplomatici italiani.* Issued by the Ministero degli Affari Esteri, Commissione per la Pubblicazione dei Documenti diplomatici. Rome: Libreria dello Stato, 1952-   There are nine series, each partially completed. Each volume has an individual editor.
   Series I. 1861-70. Vols. I-III, VIII.
   Series II. 1870-96. Vols. I-III, XXI.
   Series III. 1896-1907. Vols. I-III.
   Series IV. 1908-14. Vol. XII.
   Series V. 1914-18. Vol. I.
   Series VI. 1918-22. Vol. I.
   Series VII. 1922-35. Vols. I-VI.
   Series VIII. 1935-39. Vols. XII, XIII.
   Series IX. 1939-43. Vols. I-V.

Guides or Indexes of the Archivio Storico del Ministero degli Affari Esteri

10. Bacino, Francesco, ed. *La legazione e i consolati del Regno di Sardegna in Russia (1783-1861).* Vol. 5, Rome, 1952.

11. *Le legazioni sarde a Parigi, Berna, l'Aja, Lisbona e Madrid.* Vol. 3. Rome, 1951.

12. *Le scrittura del "Gabinetto Crispi" e le carte "Sonnino."* Vol. 7. Rome, 1955.

13. Mori, Renato, ed. *Le scritture della legazione e del Granducato di Toscana in Roma dal 1737 al 1859.* Vol. 8. Rome, 1959.

14. Moscati, Ruggero, ed. *Le scritture della Segreteria di Stato degli Affari Esteri del Regno di Sardegna*. Vol. 1. Rome, 1947.
15. *Le scritture del Ministeri degli Affari Esteri del Regno d'Italia dal 1861 al 1887*. Vol. 6. Rome, 1953.
16. Pastore, Mario, ed. *La legazione sarda in Londra (1730-1860)*. Vol. 4. Rome, 1952.
17. Piscitelli, Enzo, ed. *La legazione sarda in Vienna (1707-1859)*. Vol. 2. Rome, 1950.

Guides for the Medici period
18. Archivio di Stato di Firenze, *Archivio Mediceo avanti il Principato, Inventario* (*Archivi di Stato*, vols. 2, 18, 28, 50.). 4 vols. Rome, 1951-63. Vol. 5, index, is being published. *Archivio Mediceo del Principato, Inventario sommario*. (*Ibid.*, Vol. 1.). Rome, 1951. Reprint, 1966.

Documents, 1765-90
19. Pietro Leopoldo, *Relazioni sul governo della Toscana*, ed. by Arnaldo Salvestrini. (*Biblioteca di storia Toscana moderna e contemporanea*, Vol. 5.) 2 vos. Florence, 1969-70. Vol. 2 contains reports of his inspection visits to cities in the archduchy.

Documents, 1815-61
20. Filipuzzi, Angelo, ed. *Le relazioni diplomatiche fra l'Austria e il Granducato di Toscana*. (*Fonti per la Storia d'Italia*, Vols. 79, 84, 93, 96, 103.) Ser. 3, Vols. 1-5 (1849-59). Rome, 1966-69.
21. Saitta, Armando, ed. *Le relazioni diplomatiche fra la Francia, il Granducato di Toscana e il Ducato di Lucca*. (*Ibid.*, Vols. 40-41.) Ser. 2, Vols. 1-2 (1830-48). Rome, 1960.
22. ——— . *Le relazioni diplomatiche fra la Francia e il Granducato di Toscana*. (*Ibid.*, vols. 33-35.) Ser. 3, Vols. 1-3 (1848-60). Rome, 1959.

Documentary Collections
23. Ciasca, Raffaele, ed. *Istruzioni e relazioni degli ambasciatori genovesi, Spagna, 1494-1797*. (*Fonti per la Storia d'Italia*, Vols. 14, 20, 21, 30, 31, 83, 97.) Rome, 1951-68.
24. Colucci, Giuseppe, ed. *I Casi della Guerra, per l'Indipendenza d'America, narrati dall'ambasciatore della Republica di Genova presso la Corte d'Inghilterra (Francesco Ageno), nella sua corrispondenza ufficiale inedita*. 2 vols. Genoa, 1879.
25. Morandi, see No. 115.
26. Vitale, Vito, ed. *La diplomazia genovese. (La diplomazia italiana.)* Milan, [1941].

26a. ———. "I dispacci dei diplomatici genovesi a Parigi (1787-1793)," *Miscellanea di storia italiano,* LV (1935), 1-680.

Guides
27. Ilardi, *see* No. 7 above, pp. 107-9.
28. Vitale, Vito. "Diplomatici e Consoli della Repubblica di Genova," *Atti della Società ligure di Storia Patria,* LXIII (1934), 1-341. Sources in archives and bibliography for 1494-1814.

Lucca

Documentary Collections
29. Bongi, Salvatore, ed. *Ambasceria della Repubblica di Lucca a Enrico IV, Re di Francia.* Lucca, 1863.
30. Pellegrini, Amadeo, ed. *Relazioni inedite di ambasciatori lucchesi alla corte di Vienna (Secoli 17-18).* Lucca, 1901-3.
31. ———. *Relazioni inedite di ambasciatori lucchesi alle corti di Firenze, Genova, Milano, Modena, Parma, Torino (Secoli 16-18).* Lucca, 1901.

Guides
32. Bongi, Salvatore, ed. *Inventario del R. Archivio di Stato in Lucca.* 4 vols. Lucca, 1872-88. Lazzareschi, Eugenio, ed. Vol. 5. Pescia, 1934. Corsi, Domenico, ed. Vol. 6. *Archivi Gentilizi.* Lucca, 1961.

Mantua

Guides and Finding Aids
33. Archivio di Stato di Mantova. *Copialettere e corrispondenza gonzaghesca da Mantova e Paesi (28 novembre 1340-24 dicembre 1401). Indice,* ed. by G. Pratico, L. Mazzoldi, and G. Coniglio. Rome, 1969. (Pubblicazioni degli Archivi di Stato, No. LIX).
34. Luzio, Alessandro. *L'Archivio Gonzaga di Mantova.* Vol. II, *La corrispondenza familiare, amministrativa e diplomatica dei Gonzaga.* Verona, 1922.
35. Mazzoldi, Leonardo. "Guide all'Archivio Gonzaga. Le schede Davari," *Bollettino storico mantovano,* II, N. 8 (1957), 3-19.
36. Torelli, Pietro. *L'Archivio Gonzaga di Mantova.* Vol. I. Ostiglia, 1920.

Documentary Collection
37. Quazza, Romolo, ed. *La diplomazia gonzaghesca.* Milan, 1941. Small selection of diplomatic documents on key questions of

Mantuan foreign policy from the sixteenth and seventeenth centuries.

Milan

Guides and Finding Aids

38. Ancona, Amilcare. *Documenti sforzeschi provenienti dalla Raccolta Morbio.* Milan, 1884.

39. Fumi, Luigi. "L'Archivio di Stato in Milano al 1908. Notizie e proposte," *Archivio storico lombardo,* Ser. IV, XI (1909), 198-242.

40. Frati, Lodovico. I codici Morbio della R. Biblioteca di Brera. Forlí, 1897 (*Inventari dei manoscritti delle Biblioteche d'Italia,* ed. G. Mazzatinti, VII).

41. Ghiron, Isaia. "Bibliografia lombarda. Catalogo dei manoscritti intorno alla storia della Lombardia esistenti nella Biblioteca Nazionale di Brera," *Archivio storico lombardo,* VI (1879), 155-174, 367-397, 576-598; VII (1880), 41-72; IX (1882), 698ff.; X (1883), 736-768.

42. Manaresi, Cesare. *I Registri viscontei.* Milan, 1915. Repr. Milan, 1971. (*Inventari e regesti del R. Achivio di Stato in Milano,* Vol. I).

43. Mazzatinti, Giuseppe. *Inventario dei manoscritti italiani delle biblioteche di Francia.* 3 vols. Rome, 1886-88.

44. Natale, Alfio Rosario. "Archivio di Stato di Milano," *Archivum. Revue Internationale des Archives,* XV (1965), published in 1969, 234-242.

45. Porro, Giulio. *Catalogo dei codici manoscritti della Trivulziana.* Turin, 1884.

46. Raponi, Nicola. "Per la storia dell'Archivio di Stato di Milano. Erudizione e cultura nell'Annuario del Fumi (1909-1919)," *Rassegna degli Archivi di Stato,* XXXI, No. 2 (1971), 313-334.

47. Resti, Enrico. "Documenti per la storia della Republica Ambrosiana. (Regesto ragionato)," *Archivio storico lombardo,* Ser. VIII, V (1954-55), 192-266.

48. Santoro, Caterina. Comune di Milano. *Inventari e regesti dell'Archivio Storico Civico.* Vol. II, *I Registri delle lettere ducali del periodo sforzesco.* Milan, 1961.

49. ———. "Notizie su alcuni codici sforzeschi," *Atti e Memorie del Terzo Congresso Storico Lombardo* (1928). Milan, 1939, 47-51.

50. Vittani, Giovanni. *Gli atti cancellereschi viscontei.* Part I, Milan, 1920; Part II, *Carteggio Estero.* Milan, 1929. Repr. Milan, 1971 (*Inventari e regesti del R. Archivio di Stato in Milano,* Vol. II).

Documentary Collections

51. Cerioni, Lydia. *La diplomazia sforzesca nella seconda metà del Quattrocento e i suoi cifrari segreti*, 2 vols. Rome, 1970.

52. Gingins-la-Sarra, Fréderich de, ed. *Dépêches des ambassadeurs milanais sur les campagnes de Charles-Le-Hardi, duc de Bourgogne de 1474 à 1477*. 2 vols. Paris-Geneva, 1858.

53. Hinds, Allen B., ed. *Calendar of State Papers and Manuscripts Existing in the Archives and Collections of Milan*, Vol. I (1385-1618). London, 1912.

54. Ilardi, Vincent and Paul M. Kendall, eds. *Dispatches with Related Documents of Milanese Ambassadors in France and Burgundy, 1450-1783*. Vol. I, 1450-1460; Vol. II, 1460-1461. Athens, Ohio, 1970-1971.

55. Mandrot, Bernard de, ed. *Dépêches des ambassadeurs milanais en France sous Louis XI et François Sforza*, 4 vols. Paris, 1916-1923.

56. Natale, Alfio Rosario, ed. *Acta in Consilio secreto in castello Portae Jovis Mediolani*, 3 vols., 1477-1479. Milan, 1963-1969.

57. ———. *I Diari di Cicco Simonetta*, Vol. I. Milan, 1962.

58. ———. *Stilus Cancellariae. Formulario visconteo-sforzesco*, Vol. I. Milan, 1965.

59. Osio, Luigi, ed. *Documenti diplomatici tratti dagli Archivi milanesi*. 3 vols. Milan, 1864-77.

60. Santoro, Caterina. *Gli Offici di Milano e del Dominio visconteo-sforzesco (1216-1515)*. Milan, 1968.

61. ———. *Gli Uffici del Dominio Sforzesco (1450-1500)*. Milan, 1948.

Modena

Guides and Finding Aids

62. Archivio di Stato di Modena. *Archivio Segreto Estense, "Casa e Stato." Inventario*. Rome, 1953. (Pubblicazioni degli Archivi di Stato, No. XIII)

63. Dallari, Umberto. "Inventario sommario dei documenti della Cancelleria ducale estense (Sezione Generale) nell'Archivio di Stato di Modena," *Atti e Memorie della Regia Deputazione di Storia Patria per le Provincie Modenesi*, Ser. VII, IV (1927), 157-275.

64. Ognibene, Giovanni. "Le relazioni della Casa d'Este coll'estero," *Atti e Memorie della Regia Deputazione di Storia Patria per le Provincie Modenesi*, Ser. V, III (1903), 223-315.

65. Valenti, Filippo. *Panorama dell'Archivio di Stato di Modena*. Modena, 1963. (Scuola di Paleografia, Diplomatica e Archivistica dell'Archivio di Stato di Modena. Lezioni e Ricerche, I).

Documentary Collections

66. Dallari, Umberto. "Carteggio tra i Bentivoglio e gli Estensi dal 1401 al 1542 esistente nell'Archivio di Stato di Modena. Regesto," *Atti e Memorie della Regia Deputazione de Storia Patria per le Romagne,* Ser. III, XVIII (1900), 1-88, 285-332; XIX (1901), 246-372.

67. Del Piazzo, Marcello. *Il carteggio "Medici-Este" dal secolo XV al 1531. Regesti delle lettere conservate negli Archivi di Stato di Firenze e Modena.* Rome, 1964. (Quaderni della Rassegna degli Archivi di Stato, No. 34)

68. Foucard Cesare. "Fonti di storia napoletana dell'Archivio di Stato di Modena. Otranto nel 1480 e nel 1481," *Archivio storico napoletano,* VI (1881), 74-176.

69. Paladino, Giuseppe. "Per la storia della congiura dei baroni. Documenti inediti dell'Archivio Estense: 1485-1487," *Archivio storico per le provincie napoletane,* XLIV (1920), 336-367; XLV (1921), 128-151, 325-351; XLVI (1923), 221-265; XLVIII (1926), 219-290.

Naples

Articles and Guides

70. Archivio di Stato di Napoli. *Archivio Borbone, Inventario sommario (Archivi di Stato,* Vols. 43-44.) 2 vols. Rome, 1961, 1972. Vol. 1 important for diplomacy.

71. Cauchie, Alfred, and Van der Essen, Leon. *Inventaire des archives farnesiennes de Naples au point de vue de l'histoire des Pays-Bas catholiques.* (Academie Royale de Belgique, Commission Royale d'Histoire, Vol. 30). Brussels, 1911.

72. Coniglio, Giuseppe. "Carteggio superstiti della Segreteria di Stato borbonica degli affari esteri," *Rassegna storica del Risorgimento,* XXXIX (Jan. 1952), 30-37.

73. Pontieri, Ernesto. "Rovine de guerra in Napoli," *Archivio storico per le Province napoletane,* LXVIII (1943), 269-283.

Documentary Collections

74. Carignani, Giuseppe, ed. "Carteggio diplomatico tra il Marchese Tannucci e il Principe Albertini," *Archivio storico per le Province napoletane,* III (1878), 102-126, 211-232; IV (1879), 365-376, 497-515.

75. Coniglio, Giuseppe, ed. *Le relazioni diplomatiche fra il Regno delle Due Sicilie e il Regno de Prussia. (Fonti per la Storia d'Italia,* Vol. 71.) Ser. 3, only one vol. (1848-60). Rome, 1964.

76. Curato, Federico, ed. *Le relazioni diplomatiche fra il governo provvisorio siciliano e la Francia.* (*Ibid.*, Vol. 114.) Ser. 3, only vol. (1848-49). Rome, 1871.

76a. ———— . *Le relazioni diplomatiche fra il governo provvisorio siciliano e la Gran Bretagna.* (*Ibid.*, Vol. 113.) Ser. 3, only vol. (1848-49). Rome, 1971.

77. Moscati, Ruggero, ed. *Le relazioni diplomatiche fra l'Austria e il Regno delle Due Sicilie.* (*Ibid.*, Vol. 69.) Ser. 3, Vol. 2 (1859-61). Rome, 1964.

78. Saitta, Armando, ed. *Le relazioni diplomatiche fra la Francia e il Regno delle Due Sicilie.* (*Ibid.*, Vol. 78.) Ser. 2, Vol. 1 (1830-35). Rome, 1966.

Parma

Guides

79. Drei, Giovanni. *L'Archivio di Stato di Parma, Indice generale, storico, descrittivo ed analitico.* (*Bibliothèque des Annales Institutorum*, Vol. 6.) Rome, 1941.

Siena

Guides and Finding Aids

80. Archivio di Stato di Siena. *Guida-inventario dell'Archivio di Stato.* 2 vols. Rome, 1951 (*Pubblicazioni degli Archivi di Stato, V-VI*)

81. Archivio di Stato di Siena. *Archivio del Concistoro del comune di Siena. Inventario.* Rome, 1952. (Pubblicazioni degli Archivi di Stato, X).

82. Archivio di Stato di Siena. *Archivio di Balia. Inventario.* Rome, 1957. (Pubblicazioni degli Archivi di Stato, XXVI).

83. Bowsky, William M. "The Sienese Archive and the Pubblicazioni degli Archivi di Stato," *Manuscripta*, V (1961), 67-77.

84. Lisini, Alessandro. *Inventario delle pergamene conservate nel Diplomatico dall'anno 736 all'anno 1250.* Siena, 1908.

Turin

Documentary Collections

85. Manno, Antonio; Ferrero, Ermanno; and Vayra, Pietro, eds. *Relazioni diplomatiche della Monarchia di Savoia dalla prima alla seconda Restaruazione, 1559-1814.* (*Biblioteca storica italiana*, Vol. 4.) Turin, 1886-91.

86. Morandi, *see* No. 115.
87. Solar de la Marguerite, Clemente, ed. *Traités publics de la Royale Maison de Savoie avec les puissances étrangères depuis la Paix de Cateau-Cambrésis jusqu'à nos jours.* 8 vols. Turin, 1836-61.

Guides to the Archives

88. Bianchi, Nicomede. *Le materie politiche relative all'estero degli Archivi di Stato piemontesi.* Bologna, 1876. Must be used with care because of omissions, simplifications, and changes. Since its publication, legation archives have been sent to the *Archivio storico,* in Rome.
89. Buraggi, Gian Carlo. "Gli Archivi di Corte e la loro storica sede," *Atti della Reale Accademia delle Scienza di Torino,* LXXII, 2 (1936-37), 89-104.

Documentary Collections, 1815-61

90. Alberti, Mario degli, ed. *La politica estera del Piemonte sotto Carlo Ablerto, secondo il carteggio diplomatico del Conte Vittorio Amadeo Balbo Bertone di Sambuy, ministro di Sardegna a Vienna (1835-46). (Biblioteca di storia italiana recente,* Vols. 5-7.) Turin, 1913-19.
91. Curato, Federico, ed. *Le relazioni diplomatiche fra la Gran Bretagna e il Regno di Sardegna. (Fonti per la Storia d'Italia,* Vol. 121.) Ser. 1, Vol. 1 (1814-   ). Rome, 1972.
92. ———. *Le relazioni diplomatiche fra la Gran Bretagna e il Regno di Sardegna. (Ibid.,* Vols. 51, 52, 80, 88, 98.) Ser. 3, Vols. 1-5 (1848-56). Rome, 1961-69. Continued by Giarrizzo.
93. ———. *Le relazioni diplomatiche fra il Regno di Sardegna e la Gran Bretgna. (Ibid.,* Vols. 22, 23, 72, 73.) Ser. 3. Vols. 1-4 (1848-52). Rome, 1955-64.
94. Filipuzzi, Angelo, ed. *Le relazioni diplomatiche fra l'Austria e il Regno di Sardegna e la guerra del 1848-49. (Ibid.,* Vols. 53-54.) Ser. 3, Vols. 1-2 (1848-49). Rome, 1961. Continued by Valsecchi.
95. Giarrizzo, Giuseppe, ed. *Le relazioni diplomatiche fra la Gran Bretagna e il Regno di Sardegna. (Ibid.,* Vols. 59-61.) Ser. 3, Vols. 6-8 (1857-61). Rome, 1962. Continuation of Curato.
96. Nada, Narciso, ed. *Le relazioni diplomatiche fra l'Austria e il Regno di Sardegna. (Ibid.,* Vols. 70, 95, 106.) Ser. 1, Vols. 1-3 (1814-30). Rome, 1964-70. *Le relazioni diplomatiche fra l'Austria e il Regno di Sardegna. (Ibid.,* Vol. 122.) Ser. 2, Vol. 1, (1830-   ). Rome, 1972.
97. Saitta, Armando, ed. *La guerra del 1859 nei rapporti tra la Francia e l'Europa. (Ibid.,* Vols. 46-50.) Rome, 1960-61.

98. ———. *Le conferenze e la pace di Zurigo nei documenti diplomatici francesi. (Ibid.,* Vol. 74.) Rome, 1965.

99. ———. *La questione italiana dalle annessioni al Regno d'Italia nei rapporti fra la Francia e l'Europa. (Ibid.,* Vols. 89-92.) Ser. 3. Rome, 1968-69.

100. Valsecchi, Franco, ed. *Le relazioni diplomatiche fra l'Austria e il Regno di Sardegna. (Ibid.,* Vols. 66-67.) Ser. 3, Vols. 3-4 (1849-57). Rome, 1963. Continuation of Filipuzzi.

Venice

Documentary Collections

101. Albèri, Eugenio, ed. *Relazioni degli ambasciatori veneti al senato durante il secolo decimosesto.* 15 vols. Florence, 1839-63.

102. Arneth, Alfred Ritter von, and Fiedler, Joseph, eds. *Die Relationen der Botschaftes Venedigs über Österreich im achtzehnten Jahrhundert. (Fontes Rerum Austriacarum,* Vols. 22, 26, 27, 30.) Vienna, 1863-70.

103. Barozzi, Nicolò, and Berchet, Guglielmo, eds. *Relazioni degli stati europei letti al senato degli ambasciatori veneti nel secolo decimosettimo.* 10 vols. Venice, 1856-78.

104. Berchet, Guglielmo, ed. *Relazioni dei consoli veneti nella Siria.* Turin, 1866.

104a. Blass, Richard. *Dalla rivolta friuliana nell'autunno 1864 alla cessione del Veneto nel 1866.* A spese della Deputazione di storia patria per le Venezie. Venice, 1968. Mostly Austrian and Italian edited documents.

105. Brown, Rawdon, ed. *Four years at the court of Henry VIII, selection of despatches written by the Venetian ambassador, Sebastian Giustinian, and addressed to the Signory of Venice, January 12th, 1515, to July 26th, 1519.* 2 vols. London, 1854.

106. Brown, Rawdon; Brown, Horatio F.; and Hinds, Allen B., eds. *Calendar of state papers and manuscripts, relating to English affairs, existing in the archives and collections of Venice, and in other libraries of northern Italy.* 38 vols. London, 1864-1947.

107. Brunetti, Mario, and Vitale, Eligio, eds. *La corrispondenza da Madrid dell'ambasciatore Leonardo Donà (1570-73). (Fondazione Giorgio Cini, Fonti e Testi,* Ser. 2.) Florence, 1963.

108. Cibrario, Luigi, ed. *Relazioni dello Stato di Savoia negli anni 1574, 1670, 1743; scritte dagli ambasciatori veneti, Molino, Bellegno, e Foscarini.* Turin, 1830.

109. Cicogna, Emmanuele A., ed. "Dispacci al Senato veneto di Francesco Foscari e di altri oratori presso l'Imperatore Massimiliano

I nel 1496," *Archivio storico italiano*, Ser. 1, VII-2 (1844), 721-948, 1089-95.

110. Davis, James Cushman, ed. *Pursuit of Power. Venetian ambassadors' reports on Spain, Turkey, and France in the age of Philip II, 1560-1600.* New York, 1970.

111. Firpo, Luigi, ed. *Relazioni di ambasciatori veneti al senato, tratta dalle migliori edizioni disponibili a ordinato cronologicamente.* (*Monumenta politica et philosophica rariore*, Ser. 2, Vols. 8-11.) Turin, 1965-70.

112. Gaeta, Franco, ed. *Relations des ambassadeurs vénitiens.* (*UNESCO d'oeuvres représentatives*, Ser. 6.) Tr. by Jean Chuzeville. Paris, 1969.

113. Lazzarini, Vittorio, ed. *Dispacci di Pietro Cornaro, ambasciatore a Milano durante la Guerra di Chioggia.* (*Monumenti storici*, Ser. 1, *Documenti*, Vol. 20.) Venice, 1939.

114. Ljubic, Simeon, ed. *Commissiones et relationes venetae.* (*Monumenta spectantia historiam slavorum meridionalium*, Vols. 6, 8, 11.) Zagreb, 1876-80.

115. Morandi, Carlo, ed. *Relazioni di ambasciatori sabaudi, genovesi e veneti durante il periodo della Grande Alleanza e della Successione di Spagna (1693-1713).* (*Fonti per la Storia d'Italia*, Vol. 1 only.) Bologna, 1935.

116. Moscati, Ruggero, ed. *Relazioni degli ambasciatori veneti al senato (Secolo 18), Francia.* (*Fonti per la Storia d'Italia*, Vol. 11.) Rome, 1943.

117. Pasini, Luigi, ed. *I dispacci di Giovanni Michiel, ambasciatore veneto in Inghilterra (1554-1557).* Venice, 1869.

117a. *Il problema veneto e l'Europa, 1859-1866.* A cura dell'Istituto Veneto di Scienze, Lettere, ed Arti, 3 vols. Venice, 1966-67. Vol. I. *Austria*, by Richard Blaas; Vol. II. *Inghilterra*, by Noel Blakiston; and Vol. III. *Francia*, by Georges Dethan.

118. Segarizzi, Arnaldo, ed. *Relazioni degli ambasciatori veneti al senato.* (*Scrittori d'Italia*, Vols. 36, 49, 79, 80.) 3 vols. in 4. Bari, 1912-16.

119. Sneyd, Charlotte Augusta, ed. *A relation, or rather a true account, of the Island of England, with sundry particulars of these people and of the royal revenues under King Henry the Seventh, about the year 1500.* (The Camden Society, Vol. 37.) London, 1847.

120. Tommaseo, Niccolò, ed. *Relations des ambassadeurs vénitiens sur les affaires de France au XVIe siècle.* (*Collection de documents inedits sur l'histoire de France*, Ser. 1.) 2 vols. Paris, 1838.

Articles, Guides and Other Books

121. Andreas, Willy. *Staatskunet und Diplomatie der Venezianer im Spiegel ihrer Gesandtenberichte.* Leipsig, 1943.

122. Antonibon, Francesca. *Le relazioni a stampa di ambasciatori veneti. (Opera della bibliografie veneziana, Collana di bibliografie minori,* Vol. 1.) Padua,. 1939. This is a very important bibliography with annotations.

123. Archivio di Stato di Venezia, *Dispacci degli ambasciatori al Senato. Indice. (Archivi di Stato,* Vol. 31.) Rome, 1959.

124. Baschet, Armand. *Les archives de Venise, histoire de la Chancellerie secrète, le Senat, le Cabinet des Ministres, le Conseil des Dix et les Inquisiteurs d'Etat dans leurs rapports avec la France* .... Paris, 1870.

125. Da Mosto, Andrea. *L'Archivio di Stato di Venezia, Indice generale, storico, descrittivo ed analitico. (Bibliothèque des Annales Institutorum,* Vol. 5.) 2 parts. Rome, 1937-40.

126. Ilardi, *see No. 7.*

127. Queller, Donald E. *The office of ambassador in the Middle Ages.* Princeton, 1967.

10 LUXEMBURG

Willard Allen Fletcher
University of Delaware

Willard Allen Fletcher
University of Delaware

HISTORY

THE origins of the Luxemburg *Archives de l'Etat,* in terms of documentary collections, may be traced back to the medieval counts of Luxemburg. For the historian of diplomatic relations, the archival holdings become noteworthy with the advent of the Protestant Reformation and with the long power struggle between the Hapsburg and the Bourbon dynasties. Regrettably, the successive political domination of the Luxemburg territory by Burgundy, Spain, Austria, France, and the Netherlands resulted in the dispersal of Luxemburg's archival collections. The modern evolution of the *Archives de l'Etat* dates from the Congress of Vienna. Luxemburg, declared a grand duchy, was linked in personal union with the Netherlands in the person of William I, styled king grand-duke. The union was temporarily disrupted in the wake of the Belgian revolution and ended with the death of William III in 1890. Both the union of Luxemburg with the Netherlands and the loss of territory to Belgium, in consequence of the London Treaty of 1839, had adverse repercussions on the Luxemburg archives. Happily, the occupation of Luxemburg by Germany, in 1914–18 and 1940–44, did not result in significant permanent archival losses.

ORGANIZATION AND CLASSIFICATION

The major chronological periods into which the political archives are divided are the following:

A. Régime antérieur à 1795
B. Régime français et des Alliés de 1795 à 1815

212

C. Régime des Pays-Bas de 1815 à 1830–1839
D. Régime belge de 1830–1839
E. Régence du Pays 1839 à 1841
F. Cabinet du Référendaire et Chancellerie d'Etat à La Haye, 1830 à 1848
G. Régime constitutionnel de 1842 à 1856
H. Régime constitutionnel de 1857 à 1880
I. Budgets et Comptes des communes et etablissements publics, 1805
K. Traités et conventions (ratifications), arrangements et actes souverains
L. Secretariat du Roi Grand-Duc à La Haye
M. Conseil d'Etat, 1857–1910

Although the personal union between the Netherlands and Luxemburg remained until the expiration of the male line of succession in the Orange-Nassau line in 1890, it is customary to date the beginning of Luxemburg independence with the Treaty of London of 1839. Files of diplomatic correspondence predating that date which have remained in Luxemburg custody are relatively sparse. Dossiers on diplomatic relations, or external affairs, within each of the groups listed above vary greatly as to quantity.

Group A: A large and varied collection of treaties and conventions, extending from ca. 1300 to 1789, involving principally Luxemburg relations with the Holy Roman Empire, Spain, France, and member states of the Empire.

Group B: Dossiers include diplomatic correspondence concerning the incorporation of Luxemburg into the French state.

Group C: Included in this group are files on the decisions reached at the Congress of Vienna to transfer Luxemburg to the Dutch king. Additionally, there are files on the international repercussions of the Belgian Revolution, the membership of Luxemburg in the Germanic Confederation, and the control of the federal fortress of Luxemburg.

Group F: Diplomatic archives in this group pertain to Germanic Confederation matters, the Belgian Revolution, the partition of Luxemburg, the *Zollverein*, and the federal fortress of Luxemburg.

Group G: A large and varied collection of diplomatic files on external affairs, the Germanic Confederation, and the federal fortress of Luxemburg is included in the materials.

Group H: This group contains a very large and highly important collection of dossiers on the monumental events between 1866 and 1871. Material on the conflict in Germany in 1866–67, the dissolution of the Germanic Confederation, the French demands for compensations, the dismantlement of the federal fortress and neutralization of Luxemburg by the London Treaty of 1867, and on the Franco-Prussian War of 1870 is expecially useful.

Group K: The material in this group consists exlusively of a wide variety of treaties and conventions concluded between 1816 and 1910 with a large number of European and other states.

Group L: A small part of the dossiers pertain to negotiations concerning the dismantlement of the fortification system of Luxemburg-City.

Those archival collections which date from about 1890 are organized on the principle of provenance. Thus, files pertaining to external relations are grouped with those dossiers emanating from the Ministry of Foreign Affairs. These files, retired to the *Archives de l'Etat,* date to ca. 1940. Although the diplomatic archives are closed, in principle, for research beyond 1913, it is possible to obtain special permission to consult documents beyond that date.

The following list provides a summary of the dossiers within each of the major groups of diplomatic archives:

I. Maison grand-ducale
The collection covers the period 1783–1940 and includes material on the following subjects: House of Nassau, regency, succession, marriages, voyages, abdication, international relations.

II. Légations luxembourgeoises à l'étranger
The collection consists of diplomatic correspondence with missions in Paris, Brussels, The Hague, London, Berlin, Bern, and Washington, in the period 1875–1940.

III. Consulats luxembourgeois à l'étranger
The dossiers consist of correspondence, for the period 1917–40, with consulates in Metz, Maastricht, Longwy, Warsaw, Nantes, Paris, Aix-la-Chapelle, Berlin, Cologne, Dresden, Düsseldorf, Munich, Stuttgart, Wiesbaden Trier, Rio de Janeiro, Tokyo, Tientsin, Los Angeles, Chicago, New York, San Francisco, Prague, Biarritz, Amsterdam, Geneva, Bucharest, Vienna, Rome, Algeria, London, Rotterdam, Lisbon, Quebec, Bombay, Fribourg, Lausanne, Florence, Rabat, Ghent, and elsewhere.

VII. Légations étrangères à Luxembourg
These files, covering the period 1880–1940, contain diplomatic correspondence with foreign missions accredited to Luxemburg and physically located either in Luxemburg, Brussels, or The Hague. Among them are Liberia, Turkey, Russia, Vatican City, France, Finland, Hungary, Austria, Rumania, Portugal, Poland, the Netherlands, Norway, Japan, Great Britain, United States of America, Germany, Denmark, Belgium, Latvia, Yugoslavia,

Czechoslovakia, Lithuania, Chile, Egypt, Iran, Brazil, Greece, Spain, Bolivia, Albania, Honduras, Italy, and Argentina.

IX. Relations internationales

The dossiers, arranged by topics and covering the period 1880 to 1940, range over a very wide variety of subjects, such as matters of protocol, contacts with foreign dignitaries, political and economic affairs, Spanish Civil War, elections abroad, Italo-Ethiopian Conflict, Locarno treaties, international disarmament, propaganda, cultural relations, neutrality, League of Nations, German invasion of Luxemburg in 1914, Papal elections, international refugees, Saar Question, Balkan wars, and others.

X. Relations de voisinage

A small but very important collection of files, for the years 1890–1940, on agreements with France, Germany, and Belgium, relative to border traffic. Most of the material pertains to economic relations affecting the immediate border regions, regulations about river traffic, water rights, bridge construction, frontier incidents, exploitation of iron ore mines or farmlands along borders, canalization of the Moselle River, custom duties, and the like.

XI. Limites

A small collection of dossiers pertaining to minor frontier corrections, topographic surveys, and replacement of frontier markers.

XII. Passeports et Visas

A collection of dossiers, essentially covering the interwar period, on international travel documents, visas for temporary residence in Luxemburg, international agreements on citizenship, legislation governing passports and visas.

XV. Traités et Conventions

This is a very extensive collection of international

agreements, treaties, and protocols to which Luxemburg was a signatory during the years 1875–1940. They are organized in a number of subdivisions.

a) Legal agreements to facilitate matters of legal collaboration between states. They include accords on extradition, arbitration, exchange of legal data for judiciary affairs, imprisonment, citizenship, marriage and divorce, child custody, and others.

b) Agreements covering issues in the field of public health, drug traffic, medical training and practice, child protection, prevention of epidemics, and others.

c) Communication and work accords relative to air, rail, and road traffic and goods transportation, international communications and transmission systems, postal conventions, and others.

d) Administrative accords, mainly with neighboring states, on fishing and hunting rights, border rectifications, citizenship and naturalization, and others.

e) Agreements dealing with the after effects of war, such as prisoner exchange, care of sick and wounded, Red Cross activities, and others.

f) Economic and financial accords covering international trade, financial agreements, international payments, collaboration in research in a wide variety of fields, protection of wildlife, taxation, and others.

g) Agreements to protect copyrights, trademarks, works of art, and others.

h) Cultural agreements, designed to facilitate international collaboration in exhibits and exchanges of art works, cultural festivals, exchange of faculty members and students, and others.

i) Social and humanitarian agreements on such matters as repatriation, public assistance, and others.

j) Agreements concluded with foreign countries to protect the rights of Luxemburg subjects abroad in matters of citizenship, business affairs, judicial proceedings, military obligations, associations of Luxemburg subjects abroad, and others.

XVII.   Etrangers dans le Grand-Duché

These files pertain largely to the immigration of Italian workers recruited for the steel and iron industry, and cover such topics as social security, expulsion, political activity, and work conditions. A small number of dossiers deal with French and German workers in Luxemburg.

XVIII. Rapatriements

A small collection of files on repatriation of Luxemburg workers from abroad, and of foreign workers in Luxemburg to their homelands. Much of the material refers to the period 1910–19.

XIX.   Extraditions

A very small collection of material dealing with the issue of extradition between Luxemburg and France in the interwar period.

XX.   Assistance judiciaire

Reports, studies, and legislation dealing with the problem of cooperation with foreign states in legal cases.

XXI.   Etat civil

An important collection of dossiers, largely for the interwar period, on questions of citizenship and marriages between Luxemburg citizens and foreigners. With the approach of war, questions of citizenship raised by France and Germany created many problems.

XXII. Questions de nationalité

A small collection of dossiers on foreign, mainly French and German, legislation regarding citizenship.

XXIII. Bibliothèque et documentation

A very useful collection of reference materials in the field of international relations.

XXV. Décorations

A collection of dossiers, covering the period 1880 to 1940, on decorations awarded to foreigners, as well as on foreign decorations awarded to Luxemburg subjects.

XXVII. Departements ministériels

A collection of dossiers, primarily for the interwar period, on international agreements affecting various ministries and agencies of the Luxemburg government. Most of the material pertains to rail transportation.

XXXI. Comptabilité

A useful collection of budgetary information concerning the activities of the Luxemburg Ministry of Foreign Affairs, covering the period 1880–1935.

ADMINISTRATION, REGULATIONS, AND FACILITIES

The *Archives de l'Etat* are located in very excellent quarters at the Plateau du St. Esprit, near the center of Luxembourg-Ville. Admission is granted to researchers, upon identification and statement about research projects. Foreign scholars need not present letters of introduction; however, graduate students should present a letter of introduction from the dissertation advisor. Researchers are usually advised to discuss their research with the archivist, M. Antoine May, who will subsequently arrange for the release of documents. The researcher will have the use of a well-appointed reading room, with a reference collection readily accessible. Microfilm readers and printers are also available, and excellent reproduction facilities provide for quick service if microfilm or xerox copies of documents are ordered. Although French and German are the working languages of the staff, many of the members do speak English. Pre-1913 files on diplomatic history are open without restriction; for post-1913 material, authorization for access may be sought from the Ministry of Foreign Affairs, with the concurrence of the archivist. The archives are open Monday through Friday, except for legal holidays, from 9–12 A.M. and from 2:30–5:30 P.M.

BIBLIOGRAPHY

Although a number of finding aids have been published, the only guide to diplomatic files open without restriction to the researcher is Pierre Ruppert, *Les archives du gouvernement du Grand Duché de Luxembourg. Inventaires sommaires.* Luxemburg, 1910.

11 THE NETHERLANDS

D. P. M. Graswinckel
Formerly of the General State Archives, The Hague

and

Willard Allen Fletcher
University of Delaware

INTRODUCTION

THE Archive Service in the Netherlands was founded in 1802 when Hendrik van Wijn was appointed *archivarius* of the Batavian Republic. Satisfactory quarters for the General State Archives were obtained in 1854, the year in which the well-known historian, Dr. R. C. Bakhuizen van den Brink, was nominated state archivist. In the course of the second half of the nineteenth century public archival repositories were established in the provincial capitals, under the control of a state archivist. The supervision of these was entrusted to the keeper of the repository at The Hague, on whom the title of General State Archivist was conferred.

Gradually, the larger towns started to give greater care to their archives. Especially at the end of the nineteenth century and the beginning of the twentieth, a great deal of influence was exercised on the development of the Dutch Archives Service by the Netherlands Society of Archivists (*Vereniging van Archivarissen in Nederland*), founded in 1892.

The present organization of the state archives was regulated by the Archives Act of 1918 and by subsequent royal decrees which settled various aspects in detail. In the provincial capitals and larger towns the repositories are under the control of officials who must have passed a professional examination. For the state repositories as well as for the archives of the larger municipalities the law requires that the keeper hold a degree of *doctorandus* in history or law. In the small towns the care of the archives is left in the hands of the local secretary, who is subject to the supervision exercised by the professional archivist of the province.

ORGANIZATION AND CLASSIFICATION

Before discussing the organization of the General State Archives at The Hague certain facts peculiar to Dutch foreign relations should be pointed out. The assembly of the states general (1581-1795) consisted of deputies of the seven independent provinces, in whose councils all foreign affairs were likewise discussed. Thus, in order to obtain a profound knowledge of the foreign relations during that period, it is usually necessary that the researcher consult the archives of the provincial governments of Holland, Zeeland, Utrecht, Gelderland, Overijssel, Freisland, and Groningen, in addition to those of the states general.

In the days of the Republic of the United Provinces the maintenance of foreign relations belonged to the competence of the states general. However, one should not overlook that Holland, and particularly the states of that province along with the grand pensionary (originally called state advocate), exerted a considerable and often determinant influence on foreign policy. The dominant role of the province rests upon historical developments. Holland and Zeeland were delivered from the Spanish rule as early as 1572, whereas the other provinces were liberated some decades later. Thus, the two provinces maintained relations with foreign states well before their sister provinces. Furthermore, commercial interests played a prominent part in Dutch foreign affairs, and commerce was largely concentrated in Holland. Finally, Holland contributed more than half toward the charges of the generalty and therefore was entitled to a great deal of influence in foreign policy. The unusual constitution of the

Republic gave no special place to "foreign affairs" and therefore tended to maintain the prominent role of the province of Holland. It was not unusual that foreign affairs were discussed first of all in the states of Holland. Only after that was it ascertained whether the other provinces had objections, whereupon the matter would be taken up by the states general. It is obvious then that the resolutions of the states of Holland are often of prime importance for the study of Dutch foreign affairs prior to 1795.

The archives and collections that make up the General State Archives consist of three major sections. The first of these contains the materials from the department of the generalty: the states general, the council of state, the chamber of accounts of the generalty, and the admiralties. These collections generally extend down to March 1, 1796, when the Batavian Republic and its national assembly replaced the Republic of the United Provinces and the college of its states general. Two other major groups within the first section contain documents pertaining to the colonial administration and to the administration of the demesne lands of the house of Nassau. The second section contains all the archives of the unified state and its departments—the Batavian Republic, the kingdom of Holland, the governor-general of the Dutch departments, the sovereign principality, and the kingdom of the Netherlands—insofar as these archives have been transferred to the States General Archives. The third section is analogous to the state archives of a province—in this case the province of South Holland—although it is to be noted that the archives of the states of Holland and of other bodies that held authority over the whole of Holland, have been stored there.[1]

Archives and Collections of the First Section (United Provinces 1576-1796)[2]

   A.   *Archieven der Staten-Generaal* 1576-1796
       1. *Hoofdarchiev:*
          Resolutions (ordinary and secret) 1576 (1592)-1796;

[1] Pp. 8-9 of No. 6.
[2] Pp. 5-27 of No. 12.

dispatches (ordinary and secret) and copybooks concerning peace conferences of Münster, Cologne, Nijmegen, Utrecht, Soissons, Aix-la-Chapelle, 1643–1748; concerning Belgium (Austrian Netherlands) 1716–94, Denmark 1679–1796, England 1576–1795, France 1578–1796, German Empire (Austria, Brandenburg-Prussia, and minor clerical and temporal principalities) 1576–1795, III Italy 1594–1795, Poland 1579–1772, Portugal 1641–1795, Russia 1589–1794, Spain 1589–1794, Spain (Spanish Netherlands) 1649–1796, Sweden 1591–1796, Switzerland 1582–1796, Turkey and Barbary States 1596–1795, United States of North America 1782–95.

2. *Vervolg van hiet Archief der Staten-Generaal:*
Ciphers, loose documents, papers from clerk Fagel, papers from clerk Nieuwenhuizen (sixteenth–eighteenth century).

3. *Loketkas:*

Loose documents and files, classified in the same order as the dispatches 1576–1700.

4. *Secrete Kas:*
Secret documents, treaties, and ratifications, classified in the same order as the dispatches 1576–1700.

5. *Tractaten en Ratificatiën sedert* 1700:
Original treaties in chronological order 1700–97; original ratifications classified in order of the countries 1701–97.

6. *Aanhangsel: Legatie- en Consulaatsarchieven:*

a. *Hoofdbestanddeel*
Reports (*Verbalen*) of missions to peace conferences; reports of special and ordinary missions to foreign courts, as well as reports intended for the record office of the States-General; documents originating from Dutch embassy archives, formed and maintained abroad; etc.

b. *Archief van het Nederlandse consulaat te Smyrna, nopel,* 1612-1784

c. *Archief van het Nederlandse consulaat te Smyrna,* 1611-1817

d. *Archief van het Nederlandse consulaat-generaal te Tanger,* 1685-1835

e. *Archief van het Nederlandse consulaat te Tunis,* 1736-1813

B. *Archief van de Landraad van deze zijde van de Maas,* later *Raad van State,* 1581-1795

C. *Stukken behorende tot het Archief van de Stadhouderlijke Secretarie en Kabinet*
See also Royal House Archives. Correspondence with Dutch and foreign diplomats and deciphered secret correspondence of the Prussian ministers in London and at The Hague and of the French ambassadors at The Hague 1751 (1755)-91

D. *Archieven van de Companiën op Oost-Indië,* 1594-1603

E. *Archieven van de vereenigde Oost-Indische Compagnie,* 1602-1796

F. *Archieven van de Staatscommissie voor de zaken der Oost-Indische Compagnie,* 1790-95 and *van het Comité tot de zaken der Oost-Indische Compagnie,* 1795-96

G. *Stukken,* in 1862-63, *uit Batavia naar Nederland gezonden, voornamelijk betrekking hebende op het bestuur der hoge regering te Batavia over de Buitenkantoren,* 1602-1827

H. *Bescheiden der voormalige Nederlandse Bezittingen in Voor-Indië (Residentie Bengalen, Opperhoofdij Coromandel en Madura, Residentie Suratte),* 1703-1826

I. *Archief van der Nederlandse factorij te Canton,* 1739-1828

J. *Archief van der Nederlandse factorij in Japan,* 1609-1890

K. *Archieven ven de eerste West-Indische Compagnie,* 1621-74

L. *Archieven van de tweede West-Indische Compagnie,* 1674-1795

M. *Archieven van de Direktie ad interim der West-Indische coloniën*, 1791–92, and *van de Raad der Koloniën in West-Indië*, 1792–95

N. *Archief van de Directie van Berbice*, 1720–95

O. *Archief van de Societeit van Suriname*, 1683–1795

P. *Verzameling verspreide West-Indische Stukken*, 1614–1795

Q. *Archieven van der Nederlandse West-Indische Bezittingen en van Suriname*, 1669–1845 (1876)

R. *Stukken behorende tot archieven, die nog in Nederlands West-Indië en Surinam berusten*, 1829–1911

S. *Archieven van de Nederlandse Bezittingen ter Kuste van Guinea*, 1658–1872

T. *Familiearchieven en andere Verzamelingen:*

Van Aerssen, sixteenth–seventeenth century

> Papers of Cornelis van Aerssen, clerk of the States General; papers of François van Aerssen, ambassador at the courts of France and England

Van Aitzema, 1625–69

> Papers of Leo van Aitzema, resident of the Hanse towns in The Netherlands Boreel, seventeenth–nineteenth century

> Papers of Willem Boreel concerning various diplomatic missions; papers of Jacob Boreel Jansz., ambassador at the court of England

Boreel de Mauregnault, 1667–72

> Johan Boreel, ambassador at the court of England

Brantsen, 1782–1808

> Papers of Gerard Brantsen, ambassador at the court of France

Calkoen, 1745–46

> Papers of Cornelis Calkoen, envoy to the king of Poland, to the elector of Saxony

Van der Capellen van de Poll, 1767–84

> Papers of J. D. van der Capellen van de Poll, supporter of American independence

Van Citters, 1621 (1540)–1694

Papers of Arnout van Citters, ambassador at the court of England

Dumas, 1776 (1700)–95

Papers of C. W. F. Dumas, secret agent of the American Congress during the American Revolution and later chargé d'affaires of the United States

Fagel, 1640–1881

Papers of Gaspar Fagel, clerk of the States General and afterward grand-pensionary of Holland; papers of François Fagel, Sr., clerk of the states general; papers of Hendrik Fagel, Sr., clerk of the states general; papers of François Fagel, Jr., second clerk of the states general; papers of Hendrik Fagel, Jr., second clerk of the states general; papers of Jacob Baron Fagel, envoy at the courts of Denmark and England; papers of Robert Baron Fagel, envoy at the court of France.

De Groot, 1606–67

Papers of Hugo de Groot, ambassador of Sweden in Paris, former legal adviser of the East India Company; papers of Willem de Groot

Van Hill, 1672–75

Papers of Govert van Hill, secretary to various envoys

Ortel, 1581–90

Papers of Joachim Ortel, Dutch agent in England

De Witt, 1670–71

Papers of Johan de Witt Johansz., ambassador to Denmark, Danzig, and Poland

U. *Losse Aanwinsten, 1820–heden:*

Aanw. 1831 A I. Original letters addressed to the Swedish envoys in Paris, 1711–64

Aanw. 1882 A VI. Journal of a member of a Dutch embassy to Dresden and Warsaw, 1744–45

Aanw. 1883 A V. Copy of the correspondence of Mozes de Montaigne, Dutch agent at Frankfurt, 1688–89

Aanw. 1888 26. Report on a mission of Boelensz. co. to the court of Denmark, 1607

Aanw. 1891 nr. 7. Letters from Paris by Abraham de Wicquefort, 1645–47, 1651–53

Aanw. 1899 XXIII 13. Journal of the ambassadors François van Aerssen and Caspar van Vosbergen at the court of France, 1628–29

Aanw. 1902 XIV 8. Report on the embassy of Aerssen and Vosbergen at the court of France, 1628–29

Aanw. 1911 XV 6–9. Notes of Gerard Schaep concerning treaties and foreign relations in the seventeenth century

Aanw. 1915 XV 1, 2. Journal of Thomas Hees, resident at Algiers, 1675–80

Aanw. 1929 XIII 2. Documents concerning difficulties with Denmark over the Icelandic fishery, 1740–41

Aanw. 1930 XI 1. Correspondence of Pieter de Groot with Abraham de Wicquefort, 1672–74

Aanw. 1948 First Section III. Correspondence and notes of Professor J. E. Heeres about the sovereignty of Miangas, 1918–19

Archives and Collections of the Second Section[3]

  A. *Archieven van 1795/96 tot 1813:*

      I. *Archieven van de (zo genoemde) Wetgevende Colleges, 1796–1801*

     II. *Archief van het Wetgevend Lichaam, 1801–10*

    III. *Archief van de Staatsraad, 1805–10*

    IV. *Archieven van de met de taak der Rekenkamer belaste instanties, 1796–1810*

     V. *Archieven van het Uitvoerend Bewind, 1798–1801*

    VI. *Archief van het Staatsbewind, 1801–5*

   VII. *Archief van de Raadpensionaries, 1805–6*

  VIII. *Archief der staatssecretarie van het Koninkrijk Holland, 1806–11*

[3] Pp. 31–67 of No. 12.

IX. *Archief van de Prins-Stedehouder van de Keizer van Frankrijk in te Hollandse Departementen, 1810–13*

X. *Archieven van het Ministerie van Buitenlandse Zaken, 1795–1810*

XI. *Archieven van Nederlandse Gezantschappen en Consulaten, 1795–1810:*

   1. Duitse Rijk (Wenen), 1786–1808

   2. Keurvorstendommen Keulen, Mainz, en Münster, de Opper- en Nederrijnse Kreits en de Westfaalse Kreits (Mainz), 1778–1800

   3. Pruisen (Berlijn), 1795–1810

   4. Hanzesteden (Hamburg), 1795–1809

   5. Hessen-Kassel (Kassel), 1796–1804

   6. Württemberg (Stuttgart), 1797–1809

   7. Baden (Mannheim) (Karlsruhe), 1807–9

   8. Denemarken (Kopenhagen), 1793–1809

   9. Zweden (Stockholm), 1795–1806

  10. Rusland (St. Peterburg), 1791–1810

  11. Frankrijk (Parijs), 1795–1810

  12. Portugal (Lissabon), 1802–4

  13. Spanje (Madrid), 1795–99

  14. Turkije (Konstantionpel), 1741–1811

  15. Noord-Amerika (Philadelphia), 1795–1801

  16. Antwerpen (consulaat), 1804–10

B. *Archieven van 1813 tot begin 20e eeuw:*

   I. *Archief van de Algemene Staatssecretarie en het Kabinet de Konings, 1813–97*

  II. *Archief van de Raad van Ministers, 1823–1920*

 III. *Archieven van het Ministerie van Buitenlandse Zaken, 1813–70*

 IV. *Archieven van Commissies en andere bijzondere organen, ressorterende onder het Departement van Buitenlandse Zaken:*

   1. *Regeling der grensscheiding tussen Nederland en Pruisen en Hannover, 1815–27*

2. *Conferentie te Londen tot regeling der aangelegenheden van Nederland en België*, 1830-39
3. *Liquidatie met Oostenrijk*, 1828
4. *Regeling van de grensscheiding tussen Nederland en Pruisen*, 1816-68
5. *Regeling van de grensscheiding tussen Nederland en Hannover*, 1819-69
6. *Regeling grensscheiding Nederland-België*, 1839-52, 1864-69
7. *Regeling grensscheiding Nederland-Frankrijk*, 1816-26
8. *Commissaries grensregeling Nederland-Frankrijk*, 1816-26
9. *Scheidsgerecht Oostenrijk-Hongarije*, 1922-23

V. *Archieven van Nederlandse Gezantschappen:*
   1. Groot-Brittanië en Ierland, 1814-1914
   2. Frankrijk, 1814-84
   3. Duitse Bond en Frankfort, Hessen, en Keur-Hessen , 1816-67
   4. Oostenrijk, 1814-42
   5. Pruisen, 1814-1900
   6. Beieren, Württemberg, en Baden, 1814-67
   7. Saksen, 1828-56
   8. Hanzesteden (Hamburg, Bremen, en Lübeck), 1815-41
   9. Hannover, 1838-66
   10. Denemarken, 1815-62
   11. Zweden en Noorwegen, 1814-62
   12. Zweden, Noorwegen, en Denemarken, 1863-1910
   13. Rusland, 1814-90
   14. Turkije en de Levant, 1814-57
   15. Kerkelijke Staat, 1826-30 (the archives for the period 1842-70 are in the Vittorio Emmanuele Library in Rome)

16. Toscane, 1826-28
17. Sardinië, 1818-55
18. Zwitserland, 1817-1915
19. Spanje, 1814-1913
20. Portugal en Brazilië, 1815-21
21. Portugal, 1823-98
22. Brazilië, 1826-33
23. België, 1839-90
24. Italië, 1875-1910
25. Noord-Amerika (Verenigde Staten), 1814-1909
26. Argentinië (tevens consulaararchief), 1880-1919
27. Japan, 1870-90
28. Perzië, 1890-1906
29. Roemenië, 1889-1910
30. Servië, 1903-11

VI. *Archieven van Nederlandse Consulaten en Vice-Consulaten:*
1. Alexandria (Ver. Staten), 1815-25
2. Athene (Nauplia), 1840-43
3. Berlijn, 1867-77
4. Bern, consulaat-generaal (tot in 1867 ook van Luxemburg), 1832-1915
5. Bern, consulaat-generaal van Luxemburg, 1880-90
6. Bern, vice-consulaat, 1865-89
7. Bordeaux, 1873
8. Buenos Aires (cf. legatie Argentinie)
9. Caracas, 1859-77
10. Coruna, 1831-86
11. Cyprus, 1829-31
12. Elmina, 1827-80
13. Genève, 1850-1915
14. Guatamala, 1853-59
15. Kanea, 1828-33
16. Lausanne, 1892-94

17. Lissabon, 1814–61
18. Londen, 1814–99
19. Mogador, 1845–97
20. Mozambique, 1874–769321. Nagasaki (Desima), 1860–1908
22. New York, 1855–1911
23. Ningpoo, 1868–1908
24. Penang, 1872–1908
25. Philadelphia, 1869–1903
26. Rio de Janeiro, 1826–31 (cf. legatie Brazilie)
27. Singapore, 1863–1905
28. Stockholm, 1821–1920
29. Tanger, 1830–1907
30. Truxillo, 1826–34
31. Tunis, 1814–64
32. Yokohama, 1860–70
33. Zurich, 1850–74

VII. *Archieven der Nederlandse Overzee Trust Maatschappij*, 1914–19

VIII. *Archief van het Koninklijk Nationaal Steuncomite*, 1914–26

IX. *Archief van het Centraal Vluchtelingen-Comite*, 1914–19

X. *Archief van de Dienst der Geinterneerde Krijgsgevangenen*, 1917–19

XI. *Private Papers of Public Officials.*
1. Asbeck, F. M. van (1889–1968): Indonesia
2. Asselbergs, C. J. (1869–1949): South Africa
3. Asser, T. M. C. (1834–1913): Court of Arbitration
4. Beel, L. J. M. (1902–   ): Indonesia and minister-president
5. Beelaerts van Blokland, F. (1872–1956): foreign affairs advisor in London
6. Beelaerts van Blokland, G. J. Th. (1772–1844): South Africa
7. Bentinck-Varel-Kniphausense line (1809–1854)

8. Besier, A. G. (1758-1829): South Africa
9. Bezemer family (c. 1760-1855): East Asia
10. Blankenstein, M. van (1880-1964): Indonesia
11. Bosboom, N. (1855-1937): war minister
12. Brouwer van Hogendorp, F. de (1807-1871): Belgium
13. Buurman van Vreeden, D. C. (1902-1964): Indonesia
14. Cock Blomhoff, J. (1779-1853): Japan
15. Cort van der Lindin, P. W. A. (1864-1935): diplomatic service, minister-president.
16. Cremer, J. Th. (1847-1923): United States
17. Cremers family (18th-20th century): diplomatic service
18. Daendels, H. W. (1762-1818): Dutch East Indies, Guinea Coast
19. Dassevael, S. (1770-1838): diplomatic service
20. Dedem van de Gelder, F. G. (1743-1815) and family (16th-19th century): diplomatic service and Turkey
21. Delprat, D. A. (1890-   ): Suez Canal
22. Deventer, M. L. van (1832-1895): Brazil
23. Doeff, H. (1777-1835): Japan
24. Domela Nieuwenhuis, F. J. (1864-1935): Southeast Asia, South Africa
25. Dumonceau, J. B. (1760-1821): diplomatic service
26. Dumont Pigalle, P. A. (c. 1728-1801): diplomatic service
27. Elout, C. Th. (1767-1841): diplomatic service
28. Eysinga, W. J. M. (1878-1961): Court of Arbitration, International Court of Justice
29. Fabius family (18th-20th century): Japan
30. Falck, A. R. (1777-1843): Great Britain, Belgium
31. Gerbrandy, P. S. (1885-1961): Great Britain, Indonesia

32. Gevers van Endegeest, D. Th. (1793–1877): foreign minister
33. Goes van Dirxland, M. van der (1751–1826): foreign minister
34. Goldberg, J. (1763–1828): diplomatic service
35. Gybland Oosterhoff, H. H. A. van (1887–1937): South Africa
36. Haes, R. L. de (1818–1884): Guinea Coast
37. Hahn, J. G. H. (1761–1822): diplomatic service
38. Hall, F. A. van (1791–1866): foreign minister
39. Hamel, J. A. van (1880–1964): League employee, international affairs
40. Hiddingh, C. (1809–1871): South Africa
41. Hoffmann, H. Th. (1898–1960): Indonesia, New Guinea
42. Hogendorp, D. (1761–1822) and G. K. (1771–1834): Russia, Austria, foreign minister
43. Janssens, J. W. (1762–1838): South Africa
44. Jansen, M. H. (1817–1893): diplomatic service
45. Joekes, A. M. (1885–1962): international affairs
46. Karnebeek, H. A. (Jr.) van (1874–1942): diplomatic service
47. Keverberg, van Kessel, Ch. (1768–1841): Belgium
48. Kinckel, H. A. van (1747–1821): diplomatic service
49. Koets, P. J. (1901–   ): Dutch East Indies
50. Lansberge, J. W. van (1830–1905): diplomatic service
51. Leyds, W. J. (1859–1940): South African minister plen.
52. Limburg Stirum, J. P. van (1873–1948): Sweden, Germany
53. Logemann, J. H. A. (1892–1969): Indonesia
54. Lijnden van Sandenburg family (18th–19th century): foreign service

55. Maanen, C. F. van (1769-1846): diplomatic service
56. Maesen de Sombreff, P. Th. van der (1827-1902): foreign minister
57. Melvil van Lijnden, R. (1843-1910): foreign minister
58. Meijer Ranneft, J. W. (1887-1968): Indonesia
59. Mook, H. J. van (1894-1965): Dutch East Indies
60. Nagell, A. W. C. van (1756-1851): foreign minister
61. Nouhuys, J. W. van (1869-1963): World War II
62. Obreen, H. C. (1874-1941): South African trade
63. Pleyte, Th. B. (1864-1926): Brazil
64. Poll, M. J. M. van (1881-1948): Dutch East Indies
65. Posthuma, F. E. (1874-1943): commercial treaties
66. Raffles, Th. Stamfor (1781-1826): Java
67. Röell, J. and W. F., J. A. and W. (3 collections): diplomatic service
68. Romme, C. P. M. (1896-   ): Indonesia
69. Roosegaarde Bisschop, W. (1866-1944): Malacca, Bengal
70. Ruyssenaers, L. H. (1850-1913) and S. W. (1815-1877): foreign service
71. Sanders, P. (1912-   ): Dutch East Indies
72. Savornin Lohman, A. F. de (1837-1924): diplomatic service, Court of Arbitration
73. Savornin Lohman, B. C. de (1883-1964): diplomatic service
74. Spies, P. (1904-   ): Indonesia
75. Spoor, S. H. (1902-1949): Indonesia
76. Stikker, D. U. (1897-   ): Indonesia, diplomatic minister, secretary-general of NATO
77. Tets van Goudriaan, D. A. W. van (1884-1930): foreign minister

78. Tjarda van Starkenborgh Stachouwer, A. W. L. (1888–   ): Dutch East Indies
79. Verhuell, C. A. (1760–1832) and C. H. (1764–1845): France, Russia, and foreign minister
80. Verstolk van Soelen, J. G. (1776–1845): Russia and foreign minister
81. Veth, B. (1861–1910): South Africa, Boer War, Belgium
82. Voorst Evekink, D. van (1890–1950): Belgium, France
83. Vos van Steenwijk, R. H. de (1885–1964): diplomatic service, German boundary
84. Wasklewicz-Van Schilfgaarde, B. (1850–1937): South Africa, Boer War
85. Welter, Ch. J. I. M. (1880–1972): Indonesia
86. Zuylen van Nijevelt, H. van (1781–1853): foreign minister
87. Zuylen van Nijevelt, J. P. J. A. van (1819–1894): foreign minister
88. Zuylen van Nijevelt, J. P. P. van (1816–1890): France, foreign minister
89. Zaaijer, J.: Dutch-Belgian questions (1919–1936)

Archives and Collections of the Third Section [4]

A.   *Archieven van de Staten van Holland en Gecommitteerde Raden in het Zuiderkwartier,* 1572–1795:

Nrs. 11–280	printed resolutions 1575–1795
Nrs. 281–298	printed index on the printed resolutions 1572–1790
Nrs. 299–315	printed secret resolutions 1653–1795
Nrs. 316–317	index on the foregoing
Nrs. 325–1208	minute resolutions 1575–1795

[4] Pp. 71–103 of No. 12.

Nrs. 1226-1250 minute secret resolutions 1651-1705
Nrs. 1384-1481 registered outgoing letters 1621-1795
Nrs. 1871-2029 orignial letters and other documents submitted to the assembly of the states 1691-1763
Nrs. 2244-2577 copies of documents concerning foreign affairs, classified in order of the various countries in which the Republic had representatives 1653-1702

B. *Archieven van de Raadpensionarissen*, 1572-1795:
In respect to foreign affairs the grand pensionary of the province of Holland occupied a most important position. He was in charge of the formulation of proposals, the leading of discussions, and the drafting of resolutions of the states of Holland, thus being in effect the president of the states assembly. In his capacity as the only permanent member he was the leader and spokesman of the states of Holland in the assembly of the states general. He also took part in the sessions of the Secret Council, in which foreign affairs were discussed, as well as in meetings of other committees of the generalty. Although the Dutch representatives abroad were obliged to report to the states general and to the clerk of that college (in which case secrecy was not always maintained), they adopted the custom of addressing important and confidential dispatches to the grand pensionary in person. These facts account for the importance of the archives of the grand pensionaries in matters of foreign relations, expecially those of Oldenbarnevelt, Johan de Witt, Gaspar Fagel, Anthonie Heinsius, Simon van Slingelandt, and Laurens Pieter van de Spiegel. The archives of the grand pensionaries are kept partly as a subdivision of the archives of the states of Holland, partly as separate collections.

    1. Paulus Buys, 1572-86
    2. Johan van Oldenbarnevelt, 1586-1619

3. Jacob Cats, 1629-31, 1636-51
4. Johan de Witt, 1653-72
5. Caspar Fagel, 1672-88
6. Anthonie Heinsius, 1688-1720
7. Isaac van Hoornbeek, 1720-27
8. Anthony van der Heim, 1737-46
9. Peter van Bleiswijk, 1772-87
10. Laurens Pieter van de Spiegel, 1787-95

Provincial Archives of the Netherlands

In addition to the General State Archives the researcher should also be aware of archival collections in the provincial repositories that might be of value for certain topics in the field of Dutch foreign relations.

1. Province of Gelderland:

The archives are located at 1, Marktstraat, Arnhem. Of interest are the papers of the counts of Culemborg, concerning diplomatic relations with various countries, as well as the archives of the manor houses of Waardenburg, Keppel, and Enghuizen, relating to embassies and diplomatic missions entrusted to functionaries from Gelderland.

2. Province of Zeeland:

Archives at 38 Sint Pieterstraat, Middelburg, house the papers of Van den Warck, a Dutch envoy to Denmark and England, as well as the Verheye-Van Citters collection, which concerns peace negotiations with France 1709-13.

3. Province of Utrecht:

Archives at 201 Alexander Niemanhade, Utrecht, have these collections: the papers of G. Hamel, counsel of the states; the family archives of De Geer van Jutphaas on diplomatic and commercial relations with Sweden, seventeenth-nineteenth centuries; the family archives of Huydecoper, on relations of members of the family with foreign countries, seventeenth-eighteenth centuries; the family archives of De Pesters, on diplomatic missions of members of the family, seventeenth-eighteenth centuries; miscellaneous papers on foreign engagements, 1618–69, and concerning the Barrier Treaty, 1753–54.

4. Province of Friesland:
These archives, at B 13, Turfmarkt, Leeuwarden, house various resolutions on foreign affairs, concerning the United States, 1782; Cologne, 1673; Denmark, 1720; England, 1672, 1704; France, 1584, 1660, 1672; Lübeck, 1653; Münster, 1643–62; Poland, 1669; Portugal, 1644; Prussia, 1720, 1727; Spain, 1660, 1672; Sweden, 1644, 1719; and the Gabbema collection, a group of papers on foreign relations, including the peace negotiations with Cologne, 1579–83.

5. Province of Overijssel:
This collection, at Sassenpoort, Zwolle, contains the archives of the nobility and towns in Overijssel, as well as missives of the deputies to the army, 1706–8, 1711, 1712.

6. Province of Groningen:
Papers of interest, at 2, St. Jansstraat, Groningen, are those concerning independent actions of the province regarding East Friesland and Germany.

7. Province of Drente:
The archives are at 4, Brink, Assen, and include papers concerning boundary disputes between the county of Bentheim and the bishopric of Munster.

8. City of Amsterdam, 57 Amsteldijk:
During the Middle Ages the city of Amsterdam pursued a more or less independent policy in respect to the Hanseatic League. Particulars concerning these relations might be found in the following: the charter collection of the Iron Chapel, the grand-memorandum registers since 1474, and the resolutions of the city council since 1536. During the period 1578–1795 Amsterdam exerted a great deal of influence on foreign policy and at times maintained foreign relations of its own. For details one may consult the resolutions of the municipality as well as the correspondence of its college. Moreover, there are embassy

reports, copies of treaties with foreign powers, and missives of Dutch envoys.

The General State Archives are located at 7, Bleijenburg, The Hague. Admission to the archives is readily granted and the researcher, native or foreign, need not present any papers of identification or letters of introduction. Upon entering the reading room the investigator is given access to the index files and can place his request for documents with the attendant. Documents are released to the user upon the presentation of a requisition bulletin, and the delay necessary for bringing documents from the stacks to the reading room is very brief. The researcher is not permitted to use ink in the reading room for the purpose of transcribing documents. A speaking knowledge of the Dutch language is not essential since most, if not all, of the archivists and attendants speak English. Consultation with members of the staff on matters of research is possible but should of course be limited to essentials. All papers after fifty years are open to research without any restriction.

A well-equipped reproduction department is attached to the General State Archives, where documents from the public archives may be photoprinted or microfilmed for the use of researchers. It may be noted that transcriptions by a researcher for the use of another party are only permitted in exceptional cases. The schedule of the archives is that of government offices, thus permitting adequate periods of uninterrupted consultation.

BIBLIOGRAPHY

Guide and Reference Works

In respect to the contents of the General State Archives it may be noted that typed inventories of virtually all the materials listed above are available to the researcher at the repository at The Hague. There has also been a consistent effort to print the inventories of the archives. In 1854 R. C. Bakhuizen van den Brink, Keeper of the State Archives at The

Hague, published a survey entitled *Overzicht van het Nederlandsche Rijksarchief, eerste stuk*. It was his intention to follow this intitial survey with a second part and then to continue with annual reports. However, this plan did not materialize and it was only in 1866 that his successor, L. Ph. C. van den Bergh, issued an annual report for the minister of the interior, which was published in the *Staatsblad,* as were the reports of the years following. Beginning in 1878, the annual reports from the Keeper of the State Archives and the keepers of other state repositories were published as *Verslagen omtrent 's Rijks oude archieven,* consisting of a first series from 1878 to 1927 and a second series beginning in 1928. In the first series inventories were published as appendixes to the reports; since 1914 they are divided into two volumes, of which the first is solely consecrated to the General State Archives.

The annual report of 1928 was the first to appear without the appended inventories, and the latter were printed thenceforth as a separate publication of the Dutch government, entitled *Inventarissen van Rijks—en andere archieven.* The gap between 1854 and 1878 was filled by the publication of a survey of the administration of Bakhuizen van den Brink, published by R. Fruin in 1926 under the title *De Gestie van Dr. R. C. Bakhuizen van den Brink als archivaris des Rijks, 1854–1865,* and by the publication, in 1914, of the annual reports from 1865 to 1877.

In *Verslagen* . . . , 1926, I, 87 ff., can be found a survey of the contents of the General State Archives; the researcher's attention is also directed to the inventory of the foreign office archives in *Verslagen* . . . , XLI, pt. 1 (1918), 291–469; XLIV, pt. 1 (1921 [1923]), 111–240; XLVI, pt. 1 (1923 [1924]), 174–207.[5]

Other guide and reference works are:

1. Bakhuizen van den Brink, R. C., L. Ph. C. van den Bergh, and J. de Jonge. *Nederlandsch Rijksarchief, verzameling van onuitgegevene oorkonden voor de geschiedenis des vaderlandes.* Amsterdam, 1855-57.
2. Bakhuizen van den Brink, R. C. *Overzicht van het Nederlandsche Rijksarchief.* The Hague, 1854.
3. Bijlsma, R. *De regeeringsarchieven der Geunieerde en Nader Geunieerde Nederlandsche Provincien.* The Hague, 1926.
4. Bosmans, Cornelis J. E., and M. Visser. *Repertoire des traites et engagements internationaux concernant les Pays-Bas, 1845-1900.* The Hague, 1928.
5. Formsma, W. J., and B. van 't Hoff. *Repertorium van inventarissen van Nederlandse archieven.* Groningen, 1947.

[5] P. 7 of No. 6.

6. Fruin, R. *The General State Archives and their contents.* The Hague, 1932.

7. Heeres, Jan E., and F. W. Stapel. *Corpus diplomaticum Neerlando-Indicum. Verzameling van politieke contracten en verdere verdragen door de Nederlanders in het Oosten gesloten, van privilegebrieven aan hen verleend, enz.* 4 vols. The Hague, 1907–38.

8. Heeringa, Klaas. *Bronnen tot de geschiedenis van den levantschen handel.* 2 vols. The Hague, 1910–17.

9. Van 't Hoff, B., and M. W. Juriaanse. *Het archief van Anthonie Heinsius.* The Hague, 1950.

10. Japiske, N., and H. H. P. Rijperman. *Resolutien der Staten-Generaal van 1576 tot 1609.* 12 vols. The Hague, 1915–50.

11. Muller, S., J. A. Feith, and R. Fruin. *Manual for the arrangement and description of archives; drawn up by the direction of the Netherlands Association of Archivists.* 2nd ed. Trans. by A. H. Leavitt. New York, 1940.

12. Nederland, Ministerie van Onderwijs, Kunsten, en Wetenschappen. *De Rijksarchieven in Nederland.* 2 vols. The Hague, 1973.

13. Riemskijk, Theodorus H. F. *De griffie van Hare Hoop Mogenden; bijdrage tot de kennis van het archief van de Staten-Generaal der Vereenigde Nederlanden.* The Hague, 1885.

14. Scheltema, P. "Het historisch-diplomatisch archief van Amsterdam," *Amstel's oudheid, of gedenkwaardigheden van Amsterdam.* Vol. III. Amsterdam, 1859.

15. ——— . *Inventaris van het Amsterdamsche archief.* 3 vols. Amsterdam, 1866–74.

16. Schilfgaarde, Antonie P. *Het archief der heeren en graven van Culemborg.* The Hague, 1949.

17. Wabeke, Bertus H. *A guide to Dutch bibliographies.* Washington, D.C., 1951.

18. Bemis and Griffin. *Guide.* Dutch archives, pp. 921–23.

19. Formsma, W. J. *Gids voor de Nederlandse archieven.* Bussum, 1967.

20. Roessingh, M. P. H. *Guide to the sources in the Netherlands for the history of Latin America.* Published under the auspices of UNESCO and of the International Council on Archives. The Hague, 1968.

12 NORWAY[1]

Florence Janson Sheriff,
Wesleyan College,
revised by Daniel H. Thomas,
University of Rhode Island

HISTORY

NORWAY has been an independent state three times in its long existence since Viking days. The earliest period of sovereignty began with its emergence about A.D. 900. Norway lost its dynastic independence when united with Denmark in 1380; then Denmark, Norway, and Sweden united through the Union of Calmar in 1397. During the early part of this union, Norway had a personal relationship with the Danish crown, but, after 1537, was almost an integral part of Denmark, the Danish chancellor conducting foreign relations for both countries during both periods.

During the Napoleonic wars, when Denmark became an ally of France in 1807, Norway was the subject of much diplomatic correspondence between the nations united against Napoleon. After the Battle of Leipzig in 1813, Bernadotte, now crown prince of Sweden and allied with Napoleon's foes, invaded Denmark and forced it to sign the Treaty of Kiel, January 14, 1814, granting Norway to Sweden. Norwegians have always refused to accept this treaty. They elected a national convention, proclaimed independence on May 17, 1814, drafted a constitution providing for the Storting as parliament, and offered the crown of Norway

---

[1] The author of this chapter in the original guide was indebted to the archivists of the *Riksarkiv* for information and guidance. Others who were of assistance through correspondence were Hedvig Schaanning, Head Librarian of *Utenriksdepartementets Bibliotek*, Odd Hjorth-Sørensen, Press Attaché, and Tordis Dreyer, Assistant in Archives, Norwegian Embassy in Washington, D.C.

to the Danish heir apparent, Prince Christian Frederik. But Bernadotte threatened to enforce the Treaty of Kiel by the invasion of Norway, and, in November of 1814, the Norwegian Storting voted a union with Sweden. This was a personal union in which Norway had home rule, even control of its army and navy, but not of foreign affairs.

The union of Norway and Sweden lasted until 1905. During this period, foreign affairs for both countries remained at first under the Swedish chancellor; after 1840, with the reorganization of the Swedish administration, foreign relations were under the Swedish minister of external affairs. The Joint Council for Sweden and Norway, which always met in Stockholm, had Norwegian representatives but never achieved any control over foreign affairs. In time the growing Norwegian merchant marine found it humiliating and difficult to deal with Swedish consuls in foreign ports, and although some Norwegian consuls were appointed, this controversy finally led to the separation of the two countries in 1905. Since that time, Norway has maintained a ministry of foreign affairs, with its archives in its capital.

The first written documents in Norway's history appeared in the twelfth century, and its first commercial treaty was between Henry III of England and Haakon IV of Norway in 1217. Haakon corresponded with the Emperor of the Holy Roman Empire, with France, England, the Christian states of Spain, and with the Sultan of Tunis. Norway had moved its capital from Nidaros, old Trondheim, to the southern commercial town of Bergen, where the Hanseatic League in the next century established the fish market of Europe. The Archbishop of Nidaros remained the political influence in the north and corresponded with the pope and with various members of the clergy in Europe prior to the Reformation.

Oslo bacame the third and permanent capital, chosen by King Haakon V at the end of the thirteenth century. He constructed Akershus, the imposing castle that overshadowed the city, as the royal residence and as a fortification for the defense of the city, and kept the royal documents there. It is first mentioned as Akersnaes in a letter written by King Haakon Magnusson dated June 22, 1300, granting gifts and privileges to *Mariekirken* (St. Mary's) in Oslo. Queen Margaret, the regent of Denmark who promoted the Union of Calmar in 1397, advised the heir apparent, King Erik, to investigate his title to the throne of Norway in the letters patent at Akershus, during his tour of Norway in 1405. His donation to the Archbishopric of Nidaros was registered at Akershus. From 1572 to 1771, the Danish stattholder for Norway resided and continued the archives at Akershus; in 1809, instead of the stattholders, a commission was appointed with a Danish prince as regent. Under the Norwegian union with Denmark from 1380 to 1814, with the conduct of the foreign affairs of the two countries by the Danish chancellor in Copenhagen, the Danish kings first sent "agents" to foreign countries in the sixteenth century, and in the seventeenth exchanged ministers. Their diplomatic correspondence is in the Danish *Riksarkiv* (National Archives) in Copenhagen. The Danes have forwarded a few of the diplomatic documents relating to Norway, and the latter's *Riksarkiv* have selected and copied some others. The materials concerning the period of independence in 1814 are in the Norwegian *Rigsarkiv*. The diplomatic correspondence for the period of the union between Norway and Sweden, 1814–1905, can be found in the Swedish *Riksarkiv*, in Stockholm. The archives of the Norwegian department of foreign affairs (*Utenriksdeparte-mentets Arkiv*) — not the National Archives — contain the diplomatic documents of Norway since 1905.

The origin of the *Riksarkiv* of Norway was the collection, by medieval monarchs, of such documents as agreements, letters, and land grants preserved in the chancellor's office, and then at Akershus. Unfortunately, few medieval papers have survived. One major collection of the present archives is the materials from the *Stattholderskap*, 1572–1771, which had been kept at Akershus. Papers from various central and local authorities during the Danish period were added as time passed. Various collections and inventories followed, examples being Carl Deichman Möller's arrangement of all the kings' letters, from 1572 to 1751, and his seventeen folio volume collection of the registers and catalogues of a portion of the archives,[2] and General Gustav Grüner's arrangement of the military documents, in 1760. Norway did receive many archives from Denmark during the first half of the nineteenth century, as provided in the Stockholm Accord of 1819: some eleven hundred sacks and various cases of government documents arriving in 1820-22. This archival exchange continued until 1851, and occurred again in 1937, but it included little diplomatic correspondence.[3] In fact, the diplomatic historian is warned not to anticipate too great a number of interesting documents in the *Riksarkiv*. Another transfer of archives was that from Munich, in the 1820s, and involved Christian II's papers, which, in his flight in 1523, he had taken from Stockholm and Copenhagen to Holland. Strangely, these archives had appeared in Munich in the early nineteenth century.[4]

The Norwegian *Riksarkiv* was officially established in Oslo, in 1839. The first official archivist was the poet, Henrik Wergeland, in 1840. In 1866, the archives moved from Akershus to a wing in the newly constructed Storting building. At the present time, they are housed in a separate building at Bankplassen but will soon be moved to new quarters. Since 1845, the *Riksarkiv* has been in the Department of Church and Education but, since 1875, has enjoyed independent status.[5]

ORGANIZATION AND CLASSIFICATION OF THE RIKSARKIV

The *Riksarkiv* of Norway is the central depository for numerous government documents. They include:

1. *Archives of central authorities in Norway before 1814.* These contain no diplomatic correspondence.

---

[2] See Nos. 20, 21, and 33.
[3] See No. 22.
[4] See No. 21.
[5] See No. 30, which should be read before starting research.

2. *Archives of the common Dano-Norwegian central adminis-tration in Copenhagen before 1814*, as far as they have been delivered from Denmark. Almost all of the archives concerning foreign affairs still remain there. The diplomatic correspondence in the *Riksarkiv* is arranged as follows:

Danske Kancelli, Graendseregulering, 28 parcels exclusive of treaties, frontier descriptions, and maps.

Departementet for de Udenlandske Sager, Acter betraeffende Graendserne mellem Norge og Sverrig 1690 to 1808 (2 parcels), *Acter betraeffende Norges Tømmerflaadning gjennem de svenske Strømme* 1733-1810 (1 parcel), *Acter betraeffende Graendserne mellem Norge og Rusland* ca. 1690-1810 (1 parcel), *Prise — og Kapersager* 1747-1809 (2 parcels).

Single documents — or single parcels — of diplomatic corre-spondence can be found in *Danske Kancellis skapsaker* and in *Rentekammerets realistisk ordnede avdeling*.

3. *Archives of the Norwegian government 1814.* These archives are scanty, and some materials are in other collections. The more important documents have been published.

4. *Archives of the Norwegian government after 1814*, as far as they have been delivered by the ministries. The archives of the common Swedish-Norwegian Ministry of Foreign Affairs for 1814-1905 remain in Stockholm. The archives of the Norwegian Department of Foreign Affairs, after 1905, remain in the depart-ment. The following groups which contain documents of diplo-matic interest have been delivered by other departments:

Indredepartementet, Grenseoppgangsforretninger m.m., av-leverte 1872-98, 7 boxes.

Finansdepartementet, Opgjøret med Danmark 1815 to 1823, 15 parcels.

Finansdepartementet (Raestads avlevering 1910), Russiskfiske forhandlinger 1831-41 og 1847-54 (13 boxes), *Svenske for-handlinger 1842-45* (2 boxes), *Norsk-Svenske renbeitekon-flikter 1817-19, 1840-45, og Norsk-Svenske renbeitesaker 1828-30, 1838, 1849-50* (1 box), *Grensereguleringen mellem*

Norge og Rusland 1825-27 (3 boxes), *Handelstraktater mellem Norge og Rusland 1824-38* (3 boxes), etc.

5. *Collections.* Only two of the collections seem to be relevant to diplomatic correspondence:

Diplomsamtlinger — collections of medieval documents, some of which concern the relations between Norway and foreign countries.

The materials are all printed in *Diplomatarium Norvegicum*.

Privatarkiver — correspondence and papers of private persons, including a few diplomats and officials of the Department of Foreign Affairs: Poul Christian Holst (*privatarkiv nr. 20*), Francis Hagerup (84), Bernt Anker Bødtker (122), Jørgen Løvland (162), Carl Berner (209), Andreas Tostrup Urbye (235), Truels Wiel (238), Halvdan Koht (258), C. J. Hambro (260). See: *Privatarkiver nr. 1-243, Hovedkatalog, Utg. av Riksarkivet.* Oslo 1963.

THE UTENRIKSDEPARTEMENTETS ARKIV

Norway's diplomatic documents since 1905 are deposited in the *Utenriksdepartementets Arkiv,* at 7 Juni Plassen 1, Oslo. As preparation for their use, researchers are advised to read E.-W. Norman's manuscript paper, which is available in the archives, "The archives of the Royal Ministry of Foreign Affairs." The following description consists of quotations or close paraphrasing of portions of this paper, to which he has kindly consented.

All current outgoing and incoming correspondence goes through the archival service. Most of the instructions and reports are recorded in journals, or *Journaler,* which indicate the serial number assigned to each, the sender, the recipient, a brief indication of subject matter, the date, the number of the dossier to which it is to be deposited, and eventually any action taken on the matter. The exceptions to this are (1) documents received from various international organizations which are filed according to the symbols and serial numbers provided by the originators and (2) some categories of very routine corresondence related to these. Since Norway has always used the dossier system, all documents are placed in subject dossiers.

The guide to the dossiers is an index made up of a maximum of 100 main classes. These are listed numerically under headings such as International Affairs, Defense, Social Problems, Finance, and Trade. Each of these main classes is divided into subclasses Some of these have an identical pattern: No. 1 being Miscellaneous; No. 2, International Cooperation (conferences, expositions); No. 3, Scandinavian Relations; and No. 4, Bilateral Relations. The subclasses, in turn, contain an index of the individual dossiers, which have been assigned a number. Thus, when a researcher requests or cites a dossier, he must indicate three numbers: the main class, the subclass, and the particular dossier. (The authorities of the archives have given much thought to a reclassification under the decimal system which other Norwegian ministries have adopted, but the disadvantages are still considered to outweigh the advantages of conversion.) Since many dossiers are arranged on a geographical pattern, there is also a geographical list of dossiers. Each state or country is assigned a permanent number to be used under all main classes or subclasses. The United States, for example, is No. 47 (*Forenede Stater*, Tallet 47), and Sweden is No. 106.

ADMINISTRATION, REGULATIONS, AND FACILITIES

The *Riksarkiv* is now located at Bankplassen 3, Oslo 1, but expects to move to new quarters on Sognsvatn, in 1976 or 1977. The materials are open to the public, with the exception of a few that have been closed by the delivering authorities, and may be used only after consent by the director. The reading room is open on winter weekdays, from 9:00 A.M. to 3:30 P.M. and 5–8:00 P.M. It closes in the summer at 3:00 P.M. and on Saturdays at 1:30 P.M. It contains guides, bibliographies, published source materials, the journals of the *Riksarkiv, Meddelelser fra Riksarkivet,* and of the Norwegian Historical Society, *Historisk Tidsskrift.* The staff is most helpful in aiding researchers. It is possible to arrange for both microfilms and duplications. The director at the time of this edition is Dr. Dagfinn Mannsäker.[6]

The *Utenriksdepartementets Arkiv,* located with the ministry at 7 Juni Plassen 1, has no time or date limit for opening documents to scholars. Historians may normally expect to see documents older than forty years and may request examination of those older than twenty years. In exceptional cases, the minister may allow use of more recent materials, but this is rarely granted. Requests for research in the archives are welcomed and should be directed to E.-W. Norman,[7] *Förstearkivaren,* well in advance of projected research. They should contain a letter of introduction from the research professor, an historical association, or a university, and a description of the research topic. The hours of the archives proper are 8:30 A.M. to 3:45 P.M. week days, and until 3:00 P.M., from May 15 to September 14. Researchers use the reading room of the library. Documents may be reproduced with the consent of the archivist. In many cases, manuscripts prepared from records made available by the ministry must be submitted for approval prior to publication.

LIBRARIES AND OTHER ARCHIVES

The *Utenriksdepartementets Bibliotek* is open to the public and is also at 7 Juni Plassen 1. Its collection of 120,000 volumes and numerous maps shows an emphasis on the quality of its holdings, rather than quantity. A modern catalogue is available in the reading room. The hours are 8:30 A.M. to 3:45 P.M.

---

[6] The editors are deeply indebted to him for the information used in the revised edition and given during interviews in August, 1970, and in correspondence since that time.

[7] The editors are deeply indebted to him for the information used in the revision and which was given during interviews in August 1970, and in correspondence since that date.

weekdays, except 3:00 P.M. during the summer. Mrs. Gerd B. Krag, Librarian,[8] maintains a staff of professionals.

The University of Oslo's main library, *Universitetsbiblioteket i Oslo*, at 42 Drammensveien, was founded by an ordinance of 1811 and has occupied the same building since 1913. All books published in Norway are deposited here, and the library publishes a national bibliography. It houses about two million volumes, including over fifty thousand volumes of newspaper files, and thousands of Norwegian and foreign doctoral theses; it is responsible for a million more in the university's institutes and museums. It is open to the public and publishes a very informative booklet describing the library and its services, such as interlibrary loans, and its union catalogue of foreign books and periodicals held in about one hundred Norwegian libraries. The city library, *Deichmanske Bibliotek,* is a circulating library of a million volumes, and its reading room contains bibliographies, published source materials, and journals. This library dates to about 1790, when Carl Deichman, an Oslo merchant, donated his private collection to the city.

The Norwegian parliament (*Storting*) and supreme court (*Hoeiesterett*) have their own archives, the former one in the *Stortingsbygning.* There is also the Nobel Institute of Oslo, located at Drammensveien and Parkveien, with a reading room open to the public and a library on international affairs and peace.

Housing in Oslo may be difficult in the summer, when it is advisable to book rooms months in advance. The Oslo airport maintains a hotel booking service, and the Norwegian Railways have a housing-service window in the eastern terminal station. For a nominal fee, the latter can arrange for rental of rooms in private homes as well as hotels and pensions. The institutions mentioned are all in or near the business or downtown section of the city. It is recommended that the researcher bring a general

---

[8] The editors are deeply grateful to her for verifying and updating the bibliography.

letter of introduction from the university with which he is associated or from an historical association.

BIBLIOGRAPHY

Published Collections of Source Materials

1. Allen, C. F.: *Breve og Aktstykker til Oplysning af Christiern den Andens og Frederik den Førstes Historie.* Copenhagen, 1854. Letters and documents of the reigns of Christian II and Frederik I from the Foreign Affairs Archives.
2. Bricka, C. F. and L. Laursen. *Kancelliets Brevbøger vedrørende Danmarks indre Forhold, 1551–1615.* 13 vols. Copenhagen. Copybooks of the chancery concerning the internal affairs of Denamrk.
3. *British views on Norwegian-Swedish problems, 1880–1895. Selections from diplomatic correspondence.* Ed. for Kjeldeskriftfondet by Paul Knaplund. Oslo, 1952.
4. *Danske Kancelliregistranter, 1553–1550.* Copenhagen, 1881–82. Registers of letters of the Danish chancery.
5. Erslev, K., and W. Mollerup. *Kong Frederik den Førstes danske Registranter.* Copenhagen, 1878–79. The registers of Frederik I (1524–33).
6. Kongelige norske Videnskabersselskab (Royal Norwegian Learned Society), *Skrifter* and *Forhandlinger.* Serial publications that contain historical sources. Following are some of the publications of diplomatic correspondence.

    Nielsen, Y. "Aktmaessige Bidrag til de nordiske Rigers politiske Historie i 1813 og 1814," *Forhandlinger i Videnskabsselskabet i Christiania.* Christiania, 1877, Nr. 2. A discussion, with excerpts, of the diplomatic correspondence between Sweden and Vienna about Norway, in 1813–14.

    "Aktstykker vedkommende stormagternes Mission till Kjöbenhavn i Aaret 1814," Videnskabsselskabet i Christiania, *Skrifter,* Christiania, 1897, (Hist.-Fil.) Klasse, Nr. 3. Source material from the diplomatic archives of Denmark, England, Prussia, Austria, and Russia, concerning Norway, in 1814.
7. Laursen, L. *Danmark-Norges Traktater, 1523–1750, med dertil hørende Aktstykker.* Copenhagen, 1907–34, Danish–Norwegian treaties and documents.
8. Generalstaben (Danish General Staff). "Akstykker vedrörende Fredsunderhandlingerne med de mod Frankrig forbundne Magter," *Meddelelser fra Krigsarkivene.* Vol. IX. Copenhagen, 1902. The

diplomatic correspondence, 1813-14, between the powers allied against Napoleon.

9. Norske historiske Kildeskriftkommission (Norwegian Commission for the Publication of Historical Sources). *Historiske Samlinger.* Collections of historical sources. 3 vols., 1900-14. Some examples of this publication are given as follows:

"Diplomatisk Brevveksling om Norge mellim Wien og London (1814) og mellem Berlin og London (1813-14)," Vol. II (1907). Diplomatic correspondence.

"Diplomatiske Aktstykker fra 1814," Vol. III (1914), 179-244. Austrian and Prussian dispatches to London, and the correspondence between Bernadotte and Alexander I of Russia.

Nielsen, Y., "Aktstykker om Bodösagen," Vol. I (1900), 113-464 Diplomatic correspondence, between London and Norway, over British smuggling at Bodö.

10. *Norske Rigs-registranter.* Christiania, 1861-91, Norwegian national registers.

11. Omang, Reider. *Altmark-Saken, 1940. Akstykker i Det Kgl. Utenriksdepartements arkiv.* Oslo, 1953. Documents on the Altmark affair.

Norge og Stormaktene, 1906-14. Vol. I *1906-08.* Oslo, 1957. A Collection of documents on Norway and the great powers. Still in progress.

12. *Regesta diplomatica historiae Danicae.* Copenhagen, 1847-1907. Source materials to 1669, including some Norwegian.

13. Riksarkivet. *Meddelelser fra det Norske Rigsarckiv.* Vols. I-III. Christiania/Oslo, 1850-1933. Contains source material and papers concerning Norwegian history, as, for example, No. 27 below. Other examples: "Fortegnelse over Regjeringsraadets og Rigsforsamlingens Medlemmer" (by E. A. Thomle), *Vol. II* (1903), 321-378. Biographical notes on the members of the Norwegian Cabinet and the National Convention, 1814.

"Aktstykker vedkommende krigsbegivenheterne 1814" (by C. Aubert), *Vol. III* (1933), 1-256. Document concerning the war in Norway, 1814.

14. Udenrigsministeriet. *Danske Traktater, 1751-1800.* Copenhagen, 1882. Danish treaties.

15. Urbye, Andreas. *Karlstadforhandlingene, 1905. Referat fra de møter hvor sekretoerene var til stede.* Oslo, 1952.

16. Utenriksdepartementet. *Norges traktater, 1661-1966.* 3 vols. and a register. Oslo, 1967-70. Compilation of treaties in force.

17. Utenriksdepartementet. *Norges forhold til Sverige under Krigen, 1940-45.* 3 vols. Oslo, 1947-50. Devoted to relations with Sweden.
18. *Sveriges och Norges traktater med främmande magter, 1814-1905.* Stockholm, 1896-1934. 6 vols. The treaties of Norway and Sweden, published by the the Swedish Department of Foreign Affairs.
19. Wegener, C. F., and A. D. Jörgensen. *Aarsberetninger fra det Kongelige Geheimearchiv indeholdend Bidrag til dansk Historie af utrykte Kilder.* 7 vols. Copenhagen, 1852-83. Annual reports from the foreign affairs archives of Denmark, with supplements of the publication of source materials of Danish history, some pertaining to Norway.

Guides and Reference Works
20. Birkeland, M. *Om Arkivvaesenets Ordning. Erklaering fra Rigsarkivaren til Kirkedepartementet.* Christiania, 1877. Reprinted in *Historiske Skrifter* (Christiania, 1922). A report of the history, and the condition, of the archives, by the archivist to the ecclesiastic department of the Norwegian government, in 1877.
21. Bowallius, R. M. "Bidrag till historien om K. Christiern II:s arkiv och dess delning mellan Sverige, Norge och Danmark," *Meddelanden fran Svenska Riksarkivet* (1875-79), III, 21-66. A good discussion of the archives, obtained from Munich, and their distribution.
22. Brinchmann, Christoffer. *Norges Arkivsaker i Danmark,* Oslo, 1927. Discusses the exchange of archives between Denmark and Norway from 1820 to 1851, the archives remaining in Denmark, which includes diplomatic correspondence, and the Arne Magnusson collection (Arnamagnaenska Samlingen) at the University of Copenhagen library.
23. Bring, Samuel E. *Bibliografisk handbok till Sveriges historia.* Stockholm, 1934. This excellent bibliography contains many references to the diplomatic correspondence of Norway and other source materials for Norwegian history.
23a. Degras, *Soviet documents.* On Norway, pp. 76, 116, 185, 229.
24. Erichsen, B., and A. Krarup. *Dansk historisk Bibliografi.* 3 vols. Copenhagen, 1917-27. A Danish historical bibliography, valuable for Norwegian international affairs.
25. International Institute of Intellectual Co-operation of the League of Nations. *Guide international des archives — Europe,* Paris 1924, "Norvège," p. 224.

26. Koht, Halvdan. *Det gamle norske Riksarkive og restane fraa det.* Oslo, 1927.

27. Kolsrud, Sigurd. "Arkivregistreringa paa Akershus i 1622," *Meddelelser fra det norske Riksarkiv,* Vol. III (Oslo, 1933), pp. 257-286. A discussion of the archives lost since 1622.

28. Norman, E.-W. "The archives of the Royal Ministry of Foreign Affairs." A manuscript describing the organization of the archives and classification of the documents.

29. Den Norske historiske Forening (Norwegian Historical Society) *Bibliografi til Norges Historie.* A national bibliography published since 1916.

30. Olstad, Jan H. "Riksarkivet," *Heimen,* XX (1952), 149-154, 183-189.

31. Omang, Reidar. *Norsk Utenrikstjeneste.* Vol. I, *Grunnleggende år.* Vol. II. *Stormfulle tider, 1813-18.* Oslo, 1955-59. A history of the foreign ministry and service.

32. Secher, V. A. "Opdagelsen og Erhvervelsen af Kong Kristiern II: s Archiv fra hans Ophold i Nederlandene 1523-31," *Meddelelser fra det danske Rigsarkiv* (1906-18), I, 355-383. A discussion of the Munich archives obtained by the Scandinavian countries.

33. Secher, V. A. "Das Archivwesen im skandinavischen Norden," *Archivalische Zeitschrift* (Munich), 1879-81, IV, 249-259; V, 40-50; VI, 77-106.

34. Universitetsbiblioteket. *Norske aviser, 1763-1969. En bibliografi. I. Alfabetisk fortegnelse.* Oslo 1973. A bibliography of Norwegian newspapers.

35. Utenriksdepartementet. *Bibliografiske Opplysninger om Norsk Utenrikspolitikketter 1905.* Oslo, 1951. A bibliography on Norwegian foreign affairs since 1905, containing publications by the Norwegain department of foreign affaris and the Storting; also magazine articles.

13 PORTUGAL

Manoel Cardozo
The Catholic University of America

INTRODUCTION

The archives and libraries of Portugal, both public and private, are surpassingly rich in source materials for the study of diplomatic history in its widest sense. While especially valuable for the study of the relations of Portugal with other European states (notably England, Castile, France, the Low Countries, the Holy See, and Austria) and with the Sovereign Order of Malta, the materials are also important, as one would expect of a country with old and widespread imperial connections, for the diplomatic history of nations and territories outside Europe. Moreover, the reports from Portuguese diplomats and agents abroad on matters in which Portugal was not directly involved are an especially neglected source of information for the diplomatic history of many countries.

Despite the abundance of Portuguese sources and their relative accessibility, foreign scholars, who concern themselves with the diplomatic history of Europe, have not been fully aware of the opportunities for research in Portugal. The Portuguese language and the dispersion of the documents have served as a largely psychological barrier, while the uncertain place that Portugal has occupied since the advent of liberalism in the Concert of Europe has tended to decrease scholarly interest in Portuguese civilization. Yet most historians realize that the eight centuries of Portuguese nationhood have profound diplomatic implications and that the existing Portuguese materials, ancient as they are and covering as they do even remote areas beyond the seas, are of a singular and perennial freshness.

Arquivo Nacional da Torre do Tombo

These archives are located in the Palácio de São Bento, Lisbon. They were founded during the second half of the fourteenth century, and are open daily, except Sundays and holidays, 10:00 A.M. to 10:00 P.M. Dr. José Pereira da Silva is their Director.

These archives, generally known as the *Torre do Tombo*, retain substantially the name that they had when located in a tower of the Castle of St. George, on a hill high above downtown Lisbon. They are the largest, richest, and most distinguished of Portugal. Today, most of the papers are housed in a wing of the Palácio de São Bento, the legislative palace, where the offices of administration and main reading room are located. The vast collections of the *Torre do Tombo*, and its dependencies elsewhere in Lisbon, run into the millions of pieces. These are not fully inventoried, but many guides to the collections, in manuscript or printed form, are available.

For the study of diplomatic history, the most extensive and important single source is the *Arquivo Historico* of the Portuguese Foreign Ministry, transferred to the *Torre do Tombo* in 1950. These papers — 717 boxes and numerous bundles — include (1) the corresondence of Portuguese and foreign diplomatic missions and consulates (known as *Corespondência das Caixas*); (2) the internal records of the Foreign Ministry; (3) letters of cardinals of the Holy Roman Church; (4) letters of princes; (5) records of the Mixed Commission on the Suppression of the Slave Trade; (6) documents on the Congress of Vienna; (7) reports of the *Desembargo do Paco* (the Court Royal); (8) correspondence with France; (9) papers of the *Junta do Comércio*; (10) reports (*oficios*) of the governors of Portugal; (11) documents on the Order of Malta; (12) documents on slavery; (13) miscellaneous protests (*reclamacões*); (14) miscellaneous petitions; and (15) international treaties, acts, and conventions.

The Foreign Ministry records in this depository are more or less complete from 1756 to 1851. They are not numerous for the period before 1756; there is nothing, for example, on the period from the Restoration of 1640 to the peace with Castile of 1668; and only miscellaneous documents from 1668 to 1736, when the Archives of the Foreign Ministry were officially created. The lacunae may be attributed to two reasons: (1) the Lisbon earthquake of 1755, which destroyed so many records; and (2) the custom followed by the Marquess of Pombal (the principal minister of state from 1750 to 1777) of removing state papers from the archives, many of which were never returned, but are now, for the most part, in the Pombaline collection of the National Library of Lisbon. However, there are considerable bodies of materials transferred to the *Torre do Tombo* during the nineteenth century.

For the period before 1756 (and in some instances after that date), *Torre do Tombo* houses manuscript collections other than those of the Foreign Ministry; notably, the Collection of Bulls (from 1099), the Papers of the Portuguese Factory at Antwerp (1411–1796), the Royal Chancery (from the thirteenth century), the Corpo Chronológico (1123–1699), diplomatic correspondence and instructions (1641–1785), papers filed by drawers or *gavetas* (from the twelfth century to the present), papers of the Mesa da Consciência e Ordens (beginning with the sixteenth century), papers of the Military Order of Christ, papers of the Holy Office, the São Vicente Collection (sixteenth and seventeenth centuries), and miscellaneous treaties of the eighteenth and nineteenth centuries.

Except for the personal papers of José Luciano de Castro, which may be consulted only with the permission of the Director, all the manuscripts of the *Torre do Tombo* are available to scholars, subject to typical rules and regulations regarding their use.

Arquivo e Biblioteca do Ministéro dos Negócios Estrangeiros

These archives are located on Largo do Rilvas, Lisbon. They were founded in 1736, and are open daily, except Sundays and holidays, 9–12:00 A.M., 2–5:30 P.M. and Saturdays, 9:00 A.M. to

12:30 P.M. Dr. Alvaro Ferrand de Almeida Fernandes is Director. They are open to foreigners with the permission of the Secretary-General of the Ministry of Foreign Affairs, to whom an appropriate request must be directed, indicating the subject, time span, and purpose of the proposed investigation. Foreigners must further show their passports and present a letter of credentials from their respective embassies.

While the records of the Foreign Ministry for the period before 1851 are in the *Torre do Tombo,* those since that date are in the Foreign Ministry's own separate archives. A significant part of the collections, the so-called "Correspondência das Caixas," is in the form of numerous codices and 1,157 boxes, classified chronologically by origin. It comprises the following sections: (1) Correspondence of the Portuguese and foreign diplomatic missions, of the Portuguese consulates (for consular information before the nineteenth century, see the collection of papers of the *Junta do Comércio* in the *Torre do Tombo*), and of the government ministries; (2) Correspondence involving the Lourenço Marques Railway; (3) Boundaries; (4) Correspondence of the civil governors and of the governors of the overseas provinces; (5) The Church of St. Anthony of the Portuguese in Rome; (6) Concordats and negotiations with the Holy See; (7) Letters of cardinals; (8) The question of Bolama, Portuguese Guinea; (9) Portuguese sovereignty in Zambezia; (10) Wills; (11) The Boer War; (12) Miscellaneous manuscripts; (13) Miscellaneous subjects; and (14) Miscellaneous protests. In addition, the Archives have thousands of dossiers, classified by subject, from the several divisions of the Ministry itself, as well as hundreds of registers of forwarded correspondence, and portions of the records of some of the embassies and consulates abroad.

Biblioteca Nacional de Lisboa

This library is located on Alameda do Campo Grande 83, Lisbon, (near the campus of the University of Lisbon) and was founded in 1796. The Director is Dr. Manuel Santos Estevens.

The main reading room is open during the week, from 10:00 A.M. to 9:00 P.M., and on Saturdays, from 10:00 A.M. to 1:00 P.M. The reading room of the Rare Book and Manuscript Division is open during the week, from 10:00 A.M. to 5:30 P.M., and on Saturdays, 10:00 A.M. to 1:00 P.M. The Library is closed in the evenings, during August and September, and on the following national holidays, or holy days of obligation: January 1, Corpus Christi (a movable feast), June 10, August 15, November 1, December 1, December 8, and December 25. It is also closed on the afternoon of Good Friday, on Holy Saturday, and on Christmas Eve. To apply for a card of admission, a foreigner must have a valid passport, two passport photographs, and a letter of introduction either from his embassy in Lisbon, from a Portuguese cultural institution (such as the *Instituto de Alta Cultura*, the Academy of Sciences, and the Calouste Gulbenkian Foundation), or from a recognized foreign institution. The card of admission, when authorized, is valid until the end of the year in which it is issued, and may be renewed thereafter for a period of 14 years. A special authorization, attached to the general card of admission, is required by the Rare Book and Manuscript Division. The Library's photo-duplication service reproduces in microfilm, negative photostat, positive photograph, or electrostat form; as an additional favor to scholars abroad, the library will reproduce any item and forward the reproduction by mail. The library is housed in a splendid new building, which is heated in the wintertime.

The holdings of the Rare Book and Manuscript Division are 3,383 boxes and bundles of miscellaneous manuscripts; 12,484 codices; 12,911 prints and drawings; 12,987 rare books; and 5,363 atlases and maps. Special mention should be made of the Pombaline Collection, acquired form the heirs of the Marquess of Pombal (1699–1782), made up largely of papers of the first half of the eighteenth century, many of them of great interest for the history of diplomacy. Other manuscripts in the division include the diplomatic correspondence of the Marquess of Niza, António da Silva e Sousa, Francisco de Sousa Coutinho, Father António Vieira, the Count of Ericeira, Alexandre de Gusmão, the Count of Tarouca, Dom Luís da Cunha, Caetano Lima, the Duke of Palmela, Anselmo José Braamcamp, José Estêvão, the Count of Lavradio, the Count of Bonfim, the Bishop of Viseu, the Duke of Ávila e Bolam, and António Ribeiro Saraiva. Still other papers deal with the diplomatic relations of Portugal with various states of Europe, Africa, and Asia. The catalogue of the division is complete, and printed guides are available for some of the collections.

Arquivo Histórico Militar

Located on Largo dos Caminhos de Ferro, Lisbon, these archives were founded by decree of May 25, 1911. The Director is Colonel Luis Mendes. These archives are open during the week from 2–5:30 P.M., and Saturdays from 9:30–12:00N. Military and civilian foreigners may work in the archives with the permission of the Army Chief of Staff. Requests for admittance should be channeled through the appropriate embassy in Lisbon in advance of the proposed period of research.

The *Arquivo Histórico Militar* is one of the largest archives of Portugal. Created for the purpose of bringing together the scattered records of the Portuguese army, it has not yet achieved this ambitious goal; the papers of the Council of War (1640 to 1834), for example, are still in the *Torre do Tombo*.

The holdings of the archives are divided into threee sections. The first concerns military campaigns in Europe and in Portugal, the oldest existing documents, before 1640, being found here. The second deals with overseas expeditions and campaigns, and Brazil is included in this section. The third comprises a collection of papers on general military matters, such as the defense of Portugal, uniforms, iconography, etc. Within the three sections are papers of the extinct Secretariat of State for Foreign Affairs and War, papers on the wars of the Liberal period (the so-called Terceira [Azores] Archives), the papers of the former Inspectors-General of Infantry and Cavalry, etc. The archives are organized chronologically by subject, and the subjects are, in many cases, the wars on which Portugal has taken part.

Arquivo Histórico do Ministério das Finanças

Located on Rua de Santa Marta 61-E, Lisbon, these archives are open daily, except Sundays and holdiays. Admittance is by arrangement with the Director, who will acquaint the scholar with the rules and regulations.

Most of the material concerns domestic affairs, but certain collections are of special interest for the history of diplomacy. Among these are the archives of the royal house, which contain, *inter alia,* reports and correspondence of Alexandre de Gusmão, the private secretary of King John V and the person most directly involved in the negotiations for the boundary treaty of 1750, dealing primarily with South America. The papers of the Order of Malta, some of which are here, and those of the Council of the Exchequer will also be of use to the historian of diplomacy.

The papers are not catalogued, but there are a number of printed guides and studies. Arrangements may be made with the director to consult papers housed in annexes of the archives in Santa Lucia, Trinas, and Calçada da Ajuda, all in Lisbon.

Arquivo Histórico Municipal, Lisbon

Located on the Paço do Concelho, Lisbon, these archives are open daily, except Sundays and holidays, from 9:15-12:00 N. and from 2-5:30 P.M., and on Saturdays from 9:15-12:00 N. The Chief Archivist is Dr. Lia Arez Ferreira do Amaral, whose assistant is Dr. Idalina Mota Grilo Ribeiro Rodrigues. The archives are ultimately under the jurisdiction of Dr. Cristiano de Maia Alves, Director of the Section on Libraries, Museums, and Archives of the Lisbon municipality. The usual identity card is required of readers or, in the case of foreigners, a passport. Typewriters may be used, and photographic reproductions may be made with the permission of the director of the Section.

The papers, collected in about six thousand codices and numerous bundles and boxes, are of considerable interest for the history of diplomacy. The current records of the city government of Lisbon are kept in the *Arquivo Geral da Câmara Municipal de Lisboa*; any document over fifty years old is automatically transferred from the *Arquivo Geral* to the *Arquivo Histórico Municipal*. The collection known as the *Chancelaria Regia* begins with the first king of Portugal and extends to the overthrow of the monarchy in 1910. The collection known as the *Chancelaria da Cidade* is divided into three parts: (1) *Livros da Chancelaria* (1627–1824), (2) *Livros da Vereação* (1515–1900), and (3) *Editais e Posturas* (1419–1753). There is a miscellaneous *Colecção da Coroa* (Crown Collection) that has nothing to do with the administration of the city of Lisbon.

There are quite detailed catalogues for the several sections of the *Arquivo Histórico*, with topographical, chronological, onomastic, and subject references. Fortunately, the papers of the municipal archives of Lisbon survived both the earthquake of 1755 and the fire of 1863. It seems likely that the *Arquivo Histórico* will be moved from the present downtown location in City Hall to a new location near the future Museum of the City of Lisbon, scheduled to be housed in Pimenta Palace in Campo Grande.

Biblioteca e Arquivo da Assembleia Nacional

Located in the Palácio de São Bento, Lisbon, this library was founded in 1836 with a valuable collection of books selected from the libraries of the suppressed religious convents and moved to its present location in 1935 under the supervision of Dr. Maria das Dores Lopes de Silva. It houses thirty-seven thousand volumes and rich manuscript sources. Established for the private use of the members of the legislature, it may be used by others who are properly identified and by foreigners with credentials from the applicant's embassy, with the permission of the Secretary-General of the Assembly, Idalino Ferreira da Costa Brochado.

The archival section contains the papers of the constitutitonal monarchy, beginning with the Constituent Assembly of 1821 and extending to the overthrow of the regime in 1910, the papers of the republican congresses (1911–1925), and those of the two legislative chambers since 1935. The *processos* from the Corporative Chamber (since 1954) are also here. There are indices for all the sections of the archives, some more complete and detailed than others.

Arquivo Histórico Ultramarino

Located in the Palácio da Ega, Calçada da Boa-Hora 30, Junqueira, Lisbon, these archives are open daily, except Sundays and holidays, from 11:30 A.M. to 7:00 P.M. and on Saturdays from 9–12:00 N. Dr. Alberto Iria is their Director.

This colonial repository is part of the Overseas Ministry. Especially well known to historians for the papers of the Overseas Council (1643–1833), in its time the most important administrative agency for the Portuguese Empire, the archives contain also the papers of the administrative offices and agencies that have since superseded the Council. The archives are exclusively historical in nature, and additions to its collections are made every five years from the files of the Overseas Ministry.

The *Arquivo Histórico Ultramarino* is the largest and most important archives of Portugal for the study of the history of the former and present overseas possessions of Portugal, including Brazil. There are about four kilometers of linear shelved materials, including 4,380 codices, 2,284 bundles of manuscripts, and 810 boxes of manuscripts. There is also an uninventoried collection of miscellaneous papers.

These archives, like nearly all the others of Portugal, do not have a special section devoted to diplomatic affairs, but many of the documents have a direct bearing on diplomatic history. For the boundary disputes in South America, as well as those in the Portuguese settlements of Africa and elsewhere, the records of the *Arquivo Histórico Ultramarino* are indispensable. Actually, the history of the imperial aspects of Portuguese diplomacy cannot be adequately treated without consulting these papers.

The archives have photoduplication equipment. Typewriters and tape recorders may be used if they do not disturb the other readers. The research facilities are open to foreigners upon the presentation of certain credentials, usually a letter of introduction from the applicant's embassy. Brazilians are exempt from these regulations and need only present their identity cards or passports.

Biblioteca da Ajuda

This library is located in the Palácio da Ajuda, Lisbon, and was opened to the public in 1880. It is open daily, except Sundays and holidays, from 10:30 A.M. to 5:00 P.M., and on Saturdays from 10:30 A.M. to 2:00 P.M. The Director is Dr. Mariana Amélia Machado Santos.

The library's holdings include about a hundred thousand printed items and some twenty-five thousand manuscripts. Among its manuscript collections are the Rerum Lusitanicarum (an eighteenth century collection of manuscripts on the relations between Portugal and the Holy See, in 226 volumes), the Chancellery of King Philip III, some diplomatic correspondence, documents on the Portuguese overseas possessions, and documents on the history of Portugal (sixteenth through the eighteenth centuries).

Biblioteca Geral da Universidade de Coimbra

This library in Coimbra is open daily, except Sundays and holidays, from 9:30 A.M. to 12:30 P.M. and from 2-5:30 P.M. Dr. Guilherme Braga is its Director.

The manuscript section of the library contains about six thousand codices and boxes, and a considerable quantity of miscellaneous papers. Its materials are especially valuable for the diplomacy of the seventeenth century, notably of the Restoration. Here are papers that deal with the missions sent to the various

European courts, in connection with the recognition of John IV, first of the Bragança line, as king of Portugal. Since 1914 this library has published a *Boletim* and numerous descriptions of its manuscript collections.

Like the *Biblioteca Nacional de Lisbon,* this university library is officially classed as a national library and contains about a million volumes. There are no restrictions against the use of typewriters and photographic equipment.

Arquivo da Universidade de Coimbra

In existence in Coimbra since the sixteenth century, but opened to the public only since 1903, these archives are open daily, except Sundays and holidays, from 9:30 A.M. to 12:30 P.M. and from 2–5:00 P.M. and on Saturday, from 9:30 A.M. to 1:00 P.M. Dr. Amèrico da Costa Ramalho is director of this repository, which is housed in a modern building and provided with every convenience. It comes under the immediate control of the rector of the university. It holds the papers of the Count of Arcos and materials on the governors-general and viceroys of Brazil. Of special interest for the history of diplomacy are materials on Dom Luís da Cunha (the Portuguese delegate to the Congress of Utrecht), the Napoleonic invasions, the relations of the University with the Holy See, the Society of Jesus, and the Nova Colónia do Sacramento.

These archives have photographic equipment, but readers may use their own. Typewriters are not allowed.

Biblioteca Pública Municipal, Oporto

Founded in 1833, this library is open daily, except Sundays and holidays, from 10:00 A.M. to 11:30 P.M. Dr. António Augusto Ferreira da Curz is director.

This is the principal library of northern Portugal and, indeed, one of the largest and best in the country. Its collection of manuscripts comprises about twenty-five hundred codices and fifteen hundred bundles of papers. This collection is of considerable interest for the study of nearly all periods of the diplomatic history of Portugal, but particularly since the seventeenth century. A catalogue is available.

Foreign readers must present passports and letters of introduction from their diplomatic or consular representatives. The library has photographic equipment, but the reproduction of manuscripts requires the approval of the director. Readers may use typewriters.

Other Archives

Mention should be made of some local archives and family collections, which, although unexplored by the author, might contain diplomatic materials:

Biblioteca Pública e Arquivo Distrital in Braga, Ponta Delegada (Azores), Angra do Heroísmo (Azores), Évora, Faro, and Funcial (Madeira).

Private archives of the noble families: Pamela, Lafões, Cadaval, Fronteira, Abrantes, Ponte de Lima, Rio Maior, Alegrete, Castelo Melhor, Val de Reis, Sabugosa, and Murça.

ADMISISTRATION, REGULATIONS, AND FACILITIES

It is well for the foreigner who expects to carry out an ambitious program of research in Portugal to express the intention in advance of arrival both to the directors of the archives and libraries, and to his cultural affairs officer. Upon arrival in Lisbon, the foreigner should secure from his embassy a letter of introduction to each director of the archives and libraries of interest. By a 1931 decree, a foreigner must present a passport as well as a letter of introduction to the director in charge, but some archives and libraries outside the captial city are lenient in this respect.

Since most of the large archives are in Lisbon, it is likely that scholars will make their headquarters in the capital city. Its hotels are numerous, but substantial savings are offered by many comfortable pensões. While summer weather is pleasant in Lisbon, one should be prepared for cold, sometimes rainy winters and remember that buildings, such as the *Biblioteca Nacional*, may not be heated. Public transportation is very good.

BIBLIOGRAPHY

Guides and References

1. Almada, José de. *Tratados Aplícaveis ao Ultramar, Apêndices ê Índices.* Lisbon, 1942.
2. Almeida, Eduardo de Castro e. *Bibliotheca Nacional de Lisboa. Archivo de Marinha e Ultramar. Inventario. Madeira.* Coimbra, 1903.
3. *Bibliotheca Nacional de Lisboa. Archivo de Marinha e Ultramar. Inventario. Madeira e Porto Santo, 1613-1833.* 2 vols. Coimbra, 1907-9.
4. *Bibliotheca Nacional de Lisboa. Archivo de Marinha e Ultramar. Catalogo de mappas, plantas, desenhos, gravuras e aguarellas.* Coimbra, 1908.
5. *Inventario dos documentos relativos ao Brasil existentes no Archivo de Marinha e Ultramar.* Vols. 31 (Bahia, 1613-1762), 32 (Bahia, 1763-86), 34 (Bahia, 1786-98), 36 (Bahia, 1798-1800), 37 (Bahia, 1801-7), 39 (Rio de Janeiro, 1616-1729), 46 (Rio de Janeiro, 1729-47), and 50 (Rio de Janeiro, 1747-55) of *Annaes da Biblioteca Nacional do Rio de Janeiro.* Rio de Janeiro, 1913-36.
6. Almeida, José Gaspar de. *Índice-Roteiro dos chamados Livros dos Originais (Colecção de Pergaminhos) do Cartório do Cabido da Sé do Pôrto.* Oporto, 1936.
7. *Inventário do Cartório do Cabido da Sé do Pôrto e dos cartôrios anexos.* Publicações do Arquivo Distrital do Pôrto, I. Oporto, 1935.
8. Almeida, Manuel Lopes d', and César Pegado. *Livro 2º de Registo das Cartas dos Governadores das Armas (1653-1657).* Biblioteca Geral da Universidade. Coimbra, 1940.
9. Alves, Francisco Manuel. *Catálogo dos manuscritos de Simancas respeitantes à história portuguesa.* Coimbra, 1933.
10. Andrada, Ernesto de Campos de. "O Palacio dos Marquezes da Fronteira e os seus manuscritos," *Revista de Historia* (Lisbon), XII, Nos. 47-48 (July-December 1923), 241-68.

11. Anselmo, António. *Os códices alcobacenses da Biblioteca Nacional.* Lisbon, 1926.

12. *Archivum, Annuaire Internationale des Archives* (Paris), XIII (1963), XXI (1972).

13. Arquivo Nacional da Torre do Tombo. *Indice geral dos documentos registados nos livros das chancellarias existentes no Real Archivo da Torre do Tombo mandado fazer pelas Cortes Na Lei do Orçamento de 7 de Abril de 1838.* Lisbon, 1841.

14. *Inventario dos livros das portarias do Reino.* Lisbon, 1909.

15. Ataíde, A.P. de Bettencourt. "Bibliografia portuguesa de Biblioteconomia e Arquivologia Subsídio para o estudo do nosso problema bibliotecário e arquivístico," *Revista de Historia* (Lisbon), VIII, No. 30 (April-June 1919), 87-106.

16. Azevedo, Pedro A. d', and António Baião. *O Archivo da Torre do Tombo, Sua historia, corpos que o compóem e organisação.* Lisbon, 1905.

17. Baião, António. *O Arquivo Nacional da Torre do Tombo.* Lisbon, 1929.

18. Barreto-Feio, Florêncio Mago. *Memoria historica e descriptiva, á cêrca da biblioteca da Universidade de Coimbra e mais estabelecimentos anexos; contendo varios esclarecimentos officiaes, e reflexões bibliographicas.* Coimbra, 1857.

19. Basset, René. *Notice sommaire des manuscrits orientaux de deux bibliothèques de Lisbonne, mémoire destiné à la 10ème session du Congrès International des Orientalistes.* Lisbon, 1894.

21. Biblioteca Geral da Universidade de Coimbra. *Catálogo da colecção de miscelânea.* Compiled by José Maria dos Santos. 19 vols.

22. Biblioteca Geral da Universidade de Coimbra. *Catálogo de manuscritos.* Vols. I-XXIX, XXI-XXIII. Coimbra, 1940-1971. (Vol. XX is in preparation.)

23. Biblioteca Nacional de Lisboa. *Inventário dos Códices Alcobacenses.* 5 vols. Lisbon, 1930-32.

24. *Inventário Decção XIII — manuscritos collecçcão pombalina.* Lisbon, 1889. *Inventario Seccao XIII) manuscritos.* Lisbon, 1896.

25. Biblioteca Pública Municipal do Porto. *Catálogo dos manuscritos (códices nos. 1225 a 1364).* Compiled by António Augusto Ferreira da Cruz. Oporto, 1952.

26. Biblioteca Pública Municipal do Porto. *Documentos para a sua historia.* Oporto, 1933.

27. *Boletim da Biblioteca da Universidade de Coimbra.* 30 vols. and 5 supplements. Coimbra, 1914-73.

28. Cardozo, Manoel S. "A guide to the manuscripts in the Lima Library, The Catholic University of America, Washington, D.C.," *Handbook of Latin American Studies,* VI (1941), 471-504.

29. Carvalho, José Branquinho de. *Roteiro do Arquivo Municipal de Coimbra.* Coimbra, 1947.

30. Castro, Luís de. "O Arquivo Municipal," *Revista Municipal* (Lisbon), Nos. 18-19 (1944), 29-34.

31. *Catálogo dos Manuscritos Ultramarinos da Biblioteca Pública Municipal do Porto.* I Congresso da História da Expansão Portuguesa no Mundo, 5.a secçao. Lisbon, 1938.

32. *Catalogue de la bibliothèque de M. Fernando Palha.* 4 vols. Lisbon, 1896. [The Palha Collection is at Harvard University.]

35. Cruz, António Augusto Rerreira da. *Catálogo dos manuscritos da Restauração da Biblioteca da Universidade de Coimbra.* Coimbra, 1936.

36. Danvers, F.C. *Report to the secretary of state for India on the Portuguese records relating to the East Indies contained in the Archivo da Torre do Tombo and the public libraries of Lisbon and Evora.* London, 1892.

37. Diffie, Bailey W. "Bibliography of the principal published guides to Portuguese archives and libraries," *Proceedings of the International Colloquium on Luso-Brazilian Studies, Washington, October 15-20, 1950, under the auspices of The Library of Congress and Vanderbilt University* (Nashville, Tenn., 1953), pp. 181-88.

38. Esfèvam, José. "A Biblioteca da Ajuda," *Illustração Portugueza* (Lisbon), November 11, 1907.

39. Estevens, Manuel Santos. *Arquivo Geral e Biblioteca Central da Marinha.* Lisbon, 1945.

40. *Sinopse Cronológica da Legislação Portuguesa sobre Bibliotecas e Arquivos (1796-1948).* Coimbra, 1949.

41. Ferrão, António. *Os arquivos e as bibliotecas em Portugal.* Ciências auxiliares da história bibliografia e bibliotecografia. Coimbra, 1920.

42. Ferreira, Carlos Alberto. *Inventário dos Manuscritos da Biblioteca da Ajuda Referentes à América do Sul.* Faculdade de Letras de Universidade de Coimbra, Instituto de Estudos Brasileiros. Coimbra, 1946.

43. Figanière, Frederico Francisco de la. *Catalogo dos manuscritos*

portuguezes existentes no Museu Britannico. Em que tambem se dá noticia dos manuscriptos estrangeiros relativos á historia civil, politica e litteraria de Portugal e seus dominios, e se transcrevem na integra alguns documentos importantes e curiosos. Lisbon, 1853.

44. Figueiredo, A. Mesquita de. *Arquivo Nacional da Tôrre do Tombo roteiro prático.* Lisbon, 1922.
45. Fitzler, M.A. Hedwig. *Os tombos de Ceilão da secção ultramarina da Biblioteca Nacional.* Publicações da Biblioteca Nacional. Lisbon, 1927.
46. Fitzler, M.A. Hedwig, and Ernesto Ennes. *A Secção Ultramarina da Biblioteca Nacional. Inventários. I. Códices do Extincto Conselho Ultramarino. Estudos e Notas por M.A. Hedwig Fitzler. II. Códices do Arquivo da Marinha publicados, anotados e prefaciados por Ernesto Ennes.* Lisbon, 1928.
47. Fonseca, Francisco Belard da. *O Arquivo Geral da Alfândega de Lisboa.* Publicações da Inspecção Superior das Bibliotecas e Arquivos, Vol. 3. Lisbon, 1950.
48. Fonseca, Martinho da. *Catálogo resumido da Preciosa collecçâo de manuscritos da Casa Cadaval.* Lisbon, 1915.
49. Guimarães, J.G. de Oliveira. *Catálogo dos pergaminhos existentes no archivo da insigne e real collegiada de Guimarães.* Lisbon, 1909.
50. *Index Codicum Bibliotheca Alcobatiae.* Lisbon, 1775.
51. Lima, Durval Pires de, ed. *Livros dos Reis,* I- (Lisboa, 1957-).
52. Lima, Henrique de Campos Ferreira. *Documentos manuscritos e cartográficos relativos ao Brasil que existem no Arquivo Histórico Militar.* Lisbon, 1942.
53. Lima, Manoel de Oliveira. *Relação dos Manuscritos portuguezes e estrangeiros, de interesse para o Brazil, existentes no Museu Britannico de Londres.* Rio de Janeiro, 1903.
54. Marques, João Martins da Silva. *Arquivo Nacional da Tôrre do Tombo (ensaio de um manual de heurística e arquivologia).* Vol. I (Index Indicum). Lisbon, 1935.
55. Mellander, Karl, and Edgar Prestage. *The diplomatic and commercial relations of Sweden and Portugal from 1641 to 1670.* Watford, England, 1930.
56. Francis, A.D. *The Methuens and Portugal 1691-1708.* Cambridge, England, 1966.
57. Melo, Arnaldo Faria de Ataíde e. "Arquivo Histórico Municipal," *Revista Municipal* (Lisbon), Numbers 30-31 (1947), 21-25.

58. Morel-Fatio, Alfred. *Catalogue des manuscrits espagnols et des manuscrits portugais, Bibliothèque Nationale, Département des Manuscrits.* Paris, 1892.

59. Norton, Luís. *Noticia sobre o "Arquivo Militar de Lisboa" encontrado no Ministério das Relações Exteriores do Brasil.* Rio de Janeiro, 1938.

60. Oliveira, Eduardo Freire. *Elementos para a Historia do Municipio de Lisboa.* 17 vols. Lisbon, 1882–1911.

61. Peixoto, Jorge. "Arquivo," *Verbum Enciclopédia Luso-Brasileira de Cultura,* II (Lisbon, 1964), 1272–1303.

62. Pereira, Gabriel. *Catálogo dos pergaminhos do cartorio da Universidade de Coimbra.* Coimbra, 1880.

63. *Bibliotecas e arquivos nacionais.* Lisbon, 1903.

64. *Biblioteca Nacional de Lisboa.* Lisbon, 1898.

65. *O archivo ultramarino, Bibliotheca Nacional de Lisboa.* Lisbon, 1902.

66. Pereira, Isaías da Rosa. "Inventário Provisório do Arquivo da Cúria Patriarcal de Lisboa," *Lusitania Sacra,* IX (1972), 311–85.

67. Prestage, Edgar. *Chapters in Anglo-Porutguese relations.* Watford, England, 1935.

68. *The diplomatic relations of Portugal with France, England, and Holland from 1640 to 1668.* Watford, England, 1925.

69. Proença, Raúl de. "A Bibliotheca Nacional Breves noções históricas e descritivas," *Publicações da Biblioteca Nacional* (Lisbon), I (1918), 7–57.

70. Rau, Virgínia. "Arquivos de Portugal: Lisboa," *Proceedings of the International Colloquium on Luso-Brazilian Studies, Washington, October 15–20, 1950, under the auspices of The Library of Congress and Vanderbilt University* (Nashville, Tenn., 1953), pp. 189–213.

71. Rau, Virgínia, and Maria Fernanda Gomes da Silva. *Os manuscritos do arquivo da Casa de Cadaval respeitantes ao Brasil.* 2 vols. Coimbra, 1956–58.

72. Rebello, José Pedro de Miranda. *Extracto do Real Archivo da Torre do Tombo offerecido á augustissima rainha, e senhora D. Maria I.* Lisbon, 1904.

73. Rego, A. da Silva. *Manuscritos da Ajuda (Guia).* Vol. I. Lisbon, 1966.

74. Ribeiro, João Pedro. *Memorias authenticas para a historia do Real Archivo.* Lisbon, 1819.

75. Rivara, Joaquim Heliodoro da Cunha. *Catálogo dos manuscritos da Biblioteca Publica Eborense.* 4 vols. Lisbon, 1850-71.

76. Sampaio, Luís Teixeira de. *O Arquivo Histórico do Ministério dos Negócios Estrangeiros (subsídio para o estudo da história da diplomacia portuguesa).* Coimbra, 1926.

77. Santarém, Visconde de. *Noticia dos manuscritos pertencentes ao direito publico externo diplomatico de Portugal, e á historia, e litteratura do mesmo paiz, que existem na bibliotheca R. de Paris, e outras, da mesma captial, e nos archivos de França.* Lisbon, 1827.

78. Silveira, Luís. *Portugal nos arquivos do estrangeiro. I. Manuscritos portugueses da Biblioteca Estadual de Hamburgo.* Lisbon, 1946.

79. Tarouca, Carlos da Silva. *Inventário das cartas e dos códices manuscritos do Arquivo do Cabido da Sé de Évora.* Évora, 1946.

80. Tovar, Conde de. *Catálogo dos manuscritos portugueses ou relativos a Portugal existentes no Museu Britânico.* Lisbon, 1932.

81. Velloso, J.M. de Queirós. *O Arquivo Geral de Simancas sua importância capital para história portuguesa.* Coimbra, 1923.

Printed Collections

82. Biker, Júlio Firmino Júdice. *Supplemento á collecção dos tratados, convenções, contratos e actos publicos celebrados entre a corôa de Portugal e as mais potencias desde 1640 compilados, coordenados e annotados pelo Visconde de Borges de Castro.* Vols. 9-30. Lisbon, 1872-79.

83. Castro, José Ferreira Borges de. *Colecção dos tratados, convenções, contratos e actos publicos celebrados entre a corôa de Portugal e as mais potencias desde 1640 até ao presente.* Vols. 1-8. Lisbon, 1856-58.

84. Cruz, António Augusto Ferreira da. *Subsídios para a história das relações diplomáticas de Portugal com a Holanda (1640-1668).* Oporto, 1948.

85. Santarém, Visconde de. *Corpo diplomatico portuguez, contendo todos os tratados de paz, de alliança, de neutralidade, de tregua, de commercio, de limites, de ajustes de casamentos, de cessões de territorio e outras transacções entre a corôa de Portugal e as diversas potencias do mundo, desde o principio da monarchia até aos nossos dias.* Vol. I (Portugal e Espanha). Paris, 1846.

86. Santarém, Visconde de, and Luís Augusto Rebello da Silva. *Quadro elementar das relações politicas e diplomaticas de Portugal com as diversas potencias do mundo, desde o principio da monarchia*

portugueza até aos nossos dias. 16 vols. Paris and Lisbon, 1842–60.

87. Silva, Luís Augusto Rebello da, and Jaime Constantino de Freitas Moniz. *Corpo diplomatico portuguez contendo os actos e relações politicas e diplomaticas de Portugal com as diversas potencias do mundo desde o seculo XVI até os nossos dias.* 10 vols. Lisbon, 1862–91.

14   SPAIN

Lino G. Canedo

Academy of American Franciscan History
(Translation by Rhea Marsh Smith, *Rollins College*)

HISTORY

THE role of Spain in European international politics began to be preponderant as a consequence of the marriage of Ferdinand and Isabel. During the sixteenth century, Spain dominated the European scene under its two monarchs, Charles I and Philip II. It continued to be one of the great powers until the Peace of Westphalia (1648) and exercised considerable influence in the affairs of Europe until the French Revolution. The power of Spain began its final decline in the latter part of the eighteenth century under the inertia of Charles IV. The struggles of the war of independence against Napoleon so shattered the machinery of state, and so divided the Spaniards politically, that the catastrophe was consummated in the reign of Ferdinand VII with the loss of nearly all the overseas territories and the beginning of internal conflicts which fill the Spanish history of the nineteenth century.

It must not be concluded that only at the end of the fifteenth century did Spaniards begin to participate in European politics. As the reconquest advanced and the Arab domination in the peninsula ceased to be an absorbing preoccupation, the old Spanish kingdoms intervened more and more in European affairs. The Kingdom of Aragon (Aragon, Catalonia, the Balearic Islands, and Valencia) was the principal Mediterranean power in the fourteenth and fifteenth centuries, while Navarre was in close contact with France. Castile, politically less developed and more absorbed in its struggle with the Arabs (who continued to occupy a good part of its territory) could not give as much attention to external enterprises, but it never lacked European interests. An example of this was the candidacy of Alfonso X, the Wise, for the imperial crown which was granted to him in effect, although he never succeeded in enjoying it. This Castilian participation in European politics became more intense as a result of the so-called Schism of the West, and after its liquidation at the beginning of the fifteenth century.[1] The documentation on this theme in the Spanish national archives of today (Simancas) is very scanty, perhaps because it was neither very extensive, nor conserved with due care, or for both reasons. The itinerant condition of the Castilian court during this time did not facilitate the services of the chancellery and archives. It was quite the contrary in the Kingdom of Aragon and Navarre, which have left us magnificent diplomatic archives, especially the former. The *Archivo de la Corona de Aragón* in Barcelona, the most important in the Aragonese kingdom, contains not only sources of a medieval character, but also others that are of interest to the history of the modern diplomacy of Spain.

All these historical circumstances make a satisfactory classification of the Spanish diplomatic archives difficult. For the practical aims of this study, it has appeared preferable to consider them as independent entities, while noting the relations that exist between some, like those of Simancas, of the *Archivo histórico nacional* and of the *Ministerio de Asuntos exteriores*.

The objective — to present within the short space assigned the greatest amount of information useful for the investigator — causes deficiencies which may be overcome in part through the consultation of the works cited in the general bibliography at the end of this chapter. In addition to those which are indicated under Nos. 1, 19, and 23, that of Carini (No. 48) is especially recommended. In regard to the collections of treaties, one should refer to the *Repertorio* of López Oliván (No. 45), where the principal series are given.

[1] Some reference to Spaniards who, for example, took a decisive part in the direction of papal diplomacy during the fifteenth century, may be found in Lino Gómez Canedo, *Don Juan de Carvajal. Un español al servicio de la Santa Sede* (Madrid, Consejo Superior de Investigaciones Científicas, 1947), pp. 8–30.

For a recent general report on the Spanish archives, see Luis Sánchez Belda, "Los archivos de España. Compendio de los grandes depósitos y de su fondos principales", *Archives et bibliothèques de Belgique*, XLIII, 1971, n. 3-4. There are numerous publications on archives and libraries, in addition to the series of Guías. The quarterly *Indice histórico español* carries regularly a section on archival bibliography.

All Spanish national public archives may be consulted. Investigators need only to provide themselves in advance with the *Tarjeta de lector*, which may be obtained in any of the archives and is valid for a year. To obtain the card it is sufficient to identify oneself as a scholar or to be introduced by a scholar or an official of some cultural body of recognized standing. The criteria of admission are very broad, and the regulations that must be observed by readers and researchers are simple.

ARCHIVO GENERAL DE SIMANCAS[2]

HISTORY

These archives are in the Castle of Simancas, a short distance from Valladolid, in the dry plain of Castile. The old castle was designated in about 1539 for the conservation and custody of the papers belonging to the royal crown. In 1509, the creation of two central archives had been arranged: one in the Chancellery of Valladolid, for the original documents, and another in the Chancellery of Granada, where authorized copies of such documents would be kept. It is not known to what extent this project was realized, especially for the Archives of Granada.[3] There is evidence that many documents perished during the War of the Com-

---

[2] The history of the Archives of Simancas is narrated in detail in the *Guía histórica y descriptiva* (No. 1). See especially pp. 140-158, 343-357.

[3] It is nevertheless certain that the licentiate Salmerón had been named "Keeper of the Writings concerning the Royal Crown," in 1509. The licentiate Galindo (1519) and the licentiate Acuña (1526) succeeded him. See *Guía histórica y descriptiva*, pp. 148 ff. in No. 1.

uneros (1521), and it was this, perhaps, which inspired the selection of a place as secure as the fortress of Simancas.

The castle housed not only he documents collected in the Chancellery of Valladolid after 1509, but also other documents relating to the Crown of Castile, which after the reigns of John II and Henry IV had been ordered secured in the Castillo de la Mota (Medina del Campo) and the Alcázar of Segovia. Successively, the authorities added other groups of documents from different offices and depositories. In 1542 these were placed in the care of *licenciado* Catalán, but the first archivist in the true sense of the word was Don Diego de Ayala, appointed in 1561. Only then did the archives begin to be really organized, with the completion of the necessary facilities in the castle. Ayala was able to accomplish a great deal not only because of this intelligence and effort, but also because he enjoyed the confidence of Philip II, who gave the archives their basic regulations by the royal decree of August 24, 1588, at the Escorial. Philip IV promulgated another important regulation, in 1633, as a consequence of the inspection made by Antonio de Hoyos.

The *Archivo general de Simancas* suffered a real disaster during the French invasion at the beginning of the nineteenth century when it had to contribute enormous quantities of papers to the fantastic Napoleonic caprice of creating the Archives of the Empire in Paris. It is estimated that between 1810 and 1811 some five hundred carts[4] of documents left Simancas for Paris. In being selected for shipment, the series was disorganized and the disaster was later increased with the entrance of parties of irregular troops into Simancas. With the fall of Napoleon in 1814, all this material should have been restored to Simancas, but the French contrived to hide the most important documents on Hispanic-French diplomatic relations. The famous canon Don Tomás González, named in 1815 by a royal commission for the reorganization of

---

[4]The estimate of 500 carts is that of Paz in the introduction to the printed catalogue of these documents (No. 11 in bibliography). In the *Guía histórica y descriptiva* (No. 1), it is stated that 60 carts were taken in 1810 and 172 boxes in 1811, without affirming that these were the only ones sent.

the archives, immediately discovered this deceitful maneuver, and Spain initiated a series of official protests, unheeded by the French until 1941. Not until after this date did they return the sequestered documents (it is not known whether all were returned) to their place of origin and to the possession of their legitimate owner.

Until the foundation of the *Archivo general de Alcalá de Henares* and the *Archivo histórico nacional* (Madrid) in the second half of the nineteenth century, Simancas constituted the only general archives of Spain for official documents, with the exception of those of America kept in the *Archivo general de Indias* (Seville). For this reason, several shipments of documents were sent to Simancas after its reorganization by Don Tomás González.

ORGANIZATION AND CLASSIFICATION

This description of the *Archivo general de Simancas* is limited to the sources of a diplomatic character. The documents are divided into sections, according to their content. Each section is subdivided into series, and within each series the distribution by bundles is usually chronological.

The documents of interest for diplomatic history are conserved principally in the section called *Estado,* consisting of the papers of the Secretariat of State. Eventually they were organized into Italy and the North, assigning to the latter the affairs of Spain and Portugal. The bulk of the State documents in Simancas belong to the sixteenth and seventeenth centuries, but there are also many of the eighteenth century and some of the fifteenth century. In general, the remaining State papers for the seventeenth and eighteenth centuries are found in the *Archivo histórico nacional* (Madrid) and are continued in the ministry of foreign affairs (formerly called State), which possesses its own historical archives.

The records of *Estado* in Simancas retain their old classification by "negotiations," one for each country. The most important "negotiations" for European diplomatic history are:

1. Negotiations with Germany (1510-1733), Saxony (1738-88),

Prussia (1744–88), Poland (1746–91), and Hamburg (1725–59). A general section also covers the years 1510–1619. These sources are inventoried in summary fashion in Catalogue II, prepared by Julián Paz (No. 12). Paz also included in his catalogue (pp. 241–299) the bundles relating to Germany, which are found in the series of *Negocios notables* of the same section of State. They contain documents from 1511 to 1744. Paz likewise indicates five bundles of the section, "Royal Patronage," with documents of the years of 1493–1661, relating to "Capitulations and Treaties with the House of Austria."

2. Negotiations with Flanders, Holland, and Brussels, 1506–1795. In *Negocios notables*, there exists also, as in the case of Germany, a number of bundles with important documents relative to the negotiations with Flanders from 1549 until 1754. These sources are inventoried in Catalogue III, also by Julián Paz (No. 13).

3. Negotiations with France. This is one of the most important archival collections for the history of European diplomacy. Many of these papers remained in Paris until after 1941, as has been indicated, but they had been inventoried in 1914 by Julián Paz in Catalogue IV of Simancas (No. 14). Nearly all of these documents belong to the sixteenth and seventeenth centuries. They include dispatches, and minutes of dispatches, from the Spanish ambassadors in Paris, consultations of the Council on such dispatches, capitulations and treaties, etc. In the cited catalogue of Paz, the bundles marked with the letter "K" are of special value.

4. Negotiations with England. These are inventoried in Catalogue XVII of the *Archivo general de Simancas* (No. 17). In spite of the dates that appear in this catalogue (1480–1824), the documents begin to be abundant only after 1550. Only *legajo* 806, the first of the series, refers to the years 1480–1549. The classification of content corresponds to that of the remaining negoitations: letters and dispatches of the Spanish ambassadors in England, the corresponding consultations of the Coun-

cil, replies to the ambassadors, etc. The most modern papers, "English Embassy," added to the archives in 1841, contain the documents of the Spanish Embassy in London from 1764 to 1824.

5. Negotiations with Portugal, 1478-1784. No catalogue of this series has been published, but brief summaries can be found in the *Guía histórica* (pp. 216-222), and in the *Guía del investigador* by Alcócer (Nos. 1, 6, and 65). There is much material on the boundaries in South America. One group of papers refers to the union of the Spanish and Portuguese squadrons (1560-64) to eliminate the corsairs from the Straits of Gibraltar.

6. Negotiations with Rome. Number XIV of the series of catalogues of the archives (Valladolid, 1936) has an old inventory of this section. There is much diplomatic material, but many documents have a merely ecclesiastical character. A very important complement of these negotiations is in the archives of the Spanish Embassy to the Holy See, which are in the ministry of external affairs, in Madrid. These have a printed catalogue of several volumes.[5] Documents before the sixteenth century are very scarce.

7. Negotiations with Naples. These are inventoried in Catalogue XVI of the archives (No. 16). Many of the documents of this section refer to the internal government of the Kingdom of Naples as a Spanish possession, but diplomatic references, explicit or implicit, abound.

8. Sicily. Spanish Viceroyalty and Negotiations with Malta. This series has its inventory in Catalogue XIX of the archives (No. 18). That which was said in respect to the "Negotiations with

---

[5] *Archivo de la Embajada de Espagna cerca de la Santa Sede* (Rome, 1915-1935). The first volume (sixteenth century) was prepared by Father Luciano Serrano, O.S.A.; the four following by Father José Maris Pou y Marti, O.F.M. Another group of documents concerning the relations between Spain and the Holy See, from the source *Nunziatura di Spagna*, in the Archives of the Vatican, has been partially inventoried by José Olarra Garmendia in his *Indice de la correspondencia entre la Nunciatura de España y la Santa Sede, en tiempo de Felipe II* (Madrid, Academia de la Historia, 1940-49).

Naples" must be borne in mind, but special attention should be given to the role played by the Order of Malta in all the political affairs of the eastern Mediterranean.

9. Kingdom of the Two Sicilies. Eighteenth Century. Spanish Embassy. The catalogue of this source has been published by Ricardo Magdaleno, present director of the archives (No. 18). Since the Kingdom of the Two Sicilies included Naples and Sicily, this series continues the two preceding ones, wih a more strictly diplomatic character. There are negotiations for Denmark, Holland, Russia, Sweden, Switzerland, and the small states of Italy.

The diplomatic historian must give equal attention to certain general and miscellaneous series of the State section. Some of these, for example, are the *Registros de decretos de oficio.* Numbers 399–417 contain many documents from 1703 to 1730. *Libros* 68–79 have abundant diplomatic material, especially concerning affairs in Italy in the sixteenth century. Book 583 of *Inconexos* (Miscellaneous — Unconnected) has copies of correspondence (1746–50) of Don José de Aldecoa, minister of Spain in Sweden. Book 584 contains his dispatches from 1746 to 1749, and Book 585 has other copies by the same diplomatic representative, which cover the years 1750–52. In *Sueltos de Estado* (Loose State Papers) there are also diplomatic documents.

Besides the State section, various other sections of the *Archivo de Simancas* contain documents of interest to diplomatic history. Thus, in *Patronato* there is the series of "royal capitulations" or accords between the kings of Spain and other European sovereigns. Their interest frequently transcends the personal sphere by dealing with true treaties between nation and nation. Aside from the treaties with the Moslem states of the peninsula and those with Aragon and Navarre, there are the "Capitulations with England" (1294–1604), "Capitulations with the House of Austria" (1493–1608), "Treaties with Portugal" (1369–1593), "Capitulations with the Popes" (1452–1570), "Naples and Sicily" (1256–1599), "Milan" (1495–1579), and "Diverse Affairs of Italy"

(1251-1668). The capitulations with England and the House of Austria are inventoried in the respective catalogues of the section of *Estado*, but there is a still better inventory of all these diplomatic sources on the section of Patronage (No. 19). The "Capitulations with France," inventoried in Catalogue IV (No. 14), do not form part of the Patronage section.

In the *Gracia y Justicia* (Justice) section, there are papers relating to the relations of Spain with the Holy See and with the Pontifical Nunciature in Spain, and relating to the Tribunal de la Rota Española. Two series of this section refer to the government of the intruder king, Joseph I, brother of Napoleon (1809-13): "Intruder Government" and "Various Books" (1808-11).

In *Guerra y Marina* and *Guerra Antigua* (1386-1701), there is much diplomatic material, especially concerning the reigns of Ferdinand and Isabel and Charles I. The material relative to the latter has been inventoried in Catalogue XVIII (No. 21). Documents of diplomatic interest are found in the section *Secretaría de Guerra* (Secretariat of War) (1700-1830). There are the series "Expedition to Algers" (1775-76); "War with Portugal" (1761-63); "War of Catalonia" (1719-21); "Expedition to Sicily" (1718-22); "War with England" (1727-63); "War with France" (1793-99); "Secretaries of State," that is, correspondence with ambassadors and ministers (1724-88). In this section, there is also a series of *Inconexos* papers, which has some documents of interest to diplomatic history as, for example, the important correspnodence of the Marquis of Valladarias on the war in Germany. Documents of similar character appear in the section *Secretaría de Marina* (Secretariat of the Navy). The series, "Expeditions of Europe" (1720-83), contains papers relative to Gibraltar and Minorca, two burning preoccupations of Spanish diplomacy.

Another source which is not primarily diplomatic but is of value is the section *Hacienda* (Finance). It is sufficient to cite such volumes and subjects as: "Sums paid to the galleys of Genoa" (1612-1746); *Armada de la Liga* (Fleet of the League); correspondence with ambassadors on matters of finance (1734-75); presents to foreign courts (1785-99); war with Portugal and England (1796-99); war with France (1791-99); wars in Italy (1737-83); and sieges of Gibraltar (1776-98).

The section called *Secretarías provinciales,* which contains documents relating to the interior government of European possessions such as the Low Countries, Naples, and Milan, has also documents of importance for diplomatic history. The same may also be said for the section *Visitas de Italia.*

ADMINISTRATION, REGULATIONS, AND FACILITIES

The Archives of Simancas are administered by officials of the Corps of the Archives, subject to the General Directorship of Archives and Libraries of the Ministry of National Education. The Director is Amando Represa Rodriguez.

The archives are well arranged in the Castle of Simancas, some seven miles from Valladolid, on a good road. Communications are easy, since the archives possess their own bus which daily carries the researchers and archivists. They remain open all working days, from 9:00 A.M. to 1:30 P.M. In the months from April to October inclusive, they are also open from 4-8:00 P.M. All the documents may be consulted. A reference library, connected with the archives, may be utilized by the investigators. The archives have a microfilm office. In order to make microfilms with one's own apparatus it is necessary to have special permission.

Valladolid is a large city, with good hotels in its center, a good location for taking the archives bus. Apartments have also been completed for researchers in Simancas near the castle. The researcher who works during the months from November to March (usually intensely cold but dry) can use his afternoons to advantage in the library of the *Instituto de Historia moderna,* a center of studies installed in the principal building of the university, where nearly all the officials of the Archives of Simancas work. Besides, Valladolid has other attractions that can occupy the time of the studious: a good museum of polychrome sculpture, important architectural monuments, and the possibility of excursions to neighboring historic places with magnificent monuments such as Tordesillas, Medina del Camp, Medina de Rioseco, and Peñafiel.

From the end of June until the end of August, the climate is warm but dry. It is cooler in the evenings, which are agreeable. In short, it is a good and healthful climate.

For guides and printed collections, see Nos. 1, 6, 10, 11, 26–28, 50–53, 55, and 65.

ARCHIVO HISTÓRICO NACIONAL

HISTORY

Don Lorenzo de Arrazola, minister of justice, had intended in 1847 continue the project of establishing a central archives in Madrid, where would be assembled, as the first objective, the papers from suppressed offices, such as the Council and Presidency of Castile, the Council of the Orders, and the *Contencioso de Indias* (Court of the Indies). To this vast quantity of documents, which filled the administrative offices, there would be added the archives of the religious corporations and orders suppressed in 1835. These last sources had been concentrated in the *Dirección de Propiedades* of the Ministry of Finance but, in 1850, were turned over to the custody of the Royal Academy of History. Eight years later there was created the Central General Archives, located in the palace that the archibishops of Toledo had in Alcalá de Henares. But these archives were principally administrative in character, in accord with the ideas that Riol had already expounded in 1726.[6] There still remained the need for historical archives that should preserve the documents of imortant organizations.

---

[6] The memorial of Riol (No. 3) is important, not only as testimony of the state of the archives of the Spanish public administration, but also of the program of organization. This work of Riol has been edited by Valladares, in Vol. III, 73–324, of his *Semanario erudito*, but merits a new edition and new study.

With this objective, the *Archivo historico nacional* were established in 1866, on the basis of the monastic papers collected in the Academy of History and the archives of suppressed organizations, according to the plan of Arrazola. The new archives were placed in the building of the Academy until 1896, when they were transferred to the Palace of Libraries and Museums, located in the Paseo do Recoletos and, more recently to a new structure. Since their installation in the Palace of Libraries and Museums, they have received many materials, which have notably increased their quantity. From the General Archives of Alcalá there came, for example, the papers of State, Chamber of Castile, and others. In 1897 the papers belonging to the Council of Castile, Royal Patronage of Castile and Aragon, and others were added. Other documents from governmental offices have been added. What was left of the General Archives of Alcalá was destroyed by fire at the end of the civil war (1939). Very recently, Spain has established in Alcalá de Henares a new *Archivo general de la Administración*, with modern installations and equipment, but the Ministry of Foreign Affairs has not yet deposited any material there.

ORGANIZATION AND CLASSIFICATION

For the objectives of this guide, the section of *Estado* is especially interesting. Its sources proceed from the Secretariat of the Office of State, which, after 1714, came to be called the First Secretariat of State and in 1833 became the Ministry of State (today, of Foreign Affairs). Consequently, the central archives for the international politics of Spain are found chronologically at Simancas, the National Historical Archives, and the Archives of the Ministry of Foreign Affairs. As has already been indicated, many of the papers of the section of *Estado* of the National Historical Archives came in 1897 from the General Archives of Alcalá de Henares, where they had been taken after having remained some time in the National Library. In 1921 the section contained 8,602 bundles, distributed in the following series:

1. Council of State:
   a. Secretariat of the North, Royal Dispatches, 1587-1687;
   b. Consultations relative to the negotiations with Germany (1684-1702), Argel (1696), Sardinia (1647-1709), Flanders (1700-12), France (1700-17), Hamburg (1700-03, 1714-16, 1722), England (1700-18), Milan (1700-07), Naples (1700-07), Oran (1667-69), Low Countries (1651-1717), Portugal (1681-1717), Porto Longone (1708-16), Savoy (1698-1702), Holy See (1679-1717), Sicily (1700-17), Switzerland (1707-17), Venice (1700-13).

2. Government of Joseph Bonaparte (Joseph I). Correspondence and Files (*Expedientes*), 1808-13.

3. Supreme Governmental Committee of the Kingdom (*Junta central suprema gubernativa del Reino*), 1808-14, consisting of 84 bundles. There is a printed index (No. 25). The documents refer, in general, to the conduct of the war against Napoleon, but there are specifically diplomatic bundles. Thus, *legajo* 22 preserves the declaration of war on Denmark, because of its attitude toward the troops of the Marquis de la Romana; the alliance with England, etc.; *legajo* 56 contains documents on the intrigues of the Princess Carlotta in the Rio de la Plata; *legajo* 69 refers to the armed aid of England and the conflict of the *Junta* of the Kingdom of Galicia with the English representative; while *legajos* 71 and 77 contain communcations between the *Junta* of Galicia, cited above, and its representative in London, Don Pedro Sangro.

4. Council of Regency (successor of the committee), 1810-14.

5. Constitutional Epochs: first, 1812-14; second, 1820-23. It is concerned with consultations, orders, decrees, etc.

6. Acts of the Consultative Committee of Government (*Junta consultiva de Gobierno*), which functioned in 1825, from September 13 to December 29.

7. Council of Government, 1833–36. Contains the acts, correspondence with the different ministries, orders, and circulars.

8. Embassies and Legations: Correspondence and files of the following: Germany (1611-61, 1780-1805), Algiers (1787-1800), Austria (1804-72), Bavaria (1804-26), Belgium (1835-49), Brazil (1809-36), Sardinia (1741-1836, 1848-60), China (1843-49), Denmark (1787-1833), Etruria (1801-07), Florence (1789-1800), France (1663-66, 1730-1849), Genoa (1793-99), Greece (1834-49), Hamburg (1779-99), England (1720-23, 1725-28, 1747-98, 1802-43), Luca (1800-48), Malta (1717-98), Mexico (1837-48), Morocco (1766-1850), Naples and the Two Sicilies (1760-1836, 1847-65), Netherlands (1789-1849), Parma (1789-1801), Poland (1760-64, 1790-94), Portugal (1765-1825), Prussia (1789-1833), Cisalpine Republic (1797-1813), Russia (1761-1838), Holy See (1632-43, 1798-1800), Saxony (1739-1832), Sweden (1789-1833), Switzerland (1703-1828), Tuscany (1801-07), Tripoli (1785-99), Tunis (1784-99), Turkey (1778-1833), United States (1785-1833), Venice (1645-65, 1789-99).

9. Consulates. Correspondence and accounts, 1800-50.

10. Treaties, 1701–1869.

11. Board of Commerce and Foreign Dependencies: consultations (1700-1807); files (1815-19).

12. War of Succession: correspondence with the First Secretariat of State (1701-14).

13. Governors of Fortifications and Ports: Correspondence with the First Secretariat of State (1750-1800).

14. Maritime captures and reprisals (eighteenth and nineteenth centuries): France, Prussia, Sweden, Portugal, England, United States.

Documents of a diplomatic character may also be found in other sections. For example, in *Consejos suprimidos* (Suppressed Councils), series "Old Archives of the Council"; in "Extraordinary Council", three bundles are preserved that are related to the

Franco-Spanish War of 1793, although nearly all of the material concerns French émigrés, especially ecclesiastics; in "Council of Italy," there are papers relating to the State of Piombino (seventeenth century).

Among the documents coming form the *Junta central suprema gubernativa del Reino,* some are on the emancipation movements in Spanish America. There is a catalogue of these documents in *Papeles de la Junta central suprema gubernativa del Reino* (Madrid, *Archivo histórico nacional,* 1904).

ADMINISTRATION, REGULATIONS, AND FACILITIES

The National Historical Archives (Serrano 115, Madrid) are under the care of the Corps of Archives, subject to the Directory General of Archives and Libraries. The Director is Dr. Luis Sánchez Belda. All documents preserved in the National Historical Archives can be consulted by investigators. The archives remain open daily, from 9:30 A.M. to 1:30 P.M. and from 4-7:00 P.M. Microfilm service is available. From July 15 to September 15, they are open only from 9:30 A.M. to 1:30 P.M. They are closed to the public from December 20 to January 6.

For guides, see Nos. 1, 2, 4, 5, 24, and 50.

ARCHIVO GENERAL DE INDIAS

HISTORY

In the last third of the eighteenth century, the General Archives of the Indies were established with a view of concentrating in a single place all the papers relating to the conquest, colonization, and government of the Spanish possessions overseas. The idea was promoted by the famous annalist of the Indies, Don Juan Bautista Muñoz; and the strong will of the powerful minister of the Indies, Don José de Galvez, played a preponderant part in its rapid realization.

Basically, the new archives were formed from the American sources already existing in the General Archives of Simancas, and from the accumulated papers of the various branches of the government of the Indies (Council of the Indies, House of Trade, etc.). Among the acquisitions of papers were those of section nine, *Estado,* which were transferred in 1871 from the ministry of foreign affairs of Madrid; *Ultramar,* consisting of documents taken in 1887 from the ministry of the same name; and of the "Papers of Cuba," transferred from Havana in 1888–89.

The bulk of State Papers remained at Simancas. Toward the middle of the nineteenth century, the National Historical Archives were created in Madrid, where the papers of the modern diplomacy of Spain have been kept. Consequently, the General Archives of the Indies at Seville can be considered only secondarily as diplomatic archives. Nevertheless, these sources are important. The classification of papers could hardly be perfect in so extensive and complicated an administration as that of the Spanish possessions in America; on the other hand, those possessions were the object of conflicts, negotiations, and agreements with other countries which could not fail to leave many significant documents in these archives.

ORGANIZATION AND CLASSIFICATION

The General Archives of the Indies consist of more than thirty-four thousand large *legajos,* divided into fourteen sections, and numbered progressively within each section. These sections are: (1) *Patronato* (Patronage); (2) *Contraduría* (Accounting); (3) *Contratación* (Trade); (4) *Papeles de Justicia* (Papers of Justice); (5) *Gobierno* (Courts and Miscellaneous); (6) *Escribanía de Cámara* (Notarial Office); (7) *Secretaría del Juzgado de Arribadas, de Cádiz* (Tribunal of the Court of Arrivals, of Cádiz) and *Comisaría interventora de la Hacienda Pública en Cadiz* (Comptrolling Treasury Commission of Cadiz); (8) *Correos* (Records of Mail); (9) *Estado* (Papers of State); (10) *Ultramar* (Papers of the Overseas Ministry); (11) *Papeles de Cuba* (Papers of Cuba); (12) *Papeles de Cádiz*

(Papers of Cádiz), renamed *Consulados*); (13) *Títulos de Castilla* (Titles of Castile); (14) *Papeles de España* (Papers of Spain); (15) *Tribunal de Cuentas* (Puerto Rico and Cuba, XIX century); (16) *Mapas, planos, dibujos y estampas*. There are handwritten inventories of all these sections at the disposal of the researcher. These inventories are made *legajo* by *legajo*, are relatively detailed in respect to the first six sections, and are very summarized for the rest. However, some of the latter, *Estado* for example, do have a complete file on their material.

Documents of a diplomatic character are scattered in almost all of these sections of the archives. Consequently, it is very difficult to give useful information in a brief treatment. The section of greatest diplomatic value, or at least where these documents predominate, is the ninth: *Papeles de Estado*. The name does not imply, however, that this section contains only material relating to diplomatic relations. Perhaps it would be more exact to say that it continues the fifth section, consisting of papers of both a political and an administrative character. Yet the diplomatic references are very great in the ninth section for an obvious reason. The dominant problem in the Spanish possessions in America during the period to which the papers of this section refer (the last third of the eighteenth century and the first third of the nineteenth) is brought about by the movements for independence. Various foreign nations, such as England, France, and the United States, intervened in these movements, and the questions raised over the struggle for liberation thereby assume an international character.

The sources of the ninth section are subdivided by *Audiencias*, like section five. The papers of a general nature form a group apart, but each *audiencia* has its own specific *legajos*, which cover all the colonies in South and Central America, Cuba, Puerto Rico, Louisiana, Florida, and the Philippines. Material relating to Hispanic-North American relations can be found in the 404 *legajos* of the same section that refers to Cuba (1740–1864).

Even in sections that don not seem to have the slightest bearing on diplomatic material, as in the seventh section (*Secretaría del Juzgado de Arribadas*), there are papers on some aspects of the wars against England in America and on the expedition of Ceballos to Rio de la Plata.

Recently, the publication of the complete file of this section (No. 60) was undertaken. Its sources already had been inventoried in large part by Torres Lanzas, as seen in his work on the independence of Hispanic America (No. 61).

Other sections of the General Archives of the Indies contain, as noted previously, materials of a diplomatic character. They are found, principally in section 5, in the respective *audiencias*, as well as in the mass of material known by the name of *Indiferente*. The conflicts with the Portuguese in Paraguay and Rio de la Plata; the wars with England in the Antilles, Central America, and Florida; the boundary questions with Portugal, the United States, and France; and the frictions arising from explorations along the coast of California, all left their trace in the immense source material of this section.

The documents of section 11 (*Papeles de Cuba*), inventoried in detail by Roscoe R. Hill (No. 62), have great importance for the history of Spanish relations with the United States concerning Florida and Louisiana. In the *Papeles de Ultramar* (section 10), there are eight *legajos* relating to Louisiana and Florida (1717–1822).

ADMINISTRATION, REGULATIONS, AND FACILITIES

The General Archives of the Indies have been located, from their inception, in the old Casa Lonja (Avda. Queipo de Lla 3, Seville), which is perfectly conserved and possess a reading room, and a heating system. Except in rare cases, investigators are not permitted to make photostats of documents themselves but may use the services of authorized photographers. The Director is Rosario Parra Cala.

The archives remain open from 9:00 A.M. to 1:30 P.M. and 3–7:00 P.M. During the latter hours there is no service for getting at the *legajos* or books, so they must be requested during the former hours. On Saturday afternoons, Sundays, and holidays of a religious or national character, the archives are not open. A reading room is provided in the building below, where the researcher can seek respite from the intense heat during the months of July and August. There is a microfilm service.

For guides, see Nos. 1, 2, 23, and 60-64.

ARCHIVO DEL MINISTERIO DE ASUNTOS EXTERIORES

HISTORY

These archives were in the Royal Palace, until transferred in 1900 to the present building of the ministry. Most of the older papers, those up to the death of Ferdinand VII, had been transferred to the Archives of Simancas, the General Archives of Alcalá de Henares, and the National Historical Archives. The bulk of the documents in the Archives of the Ministry of Foreign Affairs today begin, therefore, about the second third of the nineteenth century. There are, nevertheless, small groups of documents of an earlier date.

ORGANIZATION AND CLASSIFICATION

The sources are arranged according to the different sections of the ministry. The most important sections for this study are the second, *Política* (Policy); the tenth, *Correspondencia*; and the fifteenth, which contains the so-called *Libros Rojos* (Red Books), relating to treaties and annexed documents (1855-1921).

Política contains copies of outgoing dispatches (up to 1931) to Spanish embassies and legations in all European and American countries. There is also a series of 194 bundles, relating to the First World War, 1914-18.

The section on General Correspondence contains dispatches (1831 to 1931) *from* Spanish representatives abroad, arranged by order of nations and chronologically. The Correspondence of

Consulates (since 1834) may be considered complementary to the above section on General Correspondence.

The section of Red Books mentioned above contains the uninterrupted series of treaties from 1869 to 1927. The preceding treaties, from 1801 to 1869, are deposited in the National Historical Archives.

In the portion of *Política* concerned with internal policy, there are also important documents for diplomatic history. Thus, in Civil War (*Guerra Civil*), there are papers relative to the British Legion, supplies of Great Britain, the Portuguese Legion, and the French Legion; in Candidates to the Throne (*Candidatos al Trono*), there are some concerning Ferdinand of Coburg, the Duke of Genoa, and the Prince of Hohenzollern.

The Spanish Royal House (*Casa Real Española*) has documents on the election of Amadeo I to the Spanish throne, as well as credentials to ambassadors and notifications of the new regime during the presidency of the Duke of la Torre.

The library of the ministry of foreign affairs also possesses some manuscripts of great diplomatic value. Among them are the transcripts of the diplomatic correspondence of Don Cristóbal de Moura (four large volumes) already utilized by Danvila in his well-known work on this influential representative of Philip II (No. 74); a volume with documents on the marriage of the Infanta Doña Maria, daughter of Philip III, with the Prince of Wales; the original correspondence of Don Melchor de Macanaz, Spanish plenipotentiary at the Congress of Breda (1747–48); memorials of the Marquis of Santa Cruz of Marcenado, ambassador extraordinary of Spain to the Congress of Soissons; diaries of the three divisions of demarcation of the boundaries between Spain and Portugal in South America; the original of the memoirs of León y Pizarro, the text of which notably differs from that published. See the note by Jerónimo Becker in *BAH*, LXXV (1919), 481–483 (No. 80).

In line with a general plan the ministry has been following, the archives of the embassy of Spain to the Holy See have been transferred to Madrid and deposited in these archives. This is a collection of great importance for European diplomatic history, in spite of the losses suffered from frequent fires, which damaged expecially the documents of the sixteenth and early seventeenth centuries, although many notable survivals of this period remain. There is a detailed *Indice analítico* (Rome-Madrid, 1915–35) in four volumes, dealing, respectively, with the sixteenth, seventeenth, eighteenth, and first half of the nineteenth centuries. The first volume was prepared by Luciano Serrano, O.S.B.; and the following three by José M. Pou y Martí, O.F.M. The latter also published the *Indice analítico de los codices de la Biblioteca contigua al Archivo* (Rome, 1925). This section likewise contains much diplomatic material.

On the importance of these archives of the Spanish embassy at the Holy See for European diplomatic history, specifically for the nineteenth century, one may refer to the article by Alberto M. Ghisalberti, "L'archivio dell'Ambasciata di Spagna presso la Santa Sede," *Rassegna storica del Risorgimiento*, XL (1935), 232–237. For more general information, see José M. Pou y Martí, "Los archivos de la Embajada de España cerca de la Santa Sede," *Miscellanea archivistica Angelo Mercati* (Vatican City, 1952), pp. 297–311.

ADMINISTRATION, REGULATIONS, AND FACILITIES

The archives and the library (Salvador 1, Madrid) are in the care of officials of the Corps of Archives, but are under the complete jurisdiction of the minister of foreign affairs. The Director is Pilar del Castillo. The consultation of documents after 1931 is not permitted. The authorization of the subsecretary of the ministry must first be procured. The personal files of Spanish diplomatic representatives cannot be consulted, except in very exceptional cases. The hours are from 10:00 A.M. to 2:00 P.M. For guides and printed collections, see Nos. 7, 45, and 82–83.

ARCHIVO DE LA CORONA DE ARAGON

The Catalan-Aragonese monarchy was the peninsular state that took the most active part in European politics during the Middle Ages and at the dawn of the modern period, before the achievement of Spanish unity through the marriage of Ferdinand and Isabel. Its magnificent archives correspond to its political importance. They are the best medieval sources that Spain possesses. The origin dates to the epoch of the counts of Barcelona (ninth to tenth centuries). They possess manuscripts prior to the invasion of Almansor (986). Alfonso the Chaste (died 1196) took measures for the reorganization of the royal archives, and with James the Conqueror the *Registros* (Registers) were begun, after the practice of the Vatican. James II (1291–1827), and Pedro the Ceremonious (1336–87), expecially interested themselves in the archives. To the latter is due the nomination (July 6, 1346) of the first archivist, Pedro Paseya, who died in 1348, after having left an inventory of the papers. Pedro the Ceremonious also ordered the assembly of all the sections of the royal archives in a single place.

The present name, "Archives of the Crown of Aragon," was assigned during the reign of Charles III. After 1782, this legend appeared on the official seal. It seems that the archives had not been well cared for in the seventeenth century, but in the eighteenth, they benefited from the new interest in historical studies. The Mercedarian, Father Manuel Mariano Riberta, accomplished a great work of arrangement during the occupation of Barcelona by the archduke in the War of Succession (1706–13). Later, the eminent archivist, Francisco Jávier de Garma y Durán (1740–83), attempted without success the unification in Barcelona of the four royal archives of the Crown of Aragon: Zaragoza, Barcelona, Valencia, and Mallorca. In any event, those of Barcelona, which were

---

[7] This information has been supplied by the former Director of the Archives of the Crown of Aragon, Don Jesus E. Martínez Ferrando, to whom due appreciation is hereby expressed.

the most important, were installed in new and better quarters (1770-71). The great archivist of the nineteenth century was Don Prospero de Bofarull, named in 1814, whose son and grandson succeeded him.

ORGANIZATION AND CLASSIFICATION

The Archives of the Crown of Aragon are divided into thirteen sections, of which the ones pertinent to this study are: the first (Chancellery), the third (Supreme Council of Aragon), the fifth (*Generalidad* or Corporation of Catalonia), the ninth (War of Independence), and the eleventh (Miscellaneous), which ends with the archives of the "Old Legation of Spain in Genoa," 1552-1804 (362 bundles).

The principal section for diplomatic history is the first: *Cancilleria Real* (Royal Chancellery). To this section belongs the famous series of "Registers," within which the subseries *Curiae, Curiae Sigilli Secreti, Legationum, Sigillum Secretum, Secretorum,* and *Itinerum* contain diplomatic documents. These must be consulted for each reign. There is also material of interest in the series *Cartas Reales* (Royal Letters), some fifty thousand documents. Likewise within this first section must be considered the series of parchments, in which are many documents of a diplomatic character. Such is the case for James II, whose parchments include a great quantity of royal correspondence, expecially with France and Italy.

In the third section, *Consejo Supremo de Aragón* (Supreme Council of Aragon), the correspondence of the secretariats of Catalonia (French frontier) and Sardinia (Mediterranean frontier) is of diplomatic interest. Yet, as the Supreme Council of Aragon was active in the sixteenth and seventeenth centuries, it must be remembered that foreign policy was then conducted basically from the capital of the united crowns.

There are also diplomatic documents in the fifth section, *Generalidad de Cataluña* (Corporation of Catalonia), especially on the occasions (fifteenth and seventeenth centuries) when this organization was opposed to the crown and sought foreign aid for its aspirations.

The ninth section, *Guerra de Independencia* (War of Independence), contains documents on the interference of the French in Catalonia and the reaction of the Spaniards and foreign governments before the open intervention of Napoleon. The two series of which the section is constituted, *Junta superior de Cataluña* (Superior Committee of Catalonia) and *Papeles de la dominación napoleónica en el principado,* are interesting in these respects.

ADMINISTRATION, REGULATIONS, AND FACILITIES

The Archives of the Crown of Aragon (Condes de Barcelona 2, Barcelona) are in the care of the officials of the Corps of Archives. The Director is Federico Udina Martorell.

The archives are open all working days, from 9:00 A.M. to 1:00 P.M. and 4–7:00 P.M. During the summer months the public service is reduced to a single period, from 10:00 A.M. to 1:00 P.M.

The archives have a library specializing in the history of the Crown of Aragon and related subjects. They also possess a microfilm service, with a projection machine and laboratory but, in special cases the researcher is authorized to photograph documents.

The investigator has at his disposal several manuscript inventories for each one of the sections mentioned. The sources of the "Old Legation of Spain in Genoa" are being inventoried, at present, in great detail. There are several manuscript catalogues, but none embodies specifically a diplomatic category.

For guides and printed collections, see Nos. 1, 9, 29, 35, and 85.

OTHER ARCHIVES AND SPECIAL COLLECTIONS

In this section brief references will be made to certain public and private archives that are either small or not primarily related to diplomacy, but have some documents of interest, and to manuscript collections of libraries related to diplomats and to diplomatic history.

ARCHIVO GENERAL DE NAVARRA

These archives are located in Pamplona and are under the custody of the Foral Commission of Navarre. Their principal content is the archives of the ancient *Cámara de Comptos* (Chamber of Accounts) of Navarre, the oldest documents of which date back to the end of the twelfth century, although the series does not become continuous until the end of the fourteenth century. Other sections are formed by the remains of the ancient royal archives, and by the modern archives of the *Cortes*. The Chamber of Accounts was an organization of financial control, but among its documents are materials of interest to the diplomatic history of Navarre, especially in the series of "Registries" (*Cartularios*).

No special prerequisite is required for the consultation of the archives. Microfilm service is available. The Director is Florentino Idoate Iragui.

For a guide and a printed collection, see Nos. 41 and 42.

BIBLIOTECA NACIONAL

Among the varied manuscript sources of the National Library (Avda. Calvo Sotelo 22, Madrid), materials of interest to the history on the diplomatic relations of Spain abound. For example, they contain letters, or registers of letters, of Spanish diplomatic embassies and missions of such men as the Count of Peñaranda (Peace of the Pyrenees), the Marquis of Alomodóvar (to Russia), Don Juan Carlos Bazán (to the Italian states), the Danish foreign minister to his consuls in Spain, Antonio Rebelo da Fonseca (to Austria), Antonio Galvão de Castellobranco (from Portugal to London), Marquis de la Hinojosa, Don Manuel Francisco de Lira (to the Low countries), Don Luís Méndez de Haro (Peace of the Pyrenees), Count of Ribeira (to France), ephimeri of Spain's treaties (1508 to 1713), Cardinal Granvela, Don Juan de Zúñiga (to Rome), Venetian reports (from Spain, Portugal, and France), Count of Fuentes, Infanta Isabel Clara Eugenia (to Flanders), Sir Charles Cornwallis, Count of Gondomar (to England), Duke of Villaumbrosa, Don Baltasar Patiño (to France), Don Andrés Borrego (memoir on new Spanish-American countries), and other papers on France, Louisiana, and Florida.

The Section of Manuscripts of the National Library is open to the public every working day, from 9:30 A.M. to 2:30 P.M. and from 3:30–10:00 P.M.

The researcher needs to provide himself with a *tarjeta de lector*, which is valid for one year. It is obtained in the Secretariat of the Library, after the identification of the person and the presentation of some document that proves his aptitude, if this should not be obvious from the offices, profession, or publications of the solicitor. Two photographs are required.

The library possesses a good microphotographic service.

The Director is Guillermo Gustavino Gallent.

For guides and printed documents, see Nos. 26, 37, 67, and 75.

BIBLIOTECA Y ARCHIVO DEL PALACIO REAL

The manuscript materials of a diplomatic character in this library are abundant, especially collections of correspondence of ambassadors and diplomats. Since the manuscripts are dispersed, rather than collected in a series, it is impossible to make a résumé, considering the brief space to be devoted to it in this study. It is sufficient to cite, as an example, the hundred volumes of correspondence of the famous Count of Gondomar,[8] ambassador of Spain in London, 1613–22, 1624–26. Part of this correspondence has been published in the first four volumes of the new series of *Documentos inéditos para la historia de España (1936–   )*.

Another notable lot of diplomatic letters conserved in the Library of the Royal Palace is that of Don Diego Hurtado de Men-

---

[8] The correspondence of Gondomar is not, for the most part, directly diplomatic in character, although it possesses extraordinary value for a knowledge of the life of this important personage. On the other hand, the correspondence of the son of Gondomar, Don Antonio Sarmiento de Acuña (1635–40), is extremely valuable in regard to the European politics of Spain for these years.

doza, one of the great craftsmen of the Italian policy of Emperor Charles V. Some of these letters have been published (No. 55). There are also numerous letters of Granvela, Lope de Acuña, Antonio Sarmiento, etc., and much material regarding the period of Charles V, Philip II, Philip III, and Philip IV. For the records regarding America, see No. 68.

There is also material of interest in the General Archives of the Palace, established by Ferdinand VII (1814). In general, it may be said that the documents are concerned principally with the House of Bourbon, although there are papers concerning the House of Austria. In addition to information scattered in other sections, the so-called "Historical Section" is important. It consists, among other series, of the "Confidential Archives of Ferdinand VII," sixty-six volumes. Other sections are *Condecoraciones* (Decorations) (1593-1931); "Matrimonial Contracts" (1570-1701); "Embassies" (seven boxes); "Succession to the Crown" (1700-1904); "Historico-Political Events" (1614-1868); "Treaties of Peace" (1598-1783), one box.

Bundle four of this *Archivo reservado de Fernando VII* has the dispatch sent by the Spanish ambassador in Mexico, Bermúdez de Castro, on the plan to convert that republic into a monarchy with a Spanish prince as ruler (1846), and a "confidentail dispatch" from the Spanish ambassador in Paris to the minister of state on complaints against Mexico (1861). On this collection, see José Moreno Villa in the *Revista de historia de América* (1938), pp. 57-58.

The section formed by the archives of the Great Steward and Private Secretary of His Majesty may also offer something of interest. It possesses, for example, 24 bundles of "Correspondence with the diplomatic and consular corps" (1874-1936); four bundles with the title of "Diplomatic corps" (1840-1930); "Diary of his majesty and audiences" (1902-29), 4 bundles; "International military nominations" (1904-27), two boxes.

Both the archives and the library of the palace are in charge of officials of the Corps of Archives, but are under the jurisdiction of the Council of Administration of the National Patrimony. To consult the sources, it is necessary to have the authorization of the Manager Delegate Councilor of the Patrimony, which must be requested in writing. Both the library and the archives are located in the building of the Royal Palace, in Madrid. The archives remain open to researchers every working day, from 10:00 A.M. to 1:00 P.M.; the library from 10:30 A.M. to 3:00 P.M. and from 3:30–6:30 P.M. Both close in August. The Director of the archives is Conrado Morterero Simón, and the Director of the library is Justa Moreno.

For guides to the library, see No. 8 and, for the archives, see No. 75.

BIBLIOTECA DE LA REAL ACADEMIA DE LA HISTORIA

Among the extremely rich manuscript sources in this academy in Madrid, there is much that is of interest in respect to diplomacy. Of primary value are some papers of Charles V, Philip V, Count Diego Sarmiento de Acuña (in England), Lope de Acuña y Avellandea (in Flanders), Don Luís de Méndez, Lope de Soria (in Italian states), Lopez Ballesteros Collection on Don Juan of Austria, Don Francisco Xavier de Istúriz (in England) (see No. 80), Don Pedro Ronquillo and the Marqués de Cogolludo (see No. 40), Lorenzo Folch de Cardona (judge in Valladolid) and, in the Colección Muñoz, some minutes of letters of Emperor Charles V to his ambassador to Rome, the Duke of Sessa, and to others (see No. 86).

For Guides and printed collections, see Nos. 26, 43, 44, 69, 70, and 86.

The library is located in the building of the Academy (Calle de León, Madrid), and application for its use must be recommended by some academician.

It is open Monday through Friday, from 4–7:30 P.M. but is closed during much of the summer, during September, and from December 24 until January 6.

MILITARY CENTERS

The investigator should be aware of two centers of military studies in Madrid: the *Servicio histórico militar* (Military Historical Service) and the *Museo Naval* (Naval Museum).

SERVICIO HISTÓRICO MILITAR

Its collection of "Transcribed Documents" (some 6,281) formed from the Archives of the Indies (Simancas) and from the Crown of Aragon, is important. It includes the most significant documents concerning the Spanish campaigns abroad, especially those of Flanders, Germany, France, and Portugal. In addition to these copies, the Military Historical Service also has some 7,264 original documents on the same theme. The most notable groups of manuscripts, maps, and plans, refer to Africa and overseas. Nevertheless, there is much material of European interest.

A catalogue of all these sources has been published in the *Boletín de la Biblioteca Central Militar*. The cartographic materials are being edited under the general title *Cartografía y relaciones históricas de Indias*. The second volume refers to the United States and Canada.

The Military Historical Service is located in the old building of the Museum and Library of the Corps of Engineers of the Army (Mártires de Alcalá 9, Madrid), from which it inherited many sources and the activities which it has, in part, continued.

To consult the sources, the permission of the Director-Colonel of the Service is required. It is obtained without any special formality. The Service is open from 9:30 A.M. to 2:00 P.M. Microfilming is available. The Director is José Caruana y Gomez de Barreda.

MUSEO NAVAL

Situated in the building of the Ministry of the Navy (Montalban 2, Madrid), this institution also has an important section of manuscripts proceeding principally from the defunct *Depósito hidrográfico* (Hydrographic Depository), founded in 1789. The section of interest to diplomatic history is that constituted by the "Sans Barutell Collection," so named because it was assembled after 1789 by the naval lieutenant, Don Juan Sans de Barutell. It is concerned with the history of the navy of Castile and Aragon, and contains many documents on the naval campaigns in the Mediterranean. In general, the originals of these documents are still preserved, usually in the archives of Simancas and the Crown of Aragon, but this does not annul the value of the work performed by Sans de Barutell.

Open 10:30 A.M. to 1:30 P.M., except Mondays. Microfilm service is available.

The Director is Captain (Spanish Navy) José Luis Morales Hernández.

The general naval archives of Spain are in the *Archivo Museo D., Alvaro de Bazán*, at Viso del Marqués, in the old palace of the Marquis of Santa Cruz. They have some important materials for the history of Spain's external relations. (See Nos. 84 and 87.)

ARCHIVO GENERAL MILITAR

Founded in 1898 and located in the Alcazar of Segovia, its holdings are predominantly administrative in character. They belong usually to the eighteenth and nineteenth centuries, as a continuation of the military sources of the General Archives of Simancas. Nevertheless, their indirect value for diplomatic history should not be overlooked. The copious first section, "Personnel," which continues the very interesting series of "Certificates of Military Service," conserved in Simancas, offers unexpected biographical information. The ninth section contains some documents concerning the wars in Portugal and Catalonia. Finally, the tenth section, "Historical," includes a select group of papers that have been judged as particularly important.

To consult these archives, special permission of the military authorities is necessary. It must be presented in a request addressed to the Subsecretary of the Army, Ministry of the Army, Madrid.

The trip from Madrid to Segovia, a city of great interest to tourists, is easily made by train (two hours), by bus, or by car.

The Director is Comandante D. Juan Ortiz Quintana.

SOME PRIVATE ARCHIVES

1. Archives of the House of Alba (Palacio de Liria, Madrid), containing also papers of the houses of Lemos y Monterrey, Modica, Admirals of Castile, Montijo, Empress Eugénie, and Olivares, as well as letters from Don Juan of Austria and Philip II. (See Nos. 38, 46, 59, and 66.)

2. Archives òf the House of Medinaceli (Palacio de Medinaceli, Genova 28, Madrid). (See No. 39.)

3. Archives of Altamira. Those in Spain are found in the *Instituto de Valencia de Don Juan* and in the archives of Heredia Spinola. They contain also letters of Mateo Vázquez, Philip II, and the Marquisate of Velada. (See Nos. 8, 26, 56, and 69.)

4. Archives of the House of Frias, containing the correspondence of the Count of Peñaranda. (See No. 77.)

5. Archives of the House of the Marquis del Castelar (Madrid), containing papers of Don Gonzalo Fernández de Córdoba and of Don Alvaro de Losada. (See No. 78.)

6. Archives of Don Antonio Cánovas del Castillo (Museo Fundación Lázaro, Serrano 122, Madrid). (See No. 8.)

7. Archives of Zuñiga-Requeséns (Archivo del Palan, Barcelona). (See Nos. 54, 56, and 57.)

8. Archives of the House of Albuquerque (Madrid), containing papers of the Marquis of Alcañices, the Marquis of Balbases, Don Luís Méndez de Haro, Juan de Vega, and Charles I (V).

9. Archives of the Marquises of Heredia Spinola (Madrid).

10. Archives of Count of Guaqui (Madrid).

11. Archives of the Duke of the Infantado (Madrid).

12. Archives of the Marquises of Camarasa (Seville).

13. Archives of the Dukes of Alcalá (Seville).

14. Registers of the diplomatic correspondence of the Duke of Liri, from Moscow, and of the Marquis of San Felipe, from Genoa (*Biblioteca publica de Toledo*).

At least indirect materials for the history of Spanish diplomacy may be found in still other Spanish collections. To avoid a possible erroneous conclusion, it should be added that among the rich manuscript sources of the Escorial, relatively few are of direct interest to diplomatic history. See Julian Zarco Cuevas, O.S.A., *Catálogo da los manuscritos castellanos de la Real Biblioteca de El Escorial* (3 vols. Madrid, 1924–29).

The examination of the particular bibliography of the diplomatic history of Spain found in Sánchez Alonso and in the *Manuel de l'hispanisant* (Nos. 46–47) will provide the researcher with indications of other archives.

BIBLIOGRAPHY OF GUIDES, REFERENCES, AND COLLECTIONS

1. *Guía histórica y descriptiva de los archivos, bibliotecas y museos de España*. Madrid, 1921.
2. Gómez Canedo, Lino. *Los archivos de la historia de América*. 2 vols. Mexico, 1961.
3. *Representación hecha por el secretario D. Santiago Agustín Riol del origen y estado de los Consejos, tribunales, archivos reales de la Corte y Chancillerías, el de Roma y Simancas, al Rey nuestro señor* (1726). The Academy of American Franciscan History possesses one copy of this manuscript made in the eighteenth century. This information was widely utilized in the next two listed works.
4. Vignau, Vicente. *El Achivo histórico nacional*. Madrid, 1898. Reception speech in the Royal Academy of History.
5. Desdevises do Dézert, M. G. *Les archives historiques nationales de Madrid*. Madrid, 1900. Extract from the *Bulletin historique et philologique*.
6. Alcocer, Mariano. *Archivo general de Simancas. Guía del investigador*. Valladolid, 1923.
7. Archivo general de Simancas. *Catálogo XV: Papeles sobre la introducción y distribución de la quina en España*. Valladolid, 1937.

Gerardo Masa describes the group "Finance" in the introduction, modifying that which was written by Alcocer in his *Guía* (No. 5 in the bibliography).

8. *Guía de los archivos de Madrid.* Madrid, Ministerio de Educación Nacional, 1952.

9. González Hurtebise, Eduardo. *Guía histórica-descriptiva del Archivo de la Corona de Aragón en Barcelona.* Madrid, 1920.

10. Meysztowicz, Valerianus. *Documenta Poloniae ex Archivo generali hispaniae in Simancas.* I Pars. Rome, Institutum Polonicum Romae, 1963. This is vol. VIII of the series "Elementa ad Fontium Editiones."

11. Van Durme, Maurice. *Les Archives générales de Simancas et l'histoire de la Belgique.* 3 vols. Bruxelles, 1964-1968. A very important work.

12. Archivo general de Simancas. *Catálogo II, Secretaría de Estado. Capitulaciones con la Casa de Austria y Papeles de las Negociaciones de Alemania, Sajonia, Polonia, Prusia, y Hamburgo (1493-1726).* Ed. by Julián Paz. 2d ed. Madrid, Consejo Superior de Investigaciones Científicas, 1942.

13. *Catálogo III, Secretaría de Estado. Documentos de las negociaciones de Flandes, Holanda y Bruselas . . . , 1506-1795,* 2d ed. Madrid, Consejo Superior de Investigaciones Científicas, 1946.

14. *Catálogo IV, Secretaría de Estado. Capitulaciones con Francia y negociaciones diplomáticas de los Embajadores de España en aquella corte (1265-1714).* Ed. by Julián Paz. Madrid, 1914.

15. *Catálogo XIV. Papeles de estado de la negociación de Roma, 1381-1700.* Valladolid, 1926.

16. *Catálogo XVI. Papeles de estado de la correspondencia y negociación de Nápoles. Virreinato.* Ed. by Ricardo Magdaleno. Edición del Consejo Superior de Investigaciones Científicas y Universidad de Valladolid. Valladolid, 1942.

17. *Catálogo XVII. Secretaría de Estado. Documentos relativo a Inglaterra (1254-1834).* Ed. by Julián Paz and Ricardo Magdaleno. Edition and prologue of the Duke of Alba. Madrid, 1947.

18. *Catálogo XIX. Papeles de Estado. Sicilia. Virreinato español y negociación de Malta.* Ed. by Ricardo Magdaleno. Madrid, 1951. See also the catalogue *Papeles de Estado. Reino de las Dos Sicilias. Siglo XVIII. Embajada española* (Ed. by Ricardo Magdaleno).

19. *Catálogo V. Patronato Real (834-1851).* Complete edition. Revi-

sion and final indexes by Amalia Prieto Cantero, 2 vols. Valladolid, 1949.

20.   *Catálogo VII. Guerra moderna. Guerra de Marruecos. Años 1774-1776.* Sources for its study by Mariano Alcocer, Valladolid, 1926.

21.   *Catálogo XVIII. Guerra y Marina. I: Epoca de Carlos I de España y V de Alemania.* Ed. by Concepción Alvarez Yerán. Valladolid, 1949.

22.   *Catálogo VI. Secretarías Provinciales. Títulos nobiliarios concedidos por nuestros Reyes en Flandes, Italia y Portugal* (Sixteenth and seventeenth centuries). Ed. by Angel de la Plaza, Valladolid, 1923.

23.   Peña y Cámara, José María. *Guía del Archivo de Indias de Sevilla* Madrid, Direccion Genede Archivos y Bibliotecas, 1958.

24.   Sanchez Belda, Luis. *Indice general de la seccíon de Estado del Archivo histórico nacional.* Madrid, Direccíon General de Archivos y Bibliotecas, Instituto Bibliográfico Hispánico, 1973.

25.   Archivo histórico nacional. *Indice de los Papeles de la Junta Central Suprema Gubernativa del Reino y Consejo de Regencia.* Madrid, 1904.

26.   *Colección de documentos inéditos para la historia de España.* 113 vols. Madrid, 1842-95. It was begun by Martín Fernández Navarrete, Miguel Salvá, and Pedro Sainz de Baranda. It is of great importance for the history of the European policy of Spain. There is a good catalogue in two volumes by Julián Paz, Madrid, 1930-31, cited as *Codoin.*

27.   Archivo histórico Español. *Colección de documentos inéditos para la historia de España y de sus Indias.* Valladolid, 1928. It is patronized by the Academy of Social and Historical Studies of Valladolid, under the direction of the Count of Gamazo, the Duke of Maura, Augustin G. de Amezua, Mariano Alcocer, and others. Vol. I contains documents concerning the Council of Trent; Vol. II (1929) the Invincible Armada; and Vol. III the consultations of the Council of State. Cited as *AHE.*

28.   *Calendar of letters, despatches, and state papers relating to the negotiations between England and Spain, preserved in the archives at Simancas and elsewhere . . . .* Ed. by G. A. Bergenroth [and others, among them Pascual de Gayangos]. London, 1862– Vol. XI, which ends in 1553, appeared in 1916.

29.   *Colección de documentos inéditos del Archivo de la Corona de Aragón.* Barcelona, 1864–   This collection was begun by Dr. Próspero Bofarull and continued by his son and grandson respec-

tively, D. Manuel de Bofarull and D. Francisco de Asis Bofarull, who were successively directors of the Archives of the Crown of Aragon. In a great part, it contains documents that are of interest to the history of the international policy of the Aragonese monarchy.

30. Rubió y Lluch, Antonio. *Diplomatari de l'Orient Català.* Barcelona, 1947.

31. Fincke, H. *Acta Aragonensia. Quellen zur deutschen, italienischen, französischen, spanischen, zur Kirchen- und Kulturgeschichte aus der diplomatischen Korrespondenz Jaymes II (1291-1327).* 3 vols. Berlin, 1908-22.

32. Alarcón, Maximiliano, and Ramon García Linares. *Los documentos árabes diplomáticos del Archivo de la Corona de Aragón.* Madrid, 1940.

33. Baer, Fritz. *Die Juden in dem christlichen Spanien. Aragonien. Navarra.* 2 vols. Berlin, 1929.

34. Torre, Antonio de la. *Documentos sobre las relaciones diplomáticas de los Reyes Católicos.* Barcelona, 1949-   .

35. Vincke, Johannes. *Documenta selecta mutuas Civitatis Arago-Cathaloniae et Ecclesiae relationes illustrantia.* Barcelona, 1936.

36. *Documentos inéditos para la historia de España.* Published by the Duke of Alba, Duke of Maura, Count of Gamazo. Madrid, 1936. Vols. I-IV contain letters and dispatches of the Count of Gondomar, ambassador of Spain in London.

37. Biblioteca nacional. *Catálogo de los documentos que pertenecieron a D. Pascual Gayangos, existentes hoy en la Biblioteca nacional.* Ed. by D. Pedro Roca. Madrid, 1904.

38. *Documentos esogidos del Archivo de la Casa de Alba.* Madrid, 1891. The Duchess of Berwick y Alba published them.

39. Paz y Melia, Antonio, *Series de los más importantes documentos del archivo y biblioteca del ... Duque de Medinaceli ... I: Serie historica, años 860-1814.* Madrid, 1915. Vol. II, a bibliographical series, was published in 1922.

40. Maura, Duque de. *Corespondencia entre los embajadores Don Pedro Ronquillo y el Marqués de Cogolludo, 1689-1691.* Transcription, introduction, and notes by the Duke of Maura. Madrid, 1951-52.

41. Diputación federal de Navarra. *Catálogo del Archivo General. Sección de comptos y documentos.* Ed. by José Ramón Castro, Chief of the Archives of Navarre. Vol. I, 842-1331; Vol. II, 1332-1357. Pamplona, 1952.

42. Brutails, Jean Auguste. *Documents des Archives de la Chambre des*

Comptes de Navarre. Paris, 1890. It is Fac. 84 of the Bibliothèque de l'Ecole des Hautes Etudes.

43. Real Academia de la Historia. *Indice de la Colección de Don Luis de Salazar y Castro*. Ed. by the Marquis of Siete Iglesias and D. Baltasar Cuartero y Huerta. 8 vols. Madrid, 1949–

44. *Catálogo de los documentos del Archivo de Lope de Soria, embajador del emperador Carlos V*. Ed. by E. Ibarra Rodríguez and G. Arsenio de Izaga, in *Boletín de la Academia de la Historia* (Madrid), XCVIII (1931), 363–416.

45. López Oliván, Julio. *Repertorio diplomático español*. Index of the treaties concluded by Spain (1125–1935) and of other international documents. Madrid, 1944. In the bibliography (pp. 651–669) are indicated the principal collections of treaties, supported by documents of the Spanish diplomatic archives.

46. Sánchez Alonso, Benito. *Fuentes de la historia española e hispano-americana*. Third edition corrected and brought up to date. Madrid, 1952.

47. Foulché-Delbosc, R. and L. Barrau-Dihigo. *Manuel de l'Hispanisant*. 2 vols. New York, 1920–25.

48. Carini, Isidoro. *Gli archivi e le biblioteche di Spagna in rapporto alla storia d'Italia in generale e di Sicilia in particolare*. 2 vols. Palermo, 1884.

49. Gachard, Louis Prosper. *Les bibliothèques de Madrid et de l'Escurial*. Brussels, 1875. Information and extracts from the manuscripts which concern the history of Belgium.

50. *Correspondance de Philippe II sur les affaires des Pays-Bas, 1558–1577, publié d'après des originaux dans les archives royales de Simancas*. 5 vols. Brussels, 1848–79.

51. *Retraite et mort de Charles-Quint au monastère de Yuste. Lettres inédites publiées d'après les originaux conservés dans les archives royales de Simancas*. 3 vols. Brussels, 1854–56.

52. Lonchay, H. *Les archives de Simancas au point de vue de l'histoire des Pays-Bas au XVII siècle, en compte-rendu des séances de la Commission royale d'Histoire ou recueil de ses bulletins*, 1907, LXXXVI, annexes XIII–LV.

53. Kybal, Vlastimil. *Über die Bedeutung des General-Archivs zu'Simancas für die neuere Geschichte Österreichs*. Vienna, 1910.

54. March, José María, S. J. "Don Luis de Requeséns, Lugarteniente general del mar, y la batalla de Lepanto a la luz de nuevos documentos," *Razón y Fe*. Madrid, CXXVI (1942), 200–225. Re-edited and expanded, Madrid, 1944.

55. Vásquez, Alberto, and S. Selden Rose. *Algunas cartas de Don Diego Hurtado de Mendoza*. New Haven, 1935. It contains 125 letters of Hurtado de Mendoza, who was ambassador in Venice, Rome, and Siena (1538-52). The originals are in Simancas and in the Library of the Royal Palace.

56. March, José María, S. J. *El comendador mayor de Castilla, Don Luis de Requeséns, en el govierno de Milán*. Madrid, Ministerio de Asuntos exteriores, Relaciones culturales, 1943.

57. *Niñez y juventud de Felipe II*. 2 vols. Madrid, Ministerio de Asuntos exteriores, Relaciones culturales, 1941-42.

58. Gómez del Campillo, Miguel, *Relaciones diplomáticas entre España y los Estados Unidos, según los documentos del Archivo histórico nacional*. 2 vols. Madrid, 1944, 1946.

59. Berwick y de Alba, Duque de. *Correspondencia de Gutierre Gómez de Fuensalida, embajador de Alemania, Flandes e Inglaterra (1496-1509)*. Madrid, 1907.

60. Archivo General de Indias. *Catálogo de documentos de la Sección Novena . . .* Vol. I: *Santo Domingo, Cuba, Puerto Rico, Lusiana, Florida y México*. Seville, 1949.

61. Torres Lanzas, Pedro. *Independencia de América, fuentes para su estudio. Catálogo de documentos conservados en el Archivo General de Indias de Sevilla*. First series, 5 vols. Madrid, 1912. Second series, 2 vols. Seville, 1924-25.

62. Hill, Roscoe R. *Descriptive catalogue of the documents relating to the history of the United States in the "Papeles procedentes de Cuba" deposited in the Archivo general de Indias at Seville*. Washington, 1916.

63. Torre Revello, José. *El Archivo general de Indias*. Buenos Aires, 1929.

64. Torres Lanzas, Pedro and German Latorre, *Catálogo-Cuadro general de la documentación del Archivo general de Indias*. Seville, 1918.

65. Alves, F. M. *No Arquivo de Simancas*. Oporto, 1932.

66. Alba, Duque de. *Epistolario del III Duque de Alba, D. Fernando Alvarez de Toledo, Años 1536-1581*. 3 vols. Madrid, 1952.

67. Paz, Julián. *Catálogo de manuscritos de América existentes en la Biblioteca nacional*. Madrid, 1933.

68. Bordona, Jesús Domínguez. *Catálogo de la Biblioteca de Palacio*. Vol. IX. *Manuscritos de América*. Madrid, 1935.

69. Serrano, Luciano, O.S.B. *Correspondencia diplomática entre España y la Santa Sede durante el pontificado de San Pío V*. 4 vols. Madrid, 1914.

70. Pacheco y de Leyva, Enrique. *La política española en Italia. Correspondencia de D. Fernando Marín, abad de Nájera, con Carlos I.* Madrid, 1919.

71. Rodríguez Villa, Antonio. *Italia desde la batalla de Pavía hasta el Saco de Roma, Reseña histórica escrita en su mayor parte con documentos originales, cifrados.* Madrid, 1885.

72. *Memorias para la historia del asalto y saqueo de Roma, en 1527, por el ejército imperial, formado con documentos originales, cifrados e inéditos en su mayoría.* Madrid, n.d.

73. Ayerbe, Marqués de, Conde de San Clemente. *Correspondencia inédita de Don Guillén de San Clemente, embajador en Alemania de . . . Felipe II y Felipe III sobre la intervención de España en los sucesos de Polonia y Hungría, 1581-1608.* Zaragoza, 1892.

74. Danvila y Burguero, Alfonso. *Diplomáticos españoles: Don Cristóbal de Moura, primer marqués de Castel Rodrigo (1538-1613).* Madrid, 1900.

75. *Guía de las bibliotecas de Madrid.* Madrid, Ministerio de Educación Nacional, 1953.

76. Alba, Duque de. "Achivos de España. El de la Casa de Alba," *Hidalguía,* I (1953), 145-156.

77. Frías, Duque de. "Breve síntesis del contenido del Archivo de la Casa de Frías y sus agregadas," *Hidalguía,* I (1953), 645-652.

78. Castelar, Marqués del. "Archivo de la Casa del Marqués del Castelar," *Hidalguía,* I (1953), 337-340.

79. Aguarelles, Eugenio Sarrablo. "Archivo de Su Alteza Real Don Carlos de Habsburgo-Lorena y Borbon Duque de Madrid," *Hidalguía,* I (1953), 653-660.

80. *Boletín de la Real Academia de la Historia* (BAH).

81. *Hidalguía. La revista de Genealogía, Nobleza y Armas.* Madrid, 1953-

82. *Colección de tratados de España con otras naciones a partir de 1939.* Ed. by Justo Gomez Ocerin. Madrid, Ministerio de Asuntos Exteriores, 1954.

83. Cagigas, Isidro de las. *Tratados y convenios referentes a Marruecos.* Madrid, 1952.

84. Guillén, Julio F. *Archivo General de Marina. Independencia de América. Indice de los Papeles de Expediciones de Indias.* 3 vols. Madrid, 1953.

85. *Archivos de Barcelona.* Barcelona, 1952.

86. *Catálogo de la Colección de Don Juan Bautista Muñoz.* 2 vols. Madrid, 1954-55.

87. Guillén, Julio F. *Archivo general de Marina. Indice de los Papeles de la Sección de Corso y Presus, 1784-1837.* 2 vols. Madrid, 1953.
88. Bemis and Griffin, *Guide.* On Spanish archives, pp. 898-908.
89. Degras, *Soviet documents.* On Spain, pp. 110, 145, 176.

The *Servicio nacional de Microfilm* made available in 1972 the documents of the section *Estado* pertaining to "Relaciones diplomáticas entre España y los Estados Unidos" (1737-1819) as listed in No. 58. It is Publication No. 16, consisting of 33 rolls and 24,588 frames. It sells for 73,764 pesetas.

15 SWEDEN[1]

Raymond E. Lindgren
California State University, Long Beach

HISTORY[2]

WITH Gustav Vasa's establishment of the modern state of Sweden in 1523, a search started for governmental documents and a system of organization. Unfortunately, the quest began with almost no papers, for most materials relating to earlier Swedish history had been either carried away by Christian II, by earlier rulers, or were later destroyed in the palace fire of 1525. Some papers that Christian took with him in his flight from Denmark reappeared in the archives of Munich in the early nineteenth century and, in an archival arrangement with Bavaria in 1829, these documents were sent to Oslo and some early national registers (*registrum regni*) to Sweden. Since Norway and Sweden were united at the time, part of the archives relating to the former remained in Oslo, but others came back to Sweden, after an absence of more than three hundred years. Another exchange with Denmark in 1929 returned some of the Sture papers from the fifteenth and early sixteenth centuries.

Although Gustav I arranged for the archives in Stockholm and brought documents kept at Strängnäs to the depository, it was only in 1618 that Chancellor Axel Oxenstierna ordered the creation of *Riksarkivet* (the National Archives) with a person responsible for maintaining some order in the documents of the kingdom. In 1661, another chancery order permitted research in these materials, but only after filing an application and a studied approval, a system persisting into the twentieth century.

[1] Thanks and acknowledgements are due to Dr. Åke Kromnow, *Riksarkivarie*; Dr. Göran Nilzén and FL Axel Norberg, *Riksarkivet*; Dr. Uno Villers, *Kungliga Biblioteket*; Dr. Wilhelm Carlgren, Chief of Archives, *Utrikesdepartementet*.
[2] See Nos. 10 and 12 for the history of the National Archives (*Riksarkiv*).

All important foreign correspondence, royal decrees, decisions of *Riksrådet* (Royal Council), treaties, etc., were customarily recorded in a copybook designated the *registrum regni* and later in the *riksregister* (national register). Some documents date from the reign of King Magnus Eriksson (1319-74). At the time of Gustav I one of the secretaries of the chancery (*Rikskansliet*), Rasmus Ludvigsson, classified and organized the archives from Strängnäs, which became known as the *riksens gamla archivium* ("old archives"). By the end of the sixteenth century, the state papers were again neglected and in disarray, and this condition was what necessitated the above order of Chancellor Oxenstierna and the allocation of a repository in the wing of the palace. His appointee as first official secretary of the archives was Peder Månsson Utter, who developed a system of cataloguing state papers that was followed for two hundred years and devised a special register for foreign affairs (*utrikesregister*, sometimes called *register i utrikesärenden*).

Fire in the old palace of Tre Kroner in 1697 destroyed two-thirds of the archives, including the registers of 1522 to 1648. Other valuable documents and the royal library also burned, and extremely rare documents and valuable books went up in smoke. Yet today, approximately 13,000 medieval manuscripts are still among the holdings, with others deposited in *Kungliga Biblioteket*. Following the fire, the archives were kept in much confusion in two residences in the "old city." To add to this calamity, the threat of a Russian invasion in 1709, after Charles XII's defeat at Poltava, caused the secretary of the archives, Elias Palmskiöld, to flee with the state papers by sea to Örebro. Caught in a storm, the ship almost sank, and the papers were soaked with sea water. After his return to Sweden, Charles XII brought the government documents back to Stockholm in 1716.

A new royal palace was completed in 1756, and the archives were lodged there until 1846. Their chaotic condition was not remedied until Archivist Hans Järta recatalogued them. For a time the archives were kept in a private residence, but then a new depository was established, in 1865, in the old Stenbock Palace on Riddarholmen; enlarged in 1891, it furnished a home until the latest move to completely new quarters in 1969. Archivists began transferring documents to the new *Riksarkiv* in 1968, including important collections housed around the city, but some materials remain in storage on Riddarholmen, and at other locations. The new archives at Fyrverkarbacken 13–17 (S112 60 Stockholm) are modern, well-furnished accommodations with ample reading space, a reference library of some 80,000 volumes and trained archivists to assist the researcher. The foreign ministry documents to 1920 are all now in these quarters.

The foreign affairs of Sweden were conducted by a chancellor until 1720. During the Period of Freedom (*Frihetstiden*) a chancery council, presided over by a president, took over this function. In 1772 the chancellor was reinstated and remained in charge of foreign affairs until 1840, when *Utrikesdepartementet* was established.[3] In the reign of Gustav I, an official named the *custos archivi* became responsible for the archives, but the cataloguing and care of these documents was relegated to a secretary in the chancery. In 1720 the *custos archivi* was replaced by a *hovkansler* (court chancellor), who was a member of the chancery council. The directives of the council were called *kansliprotokoll* (chancery protocols). The *rådsprotokoll* (orders in council) were passed by *Riksrådet*, which actually governed Sweden from 1720–1772.

Within the chancery, there was a special secretary for foreign correspondence. He was responsible for the maintenance of the *register i utrikesärenden*, but soon, several secretaries handled this foreign correspondence and formed a council or cabinet of foreign affairs within the chancery. Their archives now rest in *Riksarkivet*, classified under the names of the secretaries responsible for the correspondence. Papers of the presidents of the chancery council are likewise filed under their respective names. Special dossiers on international problems of the day are filed according to subject in a special section of the chancery council

---

[3] See No. 21.

archives. For the committee papers and individuals involved in diplomacy, two card catalogues in *Riksarkivet* furnish records of subject matter, names, and other items of identification which are most useful for the researcher.[4]

With the ascension to the Swedish throne of the enlightened despot, Gustav III, nephew of Frederick the Great, the Riksdag lost its power, and the office of chancellor was restored. Then, in the 1840s, many functions of the chancery were given to various departments of the new cabinet system, and one became the department of foreign affairs. *Riksarkivet* remained is this department until transferred, first to Church and Education, and then to the Department of Education where it is presently lodged. The title of *Riksarkivarie* (national archivist) was first used in 1835. With the administration of Hans Järta from 1837 to 1844 came a complete reorganization of the archives. They now became not only the depository for government documents, but also a central institution for historical research. *Riksarkivet* began publication of historical works, such as the *Svenskt diplomatarium* (1829–   ),[5] *Svenska riksrådet protokool* (1878–   ), etc., and also a journal, *Meddelanden fran Riksarkivet* (1875–   ). More recently the archives publish *Skrifter* (1931–   ) and a small bulletin on holdings, acquisitions, and news called *RA nytt* (1969–   ). Naturally, the staff has grown, and the *Riksarkivarie* now has two subchiefs, five section archivists, five assistant archivists, and quite a number of other personnel. The staff of *expedition* (desk for submission of requests by readers) proves most helpful in locating materials, since they know where and under what rubric to look.

ORGANIZATION AND CLASSIFICATION

For the study of the diplomatic correspondence and the foreign affairs of Sweden, the researcher will find the above-mentioned

---

[4] These are called *Register över frihetstidens utskottsutlåtanden* and *Personregistratur över innehållet i de diplomatiska samlingarna.*
[5] See No. 5c.

registers of foreign affairs of great value for the period up to 1809, since they consist of chronological records and copies of all correspondence expedited by the secretaries of foreign affairs in the chancery.

The correspondence itself is called *koncepten,* and these may be checked against registers. The latter are usually referred to in historical works as RR. Some registers prior to 1523 may also be found in the archives. After 1619 so-called *diarierna* (diaries), consisting of chronologically-arranged summaries of incoming or outgoing correspondence, supplemented or replaced the registers. Often other sources are the *Rådsprotokoll* (orders in council) for those periods when the Swedish kings were absent from Stockholm or later, during the Period of Freedom in the eighteenth century. The papers and correspondence of the kings and queens of Sweden, of chancellors, diplomats, and statesmen may be found in *Riksarkivet,* although since 1818 the royal family archives have been kept separately in *Bernadotte familjearkivet* with a special archivist and strict regulations on the use of materials. Treaties have been published since 1877, at first by *Utrikesdepartementet,* then by *Riksarkivet.* Since 1912 the foreign ministry has published a current public treaties series under the title of *Sveriges överenskommelser med främmande makter.*

The diplomatic materials in *Riksarkivet* are designated the *diplomatica-samling.* Before 1809 instructions to Swedish diplomats were filed under *kanslikollegium* by the name of the secretary who issued the directives. Since that date they have been filed under the countries to which the diplomats were assigned, for example: *Diplomatica Gallica* for France, etc.[6] Correspondence from foreign countries may be found in the same way. The older files are orgnaized under the Latin designation of the countries used in Europe at the time. A series of printed indexes have appeared in various numbers of *Meddelanden från Riksarkivet;* most are covered in these publications including *Americana,*

[6] See No. 29.

Anglica, Brandenburgico-Borussia, etc. Although these indexes are somewhat out of date, the *expedition* maintains a card catalog name index of letter writers.

Formerly, correspondence of diplomats and the foreign ministry was in Latin, then in German and Swedish, then in the early eighteenth century in French, German, Swedish, and Latin, and today in many languages. Materials are retained in the foreign ministry for fifty years before they are turned over to *Riksarkivet.* Some correspondence still in the foreign ministry is open for qualified persons, up to 1939 and, in special instances, approval has been given for the study of World War II materials, depending on the sensitivity of the subject. But, after May 9, 1945, the archives are completely closed. Application should be made to the Minister of Foreign Affairs, Utrikesdepartementet, Gustaf Adolfs torg 1, Stockholm. The department also has a library which is open to the public, but it contains mostly journals and other materials available elsewhere.

Collections of private papers are in various public archives, libraries, and family collections. *Bernadotte familjearkivet,* housed in the castle, is open for research, but permission must be obtained from the monarch. These materials have much nineteenth-century diplomatic correspondence, since the king acted closely with the foreign minister and often conducted foreign affairs independently. Papers of other individuals have been deposited in *Riksarkivet, Kungliga Biblioteket,* university libraries, and regional archives. A catalog by Otto Walde[7] covers these private archives to 1956 and is available at the Uppsala University Library, *Kungliga Biblioteket,* and *Riksarkivet* in xerox copy. A few valuable papers are still on estates of prominent Swedish statesmen and diplomats of the aristocracy. The following list includes a few of these collections and their location but, obviously, many more are in either *Kungliga Biblioteket* or especially *Riksarkivet:*

---

[7] See Nos. 22, 23, and 24.

In *Riksarkivet*:

Adler-Salvius papers. Important for the Thirty-Years War; contains correspondence of Hugo Grotius.

De la Gardie. Papers confiscated from Magnus de la Gardie, favorite of Queen Christina. Other archives of the family are deposited at the University of Lund and in Estonia. There is an unpublished catalogue of this collection in *Riksarkivet*.

Löwenhjelm. Baron Gustaf Löwenhjelm was the Swedish ambassador to France, and these materials cover the years 1812–1816.

Oxenstierna. Chancellor Axel Oxenstierna and nephew, Bengt, were important in Swedish history from 1616 to the 1680s; the materials have been arranged récently.

Stavsund. Papers of the Fersen family, correspondence of Queen Lovisa Ulrika and others; important papers of Hans Axel von Fersen, friend of Marie Antoinette.

Björnstjerna. General M. F. F. Björnstjerna was Swedish ambassador to England during the time of Gustav III; O. M. Björnstjerna was a later foreign minister.

Film arkiv. Microfilm of materials in the Russian archives relating to Sweden (1717–1864, 74 rolls) and to Denmark (190 rolls). Most important for the period from 1510 to 1864.

Kungliga Biblioteket:

Wachtmeister. Axel Fredrik Wachtmeister (1855–1919), foreign minister.

Mörner. Carl Mörner was a personal friend of Karl Johan (Charles Jean Bernadotte).

Östen Undén. Foreign minister of Sweden after World War II.

Engström. Lars von Engström's collection contains letters of the royal family and private individuals at the end of the eighteenth century.

Wrangel. Some of the important and more recent Wrangel family papers are included.

Other archives:

Uppsala University Library: Letters of Queen Lovisa Ulrika and the very large *Gustavianska samling* of Gustav III; also many other private papers.

Lund University: De la Gardie, J. C. Toll, Henning Hamilton and other private archives are depostied here.

Östergötlands Museum: Fersen papers, including Marie Antoinette and Barnave materials (1791–92), which were entrusted to Fersen by the French queen.

Private possession: Sten M. C. Lewenhaupt papers at Barksäter; Ericsberg has some royal family and private papers; a few remain at Trolle-Ljungby (Wachtmeister) of an extensive collection; some Wrangel papers are at Boo.[8]

Krigsarkiv: The War Department museum and archives at Banérgatan 64 preserves papers of M. A. von Ungern-Sternberg, J. A. Sandel, G. C. von Döbeln, and others important both in war and diplomacy.

Stadsarkiv, Göteborg, and *Stadsbibliotek:* special collections of residents of the city such as S. A. Hedlund, once editor of *Göteborgs Handels-och Sjöfartstidning.*

ADMINISTRATION, REGULATIONS, AND FACILITIES

Riksarkivet (Fyrverkarbacken 13–17, S112 60 Stockholm) are now under the Department of Education. The *Riksarkivarie* (National Archivist) has charge of the administration of the national and regional or county archives and private collections. The reading rooms are open from 9:00 A.M. to 7:00 P.M., on Monday, Tuesday, and Wednesday, and from 9:00 A.M. to 5:00 P.M. on Thursday and Friday; on Saturday, the room is open from 9:00 A.M. to 12:30 P.M. and from 1:30–5:00 P.M. The *expedition* is open during the week, but not on Saturday from 9:00 A.M. to 4:00 P.M. Requests for materials must be submitted prior to

[8] See again Nos. 22, 23 and 24.

4:00 P.M., but those needed for the following day's work may be kept at the desk in the reading room. From June 1 to August 31 the hours for the reading room are changed to an opening time of 9:00 A.M., arid a closing hour of 5:00 P.M. All visitors are asked to register when they enter the archives, but neither identification nor letters of introduction are necessary unless there are special personal reasons. Some catalogs of special collections — most of which are quite undependable at present — are published in *Meddelanden från Riksarkivet.* A card catalog in the circulation room on the lower floor lists most archival materials; unpublished catalogs cover special collections; and there is a separate file of some antiquity. But it is best for the novice to inquire of the archivists at the desk as to procedure. Microfilm and xerox copies of materials may be obtained, a list of prices being available on request.

Kungliga Biblioteket is located in a park called Humlegården, off one of Stockholm's busiest squares, Stureplan, S114 46 Stockholm. It is a depository for many important papers and collections. Since 1661 it has been a depository for published books in Sweden, a practice which has been extended to other libraries as well. Here may be found some collections of diplomatic papers, medieval documents, private papers, bibliographies, guides, published source materials, and Swedish historical journals. The library was started as a palace library by Queen Christina, but she took some volumes with her to Rome when she abdicated. A second library in the palace was about eighty percent destroyed by fire in 1697. A third attempt to assemble a library was made in the new palace, and this was the nucleus of the new library in Humlegården when it moved there in 1877. It now contains over a million volumes and a valuable collection of rare parchment manuscripts. The library is open to the public during the winter from 8:45 A.M. to 11:00 P.M. during the week, and from 8:45 A.M. to 6:00 P.M. on Saturday; the manuscript room closes at 5:00 P.M. on weekdays. All books or materials must be requested prior to 4:00 P.M., and it requires from one to three hours to secure them, although manuscript service takes only fifteen to twenty minutes. Registration of name and local address is expected of readers upon entering the library. Three catalogs are arranged according to title, author, and topic, together with published accession catalogs, which must be frequently used. The library provides microfilm and xerox service.

The city of Stockholm's *Stadsbibliotek* (Sveävagen 73, S113 59 Stockholm) is an excellent library but has few materials pertinent to foreign affairs. The *Riksdag* current archives are one source for materials on foreign policy, but these are available only on request and under special conditions. The city of Stockholm has archives dating back to 1474, including some transactions with the Hanseatic League. *Krigsarkivet*, previously mentioned, is at Banérgt 64, S104 50 Stockholm.

Landsarkiv (seven county archives) have been established in various districts of Sweden, since 1897, and are under the direction of the National Archivist. The one at Vadstena in central Sweden is near the ruins of the famous shrine of St. Bridget, which attracted many pilgrims in medieval times and some tourists today, and it has collections of handwritten manuscripts and other materials. Another *landsarkiv* is in the old castle at Uppsala, and another in Visby on the island of Gotland, a thriving merchant town until forced to yield an enormous treasure by Valdemar Atterdag of Denmark in 1861. The old warehouse of the Swedish East India Company in Göteborg has been converted into a museum and the city has another *landsarkiv*. The records of the archibishopric of Lund, the oldest in the north, have been placed in the local archives of this university town.

Housing in Stockholm is a most difficult matter, and it would be wise to make arrangements beforehand. The Swedish Institute in Sverigeshuset, Hamngatan 27, Stockholm, can be of assistance, as can the Swedish-American Information Service in New York, or the cultural attaché of the Swedish embassy in Washington. Since *Riksarkivet* is outside the central part of town, it is necessary to use a bus — number 62 from Norrmalmstorg — which goes near the archives at Marieberg. Because of the fluctuating prices and the high cost of living in Stockholm, the scholar should be prepared for the worst.

BIBLIOGRAPHY

Published Collections of Source Materials
1. Fryxell, Anders, *Handlingar rörande Sveriges historia ur utrikes arkiver*. 1836-43. Extracts from foreign archives concerning Sweden's history.
2. a. Klemming, Gustaf E. *Kongl. Bibliotekets samling af samtida berättelser om Sveriges drig*. Contemporary accounts of Sweden's wars in the Royal Library.
   b. *Samtida skrifter rörande Sveriges förhallånden till främmande magter*. 1881-83. Contemporary accounts of Sweden's relations with foreign powers.
   These two publications have been continued by Karl J. G. Snoilsky in 1892, by Johan A. Almquist in 1901-02, and by Arne Jörgensen, the latter in Helsinki, in 1918.
3. Kungliga samfundet för utgifvande af handskrifter rörande Skandinaviens historia. *Handlingar rörande Skandinaviens historia*. (HSH). 40 vols. 1816-60. Documents concerning Scandinavian history.
   Historiska handlingar. (HH). 29 vols. 1861—. A continuation of the above.
4. *Stockholms stadsböcker från äldre tid*. 4th series. 1876—. The archives of Stockholm, from 1420 to 1544.
5. *Riksarkivet*.
   a. *Arkivar till upplysning om svenska krigens och krigrättningarnes historia*. 3 vols. 1854-61. Archives of the Thirty Years War.
   b. *Handlingar rörande Sveriges historia*. 1859—. Historical sources including:
      Series I. "Konung Gustaf:s registratur." 29 vols. 1861-1916. Covers the dates 1521-60.
      Series III. "Svenska riksrådets protokoll." 1878—. Orders in Council from 1621—.
   c. *Svenskt diplomatarium från och med år 1401*. 1875—. Previously: *Diplomatarium suecanicum*. 1829—.
6. *Svenska riksdagsakter jämte andra handlingar, som höra till statsförfattningens historia*. 2 series. 1521-1718 and 1718-1800.

1887—. Acts of the *Riksdag* and other documents concerning constitutional developments and foreign affairs.

7. *Utrikesdepartementet.*

    a. *Sveriges traktater med främmande magter jämte andra dit hörande handlingar.* 1877—. Foreign treaties and other documents concerning foreign relations. 15 parts covering 862 to 1905. Now published by *Riksarkivet.*

    b. *Sveriges och Norges traktater med främmande magter.* 1810–1905. Separate edition of parts 10–15, above.

    c. *Recueil des traités, conventions et autres actes diplomatiques de la Suède entièrement ou partiellement en vigeur le 1er janvier 1910.* 1910. Another edition of 1910–11.

    d. *Sveriges överenskommelser med främmande makter.* 1912—. Annual publication of Sweden's foreign agreements.

8. Vitterhets-historie-och antikvitetsakademien. *Rikskansler Axel Oxenstiernas skrifter och brefvexling.* 2 series. 1888—. The Royal Academy of Literature, History, and Antiquities publication of the works and correspondence of Gustaf Adolf's chief minister and the regent, during Queen Christina's minority.

9. *Samling och studier,* utgivna av Svenskt arkiv samfund. 1956—.

Guides and Reference Works

10. Bergh, Severin. *Svenska riksarkivet.* 2 vols. 1916–17. The history of the National Archives, from 1618 to 1846.

11. Bowallis, Robert M. "Bidrag till historien om K. Christiern II:s arkiv och dess delning mellan Sverige, Norge och Danmark," *Meddelanden från Riks-Arkivet,* I:3 (1879), 21–66. A discussion of the archives taken from Sweden and Denmark by Christian II, in his flight to Holland.

12. Bring, Samuel E. *Bibliografisk handbok till Sveriges historia.* 1934. Also volume 15 of *Sveriges historia till våra dagar.* 1945. This excellent bibliography and survey of the history of *Riksarkivet,* *Kungliga Biblioteket,* and other depositories lists their contents, gives a bibliography of published diplomatic correspondence, and points out guides to archival material.

13. "Utbyte av arkivalier mellan Sverige och Danmark," *Historisk tidskrift* (Sw.), 1929, 82–84. The archival exchange between the two countries in which Sweden received documents of stadholders Svante Nilsson and Sten Sture the Elder, the so-called Sture papers.

14. Bååth, Ludvig M. "Anteckningar om det s. k. Sturearkivet," *Medde-*

landen från Riksarkivet, 1929, 165-170. Details of the Sture archives.

15. Carlander, Carl M. *Svenska bibliotek och ex libris*. 6 vols. 1904. An excellent account of private correspondence in library and private collections; almost all pertinent personal collections have been transferred to public institutions.

16. International Institute of Intellectual Cooperation of the League of Nations. *Guide international des archives—Europe*, "Suède."

17. Posse, Johan August. "Anteckningar om RA bestammelse och arkivhandlingarnas fördelning," *Meddelanden från Riks-Arkivet*, I: 1 (1877), 30-45.

18. Weibull, Curt G. "Arkivordningsprinciper. Historisk återblick och nyorientering," *Scandia*, 1930, 52-77. Since 1902, the principle of provenience has been used in the Swedish archives.

19. *RA nytt*. 1969—. Publication of *Riksarkivet* with news, lists of acquisitions and collections.

20. Beskow, Ivar (ed.). *Den svenska utrikespolitikens historia*. 5 vols. 1952 to 1961. Both its history of Swedish foreign policy since the Vikings and its bibliography make this series a standard and valuable reference item.

21. Tunberg, Sven, et. al. *Den svenska utrikesförvaltningens historia*. 1935. History of the development of the foreign office and its administration.

Guides to Special Archive Collections

22. *Otto Waldes katalog över enskilda arkiv*. Xerox copies in the Uppsala University Library, *Kungliga Biblioteket*, and *Riksarkivet*. This guide to private archives ended in the 1950s, but *Riksarkivet* has continued publication of lists of such collections. Walde's catalogue is most complete and useful, except for the current location of many collections.

23. Kommissionen for Riksinventering av de enskilda arkiven. *Bulletin*. Supplements the above.

24. Grill, Erik and Jägerskiöld, Olof. "Person-släkt-och gardsårkiv inom riksarkivets tredje section," *RA nytt*, No. 1, 1969.

25. Bergh, Severin. "Kungliga kansliets in Riksarkivet förvarade diarier," *Meddelanden från Riksarkivet*, n. f., I (24), 1910, 436-467.

26. Brulin, Johan Olof Herman. "Gadebuchska samlingen i Riksarkivet," *Nordiska tidskrift för bok- och biblioteksväsen*, 1916, 40-51. A collection of materials on the history of Swedish Pomerania by Professor Thomas H. Gadebusch.

27. "Förteckning öfver samlingen af riksregistratur i Kongl. Riks-Arkivet," *Meddelanden från Riks-Arkivet*, I: 1 (1877), 61–72. A discussion of the collection of national registers or copybooks of correspondence of the chancery handling foreign affairs.

28. Taube, Bernhard and Bergh, Severin. "Förteckning öfver samling af originaltraktater i Svenska Riksarkivet," *ibid.*, IV (1897), 99–154.

29. Taube, Bernhard and Westrin, Theodor. "Förteckningar över ministeriella handlingar," *ibid.*, I (1878–79), II (1882–84), III (1891), IV (1897), V (1901). These articles provide descriptions of materials in the diplomatic correspondence by country; the same list can be seen in Bring, 72–73, No. 12, above.

30. Bemis and Griffin, *Guide*. On Swedish archives, pp. 931–932.

31. Degras, *Soviet documents*. On Sweden, pp. 76, 117, 148, 185, 229.

16 SWITZERLAND

Lynn M. Case
University of Pennsylvania

HISTORY OF THE ARCHIVES

THERE was no national repository in Switzerland for government records and documents until 1798. Consequenly, for documentary materials on Swiss foreign affairs before 1798, one must rely on the collections scattered in the various cantonal archives.[1] The cantonal archives of Bern, Lucerne, and Zurich are the most important for the earlier materials on foreign relations. However, also of considerable value are the cantonal archives of Appenzell (Ausser Rhoden), Appenzell (Inner Rhoden), Basel, Frauenfeld, Fribourg, Glarus, Nidwald, Obwald, Schaffhausen, Soleure, and Zug. There are materials of lesser importance to be found in the cantonal archives of Geneva, Grisons (at Coire), Neuchatel, Schwyz, and Valais (at Sion). The archives of Uri were burned by the French in 1799.[2]

The first central repository for confederation documents came at the time of the establishment of the Helvetic Republic in 1798, when provision was made for national archives on December 18 of the same year. In spite of changing regimes, the archives were continued in 1803 and 1848. In 1804 they were given their permanent location in Bern, where all of the records on Swiss foreign relations since 1798 have been kept. After 1803 the archives were designated as the *Eidgenössische Archiv* and after 1848 as the *Schweizerische Bundesarchiv*.[3] With the founding of the Swiss federal government in 1848, the archives were put under

---

[1] I, 385 of No. 40.

[2] Based on information furnished by the *Schweizerische Bundesarchiv*, April 7, 1953 and June 13,1972.

[3] The French and Italian designations for the archives are: *Archives Fédérales Suisses* and *Archivio Federale Svizzero*.

the direction of the federal chancellery, but in 1861 they were reorganized on their present basis and placed under the department of interior. For many years the *Bundesarchiv* occupied part of the basement of the Federal Palace in central Bern, but in 1899 it moved to the south wing of the new Archives and Library Building in Kirchenfeld (South Bern). In 1931 the library (*Landesbibliothek*) moved to its new, modern building, and the *Bundesarchiv* then took over the rest of the space in the old building left vacant by the library.[4]

ORGANIZATION AND CLASSIFICATION

Although its name, organization, and location may have changed since its founding, the *Bundesarchiv* contains the confederation's documentary materials since 1798. Thus there are three general chronological groupings of the official documents: (1) the archives of the government of the Helvetic Republic (1798–1803), (2) the archives of the Diet (1803–1848), and (3) the archives of the central federal administration, since 1848.

The archival materials of the period of the Helvetic Republic (1798–1803), consisting of 3,775 volumes, are classified under the headings of ten authorities: (1) legislative, (2) executive, (3) finance, (6) war, (7) foreign affairs, (8) judicial, (9) treasury and office of the seals, and (10) pay commissioner (*commissaire ordonnateur*). All these sections have documentary materials relating to foreign affairs, but of course the one containing the materials of the ministry of foreign affairs is the most important. The section of material (7) is subdivided into subheadings: (*a*) minutes of proceedings (*procès-verbaux*), brief descriptions of the deliberations in the Executive Directory concerning foreign affairs; and (*b*) decisions, messages, correspondence, and instructions.

The archives of the Diet (1803–1848) are subdivided into two peroids: Period of the Mediation (1803–1813) and Period of the Restoration and Regeneration (1813–1848). The foreign ministry

[4] I, 496 of No. 42; I, 385–386 of No. 40.

materials of the Period of the Mediation, consisting of 672 volumes, are further subdivided under the following subheadings:

1. Political reports from the Swiss diplomatic agents in Paris, Vienna, and Milan.

2. Papers concerning special (*extraordinaires*) diplomatic missions to foreign countries.

3. Swiss consular papers from France and the Italian states.

4. Papers (diplomatic and consular) originating with the Swiss federal authorities concerning Swiss negotiations and correspondence with foreign countries. These are still further subdivided under the headings of German states, France, Great Britain, Italy, the Netherlands, Austria, Prussia, Rome, Russia, Sweden, Austria, Sicily, Spain, Valais, Neuchatel (except for the last subheading, these are arranged alphabetically under the German form of the name).

The foreign ministry materials of the Period of Restoration and Regeneration (1813-1848), consisting of 2,230 volumes, are arranged under the following headings and subheadings:

1. Correspondence of the federal authorities with the Swiss diplomatic representatives in Paris, Vienna, and Milan.

2. Special (*extraordinaires*) diplomatic missions to foreign countries.

3. Correspondence with the Swiss consulates in Marseilles, Lyons, Bordeaux, le Havre, Bastia, Nantes, Algiers, Lisbon, Barcelona, Genoa, Naples, Rome, Milan, Leghorn, Trieste, Turin, London, Liverpool, Leipzig, Hamburg, Amsterdam, Rotterdam, Antwerp, Brussels, St. Petersburg, Odessa, Moscow, Christiania, New York, New Orleans, Philadelphia, Madison, Galveston, Louisville, Alexandria, Mexico City, Rio de Janeiro, Pernambuco, Bahia, and Para.

4. Correspondence, negotiations, and treaties with the German states, Belgium, Brazil, Denmark, France, Greece, Great

Britain, the Italian states outside Sardinia and the Two Sicilies, Liechtenstein, Mexico, the Netherlands, the United States, Austria, Portugal, Prussia, Russia, Sardinia, Sweden, Two Sicilies, and Spain.

The foreign ministry archives of the central federal administration since 1848 have no specially prepared inventory but are classified by files according to the headings given by the registry of the political department. The main collection of diplomatic correspondence is, however, arranged under the heading of "*Rapports politiques*" and is then subdivided into the various foreign countries. There is no catalogue of this material available to outside researchers, but the following card catalogues in the research room serve as guides to other materials since 1848 and indicate their nature:

1. Catalogue of general bilateral treaties to which Switzerland is a party, listed by number, date, diplomatic personnel, and country.

2. Catalogue of boundary treaties, listed by number, date, country, and place of signature.

3. Catalogue of international (multilateral) treaties, listed by number, date, subject, country, and place of signature.

4. Catalogue of tariff treaties (*Zollauslösungsverträge*).

5. Catalogue of federal and cantonal constitutions.

Other collections in the period since 1848 of interest to foreign relations are:

1. Consular reports since 1848 (administrative, commercial, and political reports, to be found under these subtitles). These, in turn, are subdivided into various foreign countries.

2. Circular instructions. These exist, but are scattered among various subject files.

3. The *original* minutes (*procès-verbaux*) of the Swiss Federal Council (*Bundesrat*), Council of States (*Ständerat*), and the

National Council (*Nationalrat*). These contain discussions on foreign affairs and ratification of treaties.

4. The original minutes (*procès-verbaux*) of the foreign affairs committees of the two legislative houses (see above). For consultation of the material of the most recent fifty years, one must obtain the permission of the *Département politique* of the Swiss foreign ministry.

5. Private papers of former Swiss officials and diplomats. Some of these will be found under their names in the *Bundesarchiv*; others are located in the various cantonal archives. For example, those of Johann Conrad Kern, Swiss minister to France during the Second Empire, are found in Frauenfeld, canton of Thurgovia. For a guide to the location of these, see No. 40.

6. Copies of foreign documents relating to Swiss history and diplomacy, obtained since 1876 from the archives and libraries of Austria, Belgium, France, Germany, Great Britain, Italy, the Netherlands, the Soviet Union, Spain, Sweden, and the United States. Many of these collections are manuscript copies, but many others obtained since 1945 are microfilm or xerox copies. See Meyrat's article in No. 28.[5]

ADMINISTRATION, REGULATIONS, AND FACILITIES

The *Bundesarchiv* is located at 24 Archivstrasse in Bern, on the south side of the city; the telephone number is 61 71 11. Dr. Leonhard Haas is the Director of the *Bundesarchiv*.

The research room will be found in the central front area of the second floor, just in front of the staircase. One must ring to obtain entrance at the iron grill at the top of the stairs. The administrative offices are located on the same floor near the research room. The *Bundesarchiv* is open from Monday through Friday, from 8:00 A.M. to 6:00 P.M. (Actually the hours are fifteen minutes

---

[5] Information on the organization and classification of the documents on foreign affairs was obtained from No. 42 and No. 39 (pp. 338–344), and from information furnished by Dr. Leonhard Haas to L. M. Case, concerning the *Bundesarchiv* in letters of August 1948 and of June 13, 1972.

earlier than those indicated.) It is closed on Saturday and Sunday, and for two days in the spring for cleaning.

According to the regulations of the *Bundesarchiv*,[6] only the documents over fifty years old are freely available for public use. No credentials or recommendations are necessary, but the administration reserves the right to require the identification of researchers. Documents less than fifty years old will be communicated only in exceptional cases, and only with the permission of the service or department concerned.[7] Interlibrary and interarchive loans of documents (except rare or fragile ones) are made within Switzerland, but not between the *Bundesarchiv* and foreign institutions.

The researcher may obtain authorization to use a typewriter, if it does not disturb other visitors. The *Bundesarchiv* does have xerox service for documentary reproductions. For photostatic reproductions they apply to the Government Printing and Supply Center (EDMI), or to a private photographer. As a safety precaution the *Bundesarchiv* has microfilmed various important branches of its own records.

Other facilities available to researchers in the *Bundesarchiv* are:

1. A library containing, among many items, the collections of printed documents, debates, statutes, and reference works. There is also a card catalogue of this library.

2. Card catalogues of some of the collections since 1848 (see above under *Organization and Classification*).

3. For inventories and indexes of collections see the bibliography at the end, Nos. 16, 17, 22, 34.

Those who are doing research in the *Bundesarchiv* will also find the following institutions and learned societies located in Bern:

Archives Cantonales de Berne
Archives de la Ville de Berne

---

[6] *Reglement für das Bundesarchiv*, 15 Juli 1966.
[7] The minutes of the public deliberations of the two legislative houses are available, regardless of date.

Bibliothèque Nationale (Landesbibliothek)
Bibliothèque de la Ville et de l'Université de Berne
Bibliothèque Militaire Fédérale
Musée des Arts et Métiers
Musée Historique
Séminaire d'Histoire Générale et d'Histoire Suisse à l'Université de Berne
Société d'Histoire du Canton de Berne

The deliberations of the two houses of the National Assembly, when they are in session, might be of interest to visiting social scientists.

Good hotels, whether they are luxurious or moderate in price and accommodations, may be found in the center of the city, not far from the railroad station. A bus runs from this area to the *Bundesarchiv* about every ten minutes. Those who wish to find boarding houses or rooms in private homes would be advised to consult the University of Bern or Cook's tourist offices in the center of the city.

BIBLIOGRAPHY

Printed Collections of Documents

1. *Amtliche Sammlung der ältern eidgenössischen Abschiede. Die eidgenössischen Abschiede aus dem Zeitraume von 1245 bis 1798.* 8 vols. in 23. Bern, 1856–86. Collected from materials in the cantons and cities; published and distributed with the cooperation of the *Bundesarchiv*.

2. *Aktensammlung aus der Zeit der helvetischen Republik* (1798–1803). Edited by Johannes Strickler and Alfred Rufer. 16 vols. Bern and Fribourg, 1886–1966.

3. *Amtliche Sammlung der neueren eidgenössischen Abschiede. Repertorium der Abschiede der eidgenössischen Tagsatzungen aus den Jahren 1803 bis 1813.* Edited by Jakob Kaiser. Bern, 1886. A second edition of the two following items.

4. *Repertorium der Abschiede der eidgenössischen Tagsatzungen vom Jahr 1803 bis Ende des Jahres 1813.* Bern, 1842.

5. *Urkunden zum Repertorium der Abschiede der eidgenössischen Tagsatzungen vom Jahr 1803 bis Ende des Jahres 1813.* Bern, 1843. A supplementary volume to the one listed above.

6. *Amtliche Sammlung der neueren eidgenössischen Abschiede. Repertorium der Abschiede der eidgenössischen Tagsatzungen aus den Jahren 1814 bis 1848.* Edited by Wilhelm Fetscherin, under the direction of Jakob Kaiser, Federal Archivist. 2 vols. Bern, 1874–76.

7. *Offizielle Sammlung der das schweizerische Staatrecht betreffenden Aktenstücke, Bundesgesetze, Verträge, und Verordnungen, 1848.* Bern, 1850– .[8]

8. *Bundesblatt der schweizerischen Eidgenossenschaft, 1848– .*[9] A publication of the laws and decrees of the Federal Assembly, discussions and decisions of the Federal Council, proposals of federal laws and decrees, official communications of federal officials, appointments, and official acts and publications of the canton authorities.

Guides and Reference Works

8a. Bemis and Griffin, *Guide.* On Swiss archives, pp. 939–940.

9. Benziger, C. "Die Schweiz in ihren Beziehungen zu den Vereinigten Staaten von Nordamerika," *Konsular-Bulletin,* X (1931), 1 ff.

10. Bonjour, Edgar. *Geschichte der schweizerischen Neutralität.* 6 vols. Basel, 1970. Vols. IV–VI deal with the period of World War II (1939–45).

11. Ceresole, Victor. *Relevé des manuscrits des archives de Venise se rapportant à la Suisse et aux III ligues grises.* Venice, 1890.

11a. Degras, *Soviet Documents.* On Switzerland, pp. 27, 65, 110, 145, 223.

12. Faust, Albert B. *Guide to materials for American history in Swiss and Austrian archives.* Washington, 1916.

13. Gautschi, Willi. *Documente zum Landesstreik 1918.* Zurich, 1971.

14. Gauye, Oscar. "Lettres inédites d'Eugen Huber," *Revue de droit suisse,* LXXXI (1962), 91–120.

15. Gauye, Oscar. "Inventar zur Dokumentation über die Erarbeitung des schweizerischen Zivilgesetzbuches 1885–1907," *Schweizerische Zeitschrift für Geschichte,* XIII (1963), 54–100.

16. *General Repertorium der Akten des helvetischen Zentralarchivs in Bern, 12 April 1798 bis März 1803* (Bern, 1876). For materials on foreign affairs, see *Auswärtiges* under *Vollziehungsgewalt,* p. 17, Nos. 786–803.

17. *Generalrepertorium für das eidgenössische Archiv, 1803–1848.* (only in manuscript form).

---

[8] The French title is: *Recueil officiel des pièces concernant le droit public en Suisse des lois fédérales, traités, décrets, et arrêtés, 1848–1947.*

[9] The French and Italian titles are: *Feuille fédérale suisse* and *Foglio federale della Confederazione svizzera.*

18. Haas, Leonhard. "Die Schweiz und die Vereinigten Staaten von Nordamerika. Ein geschichtlicher Rückblick (1607-1917)," *Zeitschrift für schweizerische Geschichte*, XX (1940), 228-263. By the Director of the *Bundesarchiv* and based on *Bundesarchiv* materials.

19. Haas, Leonhard. *Lenin, unbekannte Briefe, 1912-1914*. Zurich, 1967.

20. Haas, Leonhard. "Spanische Quellen zur Schweizergeschichte," *Schweizerische Zeitschrift für Geschichte*, I (1951), 599-608.

21. Haas, Leonhard. *Geschichte des Schweizerische Bundesarchivs.*

22. *Inventarium des eidgenössischen Archivs von 1803-1832* (a manuscript copy existing only in the *Bundesarchiv*).

23. Kaiser, Jacob. "Les Archives Fédérales," *Dictionnaire géographique de la Suisse*, V (1908), 337-338.

24. Kern, Léon; Henri Beuchat; Leonhard Haas. *Repertorium über die Verhandlungen der Bundesversammlung der schweizerischen Eidgenossenschaft.* Vol. I (1848-74), Fribourg, 1942; Vol. II (1874-91), compiled by Walter Meyrat. Bern, 1972.

25. Kern, Leon; Edgar Bonjour. "Summarisches Verzeichnis der Abschriften aus ausländischen Archiven, die im Bundesarchiv aufbewahrt werden," *Zeitschrift für schweizerische Geschichte*, XV (1935), 422-432.

26. Largiadèr, Anton, "Die Archive der Schweiz," *Archivar*, February 1953.

27. Largiadèr, Anton. "Schweizerisches Archivwesen. Ein Überblick," *Festschrift Haus-, Hof-, und Staatsarchiv* (Vienna, 1949), I, 23-53.

28. Meyrat, Walter. "Die Manuskripten- und Abschriftensammlung des Bundesarchivs," *Schweizerische Zeitschrift für Geschichte*, IX (1959), 93-97.

29. Meyrat, Walter. "Die Bestände des Bundesarchivs als Quellen für die Familienforschung in der Schweiz," *Der Schweizer Familienforscher*, XXVI (1959), 93-97.

30. Neuhaus, Leo. "Die Schweizerregimenter in Spanien, 1734-1835," *Schweizerische Zeitschrift für Geschichte*, VII 1958), 226-230. This concerns the papers of the regiments 1, 3, and 4 in Spanish services in the Swiss archives.

31. Plüss, A. "Mitteilungen über das Archivwesen der Schweis," *Deutsche Geschichtsblätter*, X (1909), 163 ff.

32. "Reglement für das Bundesarchiv," *Amtliche Gesetzessammlung*, (1966), p. 916. Decree of the Swiss Federal Council of July 15, 1966.

33. *Reglement und Plan für das eidgenössische Archiv nebst dazu gehörender Instruktion.*

34. *Repertorium über die in Zeit- und Sammelschriften der Jahre 1812-1912 enthaltene Aufsätze und Mitteilungen schweizergeschichtlichen Inhaltes.* Published by the Allgemeine geschichtsforschenden Gesellschaft der Schweiz, and edited by Joseph Leopold Brandstetter and Hans Barth. 6 vols. Basel, 1892, 1906, 1943.

35. Reinhardt, H. *Schweizergeschichtliche Forschungen in spanischen Archiven und Bibliotheken.* Published by the Swiss Bundesarchiv. Bern, 1900.

36. Rott, Edouard. *Histoire de la représentation diplomatique de la France auprès des cantons suisses, de leurs alliés et de leurs confédérés, 1430-1704.* 10 vols. Bern, 1900-35.

37. Rott, Edouard. *Inventaire sommaire des documents relatifs à l'histoire de Suisse conservés dans les archives et bibliothèques de Paris et spécialement de la correspondance échangée entre les ambassadeurs de France aux Ligues et leur gouvernement, 1444 à 1700.* 6 Parts. Bern, 1882-94. Part VI is made up entirely of two alphabetical indexes of persons and subjects.

38. Schmutz-Pfister, Anne-Marie. *Repertorium der handschriftlichen Nachlässe in den Bibliotheken und Archiven der Schweiz* in *Quellen zur Schweizergeschichte.* New Series IV. Section of *Handbücher der Schweizergeschichte.* Vol. VIII (Bern, 1967), 1-200. This lists many collections of private papers of Swiss officials and diplomats concerned with foreign relations. (The French and Italian titles are: *Répertoire sommaire des fonds manuscrits conservés dans les bibliothèques et archives de Suisse;* and *Repertorio sommario dei fondi manoscritti nelle biblioteche e negli archivi della Svizzera.*)

39. Société des Nations. Institut International de Coopération Intellectuelle. *Guide international des archives. Europe.* Paris, 1934.

40. Türler, Henri. "Les archives fédérales à Berne. . . . Les archives cantonales," *Dictionnaire historique et biographique suisse,* I (1921), 385-388. This describes the classification plan of the *Bundesarchiv* and discusses the collections in the canton archives.

41. Usteri, Emile. "Berichte über Literatur, die schweizerische Archive betreffend, 1907-1927," *Archivalische Zeitschrift,* 3d Series. Vol. IV (1928), 279-316.

42. Wentzke, P., and G. Ludtke. "Die Archive," *Minerva Handbücher,* Part II, Vol. I (1932), 496.

43. Wild, Helen. *Bibliographie Schweizergeschichte, Jahrgang 1913-27.* Bern, 1915-20. Zurich, 1921-57. This bibliography has been continued by others since 1927, presently by Lucienne Meyers, since 1958.

44. Wirz, Caspar. *Regesten zur Schweizergeschichte aus den päpstlischen Archiven, 1447-1503.* Collected and published by the *Bundesarchiv* in Bern. 6 nos. Bern, 1911-18.

17 VATICAN CITY

Raymond L. Cummings

Villanova University

HISTORY

FROM early Christian times, the popes conserved administrative records, acts of councils, letters, and other important documents. Unfortunately, almost all of the manuscripts prior to the reign of Innocent III (1198-1216) are missing.[1] Part of the material subsequently collected was stored in the Vatican Library, founded in 1450 by Pope Nicholas V (1447-55). It took considerable time, however, before the idea developed of creating a central church archive, and it was not until 1611, during the pontificate of Paul V (1605-21), that the papacy established a special depository for Vatican manuscripts, known as the *Archivio Segreto Vaticano* (commonly abbreviated ASV), independent of the library. Its nucleus was made up of archival material collected from the library, the nearby Castel Sant' Angelo, the Apostolic Camera, and other offices.[2] The process of gathering material into the ASV has continued, but there are still documentary collections, significant for the study of Vatican diplomacy, stored elsewhere, such as the papers of families to which some of the secretaries of state and nuncios belonged.

The archival collection has sustained substantial losses over the centuries. Its movement from place to place during the Medieval and Renaissance periods, the sack of Rome in 1527, and the French occupation of 1798 were costly events in its history. Especially serious damage occurred as a result of Napoleon's decision to have the archives transported to Paris in 1810.[3]

---

[1] No. 176, pp. 88-90.
[2] No. 169, p. 552.
[3] No. 157, col. 1132.

While papal nuncios were dispatched to various countries as early as the year 1500, permanent nunciatures began to appear in the principal cities of Europe only in the second half of the sixteenth century, expecially during the pontificate of Gregory XIII (1572–1585). During most of the sixteenth and seventeenth centuries the direction of the external affairs of the Holy See was shared by a succession of cardinal secretaries on one hand and cardinal nephews on the other. The post of secretary of state was gradually evolving, but did not clearly emerge with full authority over papal diplomacy until 1692.[4] Thereafter, the influence of the secretary of state within the Curia grew impressively. During the nineteenth century, in addition to carrying out his diplomatic duties, he was given general supervision of the Papal State.

Since the opening of the Archives in 1881, by Pope Leo XIII (1878–1903), many publications of documents have appeared. German and Austrian institutes in Rome were particularly active in this respect, while notable contributions were made by Belgian, Swiss, French, Dutch, and other scholars.[5]

ORGANIZATION AND CLASSIFICATION

The Vatican holdings may be divided into the following main groups: 1) Original Secret Vatican Archives; 2) Archives of the Apostolic Camera; 3) Avignon Archives; 4) Archives of the Castel Sant'Angelo; 5) Archives of the Apostolic Datary; 6) Archives of the Consistory and the College of Cardinals; 7) Archives of Congregations; 8) Archives of Tribunals; 9) Archives of the Secretariat of State; 10) Archives of other Secretariats; 11) Archives of Nunciatures; 12) Archives of Private Persons, Religious Orders, Popes, Cardinals, etc.

Because of the complexity of the ASV there is no single, universally accepted schema of its contents. The researcher will, therefore, encounter variations of the one presented above upon consulting other guides. The most important Vatican collection,

---

[4] No. 172, p. 9.
[5] No. 161, pp. 15–18.

for modern diplomatic history, is that of the secretariat of state (*Segreteria di Stato*). However, in view of the peculiar organizational structure of the entire archival collection, it is by no means all inclusive, and the researcher is cautioned to refer to the other major collections of the Vatican. The following holdings are those which are the most valuable for research in diplomatic history.

ARCHIVES OF THE SECRETARIAT OF STATE

The materials in this rich collection are traditionally divided into three main groups, on a chronological basis: A. *Fondo Vecchio*; B. *Epoca Napoleonica*; C. *Fondo Moderno*.

A.   *Fondo Vecchio*

This *fondo,* terminating generally with the end of the eighteenth century but containing some nineteenth century material, consists of two major series: (1) *Nunziature e Legazioni* and (2) *Lettere.*

1. *Nunziature e Legazioni*

As would be expected, the reports from the nunciatures and the instructions of the Vatican secretaries of state to the nuncios abroad constitute very significant segments of the archives of the secretariat of state. The material in this group dates primarily from the sixteenth century when, as previously noted, permanent papal nunciatures were being established in the important capitals of Europe. Apart from the ordinary dispatches and coded messages, the correspondence came in time to include letters as well as enclosures. Instructions to the nuncios are preserved both in preliminary and in final drafts. It should be noted that the collection has many gaps, especially in the sixteenth century materials. Furthermore, diplomatic instructions to the nuncios were at times included in correspondence dealing primarily with nondiplomatic affairs and therefore may not always be in the archives of the secretariat of state. Some of the figures and dates given for the holdings listed below are approximate, as it is difficult to ascertain in each and every case the precise number of volumes and the exact time span covered.

Fondi Nunciature	Vols. or bundles		Index
Bavaria	49	1786–1808	1071
Colonia	339	1575–1797	1027
Corsica	11	1655–1801	1024
Fiandra	250	1553–1795	1026
Firenze	271	1532–1809	1024
Francia	727	1527–1809	1025
Genova	21	1463–1808	1024
Germania	787	1515–1809	1027
Inghilterra	32	1555–1856	1071
Malta	186	1432–1797	1024
Napoli	646	1191–1808	1024
Polonia	396	1541–1810	134
Polonia-Russia	30	1793–1806	134
Portogallo	245	1535–1851	1025
Savoia	349	1560–1803	1024
Spagna	491	1524–1808	1025
Svizzera	327	1532–1815	1028
Venezia	420	1524–1807	1024
(Legazione di)			
Avignone	381	1231–1792	1023
Bologna	395	1450–1796	1023
Ferrara	408	1597–1797	1023
Romagna	197	1524–1797	1023
Urbino	223	1624–1798	1023
Ubaldini (Arch.)	49	1187–1752	1023
Nunciature de Paci	71	1628–1716	1026

The *Archivio Ubaldini*, a family *fondo*, contains Urbino legation material, as well as Ubaldini family papers. The *Paci* collection is made up primarily of secretary of state correspondence dealing with peace negotiations and treaties.

Nunziature diverse	*308 volumes or bundles*	*Index 1026*
Colonia	1605-86	
Fiandra	1605-86	
Firenze	1607-64	
Francia	1521-1689	
Germania	1591-1807	
Inghilterra	1553-1686	
Malta	1678-81	
Napoli	1462-1686	
Nimega	1676-79	
Polonia	1563-1705	
Portogallo	1560-1684	
Savoia	1605-85	
Spagna	1560-1686	
Svizzera	1605-86	
Venezia	1596-1686	
Legazioni	1607-86	
Istruzioni	Eugenius IV-1736	
Lettere varie	1510-1724	
Relazioni, Testi, Atti politici, Affari	1546-1790	

Avvisi	*159 volumes or bundles*	*Index 1026*

a. Notices originating within the jurisdiction of individual nunciatures:

Colonia	1601-97
Finadra	1563-1746
Firenze	1651-1793
Francia	1562-1793
Malta	1667-72
Napoli	1618-1704
Polonia	1607-1770
Portogallo	1587-1672
Savoia	1616-97

Spagna	1587–1719
Svizzera	1620–96
Venezia	1605–1791
Vienna-Praga-Germania	1563–1709

b. Letters and notices from other places:

Ancona, Belgrado, Bologna, Dalmazia, Ferrara, Foligno, Forli, Genova, Inghilterra, Levanta, Macerata, Mantova, Milano, Modena, Olanda, Parma-Piacenza, Pavia, Pesaro, Ravenna, Rimini, Roma, Spoleto, Svezia.

Two secretariat of state series, *Memoriale e Biglietti* and *Emigrati Rivoluzione Francese*, are also indexed in Vatican index 1026. The former contains memorials and petitions to the pope or secretary of state, along with correspondence from the secretary of state to a variety of departments of the Curia, prelates, cardinals, and private persons. The latter consists of correspondence of diverse origin, some of it from nuncios and legates, relative to the plight of the French émigrés.

2. *Lettere*

In addition to the correspondence found in the *Nunziature e Legazione* collection, there exists the *Lettere* collection, which ranges over a wider scope, since it contains papal and curial correspondence with officials of the church, foreign governments, and private persons. Although the collection is divided into the groups listed below, it is necessary to emphasize that no rigid separation is maintained. First to be found in each group are the original communications *received* up to the year 1740, with material from the sixteenth and early seventeenth centuries being sparse; they are followed by communications *sent*, partly in copy and partly in draft. This procedure is then repeated, for the period 1740 to the end of the eighteenth century. Letters received by the secretary of state predominate. The following are the divisions of the *Lettere* series:

Volumes or Bundles

Lettere di cardinali	211	1572-1809
Lettere di vescovi e prelati	533	1500-1810
Lettere di principi e titolati	300	1515-1808
Lettere di particolari	421	1518-1809
Lettere di soldati	88	1572-1755

Consult indexes 1013-1022, 1071.

B.   *Epoca Napoleonica*

This collection, forming a link between the old and the new *fondi* within the the secretariat of state archives, is, at present, in the process of reorganization. It should be noted that part of the material for this period is to be found in the *Fondo Vecchio* (under which some guides to the archives place it), as the dates next to many of the holdings in the *Nunziature* and *Lettere* collections indicate. However, since a new system of organizing diplomatic correspondence was being introduced in the first decade of the nineteenth century,[6] another part came to form a separate collection. Everything from this period bears the mark of Napoleonic activity, the most unfortunate result of which was the loss of substantial quantities of archival holdings, much of it pertaining to the Napoleonic era itself.

Index 87 is a guide to the material of the *Epoca Napoleonica* dealing with Bavaria, France, and Italy. While most of it relates to 1800-10, there is correspondence going back to 1792, and even earlier. Index 108, entitled *Governatori* (1800-1809), refers to problems connected with the administration of the papal territories.

C.   *Fondo Moderno*

The comprehensive archival reform, finally accomplished under the direction of Cardinal Consalvi in 1816, classified the

---

[6] No. 189, and No. 188, pp. 79-81.

holdings of the secretariat of state under nine headings (*titoli*), separated into two general groups, *Interno* and *Estero*. The eight headings designated *Interno* refer to internal administrative affairs of the Papal States, which fell in some way within the competency of the secretary of state. Some of this material, from the period 1834–1870, is in the Italian *Archivio di Stato* in Rome. It is necessary for the scholar to realize that not all the diplomatic correspondence in the secretariat of state archives subsequent to 1816 can be found under the rubrics of *titolo* nine (*Estero*), for when a dispatch referred to some topic connected with internal affairs, it was generally put under an appropriate rubric of the first eight headings. For instance, important dispatches dealing with Italian events of 1859–1860 have been placed under rubric 165, which concerns the internal security of the papal territory. It is equally essential to remember that correspondence which one would expect to find under a certain rubric in the *Estero* group, e.g., *Parigi, nunziatura*, might turn up under a different rubric of the same group. This occurs if the dispatch of the nunzio pertains primarily to the affairs of another state, or to matters being handled by some other diplomatic agent. Furthermore, the designation assigned to certain rubrics is sometimes unclear. Thus, rubric 241, *Circolari ai Nunzii . . .*, contains for some years both instructions given to the nuncios and their first reports. The researcher must, therefore, cast a very wide net. The following are the divisions of the *Fondo Moderno*. The titles and holdings assigned to the rubric numbers of the *Estero* group presented below varied occasionally during the nineteenth century.[7]

Interno

Titolo	I	*Affari ecclesiastici*	*Rubriche Nr.*	1–24
	II	*Amministrazione pubblica*		25–70
	III	*Materie giudiziarie*		80–99
	IV	*Finanze*		110–130
	V	*Sicurezza interna*		149–166

[7] See No. 188, p. 110.

Estero

268. Russia, ministro
269. Prussia, ministro
270. Paesi Bassi, ministro
271. Hannover, ministro
272. Toscana, ministro
273. Malta, incaricato
274. Modena, incaricato
275. Württemberg (anche Baden), incaricato
276. Lucca, incaricato
277. Sassonia, incaricato
278. Inghilterra e Irlanda
279. Affari di America
280. Propaganda Fide
281. Congregazione degli Affari Ecclesiastici
282. Ministri di Stato
283. Vescovi esteri
284. Particolari esteri
285. Consoli pontifici in Napoli e Regno
286. Consoli pontifici in Livorno e Toscana
287. Consoli pontifici in Genova e suo stato
288. Consoli pontifici in Venezia
289. Consoli pontifici in Trieste
290. Consoli pontifici in Palermo e Messina
291. Consoli pontifici in Marsiglia e Tolone
292. Consoli pontifici in Corfù e Isole
293. Consoli pontifici in Spagna e Portogallo
294. Consoli pontifici in Malta, Corsica e Sardegna
295. Consoli pontifici in Dalmazia
295A. Consoli pontifici per gli anni 1848-1852
296. Consoli esteri Napoletano
297. Consoli esteri Inglese
298. Consoli esteri diversi
299. Condoli pontifici, disposizioni generali
300. Consoli esteri, disposizioni generali
301. (Provisioni) Delagato di Constantinopli

Invaluable instruments of research for those working in the *Fondo Moderno* are *protocolli* and *rubricelle* volumes which, dating from the first decade of the nineteenth century, are especially helpful for the period following the reform of 1816. Incoming and outgoing dispatches now began to be assigned protocol numbers, which were entered into volumes, along with the date of the dispatch, the sender, the place of origin, and, of prime importance, the rubric to which the dispatch was assigned. Sometimes, along with reference to a prior and subsequent dispatch relating to the same topic, there is a brief note on the object of the dispatch and its resolution. The protocol volumes are arranged chronologically. Index 1034 lists the volume numbers, with the protocol numbers included in each, for the years 1816-1851.

The new procedures also provided for general alphabetical inventories, referred to as *rubricelle,* which list dispatches in accord with a topical-chronological arrangement. This topical guide of several hundred volumes assists anyone trying to reassemble the correspondence of an individual nuncio or the correspondence dealing with a specific subject. Here the researcher will find under the appropriate year and topical heading dispatch numbers, a statement concerning the object of each dispatch, and its protocol number. For the years 1816-1860, he should consult index 1035. For the period not covered by indexes 1034-35, it is necessary to go directly to the volumes themselves. Despite gaps, the *protocolli* and *rubricelle* help offset the complications encountered in trying to discover the various rubrics in which papers relating to one's topic of research may be scattered. If a dispatch in a protocol volume carries next to it the initial *AE* (*Affari Ecclesiastici Straordinari*) or *BS* (*Buste separate*), it may not be consulted without special permission.

ARCHIVI DI NUNCIATURE

Complementing the correspondence of the nuncios conserved in the secretariat of state archives is the material found in nunciature archives brought back to Rome and deposited in the ASV. Although these archives constitute separate *fondi*, many guides to the ASV place them under the heading of secretariat of state. Indeed, some of their holdings have found their way into the secretariat of state archives, either in the series dealing with the country to which the nuncio involved was accredited, or in the series titled *Spogli*. The nunciature archives contain correspondence received by the nuncios, and also registers and minutes of letters sent by them to the secretary of state, other curial officials, political and ecclesiastical leaders, and private persons. The researcher may consult, for the period up to 1878, the archives of the following nunciatures:

	Volumes		Indexes
L'Aja (The Hague)	20	1802–96	1081
Bruxelles	75	1835–1904	1082
Colonia	318	c.1500–1797	1083
Firenze	425	c.1590–1859	1084
Lisbona	427	c.1580–1910	
Lucerna	451	c.1617–1873	1070
Madrid	484	c.1623–1912	1090
Monaco (Baviera)	241	1818–1913	
Napoli	410	1818–60	1085
Parigi	82	1819–1904	1086
Torino	220	c.16th–1859	
Varsavia	189	c.1587–1796	
Venezia	90	c.1658–1795	1024
Vienna	555	c.1607–1913	1055

FONDI DIVERSI

Significant quantities of diplomatic correspondence and other material, relating to the foreign relations of the Holy See, can be found among the holdings of individuals and families who played an important role in the affairs of the church. Some of the more valuable collections date from the early centuries of the modern period, when those in responsible positions tended to consider as private property all the papers which came into their possession, whether official or personal. The popes, especially from the time of the latter seventeenth century, have sought to obtain such papers from the private libraries and archives housing them, so that they might be deposited in the Vatican. Once acquired, they are maintained there as separate collections. In addition to the collections identified below, there are numerous others which may be profitably consulted, such as the *Fondo Carpegna, Fondo Confalonieri, Fondo Pio, Archivo Rospigliosi, Fondo Salviati,* etc.

a. *Carte Farnesiane* (1415-1580): Only 21 volumes of the extensive papers of Paul III and the Farnese family have come into the possession of the ASV. Most of the material is located in the archives in Parma. Among the papers in the ASV are the letters of the legates at the Council of Trent. For Vatican holdings, see index 1067.

b. *Fondo Borghese* (1485-1621): The core of this impressive collection, not to be confused with the *Archivio Borghese* or *Casa Borghese* in the *ASV*, consists of the archives of the secretaries of state under Paul V (1605-21), himself a Borghese, and under his predecessor, Clement VIII (1592-1605). It consists of four series, totaling about two thousand volumes, and constitutes a most important source for the political history of the late sixteenth and early seventeenth centuries. The nuncio correspondence from Spain, France, and Flanders is specially voluminous. See indexes 192, 193, 1052.

c. *Fondo Albani* (c.1700-21): This collection of 265 volumes contains papers accumulated during the pontificate of Clement XI (1700-21) of the Albani family. Though the bulk of the material pertains to the first decades of the eighteenth century, some of it dates from pontificates prior to 1700. See indexes 143-144.

d. *Fondo Barberini* (1300-1650): The archives of the Barberini family that are housed in the Vatican library constitute primarily the archives of the secretaries of state under Urban VIII (1623-44), but include material of other periods also. Of major interest are its *Carteggi diplomatici,* found under the series *Codd. Barb. Lat.* 6559-9808 and totaling over three thousand volumes, which contain diplomatic correspondence of the papacy.

e. *Fondo Chigi* (c.1600-1700): The Chigi archives, conserved in the Vatican library, contain principally the papers of Fabio Chigi, nunzio at Cologne and later pope (Alexander VII, 1655-67). Of particular value for seventeenth century history, this *fond* includes some papers of earlier origin, such as transcripts of sixteenth century Flanders nunciature correspondence.

f. *Archivio particolare di Pio IX* (c.1846-78): The opening of the ASV, through the pontificate of Pius IX, has made available to scholars these valuable personal papers of Piux IX which, divided into two parts, consist, first, of almost seventeen hundred items of papal correspondence and, secondly, of letters, minutes, reports, and other documents of a miscellaneous and usually official nature. There is a separate index for each part. Part I embraces some of the most important correspondence of Pius IX, up to 1874, with sovereigns, heads of states, bishops, and other persons of note. It is necessary to remember that this collection does not contain all of the correspondence of Pius IX. One must also consult the archives of the secretariat of state, the secretariat of *Litterae Latinae,* and the secretariat of *Epistulae ad Principes.*

Another collection of Pius IX papers is the *Fondo particolare di Pio IX,* in which the researcher will find family letters and also papers dealing with personal, financial, administrative, and political affairs from the time Pius was bishop of Spoleto (1827-32) until 1878. There are some letters of his predecessors dating back to Leo XII (1823-29). The documents of this *fond,* dating from the pontificate of Pius, are mostly financial in nature.

ARCHIVES OF THE SECRETARIATS

a. Secretariat of Briefs (1502, 1560-1908): Created by Alexander VI in 1502, this secretariat was reorganized in 1560 and suppressed in 1908, when it was transformed into the third section of the secretariat of state. It prepared briefs (papal letters less formal than a bull) which constituted part of the correspondence between the Vatican and ecclesiastical and temporal leaders throughout the world. Though most of this correspondence is purely ecclesiastical in nature, it sometimes bears upon political matters, particularly upon church-state realtions. Some of the briefs dating from the sixteenth and seventeenth centuries may be found in the archives of the apostolic secretariat, part of whose duties the secretariat of briefs absorbed.

b. Secretariat of *Epistolae ad Principes* (1560–1914): Correspondence, in Latin, of a more routine nature than the briefs fell within the jurisdiction of this secretariat which corresponded, on behalf of the papacy, not only with princes but also with cardinals, bishops, and nuncios. Its duties were closely tied to those of the secretariat of state, and its archives constitute a useful source for the diplomatic history of the post-Reformation papacy. For the eighteenth century, various volumes of the secretariat of state *Principi* series complement the material found here.

c. Secretariat of *Litterae Latinae* (1823–1914): Though this secretariat first appeared in the sixteenth century, "Latin Letters" before 1823 are conserved in the archives of the secretariat of *Epistolae ad Principes*. The competency of these two secretariats was not sharply differentiated. Much of the papal correspondence carried on by the secretariat of *Litterae Latinae* may be termed officious, but a portion of it, written to sovereigns, bishops, and others, merits attention.

MISCELLANEA (*VARIA MISCELLANEA*)

This *fondo*, separated into fifteen *armaria*, is composed of items that could not be easily integrated into the other collections. Much material, some of it from the secretariat of state, bearing on the history of the church from the sixteenth to the nineteenth century, such as correspondence with nunciatures, treaties, concordats, administrative documents, etc., is gathered in this collection, part of which is located in the Vatican Library. There are many indexes.[8]

ARMARIUM XLIV OF THE ORIGINAL ASV HOLDINGS

This *armarium* contains thirty-four volumes of nunciature reports, primarily of the sixteenth century. The first twenty-seven pertain to Germany; the rest concern Poland, Portugal, Spain, France, Savoy, England, Ireland, and Scotland.

Housed separately in the *Palazzo Apostolico* in Vatican City, a collection of considerable fascination to diplomatic historians of the nineteenth and twentieth centuries is the archives of the *Congregazione degli Affari Ecclesiastici Straordinari*, organized since 1967 as the *Consiglio degli Affari Pubblici della Chiesa*. Not much is known of the collection, which is presently in the process of being reorganized, but there is no doubt about its importance. Qualified scholars may seek permission to use it by writing well in advance to the cardinal secretary of state.

The best and most recent guide to the ASV is by Pasztor.[9] Another recent work, that by Boyle, is a thorough general guide with little, however, on secretariat of state material after 1800.[10] Fink's well-known monograph is still of great value,[11] while Macfarlane[12] and Gray and Chambers[13] provide excellent introductions to the archives. Complete lists of the nuncios and nunciatures from the beginning of the nunciature system, with biographical information, are available.[14] Use of the ASV is

[8] No. 161, p. 71.
[9] No. 188.
[10] No. 161.
[11] No. 168.
[12] No. 180.
[13] No. 172.
[14] Nos. 158, 175, 183.

facilitated by the existence of a large collection of indexes, nearly eight hundred volumes, with new ones constantly being added. Those not located in the *sala degli indici* must be requested from the attendants. There are two indexes of indexes in the *sala degli indici*, one compiled in 1901 and listing 681 volumes, the other listing volumes, starting with volume number 1001, compiled after 1901. Some of the new volumes supersede, in whole or in part, the older ones. The researcher is cautioned that he may have to hunt for some of the indexes as they are not in perfect order on the shelves.

ADMINISTRATION, REGULATIONS, AND FACILITIES

It would be of great advantage, to anyone intending to work in the ASV to familiarize himself with one or more of the guides noted in this chapter. Secretariat of state material is normally in Italian, but research in some of the other collections may require Latin and facility in several modern European languages. Unless the researcher is able to speak at least some Italian, he will waste much valuable time.

Beginners from America, self-conscious about their conversational Italian, will be relieved to find that the first official to whom they are directed by the attendant on duty at the entrance of the archives is Dr. Sergio Damiani, the administrative secretary, who speaks excellent English and is most gracious. Assistance may also be obtained, in English if necessary, from Msgr. Hermann Hoberg, the vice-prefect, who presides over the *sala di studio,* and from archivist Msgr. Charles Burns who, despite the press of duties which keep him away from the *sala di studio* most of the time, shares his impressive knowledge of the archives with innumerable researchers. The personnel employed in the archives is small, however, and the attendants with whom one has the most contact expect a facility in Italian. They will try to answer questions and to aid the researcher in finding and using indexes, but assistance will be strictly limited to that.

It is to be remembered that both the library and the archives are not public institutions and are open to the public only as a courtesy of the Vatican authorities. Indeed, the adjective *Segreto* in the title of the archives connotes their private character. On January 1, 1967, the terminal date of the material which may be consulted was advanced from 1846 to February 7, 1878; that is, through the entire pontificate of Pius IX. Recently the papacy has expressed the desire to open the archives to 1903, the end of Leo XIII's pontificate, but it is not certain when it will be possible to have the holdings involved ready for investigation.

Permission to work in the archives requires a letter from a university, a library, or any institution of learning. The person wishing to use the archives applies to the administrative secretary, in whose office he fills out a form; a card of admission (*tessera*), valid from mid-September to mid-July, is then issued. A photograph of the applicant must be attached. Students with proper credentials are able to obtain a *tessera* valid for a brief period of time. When first applying for permission to use the archives, it is necessary to present a passport at the Porta di S. Anna of Vatican City. To use the library as well as the archives to full advantage, the researchers should apply for a library *tessera*, which requires another letter of introduction accompanied by another photograph. An archive *tessera* entitles one to use the open shelves of the library's vast *Sala Leonina*, which is located across a courtyard from the archive's *sala di studio*, and it does permit the ordering of books. All researchers must be properly attired, which means that men must wear jackets.

To obtain volumes in the *sala di studio*, one fills out an order slip at the main desk. The call numbers to use are found in the indexes in the adjoining *sala degli indici*. Several volumes may be ordered at one time. Attendants will bring the material, generally within a short period, to a table from whence the researcher carries it to his assigned seat. He may retain it at his place from day to day. The study rooms of both the archives and the library are open from 8:15 A.M. to 1:30 P.M. daily, except on Sundays and Catholic holidays. The Christmas holiday extends from December 24 to January 1; the Easter holiday, from Holy Thursday to Easter Monday. The summer holidays begin on July 16, and end on September 15. The archives provide microfilming and photographic services. A 35 mm. exposure costs 40 lire (or about seven cents) at the present time. Inquiries should be addressed to the prefect of the archives, Msgr. Martino Giusti, Archivio Segreto Vaticano, Cittá del Vaticano.

There is no special quarter in Rome where students live. Boarding houses (*pensioni*) and rooms can be found in most parts of the city, including the area adjacent to the archives.

BIBLIOGRAPHY

Printed Collections of Documents

Austrian

1. Steinherz, S. *Die Nuntien Hosius und Delfino 1560–1561. Nuntiaturberichte aus Deutschland.* 2nd ser. (1560–1572). Vienna, 1897.
2. Wandruska, A. *Nuntius Commendone 1560–1562.* 2nd ser. Graz, 1953.
3. Steinherz, S. *Nuntius Delfino 1562–1563.* 2nd ser. Vienna, 1903.
4. ———. *Nuntius Delfino 1564–1565.* 2nd ser. Vienna, 1914.
5. Dengel, I. Philipp. *Nuntius Biglia 1565–1566. Commendone als Legat auf dem Reichstag zu Augsburg 1566.* 2nd ser. Vienna, 1928.
6. ———. *Nuntius Biglia 1566 (Juni)–1569 (Dezember). Commendone als Legat bei Kaiser Maximilian II. 1568 (Oktober)–1569 (Jänner).* 2nd ser. Vienna, 1939.
7. Dengel, I. Philipp and H. Kramer. *Nuntius Biglia 1570 (Jänner)–1571 (April).* 2nd ser. Graz, 1952.
8. Rainer, J. *Nuntius G. Delfino und Kardinallegat G. F. Commendone, 1571–1572.* 2nd ser. Graz-Cologne, 1967. This volume completed the 2nd series.
9. Rainer, J. *Nuntiatur des Germanico Malaspina, Sendung des Antonio Possevino, 1580–1582.* Vienna, 1973.
10. Dengel, I. Philipp. *Die politische und kirchliche Tätigkeit des Mons. Josef Garampi in Deutschland 1761–1763.* Rome, 1905.
11. Lindeck-Pozza, I. *Der Schriftwerkehr zwischen dem päpstlichen Staatssekretariat und dem Nuntius am Kaiserhof Antonio Eugenio Visconti 1767–1774.* Vienna, 1970.

12. Dengel, I. Philipp. "Ein Bericht des Nuntius Joseph Garampi über Böhmen im Jahre 1776," *Sitzungsberichte der kgl. böhmischen Gesellschaft der Wissenschaften. Abt. Philosophie und Geschichte*, VI (1902), 1 ff.

13. ———. "Nuntius Joseph Garampi in Preussen, Schlesien und in Sachsen im Jahre 1776," *Quellen und Forschungen aus Italienischen Archiven und Bibliotheken*, V (1903), 223-268.

14. Just, L. *Der Widerruf des Febronius in der Korrespondenz des Abbé Franz Heinrich Beck mit dem Wiener Nuntius Guiseppe Garampi*. Wiesbaden, 1959.

15. Martina, Giacomo. "Nel centenario della morte di Massimiliano d'Asburgo. La correspondenza tra Pio IX e Massimiliano." *Archivum Historiae Pontificiae*, V (1967), 373-391.

Belgian

16. Jadin, L. *Relations des Pays-Bas, de Liège et de Franche-Comté avec le Saint-Siège d'après les "Lettere di particolari" conservées aux Archives Vaticanes (1525-1796)*. Brussels, 1962.

17. ———. *Relations des Pays-Bas, de Liège et de Franche-Comté avec le Saint-Siège d'après les "Lettere di vescovi" conservées aux Archives Vatican (1566-1779)*. Brussels, 1952.

18. Cauchie, A. and R. Maere. *Recueil des instructions générales aux nonces de Flandre, 1596-1635*. Brussels, 1904.

19. Lefèvre, J. *Documents relatifs à la juridiction des nonces et internonces des Pays-Bas pendant le régime espagnol, 1596-1706*. Analecta Vaticano-Belgica. Ser 2 (A). Brussels, 1943.

20. Lefèvre, J. and P. *Documents relatifs à l'admission aux Pays-Bas des nonces et internonces des XVII et XVIII siècles*. Ser. 2 (A). Brussels, 1939.

21. Essen, L. van der. *Correspondance d'Ottavio Mirto Frangipani 1595-1606*. T. 1 (1596-1598). Ser 2 (A). Brussels, 1924.

22. Louant, A. *Correspondance d'Ottavio Mirto Frangipani 1596-1606*. T. 2 (1597-1598); T. 3 in 2 vols. (1599-1606). Ser. 2 (A). Brussels, 1932 and 1942.

23. Meerbeck, L. van. *Correspondance des nonces Gesualdo, Morra, Sanseverino avec le secrétaire d'état pontifical, 1615-1621 et annexes*. Ser. 2 (A). Brussels, 1937.

24. Meester, B. de. *Correspondance du nonce Giovanni Francesco Guidi di Bagno, 1621-1627*. T. 1 (1621-1624); T. 2 (1625-1627). Ser. 2 (A). Brussels, 1938.

25. Meerbeeck, L. van. *Correspondance du nonce Fabio de Lagonissa, archevêque de Conza, 1627-1634*. Ser. 2 (A). Brussels, 1966.

26. Brulez, W. *Correspondance de Richard Pauli-Stravius, 1634-1642.* Ser. 2 (A). Brussels, 1966.

27. ———. *Correspondance de Martino Alfieri, 1634-1639.* Ser. 2 (B). Brussels, 1956.

28. Meerbeeck, L. van. "L'instruction de l'internonce de Flandre Antonio Bichi en 1642," *Bulletin de l'Institut belge de Rome,* XXVII (1952), 395-414.

29. Jadin, L. *L'Europe au début du XVIIIème siècle. Correspondance du baron Karg de Behembourg, chancelier du prince-evêque de Liège, Joseph-Clément de Bavière, archevêque électeur de Cologne, avec le cardinal Paolucci, secrétaire d'état (1700-1719).* Brussels, 1968.

30. Lefèvre, J. *Documents relatifs à la juridiction des nonces et internonces des Pays-Bas pendant le régime autrichien, 1706-1794.* Analecta Vaticano-Belgica. Ser. 2 (A). Brussels, 1950.

31. Thielens, J. *La correspondance de Vincenzo Santini, internonce aux Pays-Bas 1713-1721.* Ser. 2 (A). Brussels, 1969.

32. Hubert, E. "La mission et les papiers du nonce Zondadari 1786-1787," *Bulletin de la Commission royale d'histoire,* LXXXIV (1922), 113-244.

33. Perniola, E. "De internuntius Mgr. Francesco Capaccini en de Belgische Omwenteling van 1830," *Mededeelingen van het Nederlandsch historisch Instituut te Rome,* 3rd series, IV (1947), 53-169.

34. Simon, A. "La Révolution belge de 1830 vue de Paris d'après les Archives Vaticanes," *Revue belge de philologie et d'histoire,* XXXVI (1948), 509-524.

35. ———. "Documents relatifs à la Revolution belge de 1830," *Bulletin de l'Institut historique belge de Rome,* XXIII (1944-46), 181-217.

36. ———. *Documents relatifs à la Nonciature de Bruxelles, 1834-1838.* Analecta Vaticano-Belgica, Ser. 2 (C). Brussels, 1958.

37. ———. *Correspondance du nonce Fornari, 1838-1843.* Ser 2 (C). Brussels, 1956.

38. ———. *Lettres de Pecci, 1843-1846.* Ser. 2 (C). Brussels, 1959.

39. ———. *Instructions aux nonces de Bruxelles, 1835-1889.* Ser. 2 (C). Brussels, 1961.

Dutch

Rijks Geschiedhundige Publicatiën

40. Brom, G. *Archivalia in Italië, belangrijk voor de geschiedenis van Nederland.* 4 vols. The Hague, 1908-15.

41. Orbaan, J. A. F. and G. J. Hoogewerff. *Bescheiden in Italië omtrent Nederlandsche kunstenaars en geleerden.* 3 vols. The Hague, 1911-17.

42. Brom, G. and A., H. L. Hensen. *Romeinsche Bronnen voor den kerkelijken staatkundigen toestand der Nederlanden in de 16ᵉ eeuw.* The Hague, 1922.

43. Cornelissen, J. D. M. *Romeinsche Bronnen voor den kerkelijken toestand der Nederlanden onder de apostolishe vicarissen 1592-1727. D. I.: 1592-1651.* The Hague, 1932.

44. Post, R. R. *Romeinsche Bronnen voor den kerkelijken toestand der Nederlanden onder de apostolische vicarissen 1592-1727. D. II: 1651-1686.* The Hague, 1941.

45. Polman, P. *Romeinse Bronnen voor de kerkelijke toestand der Nederlanden onder de apostolische vicarissen 1592-1727. D. III and IV.* The Hague, 1952-5̣5.

46. ———. *Romeinse bescheiden voor de geschiedenis der Rooms-Katholicke Kerk in Nederland 1727-1853. D.I.* (1727-1754); *D.II* (1754-1795). The Hague, 1959-63.

French

47. Richard, P. "Une correspondance diplomatique de la Curie romaine à la veille de Marignan (1515)," *Revue d'histoire et de littérature religieuses,* IX (1904), 1-47, 104-142, 321-355.

48. Paquier, J. "Nonciature d'Aléandre auprès de François Iᵉʳ," *Annales de Saint-Louis-des-Français,* I (1897), 45-58.

49. Fraiken, J. *Les nonciatures de Clément VII.* T.1 (1525-1527). Paris, 1906.

50. Lestocquoy, J. *Correspondance des nonces en France Carpi et Ferrerio 1535-1540.* Acta Nuntiaturae Gallicae. Rome, 1961.

51. Baroni, P. *La nunziatura in Francia di Rodolfo Pio* [Carpi] *1535-1537. Memorie storiche e Documenti sulla città e sull'antico Principato di Carpi.* Bologna, 1962.

52. Lestocquoy, J. *Correspondance des nonces en France Capodiferro, Dandino et Guidiccione 1541-1546.* Acta Nuntiaturae Gallicae. Rome, 1963.

53. ———. *Correspondance des nonces en France Dandino, della Torre et Trivultio 1546-1551.* Acta Nuntiaturae Gallicae. Rome, 1966.

54. Lestocquoy, J. and F. Giannetto. *Correspondance du nonce en France Prospero Santa Croce 1552-1554.* Acta Nuntiaturae Gallicae. Rome, 1972.

55. Ancel, R. *Nonciatures de France. Nonciatures de Paul IV 1554-1557.* 2 vols. Paris, 1909-11.

56. Cimber, L. [L. Lafaist] and F. Danjou. *Archives curieuses de l'histoire de France depuis Louis XI jusqu'à Louis XVIII*. Ser. 1. Vol. VI. Paris, 1835. For dispatches of nuncio Santa Croce, 1561-1565.

57. Susta, J. *Die Römanische Kurie und das Konzil von Trient unter Pius IV*. Vols. I & II. Vienna, 1904-19. For more Santa Croce dispatches, 1561-1565.

58. Hirschauer, C. *La politique de St. Pie V en France*. Paris, 1922. For dispatches of Frangipani, nuncio in France, 1570-1572.

59. Hurtubise, P. *Correspondance du nonce en France Antonio Maria Salviati*. T.1 (1572-1574). Acta Nuntiaturae Gallicae. Rome, [in press].

60. Hurtubise, P. and R. Toupin. *Correspondance du nonce en France Antonio Maria Salviati*. T.2 (1575-1578). Acta Nuntiaturae Gallicae. Rome, [in press].

61. Cloulas, I. *Correspondance du nonce en France Anselmo Dandino 1578-1581*. Acta Nuntiaturae Gallicae. Rome, 1970.

62. Toupin, R. *Correspondance du Nonce en France Giovanni Battista Castelli 1581-1583*. Acta Nuntiaturae Gallicae. Rome, 1967.

63. Blet, P. *Girolamo Ragazzoni, évêque de Bergame, nonce en France: Correspondance de sa nonciature 1583-1586*. Acta Nuntiaturae Gallicae. Rome, 1962.

64. Cloulas, I. "Les rapports de Jérome Ragazzoni, évêque de Bergame, avec les ecclésiastiques pendant sa nonciature en France (1583-1586)," *Mélanges d'archéologie et d'histoire*, LXXII (1960), 511-550.

65. Barbiche, B. *Lettres de Henri IV concernant les relations du Saint-Siège et de la France 1595-1609*. Vatican City, 1968.

66. Richard, P. "La légation du cardinal Aldobrandini (1600-1601)," *Revue d'histoire et de littérature religieuses*, VII (1902), 481-509; VIII (1903), 25-48, 133-151.

67. Barbiche, B. *Correspondance du nonce en France Innocenzo del Bufalo, évêque de Camerino 1601-1604*. Acta Nunciaturae Gallicae. Rome, 1964.

68. Leman, A. *Recueil des instructions générales aux nonces ordinaires de France de 1624 à 1634*. Paris, 1920.

69. Blet, P. *Correspondance du nonce en France Ranuccio Scotti 1639-1641*. Acta Nunicaturae Gallicae. Rome, 1965.

70. Dubruel, M. *En plein conflit. La Nonciature de France, la Secrétairerie d'État du Vatican, les Congrégations des affaires de France pendant la querelle de la Régale (1674-1694). Etude des archives romaines*. Paris, 1927.

71. Neveu, B. *Correspondance du nonce en France Angelo Ranuzzi.* T. 1 (1683-1686); T. 2 (1686-1689). Acta Nuntiaturae Gallicae. Rome, [in press].

72. Morelli, E. *Le lettere di Benedetto XIV al cardinale de Tencin dai testi originali.* 2 vols. Rome, 1955 and 1965.

73. [Salamon, Louis S. de]. *Correspondance secrète de l'abbé de Salamon, chargé d'affaires du Saint Siège pendant la révolution, avec le cardinal de Zelada 1791-1792.* Compiled by L. de Richemont. Paris, 1898. Completed in *Mélanges d'archéologie et d'histoire,* XVIII (1898), 419-450.

74. Poupard, P. *Correspondance inédite entre Mgr. Antonio Garibaldi, internonce à Paris et Mgr. Césaire Mathieu, archevêque de Besançon.* Rome, 1961.

75. Procacci, G. *Le relazioni diplomatiche fra lo Stato Pontificio e la Francia.* Fonti per la Storia d'Italia. 3 vols. (1830-1838). Rome, 1962-69.

76. Fatica, M. *Le relazioni diplomatiche fra lo Stato Pontificio e la Francia.* Fonti per la Storia d'Italia. 2 vols. (1848-1850). Rome, 1971-72.

77. Gabriele, M. *Il carteggio Antonelli-Sacconi 1858-1860.* 2 vols. Rome, 1962.

German

Preussisches (later Deutsches) Historisches Institut in Rom

78. Müller, G. *Legation Lorenzo Campeggios 1530-1531 und Nuntiatur Girolamo Aleandros 1531. Nuntiaturberichte aus Deutschland nebst erganzenden Aktenstücken.* 1st ser. (1533-1559). 1st supplement. Tubingen, 1963.

79. ———. *Legation Lorenzo Campeggios 1532 und Nuntiatur Girolamo Aleandros 1532.* 1st ser. 2nd supplement. Tubingen, 1969.

80. Friedensburg, W. *Nuntiaturen des Vergerio 1533-1536.* 1st ser. Gotha. 1892.

81. ———. *Nuntiaturen des Morone 1536-1538.* 1st ser. Gotha, 1892.

82. ———. *Legation Aleanders 1538-1539.* 2 vols. 1st ser. Gotha, 1893.

83. Cardauns, L. *Nuntiaturen Morones und Poggios. Legationem Farneses und Cervinis 1539-1540.* 1st ser. Berlin, 1909.

84. ———. *Gesandtschaft Campegios. Nuntiaturen Morones und Poggios 1540-1541.* 1st ser. Berlin, 1910.

85. ———. *Berichte vom Regensburger und Speierer Reichstag 1541-1542. Nuntiaturen Verallos und Poggios. Sendungen Farneses und Sfondratos 1541-1544.* 1st ser. Berlin, 1912.

86. Friedensburg, W. *Nuntiatur des Verallo 1545-1546.* 1st ser. Gotha, 1898.
87. ———. *Nuntiatur des Verallo 1546-1547.* 1st ser. Gotha, 1899.
88. ———. *Legation des Kardinals Sfondrato 1547-1548.* 1st ser. Berlin, 1907.
89. ———. *Nuntiatur des Bischofs Pietro Bertano von Fano 1548-1549.* 1st ser Berlin, 1910.
90. Kupke, G. *Nuntiaturen des Pietro Bertano und Pietro Camaiani 1550-1552.* 1st ser. Berlin, 1901.
91. Lutz, H. *Nuntiaturen des Pietro Camaiani und Achille de Grassi. Legation des Girolamo Dandino 1552-1553.* 1st ser. Tubingen, 1959.
92. Goetz, H. *Nuntiatur des Girolamo Martinengo 1550-1554.* 1st ser. Tubingen, 1965.
93. Lutz, H. *Nuntiatur des Girolamo Muzzarelli. Sendung des Antonio Agustin. Legation des Scipione Rebiba 1554-1556.* 1st ser. Tubingen, 1971.
94. Goetz, H. *Nuntiatur Delfinos. Legation Morones. Sendung Lippomanos 1554-1556.* 1st ser. Tubingen, 1970.
95. Schellhass, K. *Die süddeutsche Nuntiatur des Grafen Batholomäus von Portia 1573-1574. Nuntiaturberichte aus Deutschland.* 3rd ser. (1572-1585). Berlin, 1896.
96. ———. *Die süddeutsche Nuntiatur des Grafen Bartholomäus von Portia 1574-1575.* 3rd ser. Berlin, 1903.
97. ———. *Die süddeutsche Nuntiatur des Grafen Bartholomäus von Portia 1575-1576.* 3rd ser. Berlin, 1909.
98. Hansen, J. *Der Kampf um Köln 1576-1584.* 3rd ser. Berlin, 1892.
99. ———. *Der Reichstag zu Regensburg 1576. Der Pacificationstag zu Köln 1579. Der Reichstag zu Augsburg 1582.* 3rd ser. Berlin, 1894.
100. Meyer, A. O. *Die Prager Nuntiatur des Giovanni Stefano Ferreri und die Wiener Nuntiatur des Giaccomo Serra 1603-1606.* 4th ser. (17th century). Berlin, 1913.
101. Kiewning, H. *Nuntiatur des Palloto 1628.* 4th ser. Berlin, 1895.
102. ———. *Nuntiatur des Palloto 1629.* 4th ser. Berlin, 1897.

Görres-Gesellschaft

103. Dittrich, F. *Nuntiaturberichte Giovanni Morones vom Deutschen Königshofe 1539-1540.* Paderborn, 1892.
104. Reichenberger, R. *Die Nuntiatur am Kaiserhofe.* I: *Germanico Malaspina und Filippo Sega. Giovanni Andrea in Graz 1584-1587.* Paderborn, 1905.

105. Schweizer, J. *Die Nuntiatur am Kaiserhofe*. II: *Antoneo Puteo in Prag 1587-1589*. Paderborn, 1912.

106. ———. *Die Nuntiatur am Kaiserhofe*. III: *Die Nuntien in Prag. Alfonso Visconte 1589-1591, Camillo Caetano 1591-1592*. Paderborn, 1919.

Cologne nunciature

107. Schwarz, W. E. *Die Nuntiatur-Korrespondenz Kaspar Groppers nebst verwandten Aktenstücken 1573-1576*. Paderborn, 1898.

108. Ehses, S. and A. Meister. *Die Kölner Nuntiatur*. I: *Bonomi in Köln. Santonio in der Schweiz. Die Strassburger Wirren*. Paderborn, 1895.

109. Ehses, S. *Die Kölner Nuntiatur*. II: *Ottavio Mirto Frangipani in Köln 1587-1590*. Paderborn, 1899.

110. Roberg, B. *Nuntius Ottavio Mirto Frangipani 1590 August-1592 Juni*. Munich, 1969.

111. ———. *Ottavio Mirto Frangipani 1592 Juli-1593 Dezember*. Munich, 1971.

112. Reinhard, W. *Antonio Albergati, 1610-1614*. 2 vols. Paderborn, 1973.

Miscellaneous

113. Repgen, K. *Die römische Kurie und der Westfälische Friede*. Vol. I: *Papst, Kaiser und Reich, 1521-1644*. Parts I-II. Tubingen, 1962-1965.

114. Kristen, Z. *Epistulae et Acta Johannis Stephani Ferrerii 1604-1607*. I (1604). Epistulae et Acta nuntiorum apostolicorum apud Imperatorem (1592-1628). Prague, 1944.

115. Linhartova, M. *Epistulae et Acta Antonii Caietani 1607-1611*. Epistulae et Acta nuntiorum apostolicorum apud Imperatorem. 4 vols. Prague, 1932-46.

116. Pieper, A. "Die Relationem des Nuntius Carafa über die Zeit seiner Wiener Nuntiatur 1621-1628," *Historisches Jahrbuch*, II (1881), 388-415.

117. Kybal, V. and G. Incisa della Rocchetta. *La nuntiatura di Fabio Chigi 1640-1651*. Vol. I in 2 vols. Rome, 1943-46.

118. Diaz, F. *Francesco Buonvisi Nunziatura a Colonia 1670-1672*. Fonti per la Storia d'Italia. 2 vols. Rome, 1959.

119. Cornaro, Andreas *et al. Der Schriftverkehr zwischen dem päpstlichen Staatssekretariat und dem Nuntius am Kaiserhof Antonio Eugenio Visconti, 1767-1774*. Vienna, 1970. An inventory, to be supplemented later with printed documents.

120. Lill, R. *Vatikanische Akten zur Geschichte des deutschen Kultur-kampfes. Leo XIII.* Vol. I (1878-1880). Tubingen, 1970.

121. Schneider, Burkhart *et al. Die Briefe Pius XII an die Deutschen Bischöfe, 1939-1944.* Mainz, 1966.

Italian

Istituto storico Italiano per l'età moderna e contemporanea, Fonti per la storia d'Italia

122. Gaeta, F. *Nunziature di Venezia.* Vol. I (1533-35); vol. II (1536-1542); vol. V (1550-1551); vol VI (1552-54). Rome, 1958-67.

123. Stella, Aldo. *Nunziature di Venezia.* Vol. III (1566-69); Vol. IX (1569-1571). Rome, 1963, 1972.

124. Buffardi, Adriana. *Nunziature di Venezia.* Vol. XI (1573-1576), Rome, 1972.

125. Fonzi, F. *Nunziature di Savoia.* Vol. I (1560-73). Rome, 1960.

126. Villani, P. *Nunziature di Napoli.* Vol. I (1570-77). Rome, 1962.

127. Villani, P. and D. Veneruso. *Nunziature di Napoli.* Vol. II (1577-1587). Rome, 1969.

128. Bettoni, M. *Nunziature di Napoli.* Vol. III (1587-91). Rome, 1970.

129. Roveri, Alessandro. *La missione Consalvi e il Congresso di Vienna.* 3 vols. Rome, 1970-73.

130. Martina, G. *Pio IX e Leopoldo II.* Miscellanea Historiae Pontificae. Rome, 1967.

131. Pirri, Pietro. *Pio IX e Vittorio Emanuele II dal loro carteggio privato.* Miscellanea Historiae Pontificiae. 3 vols. Rome, 1944-61.

Spanish

132. Hinojosa, R. de. *Los despachos de la diplomacia pontificia en España.* Madrid, 1896.

133. Alonso, J. Fernandez. *Legaciones y Nunciaturas en España de 1466 a 1521.* Vol. I (1466-1486). Rome, 1963.

134. Olarra Garmendia, J. de and M. L. de Larramendi. *Indices de la correspondencia entre la Nunciatura en España y la Santa Sede durante el reinado de Felipe II.* 2 vols. Madrid, 1948-49.

135. Serrano, L. *Correspondencia diplomatica entre España y la Santa Sede durante el pontificado de S. Pio V.* 4 vols. Madrid, 1914.

136. Alarra Garmendia, J. de "Indices de la Nunziatura en España (1598-1621)," *Anthologica annua,* VII (1959), 409-702.

137. Olarra Garmendia, J. de and M. L. de Larramendi. [Indices de] correspondencia entre la Nunciatura en España y la Santa Sede. Reinado de Felipe III (1598-1621). 5 vols. Rome, 1960-64.

Swiss

138. Fry, K. Giovanni Antonio Volpe. Seine erste Nuntiatur in der Schweiz 1560-1564. Freiburg, 1931.

139. ———. Giovanni Antonio Volpe, Nuntius in der Schweitz. Dokumente. 2 vols. Florence, 1935; Stans, 1946.

140. Schellhass, K. Der Dominikaner Felician Ninguarda 1560-1583. 2 vols. Rome, 1930-39.

141. Reinhardt, H. and F. Stevens. Die Nuntiatur von Giovanni Bonhomini 1579-1581. 4 vols. Soleure, 1906-10; Freiburg, 1917-29.

Eastern European

142. Mosconi, N. La nunziatura di Praga di Cesare Speciano 1592-1598) nelle carte inedite vaticane e ambrosiane. 5 vols. Brescia, 1966-67.

143. Relationes Cardinalis Buonvisi in Imperatoris et Hungariae Regis curia nuntii apostolici. Budapest, 1886.

144. Boratynski, L. Iohannis Andreae Caligarii, nuntii apostolici in Polonia, epistolae et acta 1578-1581. Cracow. 1915.

145. Kuntze, E. and C. Nanke. Alberti Bolgnetti, nuntii apostolici in Polonia, epistolae et acta 1581-1585. 2 vols. Cracow, 1933-38.

146. Diaz, F. and N. Carranza. Francesco Buonvisi. Nunziatura a Varsavia. Vol. I (1673-1674); Vol. II (1674-1675). Fonti per la storia d'Italia. Rome, 1965.

147. Rouët de Journal, M.J. Nonciatures de Russie, d'après les documens authentiques. 5 vols. Rome, 1952-57.

148. Olszamowska-Skowronska, S. La correspondance des Papes et des Empereurs de Russie, 1814-1878, selon les documents autheniques. Miscellanea Historiae Pontificiae. Rome, 1970.

149. Lefevre, R. "S. Sede e Russia e i colloqui dello Czar Nicola I nei documenti vaticani (1843-1846)" in Gregorio XVI: Miscellanea commemorativa. Roma, 1948. Part II, pp. 159-293.

150. Welykyi, A. G. and G. Harastej. Litterae nuntiorum apostolicorum historiam Ucrainae illustrantes 1550-1850. 13 vols. to date (1550-1683). Rome, 1959-

Other

151. Biaudet, H. Le Saint-Siège et la Suède durant le seconde moitié du XVI siècle. Notes et documents (1570-1576). Paris, 1906.

152. ————. *Documents concernant les relations entre le Saint-Siège et la Suède durant le seconde moitié du XVIe siecle.* Part II. Vol. I (1576-1577). Geneva, 1912.

153. Borg, V. *Fabio Chigi, Apostolic Delegate in Malta (1634-1639): An edition of his official correspondence.* Vatican City, 1967.

154. Holy See. Secretaria Status. *Actes et documents relatifs à la Seconde Guerre Mondiale.* Ed. by P. Blet *et al.* 5 vols. to date. Vatican City, 1965-

Guides and Reference Works

155. Ambrosini, M. L. *The secret archives of the Vatican.* London, 1970. A popular treatment, with bibliography.

156. *L'Attivita della Santa Sede.* A yearbook with a section devoted to the *ASV* and notices of recent works based on material drawn from it.

157. Battelli, Giulio. "Archivio Vaticano." *Enciclopedia Cattolica,* XII (1954), cols. 1131-1134.

157a. Bemis and Griffin, *Guide.* On Vatican archives, pp. 937-939.

158. Biaudet, H. *Les nonciatures apostoliques permanentes jusqu'en 1648.* Helsinki, 1910. See also Nos. 175, 183.

159. *Bibliografia dell'Archivio Vaticano.* 4 vols. Vatican City, 1962-66. Attempts to list any book or article which has used ASV material since 1881.

160. Blet, P. "Acta Nunticturae Gallicae," *Archivum Historiae Pontificiae,* I (1963), 413-422.

161. Poyle, Leonard. *A survey of the Vatican Archives and of its Medieval holdings.* Toronto, 1972. Those who are not medievalists will also profit from this work.

162. Brezzi, Paolo. *La diplomazia pontificia.* Milan, 1942.

163. ————. "La diplomazia pontificia," *Vaticano.* Edited by G. Falloni and M. Escobar. Florence, 1946.

164. Brom, Gisbert. *Guide aux archives du Vatican.* Rome, 1911. Outdated. The footnotes contain many references to publications from Vatican archival sources.

165. Cardinale, Igino. *Le Saint-Siège et la diplomatie: aperçu historique, juridique et pratique de la diplomatie pontificale.* Paris, 1962

166. Del Re, Niccolo. *La Curia Romana.* 3d ed., rev. Rome, 1970.

167. Dörrer, Fr. "Der Schriftverkehr zwischen dem päpstlichen Staatssekretariat und dem Apostolischen Nuntius Wien in der Zweiten Hälfte des 18. Jahrhunderts," *Römische historische Mitteilungen,* IV (1960-61), 63-246.

168. Fink, Karl A. *Das Vatikanische Archiv.* 2d ed. Rome, 1951.

169. ———. "Vatican Archives," *New Catholic Encyclopedia.* Vol. XIV, 1967.

170. Giblin, Cathaldus, ed. *Collectanea Hibernica: Sources for Irish history.* No. 1. Dublin and London, 1958. Provides an introduction to whole "Nunziatura di Fiandra" collection.

171. Giusti, Martino. *Studi sui Registri di Bolle Papali.* Vatican City, 1968.

172. Gray, R. and D. Chambers. *Materials for West African history in Italian archives.* London, 1965. The title does not indicate its wider importance.

173. Halkin, Léon E. *Les archives des nonciatures.* Brussels, 1968. Provides an extensive bibliography of printed collections of nuncio correspondence, and of indexes to and works based upon nuncio material in the ASV.

174. Jedin, H. "Osservazioni sulla pubblicazione delle *Nunziature d'Italia,*" *Revista storica italiana,* LXXV (1963), 327–343.

175. Karttunen, L. *Les nonciatures apostoliques permanentes de 1650 à 1800.* Geneva, 1912.

176. Katterbach, Bruno. "Archivio e archivistica," *Enciclopedia italiana.* Vol. IV, 1929.

177. Kramer, H. "Die Erforschung und Herausgabe der Nuntiaturberichte," *Mitteilungen des Osterreichischen Staatsarchivs,* I (1948), 492–514. Gives a broad picture of nunciature publications.

178. Kraus, A. *Das päpstliche. Staatssekretariat unter Urban VIII, 1623–1644.* Rome, 1964. Provides a scholarly guide to the Secretariat of State archives.

179. Leflon, J. and Latreille, A. "Répertoire des fonds napoléoniens aux Archives Vaticanes," *Revue historique,* CCIII (1950), 59–63.

180. Lutz, G. "Die Bedeutung der Nuntiaturberichte für die europäische Geschichtforschung und Geschichtsschreibung." *Quellen und Forschungen aus italienischen Archiven und Bibliotheken,* LIII (1973), 152–167.

181. Macfarlane, Leslie. "The Vatican Archives: with references to sources for British medieval history." *Archives,* IV, No. 21 (1959), 29–44; No. 22 (1959), 84–100.

182. ———. "The Vatican Library and Archives: Opportunities for English-speaking students," *The Wiseman Review,* (Summer, 1961), 128–141.

183. Marchi, Giuseppe de. *Le Nunziature Apostoliche dal 1800 al 1956.* Rome, 1957.

184. Mercati, Angelo. "La Biblioteca Apostolica e l'Archivio Segreto Vaticano," *Vaticano*. Edited by G. Falloni and M. Escobar. Florence, 1946.

185. Meysztowicz, V. *De Archivo nuntiaturae Varsaviensis*. Rome, 1944.

186. Pasztor, Lajos. "L'Archivio della Segreteria di Stato tra il 1833 e il 1847," *Annali della Scuola Speciale per Archivisti e Bibliotecari dell' Università di Roma*, X (1970), 104-148.

187. ———. "La Congregazione degli Affari Ecclesiastici Straordinari tra 1814 e il 1850," *Archivum Historiae Pontificiae*, VI (1968), 71-112.

188. ———. *Guida delle fonti per la storia dell' America Latina negli archivi della Santa Sede e negli archivi ecclesiastici d'Italia*. Vatican City, 1970. A far broader guide than the title indicates.

189. ———. "Per la storia della Segreteria di Stato nell' Ottocento. La riforma del 1816," in *Mélanges Tisserant*. Vol. V. Studi e Testi. Vatican City, 1964.

190. ———. "Per la storia della Segreteria di Stato durante il triennio 1848-1850," *Annali della Fondazione Italiana per la storia amministrativa*, III (1966), 307-365.

191. Rainer, J. "Quellen zur Geschichte der Grazer Nuntiatur (1580-1622)," *Römische historische Mitteilungen*, II (1959), 72-81.

192. Repetti, A. *La diplomazia vaticana: aspetti giuridici ed evoluzione storica delle relazioni internazionali della Santa Sede*. Diss. Genova, 1971.

193. Sauer, Edith. "Zum Thema Nuntiaturberichte: Aus Erfahrungen mit Nuntiaturberichte des 19. Jahrhunderts." *Römische historische Mitteilungen*, XIV (1972), 111-121.

194. Savio, P. *De actis nuntiaturae Poloniae*. Rome, 1947.

195. Vecchi, M. *Ambasciate estere a Roma*. Milan (SISAR), 1971.

196. Wagner, W. "Die Bestände des Archivio della Nunziatura Vienna bis 1792," *Römische historische Mitteilungen*, II (1959), 82-203.

197. Weber, F. J. "The Secret Vatican Archives," *American Archivist*, XXVII (1964), 63-66.

198. Wright, A. D. "Libraries and archives: Italy and the Vatican," *History*, LVI (Feb., 1971), 50-54. A useful, brief introduction.

18 THE UNITED NATIONS AND OTHER INTERNATIONAL ORGANIZATIONS

THE UNITED NATIONS

Robert Claus, *Archivist, Connecticut State Library*

INTRODUCTION

A FEW years ago, when an international organization of major importance had completed its program and was about to disband, responsible officials seriously proposed that its archives be destroyed as soon as the official history had been compiled. Fortunately this was not done, but the records of international agencies are perhaps unusually vulnerable to this kind of thinking. Such agencies commonly publish voluminous documentation on their activities, so that proceedings of meetings, study reports, proposed resolutions, and records of performance are likely to be widely available in printed form. Even when copies are limited, the multipartite nature of the organization ensures that much of the basic material will be held by several governments, as well as in the agency's own archives. It is true, too, that what might be called the material for a diplomatic history of an international organization — that is, the inside story of the interaction of the views and interests of the various constituent governments — is perhaps more likely to be found in the archives of those governments than in the records of the agency itself.

Parly because of these circumstances, the archives of international organizations — except for their published documents — have been used relatively little for scholarly research. Another reason, of course, is that most of the major international agencies are still young, and their records generally remain closed to scholarly research. As is noted below in the League subsection, it was only in 1969 that standard rules of access to the League of Nations archives were promulgated. The United Nations and its associated agencies, most of them now in their third decade, have not yet followed suit, but perhaps the passage of a few more years will see some favorable developments in this respect.

Even now, however, there are substantial bodies of records from international agencies available to scholars — the archives of some of the older or defunct agencies and, under *ad hoc* arrangements, at least some of the records of more recent organizations. These papers often include unique and exciting materials not available elsewhere, dealing particularly, of course, with the design and implementation of the agency's program and with the story of the development of the organization and its work, but also often including much material on relations between states and on economic, social, and political conditions in one or many countries.

The United Nations Archives in New York contains the records of the United Nations itself and those of a number of earlier agencies. As an organizational entity, the archives began as a small filing unit at the San Francisco Conference of 1945. Now a section in the United Nations Secretariat, it has a staff of about thirty archivists, records management officers, and clerks and is responsible for all noncurrent records of the United Nations, and for the archives of other agencies that have been placed in United Nations custody.[1] Current records and documents, to which reference is also made in the descriptions below, are the responsi-

---

[1] A single exception of major importance is the archives of the League of Nations, held by the library of the United Nations Office at Geneva and described later in this chapter.

bility of other Secretariat units, the Registry Section, and the Dag Hammarskjold Library, respectively.

The Archives Section maintains its records in some forty "record groups" based on the provenance of the materials, each group normally comprising the papers of an independent agency or a major unit of the United Nations. "Registration sheets" serve as brief guides to the contents of each record group, and other guides and indexes provide more detailed reference tools. Most of these guides are unpublished, but copies are made available to searchers. The more important ones are listed in the bibliography.

The United Nations Records

The United Nations, established after a series of international meetings and conferences (among them the Atlantic Meeting, and those of Teheran, Yalta, Dumbarton Oaks, and San Francisco) came into being on October 24, 1945, and held its first meeting on January 19, 1946. Its basic structure had been outlined in the Charter drawn up at the San Francisco conference, while rules of procedure and arrangements for the first session had been prepared by a preparatory commission meeting in London at the end of 1945. The principal organs are the General Assembly, the Security Council, the Economic and Social Council, the Trusteeship Council, the International Court of Justice, and the Secretariat. Their functions are too well known to warrant repetition here.

To understand the records, however, one must understand that United Nations programs and policies are determined in the first instance by representatives of the member states participating in the General Assembly and the councils and other bodies. These representatives are employees each of his own government, and their papers belong to the individual governments rather than to the United Nations. However, the records of their joint activity — minutes of meetings, proposals advanced, resolutions passed, reports prepared and accepted — are records of the United Nations body concerned and are usually published.

The Secretariat, headed by the secretary general, meanwhile provides all essential services for the meetings of the General Assembly and other organs, and is responsible for implementation of the decisions they make and the programs they authorize. Thus the Secretariat collects and prepares a vast amount of data on all subjects of concern to the United Nations, assists in administering a substantial technical cooperation program to help developing countries, and carries on many other related functions. Not the least of these is the handling and filing of all the correspondence, documents, and working papers arising out of its own work and the work of the Assembly and the other organs.

For our purposes here, four types of United Nations archival materials may be described:

1. The United Nations document series, published in print or mimeograph, are available for the most part to the public by sale or at the Dag Hammarskjold Library in New York or in the United Nations Information Centres and depository libraries throughout the world.[2] Including the *Official Records* of the General Assembly and other organs, these are the basic records of their work. They are extremely voluminous, but access is facilitated by symbols representing the producing organ or suborgan, identifying the type of document (resolution, summary record, working document, etc.), and placing them in chronological order. The library publishes various indexes to the documents, as noted in the bibliography, and it also maintains a complete collection and a reference service.

2. The Registry files, or the central correspondence files of the Secretariat, containing the bulk of the correspondence and memoranda produced or received by the United Nations. These are filed according to a subject classification system, with major headings (e.g., economic affairs, technical cooperation, political questions, personnel, finance, administration) roughly parallel to the struc-

[2] The Archives Section also has them on 16mm. microfilm, and a program for producing an indexed microfiche version is under way, in the Dag Hammarskjold Library.

ture of the Secretariat. Indexes are maintained for some types of communications, but the classification scheme serves as the main control and guide. Most files from January, 1946, to the end of 1968, except for a small proportion discarded as valueless, are in the archives (about 3,400 feet). Current and more recent files (about 1,400 feet) are in the Registry Section at the headquarters building. Access to any Registry files is limited to official use, or to researchers individually receiving special authorization.

3. Departmental, mission, and commission records. This large class includes Secretariat administrative papers (e.g., purchase orders, voucher, personnel files) and working papers, which, because of their nature, are not filed in the Registry, as well as some sensitive or special records kept by the secretary-general or other officials. It also includes the records of overseas offices and special missions, commissions, and suborgans (e.g., the United Nations Emergency Force [in the Middle East], 1956–1967, and the United Nations Organization in the Congo, 1960–1964). Records from all these sources now held by the archives amount to perhaps 10,000 feet, At least as many more are still kept in the offices which accumulated them. Like the Registry files, they can be made available, for nonofficial use, only with special authorization.

4. Certain specialized collections of United Nations records. The film footage library of the Office of Public Information has thousands of feet of motion picture footage and documentary films on United Nations activities, as well as significant film material accumulated by the League of Nations and the United Nations Relief and Rehabilitation Administration. Both the archives and the photo library of the Office of Public Information have valuable collections of still photographs. Of particular interest is the archival collection containing sound recordlings (mostly on tape) of the proceedings of the General Assembly and other major United Nations organs, 1946 to the present.

San Francisco Conference Records, 1945

The United Nations Conference on International Organization met at San Francisco on April 25, 1945, for the purpose of agreeing upon a structure and terms of reference for the United Nations organization that had long been envisaged. Basing their work on a draft prepared by the 1944 meetings at Dumbarton Oaks, the representatives of the fifty participating governments signed the United Nations Charter on June 26, 1945 and, at the same time, set up a preparatory commission to arrange the first United Nations General Assembly.

The conference acted through four general committees — on conference direction, credentials, procedure, and draft coordination — and four commissions to plan the charter sections, dealing respectively with general provisions, the general assembly, the security council, and judicial organization. Each commission was divided into two or more technical committees. A secretariat, headed by Alger Hiss of the United States, provided conference services.[3]

The records fall into the following groups:

1. Documents (twenty-seven feet). The principal conference records, printed or mimeographed and bound, containing the resolutions, minutes, committee reports, and draft texts that led to the final Charter. They are valuable and much used sources for interpretation of the intent of the founders with regard to the charter provisions. Classified by committee symbols, most have been published and indexed (see bibliography).

2. Unpublished verbatim minutes of committee meetings (six feet).

3. Conference correspondence and general files (thirteen feet).

4. Commission and committee working papers (nine feet).

5. Credentials, charter texts, and related materials, presentation and publicity files, photographs, and sound recordings (twenty-six feet).

United Nations Preparatory Commission Records, 1945–46

Established at the San Francisco Conference in June, 1945, the commission met only briefly at that time and convened its

---

[3] Most secretariat files are in the National Archives of the United States. The signed copy of the Charter is in the Treaty Office of the U. S. Department of State. The participants in the Dumbarton Oaks Conference often kept their records, but many are in the custody of the above National Archives.

executive committee in London on August 16, for the purpose of preparing for the first United Nations General Assembly and formulating recommendations concerning transfer of League of Nations assets, organization of the secretariat, and other matters. The executive committee reported to the full commission on November 24, and the latter adopted the final report and adjourned on December 23, 1945. The commission was superseded by the United Nations Secretariat, when the secretary-general took office on February 2, 1946.

Both the executive committee and the preparatory commission carried on their work by means of a series of committees, each entrusted with the task of discussing and formulating recommendations concerning one aspect of the work of the United Nations. A secretariat, headed by Gladwyn Jebb, assisted the committees in their work.

There are four principal groups of records:

1. Official documents, August-December 1945 (four feet). Classified by committee symbols and indexed.

2. Verbatim records of meetings of the commission, its technical committees, and the executive committee, June 1945–February 1946 (three feet).

3. Working papers of the technical committees, 1945–46 (one foot).

4. Correspondence files, classified by subject, with card indexes, 1945–46 (six feet).

United Nations Information Organization Records, New York, 1941–46

This was the successor of one of the two information centers established by the Inter-Allied Committee in 1940 and 1941 to serve as clearinghouses for news and information of the Allied governments. It consisted of an Information Office and a United Nations Information Board, which controlled the various technical committees on press, radio, films, etc. Its work and records were taken over by the United Nations department of public information in February, 1946. The records of the parallel and cooperating London organization are not in the custody of the United Nations.

The UNIO records in the United Nations archives consist of:

1. Reference materials produced or distributed by UNIO, dealing with the activities of the Allied governments and with the San Francisco Conference, and including press releases, periodical reviews, bibliographies, studies, reports, photographs, and sheet music, 1941–46 (fifty-six feet).

2. Administrative records, including accounting papers and minutes of the Information Board and its committees, 1941–46 (three feet).

United Nations War Crimes Commission Records, 1943-48

The commission was established on October 20, 1943, by a meeting of Allied and Dominion representatives convened for the purpose at the Foreign Office in London. The first official meeting was held on January 11, 1944, and the commission continued its work actively until the end of March 1948.

Composed of representatives of its member governments, the commission performed valuable functions in connection with the development of principles of international law and planning for international tribunals. Its primary task, however, was to collect, investigate, and record evidence of war crimes, and to report to the governments concerned those instances where the available material appeared to disclose a prima facie case. In carrying out this function, the commission was assisted by national offices established by each of the constituent members. Formal charges against alleged or suspected war criminals were submitted by the national offices, along with supporting data, and the commission then determined whether there appeared to be sufficient evidence to warrant the listing of the persons charged as war criminals in order that they might be detained and prosecuted by the member governments. The commission took no part, however, in the detention of persons listed or in the prosecution of the cases, and it should be noted that only a very small proportion of the persons listed as war criminals have ever been prosecuted.

The commission carried on its work by means of a research office and three main committees, which dealt respectively with facts and evidence, enforcement, and legal questions. A Far Eastern and Pacific Sub-Commission was also set up in Chungking in October 1944.

The following are the major groups of records:

1. Minutes of meetings, 1943–48 (one foot).

2. Documents (mimeographed), 1943–48 (one foot).

3. Research office publications and reference files of related materials, 1944–48 (two feet).

4. Charge files containing formal charges, with papers submitted in evidence and other related materials, 1943–48 (forty-five feet). Indexed by name of suspect. (These files may be used only for official United Nations purposes.)

5. Reports and transcripts of the proceedings of national military tribunals and of the International Military Tribunal for the Far East, 1944–48 (one hundred feet).

United Nations Relief and Rehabilitation Administration Records, 1943–49

UNRRA was established on November 9, 1943, when forty-four nations (later increased to forty-eight) signed an agreement, the purpose of which was to "plan, co-ordinate, administer or arrange for the administration of measures for the relief of victims of war in any area under the control of any of the United Nations, through the provision of food, fuel, clothing, shelter and other basic necessities, medical and other essential services" (Article I, 2). The more important predecessor organizations were the Office of Foreign Relief and Rehabilitation Operations of the United States Department of State (OFRRO), set up on November 21, 1942, and the Inter-Allied Committee on Post-War Requirements (Leith-Ross Committee), set up in London in September, 1941.

The agreement provided for a council, on which each member government was represented and which met in six sessions from November, 1943, to December, 1946; a central committee, consisting initially of China, U.S.S.R., U.K., and U.S.A., to make policy decisions between council sessions; a committee on supplies and various regional and special committees; and a director-general to serve as the chief executive and administer officer. Under the latter's direction, a staff numbering almost twenty-five thousand was recruited and organized in a large number of offices all over the world. Its headquarters was in Washington, D.C., and a major field office, the European Regional Office, was set up in London.

UNRRA operations came to an end in the latter part of 1946, but the demobilization of the staff and the liquidation of property and accounts continued until March 31, 1949, when the records and a few remaining functions were taken over by the United Nations.

The UNRRA files contain vast quantities of unexploited data on all aspects of UNRRA's work, on its policies, techniques, and administrative organization and procedures, and on economic, social, and political conditions in nearly all areas of Europe and China during the critical postwar years. Nearly half of the records have been destroyed, but those were primarily the routine files dealing with individual purchases and shipments. The remaining archives should interest almost any scholar working in the field of international affairs, or European or Asiatic history, during the decade of the 1940s.

Many UNRRA publications are easily available; the council journals, the director-general's annual reports, the periodic financial reports, and many other informative documents were printed and widely distributed, and an official history (noted in the bibliography) was published.

The records fall broadly into the following groups:

1. Documents and publications, 1943–49 (twenty-five). Printed or mimeographed; classified, listed, and indexed.

2. Headquarters records, divided as follows:

Executive Office, 1943–49 (380 feet). Papers of the director-general, the general counsel, the public information division (with a fine collection of photographs), the historian, and others.

Bureau of Administration, 1943–49 (twelve hundred feet). Personnel files and classified central registry files covering all phases of UNRRA work.

Bureau of Supply, 1943–48 (470 feet). Detailed records of the operating divisions dealing with agricultrual rehabilitation, industrial rehabilitation, food, clothing, textiles and footwear, and with procurement and shipping generally.

Bureau of Areas, 1944–45 (sixty feet). The files of a short-lived bureau set up to coordinate field work.

Bureau of Services, 1943–48 (one hundred feet). Material pertaining to repatriation and welfare work, displaced persons programs, and relations with associated voluntary agencies.

Controller, 1943–49 (260 feet). Accounting, budget, and statistical records, containing much useful data on the source and distribution of funds.

3. European Regional Office (London), 1944–49 (340 feet). A large and valuable classified subject file dealing with all aspects of operations in Europe, together with some accounting files.

4. Mission files, 1944–48 (fifteen hundred feet). Papers of the offices in countries listed below. Some of them were engaged in distributing supplies, maintaining welfare services, or operating displaced persons camps; some were purchasing missions; still others were merely shipping offices.

Albania	Ethiopia	Italy	Trieste
Austria	Finland	Korea	Turkey
Belgium	France	Luxemburg	Ukraine
Byelorussia	Germany	Norway	Yugoslavia
China	Greece	Philippines	Balkans
Czechoslovakia	Hawaii	Poland	Middle East
Denmark	Hungary	Sweden	Southwest Pacific
Dodecanese	India	Switzerland	Latin America

International Penal and Penitentiary Commission Records, 1893-1951

The International Penitentiary Congress in London in 1872 was the first of a series that met about every five years "to collect reliable prison statistics, to gather information, and to compare experience as to the working of different prison systems and the effects of various systems of penal legislation; to compare the deterrent effects of various forms of punishment and treatment, and the methods adopted, both for the repression and prevention of crime." By 1896 formal regulations were adopted providing for equal representation of all member states on the commission and establishment of a small executive committee. A secretary-general was responsible for the administration of the affairs of the commission, and in 1926 his office became a permanent bureau. In 1929 the commission adopted the more accurate title that appears in the heading above. After a period of relative inactivity during the war years, 1939-45, the commission in 1946 offered its assistance to the United Nations and, after some years of negotiation and planning, the commission was integrated within the United Nations by a resolution of the General Assembly on December 1, 1950. Its work is now carried on by the department of economic and social affairs of the United Nations Secretariat.

The records of the commission consist of:

1. Accounting records, 1893-1939, including records of contributions, treasurer's reports, ledgers, and permanent bureau accounts (one foot, six inches).

2. Secretary-general's correspondence, 1910-26, filed chronologically with a log index (one foot, ten inches).

3. Registry files of the permanent bureau, 1925-51, classified by subject (thirty-five feet).

ADMINISTRATION, REGULATIONS, AND FACILITIES

The Archives Section is a part of the Communications, Archives, and Records Service of the United Nations Secretariat. Its stacks, offices, workrooms, and reading rooms are located on the third and fourth floors at 30-10 41st Avenue, Long Island City, New York (about ten minutes by car from United Nations headquarters). Reference service is available weekdays between 10:00 A.M. and 5:00 P.M., or by mail or telephone, and there are microfilm and photocopy machines and microfilm readers on the premises.

The regulations governing access to the archives vary widely, and it is suggested that scholars initiate their inquiries by mail or telephone. The chief archivist is glad to assist as far as possible in facilitating the handling of requests to consult records, whether in archives or elsewhere in the United Nations.

The other principal custodians of United Nations records mentioned in the text above (the Registry Section, the Dag Hammarskjold Library, and the Film Footage and Photo Libraries of the Office of Public Information) are located at United Nations headquarters, 1st Avenue and 42nd. Street, New York, N.Y. 10017. The sound recordings collection is also in the headquarters buildings, room GA-19, where indexes and listening rooms are available, and where tape copies of recordings may be ordered at cost.

Among the international organizations known as the "United Nations family" and which have headquarters in Geneva, three possess archives beginning before the Second World War and maintain services for their preservation and use. From the standpoint of diplomatic history, the most important records are obviously those of the League of Nations, which now belong to the United Nations; they are the subject of the next section of this chapter. The other portions concern the archives of the International Labour Office, whose activity, in part diplomatic, has been substantial since its creation in 1919, and the International Telecommunication Union, earliest of the organizations, with some files more than a hundred years old. The descriptions of the archives of the ILO and ITU have been kindly prepared, unofficially, by the organizations concerned.

THE LEAGUE OF NATIONS

Yves Pérotin *World Health Organization*
(Translation by Robert Claus, *Connecticut State Library*)

THE archives of the League of Nations, in comparison with those of the other international organizations, present a special case, though a classic one, in terms of archival management. Since the agency has gone out of existence, its archives consist of closed *fonds* and can no longer grow, except by the accession of private papers, the retrieval of missing items, or the reintegration of files still used by the United Nations at Geneva.

HISTORY

The League of Nations had a secretariat before it had an official existence; this explains why the earliest archives go back to 1919, even though the organization theoretically did not begin to function until 1920. The latest documents, too, run not to 1940, as is often said, but to 1946 or — for those dealing with liquidation — into 1947.

The archives consist of several *fonds*, each with its own history. The principal one, the *Fonds du Secrétariat*, was accumulated primarily at Geneva, but it includes papers from the early period in London and, in its later part, some American segments. It is the result of the work of the Secretariat as the auxiliary of the other organs of the League — the Council and the Assembly, their commissions and conferences, etc. — and as the operating agency for the League's business. The records thus constitute the archives of the headquarters; they include the files of the central Registry as well as those maintained apart from the Registry, which were commonly called "Section files." The Secretariat archives were subjected to various moves within Geneva, as well as some partial transfers of varying duration, outside Geneva. Since 1969 they have been brought together again in the Palais des Nations, and, despite some losses, about eighty percent of them remain intact and in good order.

Besides these central organs, the League of Nations created a number of other administrative units, very diverse in status but more or less integrated into the system, which functioned for various periods in various parts of the world: external offices, commissions for administration or for government, arbitral jurisdictions, institutes, etc. These units also produced archives which formed the *Fonds extérieurs,* with various closing dates. After their respective terminations, these were regrouped according to a relatively coherent policy (resulting, however, in some anomalies); certain records were inserted in the Secretariat *fonds;* others, to be listed below, were also gathered together in Geneva but without losing their character as distinct, autonomous groups (sometimes after dividing them with the governments); still others were left in place and most often lost.

In addition to these two groups — the *Fonds du Secrétariat* and the *Fonds extérieurs* — a very special group, called the *Fonds mixte Nansen,* grew up little by little out of the work of the organs and services successively responsible for aid to refugees under the aegis of the League of Nations and more or less strictly controlled by it.

In 1946 all these groups were turned over to the United Nations under the global (and justified) title of "Archives of the League of Nations" at the time of the transmission of the property of that organization. The files which were not then transferred to New York were concentrated first in the Registry and in various storage rooms of the European Office of the United Nations; in 1956, still in the Palais des Nations, they were entrusted to the Library and installed in its stacks, where they were ultimately joined by certain *collections,* some *fonds privés,* and the segments that had been temporarily kept elsewhere. The total measures about two thousand linear meters.

The decision to transfer the archives to the Library was taken after studies had shown a diminishing administrative use of the records, and an increasing interest in their historical significance. The same considerations led to the establishment of provisional procedures for the consultation of the documents by private readers, procedures involving the examination of each request for access and a review of the files requested. By the beginning of the 1960s, however, requests for access became so pressing as to make these procedures difficult; at the same time it became evident that the guides or indexes appropriate for research were lacking. A subvention from the Carnegie Endowment for International Peace made it possible to resolve the most urgent problems through the financing of the "League of Nations Archives Project," which was carried on from 1966 to 1969. The project consisted of two elements: a committee responsible for recommending to the secretary-general of the United Nations a statement of regulations for the League of Nations archives; and a working team, directed by an expert archivist, who both served as rapporteur for the committee and undertook, with his associates, to reorganize the archives and prepare guides to them. The project was completed on schedule, and the League archives now have explicit rules of access and the indispensable working guides. With other elements (a museum, a "manuscript collection" autographs, etc.), they make up the holdings of the Historical Collections Section of the United Nations Library at Geneva. It is under the direction of a professional archivist, and a temporary reading room has been equipped for use. Unfortunately the quarters are less than satisfactory and the staff is inadequate in number.

DESCRIPTION OF THE ARCHIVES

1) *Fonds du Secrétariat (1919-47)*

This *fonds* comprises the Registry files and Section files, physically arranged in two separate groups in the stacks. According to the administrative units which produced the files in one or the other category, they are:

Office (or Cabinet) of the Secretary-General (Registry).
Section for Administrative Commissions and Minorities.
Economic and Financial Section(s).
Social Questions and Health Section(s).
Information Section.
Legal Section.
Intellectual Cooperation and International Bureaux Section.
Mandates Section.
Political Section.
Transit and Communications Section.
Disarmament Section.
"Liaison with Latin America."
Files accumulated by several political or technical sections.
Finance Administration and Treasury.
Internal and Personnel Services.
Library.
Publications and "Documents" Services.

2) *Fonds mixte Nansen (1920-47)* (Prisoners of War, Displaced Persons, and Refugees).

These groups, very complicated, comprise principally:

League of Nations Registry files (1920-24) left by the High Commissioner's Office, when it transferred to the ILO.

Some series of files inherited from the Nansen Office and its successors, including the central files from Geneva, the archives of the missions, offices or delegations in the USSR, London, Belgrade, Greece, Berlin, Vienna, and Warsaw, and the London files of the High Commissioner (1920-43).

The private papers of the High Commissioner for Refugees from Germany, established in London (1933-36).

The Section files (1921-38) and the later segment (1933-47) of the Registry files of the League of Nations Secretariat, concerning refugees.

3) *Fonds extérieurs:*

Commissariat and delegation for the financial reconstruction of Austria (1922-37).

Commissariat and delegation for the financial reconstruction of Hungary (1923-29).

Independent Office for the Settlement of Greek Refugees (1925-30).

Mixed Commission for Greek-Bulgarian Reciprocal Emigration (1920-31).

Mixed Commission for Exchange of Greek and Turkish Populations (1923-34).

Governing Commission for the Saar (1920-35).

Plebiscite Commission for the Saar (1931-35).

Supreme Court for the Saar Plebiscite (1935-36).

Mixed Commission for Upper Silesia (1922-37).

Mixed Arbitral Tribunal for Upper Silesia (1932-37).

Electoral commission for the Sanjak of Alexandretta (1937-38).

Office in Berlin (1927-33).

Office in London. Economic and Financial Section (1920-40).

Princeton Mission (archives of economic, financial, and transit units transferred during the war, with older files from Geneva [1919-46]).

Washington Office. Detached units of the Opium Central Committee and the Narcotics Control Bureau (1941-46).

4) *Collections*

The most important "collections" are the publications (printed) and the documents (generally multigraphed for information or distribution), of which the most complete set is kept in the Library of the United Nations at Geneva[1]. Now Research Publications, Inc. (12 Lunar Drive, Woodbridge, Conn., 06525

[1] The remaining stocks of publications were turned over for sale to Oceana Publications, of New York.

USA) has microfilmed the monumental collections, *League of Nations documents and serial publications, 1919-1946,* which can be purchased by subject classes as well as in entirety, and has an excellent guide, *League of Nations documents, 1919-1946: A descriptive guide and key to the microfilm collection,* edited by Edward A. Reno, Jr., (3 vols., 1973-75). Although in essence they are an integral part of the archives, the collections are generally maintained apart from them; the following collections are directly attached to the archives:

Conventions, ratifications, and other diplomatic instruments.
Daily Synopsis (résume of registered correspondence).
Bulky Enclosures (oversize annexes or attachments to Registry files).

5) *Fonds privés*

Drummond papers (1920-33), two files.
Avenol papers (1924-46), one carton.
Mantoux papers (1919-25), two cartons.
Tyler papers (1931-39), seven files.
Loveday papers (1921-49), twenty-nine cartons.
Van Asbeck papers (1925-38), one file.
Archives of the International Union of League of Nations Associations (1921-39), thirty-six cartons.
Archives of the International Association of Journalists Accredited to the League of Nations (1921-39), twelve cartons.

The preceding list by itself can only hint at the richness of the archives of the League of Nations. They all deal, directly or indirectly, with the relations between governments and peoples, even though they are of course most valuable for the history of the League of Nations itself. It is evident that the records contain much unpublished material for diplomatic history or, more broadly speaking, for political history on such topics as disarmament, minority questions, and mandates.[2] Less evident, but no less certain, is the importance of the archives from the point of view of economic history (technical assistance, statistics, the Bruce Plan, etc.). Researchers in other disciplines — some unexpectedly, like the history of science, technology, sociology, and medicine — will find useful material. In brief, there is a mine of material here which researchers have barely scratched.

ACCESSIBILITY

The regulations on the use of the archives may be summarized as follows: whereas the general rule is that files remain closed for forty years, special permission may be granted for research in more recent materials, and certain files which deal with domestic and personnel matters or are unofficial communications remain closed for sixty years. Reproduction of documents other than whole groups or large series is permitted.

THE INTERNATIONAL LABOUR ORGANISATION[3]

HISTORY

THE International Labour Organisation was created in 1919 by the Paris Peace Conference in organic relation with the League of Nations; on the dissolution of the League in 1946 it entered into an Agreement with the United Nations, becoming the first specialized agency associated with that body. In one fundamental respect, the Constitution of the ILO, originally forming Part XIII of the Treaty of Versailles, differentiated it from the League and continues to differentiate it from the United Nations. Whereas in

---

[2] This is insofar as the events involved took place within the scope of the League of Nations. Thus, with regard to Locarno, one would look in vain for original documents other than those dealing with general political considerations or with observations on the compatibility of the Treaty with the Covenant.

[3] The British spelling for the name of this organization is used throughout this section.

the General Assembly and Councils of the United Nations, as in the similar organs of the League, only the governments are represented, in the Conference and Governing Body of the ILO, the governments, employers, and workers of member states are represented, sitting on a basis of equality. In virtue of this tripartite composition, which is reflected in the meetings of almost all the ILO's deliberative bodies, it is unique among international organizations.

The earliest archives of the ILO consist of papers of the Organizing Committee set up immediately after the adoption of the constitution to prepare for the first Conference (Washington; October-November, 1919). The International Labour Office (the secretariat, executive agency, and publishing house) began to function in January, 1920, in London and was transferred in July, 1920 to Geneva, where it has continued to operate, except for a period during and immediately after the Second World War when the working center was transferred to Montreal.

It is significant that the original internal organization of the Office comprised a Diplomatic Division, a recognition that diplomacy should not be merely a matter of political relations but should extend to the social, economic, and other problems within the field of action of the ILO.

DESCRIPTION AND REGULATIONS

The archives of the ILO consist mainly of what some archivists have called, rather contemptuously, "mere by-products of administration." Consisting of cardboard covers or jackets in which communications, minutes, and other papers are placed, the files are opened (i.e., brought into use) and maintained in a central Registry, or, in cooperation with it, in a filing station in the administrative, editorial, research, or operational unit concerned. An inscription on the jacket indicates the number and brief descriptive title of the file. In the jackets, minutes of headquarters' officials are placed on the left side, and on the right side all other papers relating to the topic of the file, such as communications from governments, organizations, or individuals, together with copies of outgoing communications from the ILO. The papers are arranged in chronological order.

Files are normally classified in series by subject. A file reference consists of two components — letters and numbers. The letters distinguish the subjects; e.g., SH is Occupational Safety and Health, and ILC is International Labour Conference. The numbers indicate subdivisions of the subject and the country. In the file reference "SI 4-0-5," "SI" indicates Social Insurance, "4" Health Insurance, "0" Requests for Information and "5" Austria.

In a very limited number of cases, files are marked "Confidential," indicating that the contents are restricted or classified.

By 1966 the files totalled approximately 225,000; of these, 107,000 were in active storage, 80,000 in inactive storage, and 38,000 in archival storage. In 1966 the ILO began a double operation: to appraise the archival value of its files in inactive storage and, by a measure of preselection, to facilitate in the case of newly opened files the process of determining their ultimate passage into archival storage.

In assessing the archival value of accumulated files, three criteria have been used. Files have been preserved (A) if they contained contractual or other legal obligations, (B) if the contents constituted precedents, or (C) if the papers were of historical interest or value. Historical interest or value has been interpreted in a broad sense to include interest for independent researchers engaged in study on labor, industrial, social, and economic policy.

Concurrently with the appraisal operation and records retirement program, as new files are opened, they are designated either for limited retention periods or for indefinite retention. The retention periods (0, 5, 10, or 25 years) allocated to each file are the periods on the expiration of which, dating from the time when the file passes into the inactive category, it would be reviewed for the decision whether to destory or to preserve in the archives.

The following are illustrations of record groups included in the archives:

(A) Files relating to prewar sessions of the Conference and Governing Body which contain, in chronological order, correspondence with governments and employers' and workers' delegates or representatives, credentials of delegates, reports, minutes of committees, and other records;

(B) Records left on the death of Albert Thomas in 1932, and subsequently transferred to the archives — a vast collection of his papers, almost all relating to the work of the ILO, and files and other papers transferred to the work of the ILO, and files and other papers transferred to the archives after the resignation of Harold Butler and the retirement of Edward Phelan;

(C) Some ten thousand files containing periodical reports of Branch Offices and National Correspondents relating to over fifty countries from 1920 to 1965, including a wealth of unpublished matter of an economic and social nature;

(D) Series of files on technical cooperation in developing countries, concerning initiation, organization, administration, and follow-up of hundreds of projects and programs, classified by country and functionally arranged in relation to the main activities of the ILO, on which cooperation has been afforded.

In addition to such record groups, the archives hold a collection of original texts of legal and constitutional agreements and instruments, such as authentic texts of conventions and recommendations adopted by the Conference, and texts of agreements and other formal arrangements with member states of the ILO, and with the United Nations and other international and regional organizations. Other miscellaneous collections include photographs, film strips, and sound discs, illustrating the history of the ILO, and the official collection of ILO postage stamps and postal history.

Two classes of "ILO records" are not normally held in the archives, viz. (A) printed ILO publications and (B) mimeographed matter; those are kept in the Central Library and Documentation Branch.

The preparation of a guide, and other instruments to facilitate research, is under active consideration, on the basis of a report made by a consultant.

ACCESSIBILITY

The Director-General considers applications for research in the archives. Forms are available from the Registrar, CH-1211, Geneva, Switzerland, and applicants are asked, *inter alia*, to indicate the subject of their proposed search and to give references. When granted, access normally provides for consultation of all files in archival storage, except those containing records less than ten years old, confidential material, and records containing correspondence with governments, organizations, or individuals, which if opened to external consultation, might result in embarrassment either to the ILO or to the government, organization, or individual concerned.

THE INTERNATIONAL TELECOMMUNICATION UNION

Mme. G. Pérotin, *Archival Service, ITU*

HISTORICAL BACKGROUND

THE International Telecommunication Union is the direct successor of the *Bureau international des Administrations télégraphiques,* which was created in 1868 by a conference of plenipotentiaries in Vienna and began to function in Berne on January 1, 1869. This is the oldest of the four international bureaus that were placed under the surveillance of the Swiss Federal Council, and it was to serve as a model for those which followed: the Universal Postal Union, founded in 1876 (and sometimes confused with the ITU), the *Bureaux de la Propriété industrielle, littéraire, et artistique,* and the *Office central pour les Transports internationaux par Chemins de Fer.*

The birth of the ITU had indeed been preceded by several other multilateral diplomatic agreements, such as the Austro-German Union which in 1852 joined not only Prussia and Austria but several other German states and the Netherlands. But the ITU constituted the first true effort at an international administration whose motivation can be found in the technical development and the growth of industrialization which characterized the last half of the nineteenth century. From this combination of a desire for international cooperation foreshadowing the twentieth century and a kind of scientism very representative of the preoccupations of the time were born the archives which are irrefutable evidence of the first efforts toward regulation, planning, and coordination on a supranational scale. They document some interesting examples of the procedures of European diplomacy in the second half of the nineteenth century and the beginning of the twentieth.

In studying these archives, one should not lose sight of the fact that they are complemented by very valuable materials in Series E of the Swiss Federal Archives at Berne.

In 1948 the International Telecommunication Union joined the United Nations' family and moved its headquarters from Berne to Geneva. When a second move took place in 1960, it appears that massive and ill-planned disposals of records occurred.

At the present time, an archives service, created and organized by a professional archivist, is concentrating on arranging and inventorying the existing *fonds,* starting a retirement program for semiactive or inactive records, and preparing reference systems. The service benefits from its privileged situation as an office attached directly to the office of the secretary-general. In quarters recently occupied, the archives have adequate storage areas, a microfilm workroom, and a reading room.

DESCRIPTION

1) *The Printed Archives*

The preservation of the collections of printed documents and publications of the ITU is a responsibility of the archives. This collection comprises on the one hand the documents accumulated by the General Secretariat (*Journal;* documents of telegraph and radio conferences, and related nomenclatures, etc.) and on the other hand the documents issued by the different specialized secretariats: the International Telegraph and Telephone Consultative Committee (CCITT), which succeeded the International Telephone Consultative Committee created in Paris in 1925, the International Radio Consultative Committee (CCIR), created in 1927, and the International Frequency Registration Board (IFRB), founded in 1947.

The classification, indexing, and cataloguing of these materials is nearing completion. Since 1971 a systematic program of microfilming is filling the gaps, which are inevitable in a series of publications a hundred years old and frequently moved from place to place. Nevertheless, this collection must now be the most complete set of ITU documents and publications in existence.

2) *The Manuscript Archives.*

Beginning in 1869, the office at Berne operated on the model of a German *Registratur,* carefully recording all incoming and outgoing communications in large registers. This practice ceased about 1950, when the ITU attempted to install a registry along the lines of those in the League of Nations and the International Labour Office. This date practically coincided with the entry of the ITU into the United Nations system, which brought with it in particular a very great financial change, both in the mode of financing and in accounting methods. Consequently, with the holding of the first great postwar conference of plenipotentiaries at Atlantic City, it was deemed preferable to close the Berne *fonds* at that time to facilitate its operations. For the time being, the *fonds* remains in its original state, and, in spite of apparently random disposals which took place after 1918, it is the part of the archives, so far unexploited, which seems to offer the greatest research resources.

The period from 1950 to 1970 is represented by a series of files of which about thirty percent deal with technical assistance activities, while the bulk of the remainder emanate from the various administrative departments, especially that of External Relations. Since 1968, archivists have progressively implemented a system for classification and codification of files, which is more flexible and consequently better adapted to the rapid growth of the agency.

In addition, the archives include the instruments of ratification of the conventions, while the conventions themselves are always kept in the archives of the host country of the conference which drew them up.

ACCESSIBILITY AND GUIDES

Subject to normal kinds of reservations, scholars can gain access through the Archives Service. Consultation of these rich resources is limited only by lack of reference systems. A program for preparing guides has been started, and the first results appeared in 1971 in a retrospective analytical table of the *Journal télégraphique,* which celebrated its centenary in 1969. This project is being done by means of a computer, enabling the publication of new editions at ten-year intervals.

Although it is the ancestor of all the intergovernmental organizations, the ITU is still relatively little known. Its archives are far less technical than one would at first think, and it is believed that, even for the non-specialist in telecommunications, they constitute an unexplored research area full of promise. The special attention devoted to the archives by the present ITU administration on the eve of the first world space communications conference demonstrates that, from Morse telegraph to satellite, the ITU has recognized its responsibility to retain a good memory.

BIBLIOGRAPHY

United Nations Documents
1. *Checklist of United Nations documents.* 20 vols., New York, 1949–53. (ST/LIB/SER.F/2-). Documents list with indexes and explanatory notes of major organs' meetings from 1946 to 1950 (when the *Documents index* begins). Incomplete: Does not include the General Assembly.

2. *United Nations documents index,* Vol. I, no. 1- ; January 1950-
(ST/LIB/SER.E/1-). Monthly with annual cumulations. Lists
and indexes all documentation of the United Nations.
3. *Indexes to proceedings.* (ST/LIB/SER.B/-). In four series: General Assembly (A), Security Council (S), Economic and Social
Council (E), Trusteeship Council (T). A bibliographical guide to
the proceedings and documentation, with agenda, subject, and
speech indexes, list of documents and introductory notes. Incomplete, except for the General Assembly series.
4. Groesbeck, Joseph. "Introducing UNDEX," *Special libraries* (New
York) 61 (July-August 1970) 265-270.
5. ———. "United Nations documents and their accessibility," *Library resources and technical services* (Chicago) 10 (summer
1966), 313-318.
6. Winton, Harry N. M. "United Nations documents," *Drexel library
quarterly* (Philadelphia, Pa.) (October 1965), 32-41.

United Nations Registry Files
7. Core, Ofra. "The United Nations correspondence classification
manual," *The American archivist,* 24 (July 1961), 317-322.

United Nations Archives
8. Registration sheets. Compiled in the archives, one for each "record
group" and available to searchers in ditto or mimeograph form,
these contain a note on the history and organization of the agency
concerned; a list of the record series with dates, arrangement, and
volume; a list of further guides and a statement of rules of access.
9. *Index to microfilm of United Nations documents in English.* 1946
to 1961. December 1963. (Archives special guide no. 14). And
Supplement No. 1. 1962-67. March 1970. Available to purchasers of
the microfilm.
10. Guide to sound recordings in the custody of archives of the United
Nations as of 31 December 1968. 5 November 1969. Mimeo, 29 p.
(ST/OGS/SER.A/Rev. 3). United Nations archives reference guide
No. 22/Rev.3.

San Francisco Conference
11. *Documents of the United Nations Conference on International
Organization, San Francisco, 1945,* 22 vols.; London and New York,
United Nations Information Organizations and United Nations,
1946-56. A photo-offset published series; contains a subject index.
12. Registration Sheet: Records of the United Nations Conference on
International Organization (UNCIO), San Francisco, 1945. Revision 2, September 1960. Ditto, 13 p.

13. Bruce, William J. "The San Francisco UNCIO documents," *The American archivist*, 9 (January 1946), 6-16.

United Nations Preparatory Commission

14. Dougall, Richardson. "The archives and documents of the Preparatory Commission of the United Nations," *The American archivist*, 10 (January 1947), 25-34.

15. Index to the documents of the United Nations Preparatory Commission, 1945-1946. United Nations archives reference guide No. 1. 1947. Mimeo, 37 p.

16. Index to the documents of the executive committee of the United Nations Preparatory Commission, 1945. United Nations archives reference guide No. 2. 1948. Mimeo, 85 p.

United Nations War Crimes Commission

17. *History of the United Nations War Crimes Commission and the development of the laws of war.* War Crimes Commission, London, H.M.S.O., 1948.

18. Registration: Records of the United Nations War Crimes Commission, London, 1943-49. Revision 1, January 1956. Ditto, 16 p.

United Nations Relief and Rehabilitation Administration

19. Woodbridge, George, and others. *UNRRA, The history of the United Nations Relief and Rehabilitation Administration.* 3 vols.; New York, 1950.

20. Registration Sheet: Records of the United Nations Relief and Rehabilitation Administration, 1943-1949. Revision 5, November 1960. Ditto, 20 p.

League of Nations

21. Pérotin, Yves. Guide to the archives of the League of Nations, Mimeo, 97 p., also (and originally) in French. Scholarly institutions may obtain copies from the library in Geneva.

22. *Répertoire général des archives de la Société des Nations.* 3 vols. Photoprinted. Available in the archives in Geneva and New York. Somewhat similar in organization to the above section on *Description of archives.*

23. Degras, *Soviet documents.* On the League and disarmament, pp. 91, 129, 158, 203.

24. Registres de classification. Two series; kept since 1938; useful complements of *Répertoire général*, although they preceded it in time. Available only in the Library in Geneva.

25. Yves, Victor, and Ghebali, Catherine, Carnegie Endowment for International peace. *A repertoire of League of Nations serial*

documents, 1919-1947. 2 vols., Dobbs Ferry, N. Y., 1973. Bilingual with introduction to use, lists, and nature of serials and documents.

26. Index. An enormous number of reference cards serving as guides to files and even individual documents in the archives in Geneva and maintained there only.

27. Pérotin, Yves. "L'ouverture des archives de la Société des Nations," *Annales d'études internationales,* no. 1 (1970), 180-190. Discusses the historical value of the archives.

28. "Facilitating access to the League of Nations archives," *The American archivist,* 35 (January 1972), 23-34. Problems involved in the above guide.

29. Walters, Frank P. *A history of the League of Nations.* 1st ed., 2 vols.; London and New York, 1952.

International Telecommunication Union

30. *L'union télégraphique internationale,* 1865–   Berne, 1915.

31. Codding, George Arthur, Jr. *The International Telecommunications Union.* London, 1952.

UNESCO
Luther H. Evans, *Columbia University*

THE predecessor of the United Nations Educational, Scientific, and Cultrual Organization was the International Committee on Intellectual Cooperation, established by the Assembly of the League of Nations in 1921, and the Committee's secretariat, the International Institute of Intellectual Cooperation, organized in 1926 by an agreement between the League and France. The Committee and its Institute had a wide range of interests in the life of the mind, and enjoyed the support and participation of many of the intellectual, artistic, scientific, and cultural leaders of the world, including a number from countries which were not members of the League.

The virtual disappearance of the League of Nations on the outbreak of World War II naturally led intellectuals as well as governments to turn attention to the matter of what should follow the League, the Committee, and the Institute at the end of hostilities. An important step in the creation of UNESCO was the establishment, in the autumn of 1942, of the Conference of Allied Ministers of Education. This informal group, representing European governments in exile in London, began at the invitation of the British government and the British Council. It concerned itself at first with the restoration of the educational systems of the occupied countries. It expanded its interests and participants and on July 31, 1945, published a draft constitution for a permanent international agency in the field of education and culture. This became the basic document for a conference to be held in London.

UNESCO was established pursuant to the constitution signed in London on November 16, 1945. The conference which drafted the constitution was attended by representatives of 44 nations which had adhered to the Declaration of the United Nations of January 1, 1942. It had been called by the British and French governments for the purpose of creating, in the field of education and culture, a specialized agency of the United Nations, as envisaged in what became Article 57 of the UN Charter. The latter provides for agencies "established by intergovernmental agreement and having wide international responsibilities, as defined in their basic instruments, in economic, social, cultural, educational, health, and related fields." The conference itself, within its discretion to define the agency's responsibilities, added "Scientific" to the name of the agency and increased its functions to include mass communications and, in general, a supporting role to the United Nations. A supplementary agreement of the same date provided for the immediate establishment, without the necessity of ratification, of a Preparatory Commission and a Secretariat, to serve until the official launching of the organization. The Commission and the Secretariat were based in London until September 15, 1946, when they transferred to the Hotel Majestic in Paris. The first session of the plenary body, the General Conference, opened in Paris on November 4, 1946, the date of the ratification of the constitution by the twentieth state, France.

ORGANIZATION AND CLASSIFICATION

The collections in the Archives of UNESCO consist of the archives (1) of the International Institute of Intellectual Cooperation, (2) of the Allied Ministers of Education, (3) of the Preparatory Commission, and (4) of UNESCO proper.

UNESCO received the archives of the Institute in 1946 and has maintained them as a separate collection. It should be pointed out, however, that a considerable part of the source material on the League's work in this field, particularly the activities of the Committee and of the League Assembly, are in the League of Nations archives, located in the Palais des Nations, the present European headquarters of the United Nations in Geneva. The Intellectual Cooperation archives consist of 6,000 "records (files)" and 948 publications, including duplicates. An unpublished inventory of the files is maintained, and there are printed catalogues and a card inventory of the publications, including periodicals. For the "documents" of the Institute there is a separate card-register. There is also a typed list of letters and telegrams to and from Einstein, Freud, and others. The holdings cover the period 1925–46.

The second collection, the archives of the Conference of Allied Ministers of Education (CAME), cover the period 1942–45. It contains 200 "records (files)", and a card index, in English, of "documents" which are also registered in the shelf-lists. In addition, there is a two-paged typed "List of [CAME] records and documents [in bound volumes] to be consulted in UNESCO archives." These materials have importance beyond their relevance to the establishment of UNESCO. They have much to say about the problems of educational reconstruction in occupied European countries and about many of the substantive matters which have concerned UNESCO: books and periodicals; audio-visual aids; scholastic equipment; protection and restoration of cultural material; denazification of education; and the problems of teaching science, history, etc.

The archives of the Preparatory Commission, though they might have been integrated with the archives proper, have been held separately, and this decision may have been wise, since it makes it possible to discern the outlines of the thinking which went into the presentation of the first draft program to the General Conference. The material is listed simply as 900 "records (files)" which cover the period from the London conference to the opening of the first session of the General Conference (November 1945–November 1946). They are listed in an unpublished inventory of the files, and the "documents" are listed in a card index, in French, as well as in the shelf-lists.

The main group of archives is naturally those of UNESCO proper. As of December 31, 1973, holdings numbered:

Records (files)	140,700	
Agreements	2,800	
Documents	428,800	(2 copies of each language issue)
Publications	25,600	(2 copies of each language issue)
Periodicals (issues)	16,500	(2 copies of each language issue)
Microfiches	17,400	(since 1973)
Total pieces	631,800	

It is interesting to note the recent growth of the collections. The "records (files)" of UNESCO origin, at the end of each of the years 1970–73, were:

1970	40,717	
1971	88,110	(increase of over 116 percent)
1972	127,726	(increase of over 44 percent)
1973	132,200	(increase of over 3 percent)
1974	140,700	(increase of over 6.1 percent)

Other increases in materials of UNESCO origin were:

Documents	326,811 to 385,243, over 17 percent
Publications	7,435 to 9,145, over 23 percent
Periodicals (issues)	13,310 to 15,469, over 16 percent

Total holdings increased by 20 percent in 1970, and from that year to the end of 1974, by 50.2 percent (to 631,800). A reason for the irregular growth of "records (files)" is that the Registry Division transfers most categories of them in large blocks, after subject files have been built up over a period of years and have become relatively inactive.

The collections were said in mid-1971 to occupy 2,250 linear meters, and those in the Registry, 1,290.52 meters.

The "records (files)" have inventories. The "agreements" have subject and geographical card indexes. The "publications", including "periodicals", published by UNESCO, are listed in printed catalogues, principally in the *General catalogue of UNESCO publications,* 1946–1959, a *Supplement . . .* 1960–63, and *Second Supplement . . .* 1964–67. From 1951 they are also in the *List of UNESCO documents and publications* (as from 1949 to April 1973, in English and French). There is also a list of publications of Regional Centres of UNESCO, and UNESCO-sponsored publications, May-December 1973. UNESCO-sponsored publications are included in the above sources and, since 1957, in the *List of UNESCO documents and publications.*

The "documents" collection is very extensive and complex, and so are the indexes. The grouping and the controls may be briefly stated as follows:

1. The General Conference. (a) For the "records and proceedings" there are published indexes for all but the eleventh to the thirteenth sessions, in English, French, and Spanish for 1946–54, plus Russian since 1954, and a French card index for the eleventh to the fifteenth sessions. There is also an unpublished cumulative French index to the proceedings for the first nine sessions. For the fourteenth and fifteenth sessions an index of the Conference documentation was published as a separate volume. (b) For the "resolutions" of the Conference, there are published indexes. (c) For the "programme and budget" documents, there are published indexes for 1952–62 and 1973–74. (d) "Working documents" are

included in the *List of UNESCO documents and publications,* from the fourth to the thirteenth sessions, and a card index (in French) list for the first to the thirteenth sessions is maintained. Beginning with the fourteenth session, these are also listed in the *United Nations documents index,* and published separately.

2. The Executive Board. The "resolutions" are covered by cumulative published indexes, in French and English, in volumes for 1946-54, 1954-58, 1958-66, and 1966-72. They are also in the *List of UNESCO documents and publications.* For "working documents" there is a card index.

3. The Secretariat. The "general series" of documents are included in the *List of UNESCO documents and publications* since 1949, and included in the *UN documents index* from 1952-62. Since 1968 index cards have been provided, in English and French, to UNESCO National Commissions and depository libraries. The "working series" are covered by a card index maintained in the Archives.

All of the documents mentioned above are also registered in the shelf-lists.

Since 1972 the record and publications, including UNESCO sponsored publications, are listed in the Computerized Documentation Service. Since 1973 "microfiches" (13,843) have been made of many items, particularly reports made by UNESCO experts in Member States, 1947-69.

The Archives unit does not possess certain materials of interest to its custodians, but the matter of including them is under consideration: films, photographs, phono-records, magnetic tapes of General Conference and Executive Board proceedings, and microfilm negatives.

Files accumulate in various segments of the Secretariat, and from there most of them go to the Registry Division, in the Bureau of General Serivces. Certain material goes to the Archives without ever passing through the Registry. Thus, records of the Personnel Division, and of the Controller, go directly there after two to five years. By August 1966, 2,078 files on personnel and 3,378 files of pension fund records had been transferred to the Archives. Such records are referred to in "Disposition schedules of the United Nations" (UN document CGS.195/3/15). Such records are required to be preserved either for long periods or permanently. Unpublished manuscripts are also sent directly to the Archives.

The Registry has the responsibility for establishing filing rules for correspondence, etc.; for setting up dossiers for correspondence; for giving service on files to the various units; for verifying that the dossiers are complete and in good order; and eventually for the transfer of material to the Archives. It has the duty to weed the files of useless and duplicating material. Even after material is transferred to the Archives, the Registry plays a role in decisions concerning the further discard of material.

The Registry uses the Universal Decimal Classification in organizing the files, and Library of Congress subject headings. It also prepares and publishes inventories and indexes of material in its custody. The Registry makes files by subject on most of the material in its custody, and issues published indexes of them by ten-year periods, and only then are they transferred to the Archives. Earlier, the routine was to make transfers irregularly and without full integration of files (received from different offices) by subject. This kind of transfer had been ordered in 1952, but was revoked for the purpose of preparing integrated subject files for easier reference use in the conduct of current business. This type of organization of material is of great importance in the efficient use of historical research material when it reaches the Archives, as well as in the management of the current business of the Organization when the material is in the Registry.

The Registry Division published an *Index of inactive correspondence files*, Series 1946-56, to facilitate research there. It is organized in one alphabetical sequence, and includes subjects, countries, institutions, organizations, and persons. Persons and organiaztions named are principally those which have played a part in UNESCO projects, missions, fellowships, etc. Many index entries relate to the preparation of publications. Under main entries, which determine the alphabetical sequence of the index, there are many sub-entries and even entries under sub-entries, and after each is a file number, and frequently sub-numbers, letters, names, and symbols for further identification. A few excerpts will serve to illustrate the system:

EDUCATION-Primary-Latin America-	
Meeting 1950-Uruguay	372(8) A 074 (892) "50"
AFRICA-Social Impact-Industrialization	338.924: 3(6)
HUMAN RIGHTS-Argentina, Complaints	342.76 (82)
HUMAN RIGHTS-Bulgaria, Complaints	342.76 (497.2)
UNIVERSITY-Brazil-TA-Reports	378.4 (81) TA A 187
-Latin America	378.(8)
YUGOSLAVIA-Fellowships 1946/56-Ivanusic	376 (497.1)-"56" Ivanusic

In the last entry, "Ivanusic" is not listed in the main alphabet. Indeed, only twenty-two personal names are mentioned in it in the letters A-C (62 pages), and eight of these are the names of historical personnages. Fellowship holders are listed only as sub-entries under country or residence as fellowship grantees.

The entries and sub-entries, etc., carrying numbered file references total approximately twenty to the page, or an estimated fifty-six hundred in the entire *Index*. Since there are frequently multiple references to the same file, the number of files is considerably smaller than might appear. Many "see" references are included, without file numbers being given.

As has been pointed out, discretion as to weeding and periods of retention is exercised to some extent by originating units, by the Registry in putting together its permanent files, and by the Archives in cooperation with the originating units and within limits set by policy directives of the UN and UNESCO.

Periods of retention are established in terms of a general plan:

Dossiers of candidates — five years.

Alphabetical and chronological files kept in Secretariat offices — five years (except those of the Director-General's office, which are unlimited)

Medical dossiers on individuals — thirty years
Dossiers on employees — seventy-five years
Most other files — unlimited

ADMINISTRATION AND REGULATIONS

The Archives Section and the UNESCO Library are a unit in the Department of Documentation, Libraries, and Archives, which in turn is part of the Division of Communications of the Secretariat. The staff consists of eight positions, including a Chief of Section, and two archivists in charge of reference and indexing, and five clerks.

As a general rule the materials are open after thirty years, but exemptions may be given in favor of "researchers proving a legitimate interest in material of more recent date." Even within the open period, applicants may be refused access to "documents which are unmistakably still of confidential or secret nature." A researcher "may be required to submit the manuscript of his work to the Director-General" of UNESCO before publication. Researchers are warned that the Organization "is not in a position to release them from any obligations in respect of copyright held by persons whose works may be found in the archives."

The "inviolability" of the archives is protected by the Headquarters Agreement between UNESCO and the French government in 1955, and by the Convention on Privileges and Immunities of the Specialized Agencies adopted by the UN General Assembly in 1957.

The archives are located in relatively new space below ground level in the main structure of UNESCO Headquarters at 7 Place Fontenoy, 75007 Paris. Here are to be found offices, work space for the staff, a reading area, bibliographical indexes and other tools, and a considerable body of material, most of it published. The large vault space is located nearby and is well arranged and secured. The building was opened in August, 1958, but the space occupied by the Archives is of more recent construction. The Archives unit is open to users from 9:00 A.M. to 12:30 P.M., and

2-6:00 P.M. on working days. There is space for eight to ten readers, and typewriters are permitted. A microfilm reader is available.

BIBLIOGRAPHY

1. Ascher, Charles S. *Program-making in UNESCO, 1946-1951.* Chicago, 1951.
2. Cassin, René. "Il y a vingt ans, naissance de l'UNESCO," *Le Monde,* Paris, November 2, 1966.
3. Cowell, F. R. "Planning the organisation of UNESCO, 1942-1946; a personal record," *Journal of world history,* X (November 1, 1966), 210-236. Has bibliography.
4. French, Hope Sewell. "Analysis of minutes and documents relating to the Conference of Allied Ministers of Education, London," UNESCO Archives, CAME /01.
5. Ghebali, Victor-Yves. *La France en guerre et les organizations internationales, 1939-1945.* Publication of the Faculté de Droit et des Sciences économiques de Grenoble, Paris, 1969.
6. Mylonas, Denis. "La Conférence des Ministres alliés de l'Education." Mimeographed, London, 1942-45 and Geneva, December 1967) plus annexes.
7. Laves, Walter H. C., and Thomson, Charles A., *UNESCO: purpose, progress, prospects.* Bloomington, Indiana, 1957.
8. Chapter on UNESCO, *Worldmark encyclopedia of the nations.* New York, 1960.
9. Publications of the International Council of Archives, particularly *Archivum,* 1952-

Index

Aabenrea, archives in, 45
Abercorn papers, 146
Aberdeen papers, 144
Abö Academy, Library of, 60, 64, 66
Abrantes family papers (Portugal), 267
Absalom (Bishop of Roskilde), 43
Abyssinia. *See* Ethiopia
Acuña y Avellandea, Lope de (Spanish diplomat), 302
Adams, William Dacres, papers of, 149
Adler, J. G., papers of, 50
Adler-Salvuis papers (Stockholm), 320
Admiralty Library (London), 145
Aehrenthal, Lexa von, papers of, 11
Aerssen, Cornelis van, papers of, 226
Aerssen, François van, papers of, 228
Africa, 40; in Belgian MSS, 29, 31; in French MSS, 91; in German MSS, 93, 121; in British MSS, 138, 143; in Portuguese MSS, 259, 264, 265; in Spanish MSS, 303; in Vatican MSS, 368; in Italian MSS, 368
Ageno, Francesco (Genoa), reports of, 202
Agnello, Benedetto, papers of, 174
Agriculture, international: in Dutch MSS, 232.
Agustin, Antonio (nuncio in Germany): papers in Vatican MSS, 363
Aitzema, Leo van, papers of, 226
Aix-la-Chapelle, Congress of: in German MSS, 99; in Dutch MSS, 224
Akershus, archives of: Norwegian, 244, 246
Åland Islands: in Finnish MSS, 62
Alba House of, papers of (Madrid), 305, 309, 311, 312
Albani archives: in Vatican MSS, 351
Albania: in Luxemburg MSS, 216; in UN MSS, 380
Albergati, Antonio (nuncio in Cologne): papers in Vatican MSS, 364

Albert I (King of the Belgians), papers of, 36, 37
Albertini (Prince of Naples), 206
Albuquerque, House of: archives, 305
Alcalá, Dukes of: archives (Seville), 306
Aldecoa, Don José de (Spanish diplomat), 282
Aldobrandini, Cardinal, (legate in France): papers in Vatican MSS, 361
Aléandre (nuncio in France): in Vatican MSS, 360
Aleandro, Girolamo (nuncio in Germany): papers in Vatican MSS, 362
Alegrete family papers (Portugal), 267
Alexander VII (Pope), (Fabio Chigi), papers of, 352
Alexander (Prince of Hesse), 111, 134
Alexander I (Czar of Russia), 253
Alexander II (Czar of Russia), 56
Alexandretta: in League MSS, 387
Alexandria, Va. (USA): repository of captured German MSS, 95, 97
Alfieri, Martino (nuncio in Belgium): papers in Vatican MSS, 359
Alfonso the Chaste (King of Aragon), 294
Algeria: in Dutch MSS, 228; in Spanish MSS, 283, 287, 288; in Swiss MSS, 330
Allgemeines Staatsarchiv (Bavarian), 105–6
Allies, the (World War II): and German archives, 94–95, 97, 115, 121–23, 125
Almodóvar, Marquis of (Spanish diplomat), 299
Alsace-Lorraine: in Prussian MSS, 101
Altamira Archives (Valencia), 305
Altmark affair: in Norwegian MSS, 253
Amadeo I (King of Spain), 294
Amadeus VI (Duke of Savoy), 192
Amberg, archives in, 108
American Historical Association, 95, 121

409